Faith, and Reason, EarthHistory

Faith, Reason, and EarthHistory

A PARADIGM OF EARTH AND BIOLOGICAL ORIGINS BY INTELLIGENT DESIGN

ANDREWS UNIVERSITY PRESS

BERRIEN SPRINGS, MICHIGAN

1997

To Kim, Dennis, and Jenelle

Cover design: Randy Siebold: randy@andrews.edu
Text design: Carol Loree

©1997 ANDREWS UNIVERSITY PRESS
213 Information Services Building
Berrien Springs, MI 49104-1700
616-471-6915
E-mail: aupress@andrews.edu

Printed in the United States of America
02 01 00 99 98 97   5 4 3 2 1

ISBN 1-883925-15-0

Library of Congress Cataloging-in-Publication Data

Brand, Leonard, 1941-
     Faith, reason, and earth history : a paradigm of earth and biological origins by intelligent design / by Leonard Brand.
          p. cm.
     Includes bibliographical references and index.
     ISBN 1-883925-15-0
     1. Natural history--Religious aspects--Christianity.
     2. Religion and science. 3. Creationism. I. Title.
BS660.B73 1997
231.7'652--dc21   96-40000
                                                   CIP

Foreword

We have probably at one time or another all been impressed with the spectacular and often mysterious transformations which occur in different organisms during development—from the mere growth of miniature arachnids to the radical metamorphism of butterflies; from the hurried development of dipterans, to the lazy extended transformations of 17-year locusts. In my mind, the growth of young-age creationism in this century is as spectacular and mysterious as the best of embryology.

Young-age creationism began this century in a grass-roots movement protesting evolution and historical geology. This early developmental phase was more or less sloughed off with the publication of *The Genesis Flood* by theologian John C. Whitcomb, Jr., and engineer Henry M. Morris. This molting replaced the often divisive protests with an immensely popular Biblio-scientific model more acceptable to evangelical Christians. In the 35 years which have elapsed since the publication of *The Genesis Flood*, the external form of the creation model has appeared to change relatively little. Vestiges of the earlier anti-science furor have persisted, evident in a myriad of anti-evolutionary publications, films, debates, student protests, and even court cases. This period of creationist history was also firmly committed to a positivist philosophy of science which, ironically enough, relegates all origins studies—including creationism itself—to the arena of non-science. Dominated as it has been by non-scientists, this phase of creationism has also been prone to rather frequent error. Yet, beneath the surface of this unsettled cocoon, changes were afoot. In an evangelical climate somewhat conducive to creation thought, an entire generation of young-age creationists have been pursuing their formal education. In the last decade or so, they have begun to emerge from their own personal cocoons of formal education with advanced degrees in a variety of fields of science. This new breed of creationists is poised to transform creationism once again.

Coincident with the important but largely unseen changes in creationism have been important changes in several disciplines of human thought. In the philosophy of science, the positivist point of view has fallen on hard times, taking hits from presuppositionists, feminists, post-modernists, and many others. This barrage has effectively destroyed any clear line of demarcation between science and non-science, allowing—at least in principle—even creation science a place to stand in the playing field of scientific ideas. At the same time, in the field of biology, a century of research under the banner of gradualistic evolutionary theory has not produced the expected answers to the biggest questions. Even after being wedded to modern genetics in the early part of this century, gradualistic Darwinism has failed to adequately explain fossil record patterns. This has forced the development of a punctualist view for the origin of species and a plea for an analogous punctualist's view for the origin of major groups of organisms. The latter has not been forthcoming. These and other challenges for evolutionary theory seem to have caused an increasing number of serious biologists and paleontologists to consider alternatives to macroevolutionary theory—although many times not publicly. At the same time, in the field of geology, the geologic gradualism of the nineteenth century has given way to neocatastrophism. In the last two decades it has even become increasingly fashionable to consider global-scale catastrophism. Thus, as creationists stand readied to enter the competition in a serious manner, and philosophers of science have again stripped away the rules preventing them from participating, the events of abrupt appearance and global catastrophism, which have always been the strongest events for young-age creationist competitors, are again thrust into the forefront of international science.

I believe we stand at the threshold of an exciting metamorphism for creationism. I believe that transformation will replace the spirit of error with the spirit of correction, the old creation model with a better one, and the old philosophy of science with an improved one. I would suggest that this work by Leonard Brand will play an important role in that metamorphism. As events in a metamorphism must be, Leonard Brand's book is quite different from those which have come before. Creationist books, because of their typical proneness to error and their science-bashing spirit, often give evolutionists the impression that creationists are deceitfully altering scientific data to fit their preconceptions. Even Christians—evolutionists and creationists alike—have been disturbed by this spirit. I think this book will not give a person that impression. Leonard Brand is an amiable man—hard not to like. I believe that spirit comes through in this volume, where it is more than words he shares when he says, "Above all it is essential that we treat each other with respect, even if we disagree on fundamental issues." This is one of the very few creationist works where I think evolutionary theory and thus evolutionists (even theistic evolutionists) have been treated with respect. Leonard Brand also introduces some essential pieces of the emerging creation model which will be replacing the one currently in vogue. This work is also one of the first to have shed the positivist philosophy of science. And it *is* the first creationist work to patiently and accurately explain to the non-scientist what science really is about. At the same time, Brand is a published biologist. He thus brings into the book a rich assortment of biological examples, lacking the typical errors which have dominated creationist literature of this century. I think evolutionists and creationists, scientists and non-scientists, theologians and non-theologians alike will profit from reading this volume.

As a child I can remember warm Fourth of July evenings in Northern Illinois when those folks who set out the fireworks and the firemen who protected the plains from prairie fires scurried about setting everything in proper place and order. There was an excitement of anticipation in the air, even as the fireworks display began. The display rolled along slowly, gradually revealing one beautiful burst after another, punctuated from time to time by a loud report or two. I would fidget as I excitedly wondered if the most recent burst of two or three quick explosions was signaling the climax of the show. Then it would happen. . . the entire sky would seem to spill color about us and I would thrill at the spectacle. I would encourage the reader to consider this volume not as the consummation of the show, but as an important display coming before its climax. I suspect Leonard Brand's work is one just preceding a most spectacular explosion of creationist works. I do hope that this book's spirit of model-building, mutual respect, and accuracy, as well as its creation model and philosophy of science, become examples for all creationist works to follow.

Kurt Wise, Ph.D.
Bryan College

Preface

The following pages present an overview of how the scientific method works, and then apply that understanding to an analysis of data in biology and earth science to illustrate how a scientist who is a creationist thinks, finally outlining an alternate interpretation of earth history. Many scientists contend that a person who believes in creation cannot possibly be a good scientist, that creationism is incompatible with the scientific method. The creationist activities of some individuals *are* incompatible with science, but it is no more fair to say this of all creationists than it would be to generalize from a few untrained evolution enthusiasts about all evolutionists. A central thesis of this book is that a creationist can indeed be an effective scientist and that that thesis is supported by personal experience and observation of individuals who are creationists and are also productive scientists. The approach taken here also is based on the observation that it is inappropriate and incorrect to characterize non-creationist scientists as stupid or uninformed people who believe in a ridiculous theory. We may indeed differ on some important philosophical issues, but the non-creationist scientists whom I know are very capable, knowledgeable individuals who can give a lot of good evidence to support what they believe is the correct understanding of earth history. A constructive approach to an alternate view of earth history needs to concentrate on careful analysis of data and the development of credible interpretations of the data.

The useful term "informed intervention" was used in the book by Thaxton et al. (1984) and was brought to my attention by my friend Bob Chilson. I use that term to refer to the concept of creation for a couple of reasons. The biblical creation, in the strict sense, is what happened at the beginning. Much of what creationists talk about involves earth and biological history that occurred after the initial creation. Informed intervention is a more inclusive term—a view of history that recognizes the important role of intelligent intervention in history, including creation, intervention in geological history, and God's communication to us through the Scriptures. This view of history also must deal with the biological and geological changes that have resulted from the normal operation of natural processes to make a unified picture of earth history. To try to include all of this in the term "creation" is like including all of evolutionary and geological theory in the term abiogenesis (origin of life by biochemical evolution). Clear communication requires words that are not confusing. For this reason, I refer to the philosophical approach presented here as interventionism.

This term does not define the nature of the intervention and could include a variety of interpretations from the concept of a God who starts the universe and leaves it to develop, to theistic evolution, and to more literal interpretations of the Bible. I discuss here one version of informed interventionism which reflects my confidence in the Scriptural account of origins.

In the scientific community, terms like creation, creationist, and creationism have acquired very negative connotations, and it's not just because of disagreement over the concept of creation. For many, these words conjure up an image of court battles over what should be taught in high-school science classes, debates, careless science, and sarcastic and derisive comments about "those evolutionists." The term "informed intervention" (also interventionist and interventionism) does not include any political agenda. My goal is to discuss these issues in a way that does not drive apart those who disagree from those who agree with me, but that helps us to understand each other.

It is somewhat dangerous to publish information like this because some may give it more authority than it deserves. George McCready Price published books on creationism and geology several decades ago, and there are people today who react to challenges to his writings as if the Bible itself were being challenged. A book, and particularly this one, should not be used to get "the answers;" it should be read as one person's thinking on the topic at this time. As new information becomes available and as science changes, part of the information in this volume will need to change with accumulating data.

It is assumed that the reader is familiar with basic biological concepts, but no previous knowledge of geology is assumed. The focus is not to present a comprehensive analysis of the works of philosophers of science, nor is it to present new data on geology or evolutionary biology. It is to present adequate information providing a basis for discussion of the issues, and the emphasis is on the question of how to integrate these topics into a coherent approach to an interventionist paradigm of earth history.

The biological portion of my research experience and training has emphasized small mammals, and thus, many of my examples involve them. One who studies insects or plants, for exambple, would no doubt use quite different examples and may even have a different perspective on certain aspects of evolutionary theory. In this volume, mammals play an important role in introducing a particular way of thinking about origins.

Many individuals have contributed to the development of the ideas contained herein, and it would be impossible to thank them all or, in many cases, even to remember who was involved in various stimulating discussions in the hallways or at meetings. Questions from the students in my classes have challenged me to search for better explanations, and discussions with other friends, especially those who disagree with me, have often clarified issues. The following individuals have read and criticized all or part of a previous version of the manuscript: Earl Aagaard, John Baldwin, Gerry Bryant, Brian Bull, David Cowles, Raoul Dederen, Joseph Galusha, Thomas Goodwin, James Hayward, George Javor, Phillip Johnson, Elaine Kennedy, Arthur Shapiro, William Shea, Bernard Taylor, Lewis Walton, Clyde Webster, Kurt Wise, and several anonymous reviewers. They did not always agree with my approach, but they all contributed to making this a better book. Chapters 11 and 12 resulted from articles written in collaboration with Ronald Carter and Jim Gibson, respectively. Their contribution to improving the quality of the discussion on these topics was substantial.

Except where otherwise noted, photos are by Mark Ford or myself and other illustrations are by Carole Stanton, Robert Knabenbauer, or myself.

Leonard Brand
March 7, 1996

Contents

The Impact of Darwinism

For nearly nineteen hundred years most of the Christian world accepted without question the creation account in the book of Genesis. Then, in a few decades, Charles Darwin and his colleagues changed all that. Now, evolution, for many people, is the only valid account for the origin of living things. Why did Darwin's theory have such an impact? Has it made the Christian's belief in a Master-Designer untenable? Or have some factors been overlooked? The following pages outline an approach to these and similar questions that affirm the integrity of the scientific process while maintaining a context of faith.

Darwin's theory of evolution has been very successful as a good scientific theory. Some years ago, an article was published entitled "Nothing in Biology Makes Sense Except in the Light of Evolution" (Dobzhansky 1973). That article illustrates the scientific community's confidence in the evolution theory and the extent to which it has been successful in organizing and explaining a broad range of biological data.

Chipmunks are an example of this success (Fig 1.1). Only one species, *Tamias striatus*, lives in the eastern half of the United States, but the western states have twenty-one species of chipmunks (Hall 1981). Why are there so many species in the West but only one in the East? The evolution theory provides an answer. The West has a great variety of habitats suitable for chipmunks: dense brush, semidesert Pinyon Pine forests, Yellow Pine forests, high altitude Lodgepole Pine forests, etc. Many unsuitable habitats such as deserts or grassy plains separated small populations of chipmunks in isolated geographic pockets. As each population became adapted to its habitat, some populations became different

Figure 1.1
Diagrammatic illustration of the distribution of chipmunk species in the United States. Each symbol is in the middle of the geographic range of a species.

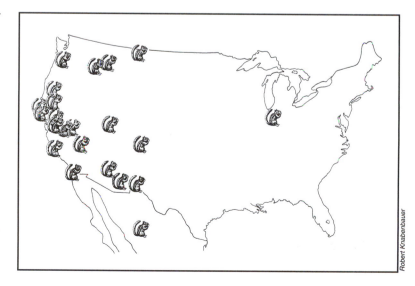

Robert Knabenbauer

species through the action of natural selection. However, in eastern United States, the original forest environment was relatively uniform and few natural barriers were adequate to isolate small populations of chipmunks and, thus, to produce new species.

Evolution not only provides explanations such as these but also suggests experiments to test these explanations. In many cases, the theory successfully predicts the outcome of the experiments, giving scientists great confidence in evolution.

The history of science shows that even very successful theories sometimes need improvement or replacement. Therefore, it is appropriate to continue examining the foundations of evolution and ask hard questions. Are all parts of the theory equally well supported? Have we overlooked or underestimated some important evidence? Do aspects of our logic need to be cleaned up? Such probing benefits both science and religion if appropriately conducted. We must be honest with the uncertainties in the data and be careful to distinguish between data and interpretation. We must approach the task with humility and open-mindedness, even if the data point to dimensions of reality beyond our current understanding. Above all, it is essential that we treat each other with respect, even if we disagree on fundamental issues.

The success of science has encouraged a tendency to believe whatever science claims. I believe that an understanding of both the strengths and the limits of science can enable us to relate to it more realistically. Therefore, we begin this exploration by examining the scientific process (chapters 1-4) and comparing conventional and interventionist approaches to science (chapters 5 and 6). We then apply our understanding of the scientific process to a comparison of different theories of origins (chapters 7-16).

Definition of Science

Science can be defined as a search for truth through repeated experimentation and observation. Another approach points out that science consists of two parts: first is the content of science, the things that science has learned and the system of organizing that knowledge. Certainly this is an important part of science; but if we stop here, we miss the most exciting and valuable part of science —the process of searching and discovering something new. Through the next few chapters, we seek to better understand this process of discovery.

The Scientific Process

Scientists, in the process of discovery, formulate hypotheses or theories, collect data, conduct experiments to test theories, and develop generalizations called scientific laws. I find that the most useful way of understanding the scientific process is to describe it as a two-step process: (1) collect data and (2) interpret data.

The activities of a scientist can all be clustered into these two categories. Collecting data is an absolutely essential step in science. It can be exciting or it also can be quite routine. The second step is figuring out what the data mean. It is the most rewarding and creative aspect of research—that which contains the realm of ideas and the application of those ideas to make sense of the data and to formulate a plan for further data collection.

Some people think that scholars in the humanities are creative and that scientists are not. But only the truly creative scientist is likely to contribute to genuine scientific progress. Science is quite free-wheeling, and different people operate in different ways within the basic framework of data collection and interpretation, repeating these two steps in a cycle over and over. Working in a lab or field-research site, people learn to do science from experienced scientists. (A good summary of these concepts is in National Academy of Sciences 1989, 1995.)

When the scientist has an idea, it is expressed as a question that can be addressed with the scientific method.

For example, while watching squirrels, we hear them make a sound. Are the squirrels communicating? And if so, what are they communicating to other squirrels? If we are in the desert and see several types of rock formations containing fossils, we may ask how those rocks and fossils originated. What is the process by which they got there? After posing questions, we try to determine what kind of data are needed to answer them. It is often necessary to break a question down into more specific questions.

What type of data could answer the question about the squirrel calls? It would help if we at least knew under what circumstances those calls were given. For example, is the call given when a predator is approaching, or when a neighboring squirrel comes close to the caller's food cache? As we observe the squirrels, we write down everything about the circumstances. These data could begin to answer our questions. The rocks and fossils are a little harder; we can't watch them form, but we can observe what is going on when rivers and streams and ocean currents deposit sand, mud, or other sediments. We can compare these modern processes, with the characteristics of the rocks to see which deposit is most similar to the rocks.

After designing an experiment and

collecting the data, we can evaluate whether the question has been answered. Researchers often find that they have part of an answer, but this part often raises additional questions—sometimes more than it answers. But as long as this process generates a stream of meaningful questions that help us to decide what experiments to do next, we can continue to make progress.

Pretend that we are archaeologists who have discovered several broken pieces of glass from an ancient ruin (Fig. 1.2). We can't argue, if we are honest, with our data—the shape of the objects or what they are made of. These facts are not just opinions; they are objective data—features that can be weighed, measured, defined by anyone with the same results. But, no matter how accurately we weigh and measure, the data are still just broken pieces of glass. The research is incomplete until we can make sense of the data—interpretation.

Interpretation involves determining relationships between pieces of data. In this case, the relationships need to be expressed in terms of what an object was and how it was used. We probably could not answer these questions directly from the data since they only tell us what the broken pieces of glass are like. We have to relate them to what we already know about similar objects, and archeological theories. Then we can devise a hypothesis as to what the glass object was like (Fig. 1.3A). We must use creativity and imagination in this process, but we can't let them run wild. The data create definite boundaries for our hypotheses—the color patterns should make sense and the curvatures of the reconstruction must fit the shape of the glass pieces.

Is our hypothesis correct? How would we know? Actually, a lot of data are missing, so we can't be sure. As often happens in science, another scientist looks at our interpretation of the data and decides that it is not done correctly, so he or she develops another hypothesis (Fig. 1.3B). Broken vases and jigsaw puzzles are likely to go together only one way. However, if the majority of the pieces are missing, we can probably arrange the remaining ones in several different ways that look logical. For this reason, there can be differences

Figure 1.2
Pieces of glass "discovered" by archaeologists.

of opinion about our glass object. In science, especially in fast-moving fields, interesting dialogue is common between people who have different interpretations. But what we ultimately want to know is which hypothesis is more correct. How do we determine this? The only way is to search for more data.

Let us say we are successful in our search and find two more pieces. One has a ridge on each end. This makes it look as though the second hypothesis is on the right track. But the other piece with a flared top doesn't fit either hypothesis. So after more study of the data, we develop a new hypothesis that fits all the current data (Fig. 1.3C). Now, is it correct? That is not certain, since we don't even know how much data is missing. In this case, we are going to cheat and look at the original (Fig. 1.3D). Part of our hypothesis was about right, but other features were still incorrect.

The glass vase illustrates the self-correcting aspect of science: as we gather more data, we move closer to a correct understanding. The accumulating data show where problems in our hypotheses or theories still lie and help us to think of better ones. Of course, complications appear along the way. What if the glass pieces are actually part of something quite unrelated to vases, but we are considering only hypotheses about vases?

That can slow down the scientific process.

Factors That Make a Theory Useful to Science

A good scientific theory or hypothesis has several specific characteristics. First of all, it organizes and explains

Figure 1.3
Hypotheses of the shape of the vase (A, B, and C) and the original vase (D).

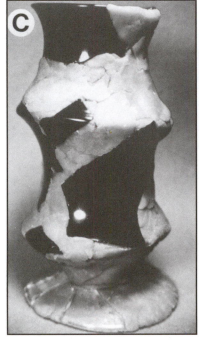

previously isolated facts. When a new field of inquiry is just beginning, one may have a lot of facts, but it is hard to see how they relate to each other, and people may have different ideas on how to put them together. A successful theory makes sense of these previously unrelated facts.

Data from studies on bats illustrate this concept. In the 1790s, a priest named Spallanzani did some fascinating experiments with bats (Hill & Smith 1984). He covered the eyes of some bats and the ears of others. From the results, he reached the conclusion that bats have to use their ears, not their eyes, to navigate successfully. Spallanzani couldn't hear the ultrasonic sounds the bats were using; consequently, his conclusions didn't make very much sense with the knowledge available at that time. But the data still supported his conclusion.

The prominent scientist Cuvier responded by proposing a theory that bats use a highly specialized sense of touch to find their way around in the dark. He had no evidence for his theory, but he was more prestigious in scientific circles and more scientists accepted his explanation (Hill & Smith 1984). Over 100 years later Spallanzani was vindicated when the theory of echolocation made sense of his observations. Now it has been demonstrated that bats give out ultrasonic cries, listen to the echoes, and use them to find their way around.

A good theory also suggests new experiments and stimulates scientific progress. Experiments are not selected randomly. They are generally chosen because some theory suggests that they will yield new insights, or they are done to test a theory. This introduces another characteristic of a good scientific theory—it should be testable. We should be able to think of data that has the potential to falsify the theory. If it is not possible to do that, then the theory is not very useful.

In reality, unless a theory is quite narrow and limited, it may not be feasible to test the theory directly. A broad theory may suggest more specific hypotheses which can be tested; and if these hypotheses withstand efforts to falsify them, confidence in the theory grows.

To illustrate what is meant by a testable hypothesis, compare these three hypotheses:

1. Ants behave the same way in undisturbed underground tunnels as in glass observation chambers.
2. Goldfish need oxygen to live.
3. Extrasensory perception exists.

Which of these three can be tested? How would you prove or disprove hypothesis number 1? Probably there is no way to find out what ants do many feet underground without seriously disturbing them. If we disturb them, we cannot possibly determine what they are doing in *undisturbed* tunnels. If we really want to understand ant behavior, we have to know the answer to this question, yet it is unanswerable. Science often has to simply live with this sort of thing. Hypothesis number 1 seems to be untestable.

Is hypothesis number 2 testable? A suitable experiment would be to seal up the goldfish bowl and see what happens, or provide the fish with an artificial atmosphere that doesn't contain oxygen. If the experiment is done and the fish still live, hypothesis number 2 has been disproved.

Can hypothesis number 3 be tested? One can design an experiment where a man who claims to have extrasensory perception is asked questions about thoughts or events in another place. If he can answer the questions correctly, it would show that something unusual is happening, but we still would have to determine exactly what it was. However, if he could not answer the questions, he could always say that he usually can do so but was unable to because the scientist was watching him. If that happens, what are we going to say? The experiment could not disprove the concept.

Some disproofs of theories seem to be quite definitive, but it is wise not to be too quick to claim to have disproved them. In some cases, seeming disproof may turn out to have overlooked something and not be a disproof at all. That doesn't weaken the principle that a scientific theory should be testable. It just means we should keep an open mind to new data that may change the picture.

The experiments done to test a theory or hypothesis should be repeatable. I should be able to define my experiment in precise, quantitative terms so somebody else in another lab can do the same experiment and get the same result. Hypotheses about subjective concepts like human opinions or attitudes are very difficult to test with repeatable experiments.

The last characteristic of a useful theory is that it predicts the outcome of untried experiments. There is a reason this is necessary. If I do some experiments to test a theory, and then, after they're done, I figure out a way to explain how they fit the theory, it is not very convincing. However, if before doing the experiment, I say that this theory predicts a specific result and then I get that result, it gives increased confidence in the theory. For example, in 1790 Spallanzani made a prediction, as it were (although I don't know that he said it this way), that if we could hear all that a bat hears, we would hear the sounds that a bat uses for navigation. Over 100 years later that implied prediction was tested, and Spallanzani was right. This gave great credibility to the theory of echolocation (Hill & Smith 1984).

Another look at these characteristics of a useful theory reveals that we haven't said that it has to be true. We hope it is, but how would we know? Isn't that what we are trying to find out with our experiments? We don't know ahead of time whether or not the theory is true; we have to wait for the results to come in, and often that can take a long time. In fact, many theories that are no longer accepted had all the characteristics of a useful theory for quite some time, even hundreds of years. A theory can be wrong and still lead to significant scientific advancement before we find

---

Characteristics of a Scientifically Useful Theory:

1. Organizes and explains previously isolated facts

2. Suggests new experiments to be done, stimulating scientific progress

3. Is testable—can potentially be disproved

4. Is based on repeatable experiments

5. Predicts the outcome of untried experiments

---

out it is wrong. We discuss this concept more in a later chapter.

The Source of an Idea Is Not What Determines Its Scientific Value

How do we get the ideas that we formulate as hypotheses? Sometimes chance observations lead to an idea. The scientist Archimedes had an interesting experience as the result of a task given to him by the king. The king was given a crown by some of his subjects. They told him it was pure gold, and the king asked Archimedes to find out if they were telling him the truth. This was a delicate task, because somebody's head might be on the line. Archimedes was thinking about this, the story goes, as he went to the public bath. His alert mind noticed that when he got in the tub, the water raised along the side. An idea popped into his head: perhaps when an object is put into water it displaces a volume of water equal to the volume of the object. He was so excited he forgot his clothes and ran down the street yelling, "Eureka (I found it)!"

That part of the story may be apocryphal, but apparently he did get information from his bath observations that helped him accomplish his task. By putting the crown in water, he could determine its volume. Then he could weigh it and calculate its density, which was not the density of gold. Someone probably lost his head over that, but it wasn't Archimedes.

Another example comes from my research on white-footed mice (genus *Peromyscus*, Brand & Ryckman 1968). I needed to catch some mice on the dry, barren islands in the Gulf of California. My assistant and I set up our traps in the valleys in typical *Peromyscus* habitat, and we caught only two or three mice per 100 traps, as would be expected.

While walking along the beach looking for rattlesnakes and bats, we saw something scurry over a rock. Out of curiosity, we started turning rocks over and found a *Peromyscus.* We knew that *Peromyscus* don't live on beaches. But when we set all of our traps along the beach, we caught 30 mice instead of the expected three. The mice on these islands have moved into a unique habitat, apparently making use of the food supply that is washing in from the ocean. A chance observation of a mouse going over the rock led to a discovery that we would never have made otherwise.

As we look back at our scientific progress, we have to recognize that chance observations were involved more often than we might like to admit. In fact, an alert scientist takes careful note of any unusual result or observation that could lead to a new discovery. Of course, the chance observations must be followed up by careful investigation if they are going to benefit science.

Previous experience or known theories are also important in suggesting ideas. It is known, for instance, that if two birds are in conflict over a territory, the bird who is defending its own territory has a psychological advantage and nearly always defeats the intruder.

When I was in graduate school, some of us were studying chipmunks and wondered if a similar process of territory conflict might occur in the behavior of chipmunks. Another student did experiments on eastern chipmunks, and I studied western ones. We found that, to a certain extent, territoriality affects dominance in chipmunks (Brand 1970; Dunford 1970). They are less territorial than birds, but chipmunks do become more dominant, or at least more aggressive, when close to their nests. Known concepts about birds helped us to devise testable hypotheses on chipmunk behavior.

Scientists sometimes mention that an idea came to them in a dream or just popped into their heads. This seems very unpredictable. How can science function that way? Ideas can come from all kinds of places in all kinds of ways. Where an idea comes from cannot be defined in objective terms (Cromer 1993, p. 148; Popper 1959, p. 31, 32), so what does that do to science? The characteristics of a scientifically useful theory provide a simple answer—can the theory be tested? Where an idea comes from is irrelevant. If we can do experiments to test it, any idea can be scientifically useful.

Picture a scientist visiting a primitive culture and watching a witch doctor treat patients with magical herb cures. She hopes to find some plants with medicinal value. Is that an acceptable source for scientific ideas, or must those ideas arise through the normal scientific process? Since she can test the plants to see if they really are medicinal, it doesn't matter where the idea comes from.

Data Do Not Lead Scientists Automatically to Truth

Some influential people, like Francis Bacon, have promoted the idea that data faithfully lead us to truth (Popper 1963). However, Bacon was overly optimistic. The data almost never directly suggest the interpretation; and data don't guarantee that our interpretation will be correct. The scientist has to relate the data to theories and "known facts," and has to be creative in order to interpret them. In our study of the broken glass pieces, we had to relate those data to information we already knew in order to develop an interpretation. Of course, some of the theories and "known facts"—and thus the interpretation—may be wrong. Scientific explanations develop through time as we interpret and test data and learn from our mistakes.

When the data do not all seem to point to the same conclusion, science chooses the conclusion that seems to be supported by the greatest weight of evidence. Since we only have part of the potential data, the apparent weight of evidence at a given time may actually point in a wrong direction. All science can do is accept the weight of the available evidence while trusting that continued research will reveal such mistakes in time. Of course, in evaluating the weight of evidence, some sources of information may be considered much more reliable than others. This has implications for informed interventionists who question some important scientific theories. We will return to this point later.

Is Some Truth Outside of Science?

There must be true answers to our questions about nature, and our theories and scientific models are tools that assist us in the search for those ultimate truths. Yet an idea that is true in an ultimate sense may not be scientifically useful (Fig. 1.4). To say that something is "not scientific" could mean two very different things. It could mean that the idea is false, or it could mean that science cannot determine whether it is true or not; it cannot be tested. If we were able to see from God's perspective, we could define a portion of human ideas as true and recognize others as false. We would find that science is able to test some of these true ideas and to convince us of their truth. Science can also test some of the false ideas and show that they are false. Other ideas can't be tested scientifically. This includes ideas in both the "true" and "false" categories.

Consider our question about the reality of extrasensory perception, for example. Whichever category it belongs in, science can't tell us for sure whether it is true or false. Consider an extreme example—the hypothesis that we all were invented five minutes ago with memory of a past human history that actually didn't exist, and that all of the physical human artifacts to go with that imaginary history were also created five minutes ago. I firmly believe that this hypothesis is false, but just try to devise a scientific test to falsify it! Understanding these limits of the scientific method can help us decide which questions science can be expected to answer reliably.

There are things in religion that are not amenable to scientific investigation; science can't test them. This doesn't mean they are false; they just may be outside the realm of what science can deal with. Did Jesus actually heal people? We each have our opinion, but science can't tell us the answer to this question. It can't begin to touch that and many other areas. An honest approach to the philosophy of science or religion needs to admit these human limitations.

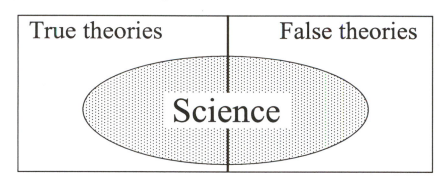

Figure 1.4
Relationship of science to true and false theories. Some theories in each category can be tested and some cannot. Of course, we do not know what percentage is in each category.

Limitations of Science 2

I once heard a theologian state that he would lay every belief and doctrine on the line to be accepted or rejected according to the findings of the physical sciences. Is that realistic or necessary? Or could it be, in some areas of inquiry, that so much confidence in the scientific process is not appropriate? Developing an intelligent, informed answer to this question requires an understanding of the limits of science (see Fig. 1.4). This discussion also helps us provide a foundation for discussing the relationship between science and faith.

Limits in Sample Size

As a student, I was very idealistic about science. I remember how shocked I was to learn that science doesn't give us absolute answers. One reason it can't is that we never have all the data. A hypothetical research project illustrates how this affects the scientific process.

This research aims to determine the abundance of a certain kind of virus in the human mouth.

Some viruses are present in everyone. They may have no evident effect on a healthy individual; but if one's resistance is lowered, they can cause problems. Obviously, it is impossible to check everyone on earth for the abundance of viruses, so our only practical option is careful, selected sampling. The smaller box in Figure 2.1A represents a sample of individuals chosen from the total population, represented by the open box. (In reality, the size of our sample compared with the total population is much smaller than this.)

Even if the sample is small, it is unrealistic to think that we can collect and count every virus, so we still have to reduce our data set. We devise a standard sampling technique, taking only a milliliter of saliva from each mouth as a sample (Fig. 2.1B). Even in that sample probably millions

**Figure 2.1 A,B,C
Successive steps in defining
the sample to be used in the
study of virus abundance.**

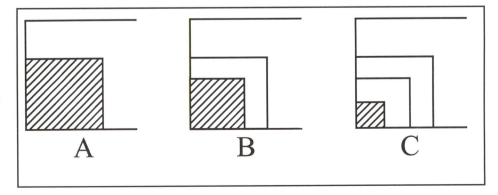

of viruses exist so we are not likely to be able to count them all. To solve this problem, we dilute the sample and take a small percentage of it, count the viruses, and estimate how many were in the total sample. As a result, we have to base our conclusions on a very small bit of data compared with what we want to know (Fig. 2.1C).

When we get that number of viruses, it still is not going to be the same for every person. A few people have a small number of viruses and a few have a very large number, but the largest number of people are in the middle (Fig. 2.2). This is a very common type of statistical distribution of data called a normal probability distribution. Our result is not an absolute answer; it is a statistical distribution from this small sample.

All research is like that. We never have all the data; we study a sample. A few years ago, I was doing research on chipmunks in northern California (Brand 1976). Golden-mantled ground squirrels also were common, and they behaved differently from chipmunks. The chipmunks commonly climbed trees, but the golden-mantled ground squirrels did not. After making this observation many times at various locations, I could have concluded that golden-mantled ground squirrels don't climb trees. That would have

been a well-supported conclusion based on a substantial number of observations. Then I went to the eastern side of the Sierra Nevada Mountains in the dry Pinon Pine forest. I don't know why the golden-mantled ground squirrels behaved so differently there, but they were climbing all over in the trees. If I had made a conclusion and published it based on my earlier sample, I would have been wrong because my sample had not been big enough at that point. My conclusion would have been valid for some populations of the squirrels, but it would not have been a correct generalization for all golden-mantled ground squirrels.

As scientists, we analyze the sample we are able to collect, and we never know just when enlarging the sample will change the picture completely. Practical realities dictate that we have to live with this uncertainty, but it doesn't reduce the value of science. It just reminds us that science is a continuing search that never runs out of interesting questions to stimulate our curiosity.

Experimental Design

Good experimental design is important since it guides us in collecting the most helpful type of data. Sometimes experiments don't tell us what we think they do because we have not used a proper design. An old

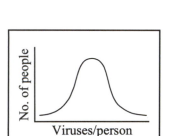

**Figure 2.2
Normal statistical distribution of virus abundance.**

joke illustrates this point with the help of an imaginary trained flea named Herman. Now I want to find out where Herman's ears are. Not all creatures have ears where we expect them to be. Some insects have ears on their legs, on their abdomen, or even on their antennae. First, we see if he wants to perform today. "Jump, Herman," I say, and he jumps. He obviously heard me. So let's see if we can find his ears. Perhaps he has them on his antennae, so we remove his two antennae. "Now, Herman, jump!" You may not be able to see him, but he jumped, so his ears are not on his antennae. Where else might they be? Maybe on his front legs. So we take his front legs off. "Herman, jump!" No problem—he still jumps. His ears apparently are not on his front legs. Often insects have ears on their back legs, so let's take them off. "Now, Herman, jump!" Herman doesn't jump, so his ears must be on his back legs. I hear you laughing, but why? What is the problem? Of course he has to have his back legs to jump. The example is obviously absurd, but it illustrates a very real problem in logic, which in many other situations would not be so obvious. We can make this same mistake and collect data that actually answer a different question from the one we thought we were answering. It is not always so clear that this has happened.

Consider another brief example:

If I am out of gas my car won't start. My car won't start. Therefore, I am out of gas.

Do you agree with that? The problem with the conclusion is that there could be another reason why the car won't start. This seems obvious; but if we are studying very complicated and sophisticated processes, it can be more difficult to see if we have made this same mistake in our logic. Now compare that with the following example:

If I am out of gas my car will not start. My car does start. Therefore I am not out of gas.

The difference between these two examples is very important for the scientific method. The first one tries to say that we can prove something—that the car is out of gas—because it will not start. It is not possible to prove things in science, because there can always be other complicating factors we haven't considered. The second example uses a different approach— "disproof" or falsification. Proving something wrong and thus eliminating a bad theory or hypothesis is easier than proving something right. So the second example is more realistic (Popper 1963). If a theory withstands efforts to disprove it, and is not disproved, then we have more confidence in it. This is more like the way science works.

An important part of experimental design is the use of experimental controls. The word "control" has a specific meaning in science. "Scientific control" does not refer to keeping the experimental conditions constant, although that is also important. A control is a known and previously tested standard for comparison with our experimental data. The control is just like the experimental situation in every way except for the specific point that is being tested.

The following partly hypothetical example tests Spallanzani's conclusion that bats use their hearing to navigate in the dark. We observe bats flying in a dark room with wires strung from floor to ceiling to see how well they can navigate. Normal bats are very good at avoiding obstacles, and they touch the wires only 1.3 times per 15 minutes. To see if Spallanzani was right, we put earplugs in the bats' ears. They now touch the wires an average of 26.7 times per 15 minutes and soon stop flying, so they must need their ears to navigate.

This is a great experiment, but does it mean what we think it means? What can we compare it with? To see what we really have done to the animals, we must have a control as a standard against which to compare the experiment. This is a real experi-ment that was done by Spallanzani in 1798 (Hill & Smith 1984), but I don't have his actual data. He found that bats with earplugs don't navigate very well, but maybe a bat with a plug glued in its ear is just too uncomfort-able to use its navigational ability. To test this, a control was done in which both the control and the experimental bats had little brass tubes glued in their ears. The tubes in the control bats were left open so they could hear, but the experimental bats had their ear tubes plugged. Both groups had the same amount of discomfort and extra weight, but the controls could still hear because the tubes were open. The control bats were just about as successful as the normal bats, and so it does verify the original conclusion.

This example illustrates how essential the control is for clarifying whether we are testing what we thought we were testing. Sometimes even good scientists don't use ade-quate controls, and sometimes we don't know enough about the pheno-menon to know what controls are needed. Does this mean that we can't do the research? No. As we do more experiments, we learn what controls we should have had earlier, so we repeat the experiments with adequate controls.

The nature of our experimental design is extremely important, but it is not always easy to know when we are using poor logic. As we do more experiments, we learn what mistakes we made earlier, so we go back and repeat the experiments with a better design. This tells us that science is a dynamic process that changes and improves as time goes on. It also tells us that we can't take scientific conclusions as absolute truth, but as statements which may need revising as time goes on.

Quantitative Data

In the process of a study of fossil tracks (Brand 1979), I was observing modern animal behavior for comparison. A paper by another scientist stated that salamanders in water don't walk on the bottom, but swim from place to place. I wanted to determine if that was correct. I spent a couple of hours catching some of the abundant salamanders in a mountain pond and watching their behavior. Then I made an entry in my notebook that the statement was mostly right—that although the salamanders do sometimes walk on the bottom, they usually swim.

When I was through catching animals, I began collecting quantitative data. With watch in hand, I timed the activities of many salamanders to determine how much time they spent walking on the bottom. Watching slow-moving salamanders can be a

boring activity but, with patient accumulation of data, it became evident that about 75 percent of their locomotion is walking on the bottom. Why was my first conclusion without quantitative data so completely wrong? To a human observer, a salamander slowly plodding along on the bottom of a pond is not very conspicuous. The one that attracts attention is the one that is swimming up to the surface to get air. Minds are not made like computers; they don't evaluate equally all incoming data. If they did, we would go crazy trying to keep track of so many details. Minds are designed to pick out the obvious, important things. Consequently, they are not good at comparing a very obvious action with something that is subtle. Counting or measuring the phenomena being studied helps us avoid the partial and sometimes misleading impressions that often result from non-quantitative observations.

Can a Scientist Be Biased?

Scientists are human, so we have to consider the possibility that biases could exist (see *Sigma XI* 1991). Unfortunately, more outright fraud occurs than scientists would like to admit. One geologist published over 350 scientific papers on the geology of the Himalayan Mountains in Asia over a 25-year period and was acknowledged as a world expert on the subject. Then it was discovered that he had been buying fossils that weren't from the Himalayas at all. He had published papers describing where in the Himalayas these fossils had been found, drawing conclusions on the stratigraphy and ages of the rocks from the fossils. He had never even been to some of the areas where he claimed to have collected the fossils and studied the geology (Oliwenstein 1990). The man probably wanted to make a name for himself, and he certainly did!

An editorial from the *American Scientist* journal stated,

> I believe there are very few scientists who deliberately falsify their work, cheat on their colleagues, or steal from their students. On the other hand, I am afraid a great many scientists deceive themselves from time to time in their treatment of data, gloss over problems involving systematic errors, or understate the contributions of others. These are the 'honest mistakes' of science. The scientific equivalent of the 'little white lie' of social discourse. The scientific community has no way to protect itself from sloppy or deceptive literature except to learn whose work is suspect as unreliable. (Branscomb 1985, p. 421-423)

The article goes on to discuss the fierce pressures on young science faculty—many must be successful in their research and in publishing their results in order to be promoted or even to keep their jobs. If research is not going well, the pressures become very strong, as the editorial points out, to use the little white lies to make things look better. It is tempting to interpret the data optimistically.

Unconscious bias results from things affecting our thinking that we are unaware of. Let's consider an example. I was studying fossil vertebrate trackways in the Coconino Sandstone, a deposit of cross-bedded sand like the deposits formed by sand dunes. I was at an abandoned, commercial quarry looking for tracks on the sloping surfaces of the cross-beds (Fig. 2.3). A biology student research assistant, with no geological training, was looking for tracks on the exposed top of a series of cross-beds that had been eroded flat (Fig. 2.3A). I was about to tell him there wouldn't be any tracks there when he called me over to look at the numerous ones he had found. I had assumed that trackways would be only on the sloping cross-beds. Without help from this "naive" biology student, I probably would never have found the tracks on the flat surface. I had an unconscious bias that prevented me from seeing what was right in front of me.

In the nature of some data, sometimes a potential for built-in biases exists that we also have to be aware of. An example comes from a study on a fossil forest in the Yellowstone Park area. The hills there are composed of many layers of

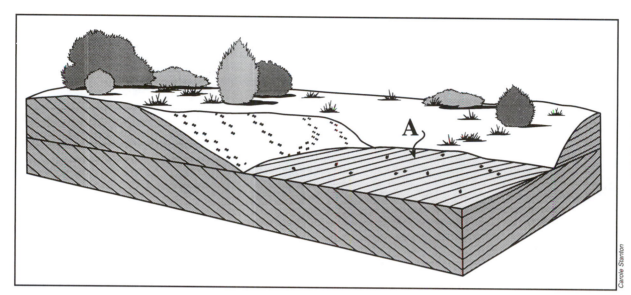

Carole Stanton

volcanic material containing fossil trees. It is of interest to know whether the horizontal fossil trees are oriented primarily in one direction. Figure 2.4 shows a section of a hillside with part of the ground removed to expose the fossil trees. If the overlying rock was still in place, we would see four trees oriented in the direction toward the right and none oriented at right angles to them. There does seem to be a preferred orientation. But when the rock is lifted up, we find that this conclusion is not true. The confusion arises because a long tree lying at right angles to the cliff face is visible for a long time. However, a tree trunk lying parallel to the cliff face would be exposed for only a short time before it falls down the hill. This natural bias can be neutralized by finding a second cliff facing approximately at right angles to the first one. The two cliffs would each have a bias in the orientation of the trees, but those

biases ought to cancel each other and give a true picture. Many similar situations occur in which an inherent physical bias in the data leads a careless researcher into a trap.

Logic: An Important Tool for the Scientific Search

Logic is always used in interpreting data. The nature of the logic that we use must be carefully considered, along with the limits of that logic. Deductive and inductive reasoning are both important in science.

Figure 2.3
Cross-bedded sandstone showing a cross section of the sloping cross-bed surfaces. Above, (A) indicates the horizontal top surface of the lower set of cross-beds. This surface was exposed by erosion of the cross-beds that were above it.

Figure 2.4
Block diagram of a portion of the Yellowstone fossil forests. A section of sediment has been lifted to expose the fossil stumps and logs on one horizon.

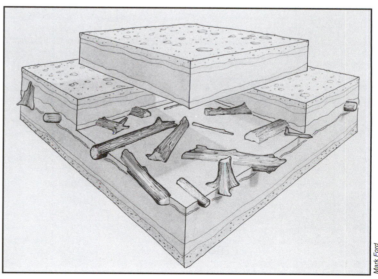

Mark Ford

Deductive logic starts with a generalization and uses that generalization to interpret the data in a specific case. This type of logic has one critical limitation: the conclusion is only as valid as the assumption.

Earlier in my experience as a researcher, I might have seen some small squirrels in a tree and concluded that they were chipmunks since ground squirrels don't climb trees. That is a correct use of deductive logic, but the conclusion is not reliable because it is based on a false assumption about ground squirrels.

If the assumption turns out to be wrong, the conclusion is wrong. Does this mean that deductive logic is not useful? No, but we need to be aware of its limitation. Science moves on, and we must realize that scientific conclusions are tentative. They may hold up or they may not; we just have to wait and see.

The other approach is inductive reasoning. Induction is one of the very key types of thinking used in science—perhaps the core of science. Induction begins with individual observations and uses these observations to develop generalizations. The virus research that we discussed is an example of inductive reasoning. We started with many specific data points and then made a generalization as to how abundant viruses are in mouths, implying that they would be about that abundant in the total population.

These generalizations are essential in science. The generalization becomes the assumption that helps us interpret the data from another experiment. The logical process follows a circular path—induction, then deduction, then collection of more data to use in induction, etc. The problem with induction is that we really can't predict the unknown. The virus level may be quite different in some other place.

Induction is only useful if we can generalize or predict, and we really can't do that. A resolution to this problem is quite important in order to understand science. Scientists and philosophers of science have directed some interesting and disturbing statements to this issue. "Just because certain generalizations are demonstrably consistent is no sound reason for extending the process to the unknown. Alternatives should be kept under consideration" (Roth 1965).

This may sound like we are really putting down scientific logic, but there are answers to the dilemma.

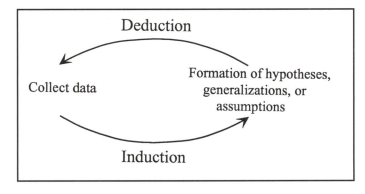

The ability of induction to deal with a future case collapses, and since this is the only useful aspect of induction, we are faced by total collapse. Thus I must report to you that discouraging news has leaked out of the citadel of logic. The external walls appear as formidable as ever, but at the very center of the supposedly solid fortress of logical thinking all is confusion. (Goodman, quoted by Weaver 1961)

These problems in science were rather disturbing to me when I first learned of them. Do they mean that science is not useful? No, obviously not.

As practical tools, no one doubts the continuing value of the armaments. But in terms of ultimate and inner strength, the revelations are astounding indeed. The ultimate basis for both types of logical thinking is infected, at the very core, with imperfection. (Goodman, quoted by Weaver 1961)

I believe the phrase "practical tools" is the answer to the dilemma. If we expect science to be able to predict with accuracy what we will find in our next observation, then we often are going to be disappointed. These two types of logic are very important tools that we must use, but they don't bring us some kind of absolute truth. We can recognize their role as being extremely useful and valuable, but we can also be realistic and be aware that logic is only a tool that helps us organize our thinking. In our research, we make the generaliza-tion that the logic suggests; it helps us to see what experiment we should do next. It helps us think in an organized way, but it does not give us absolute truth.

To illustrate this concept further, consider an example from an actual research project (Brand 1974):

Data from field observations: all chipmunk nests found in this study were found high in trees.

Conclusion: chipmunks nest in trees

This sounds logical. I collected data, used induction, and reached the conclusion that chipmunks nest in trees, at least during the summer. In a sense, that is predicting that other chipmunk nests will be in trees as well. What is the correct interpreta-tion of that conclusion? Here is one way to look at it:

"CHIPMUNKS NEST IN TREES."

It is an absolute conclusion; that's the way it is. Another way to look at this conclusion can be illustrated by restating it as follows:

Under the conditions of this research, in the places where the research was conducted, the nests that could be found were in trees. "Chipmunks nest in trees" is a hypothesis to be explored further.

Now we have a realistic under-standing of what we have found. This is a hypothesis based on what we know so far. It may not hold up in the future after more research, but it is still a useful summary of where we are at this point in our understanding of chipmunks.

Another helpful analogy is provided by comparing inductive and deductive reasoning to the information or "tools" needed to read a road map. If we correctly use these tools and make the right choice at a highway intersection, that does not mean that we have reached our destination. The highway will bring us to other decision points where we must use the same tools again. If we persist in wisely using these logical tools, we will continue to make positive progress in our journey. Science is always a progress report of where we are in this dynamic search for understanding.

Occam's Razor

Another logical tool that science sometimes uses is the concept of Occam's razor. In choosing between opposing hypotheses, we prefer the simpler hypothesis. For example, a bird's ability to find its way home again after a 5,000 mile migration could be interpreted as (1) the operation of higher reasoning ability or (2) instinct. Occam's razor indicates a preference for the simpler mechanism—instinct—rather than assuming a more complicated mechanism.

However, the problem with this concept in many cases is how to define "simpler" in objective terms. Occam's razor is not a way to determine which hypothesis is correct; it is simply another practical tool to help us decide which hypothesis to use to guide our research until there is sufficient evidence to help make the choice on a sounder basis.

The Scientific Perspective in Space and Time

The perspective from which we view many things affects whether we can gain a realistic understanding of them. From a valley, mountains look very high, but the view from a spaceship provides a more accurate perspective. In reality, mountains are tiny wrinkles on the surface of the earth, but they don't look that way from our normally limited perspective. Humankind is small compared to the universe, so it took us thousands of years to discover that the earth rotates around the sun.

We also view our world from a limited perspective in time, and this makes it more difficult for us to study historical events. Earlier, we discussed the reconstruction of a glass vase. When we are attempting to answer historical questions about glass vases, our main problem is that we cannot go back in time and observe what happened. Some time in the past, people were making those vases and using them (Fig. 2.5). A scientist who lived then could observe how they were made and what they were used for, and could have all the data to reach reliable conclusions. Time passed, people died, and all we have left is some broken glass. Most of the data are gone; consequently, the conclusions that can be reached from study of this evidence have very definite limits.

When studying earth history, we have the same problem as with the vases. A scientist who lived throughout earth's history and observed the formation of rocks and fossils and the changes in living things would have all the data to reach sure conclusions. Today scientists have to rely on the fossils and rocks for the study of earth history and the history of life. These provide limited circumstantial evidence, but much of the crucial data are gone forever.

The study of things that happen now is what science does best. The physiology of blood flow can be studied in rabbits that have blood flowing in their veins right now. Experiments can be done in the laboratory over and over again until we understand what is happening inside of the rabbits. In much of physics, biology, chemistry, and other disciplines,

the same is true. It is also at least partly true in the study of the genetic process that controls micro-evolutionary changes in populations of organisms today. In the study of the past, however, science has a problem. No one has ever seen a mountain rise or observed the formation of rocks in the geologic column. Yet, it is still fascinating to study those phenomena, and it is helpful to put things in a historical perspective—e.g., wars and tensions between nations are more easily understood if we consider the history of past conflicts rather than considering only the current situation. One difference in the study of earth history is that science doesn't have a written historical record. We try to reconstruct that history and we can make some progress, but we must be aware of serious limitations in the study of ancient events.

In discussions of the history of life, statements that evolution is as

Figure 2.5
As time passes after an ancient event, the amount of evidence available for studying that event is reduced.

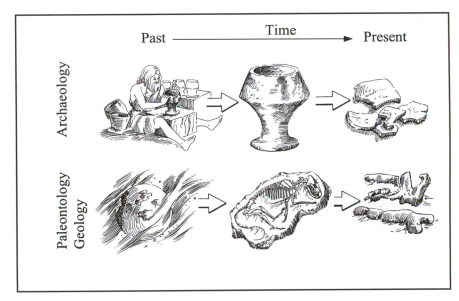

much a proven fact as the law of gravity sometimes appear. It seems they refer not only to the genetic process of change, but also to the origin of all life forms by evolution. Can we honestly make that type of statement? The study of the history of life is the study of a series of events that happened some time in the past. We can't make those events happen again. Thus, it is unrealistic to say that the historical dimension of evolution (or any other theory about the past) is as much a proven fact as the law of gravity. A very great difference exists between these two phenomena.

How does geology deal with this problem of history? I illustrate the answer with an example, the study of cross-bedded sandstones (Fig. 2.6). Geologists study the origin of these sloping cross-beds by comparing the features of the sandstone with situa-

tions where sand is being deposited today. They dig trenches into desert dunes and compare the details of the layers of sand inside the dunes with the layers of sandstone to see if the dunes are a reasonable analogue for the rock formation. Could the sand in this sandstone have been deposited in the same way as the sand in a modern desert dune? Other analogues must also be examined and compared with the desert dunes to determine which has features most like those of the rock formation. It is like taking a multiple-choice quiz:

Which is the correct modern analogue for the sandstone?

A. desert dunes
B. river sandbars
C. river delta
D. ocean beach deposits
E. under-water dunes

The most significant difficulty in this process arises if the true answer is actually "none of the above." We probably would not have any way of knowing that and we would choose one of the analogues observed. In this case, science becomes, as one philosopher put it, "an organized way of going wrong with confidence."

What if the rock formed in a very large-scale flood larger than anything observed today? Such an

**Figure 2.6
Cross-bedded sandstone in
The Navajo Sandstone, Zion
National Park.**

event would no doubt involve processes very similar to some of the options listed above. The difference would be in scale—both extent and speed of deposition. The process in many respects might mimic one or more of the modern processes; so even though the rock might be the result of a large-scale flood, we wouldn't know it. We would likely choose a smaller scale modern analogue as our answer. Of course, a large-scale event should leave some characteristic features in the sediments; but having never observed such an event, we might be slow to recognize these features. Indeed, we might have only a vague idea of what to look for.

In the study of history, we can't be sure we have the right analogue; yet we must have it to reach the right conclusion. Consequently, a considerable amount of humility and tentativeness is in order when we study what has happened in the past. That is true for non-interventionists and interventionists alike. Does that mean that geology and paleontology are not effective sciences? Not at all. It just means that scientists in those fields have to be at least as cautious as other scientists, and often more cautious so as not to make the unwarranted claim that they know for sure what happened some distant time in the past.

Hopefully, this helps us to under-

stand that when we discuss evolution and informed intervention, none of us, no matter what philosophy we start from, is in a position to make dogmatic, scientific statements about somebody else's point of view on the subject. Ridiculing someone who also is searching honestly for understanding, is never constructive.

Science and Objectivity

Understanding the nature and limits of objectivity in science places us in the best position to compensate for the problems these limits can produce.

A theory that is well entrenched is not easy to change. A scientist may find it difficult to be objective in evaluating a favorite theory. Neither is it easy to buck the tide and go against a popular theory.

Our vision can become restricted by what we learn in school. We go to high school, to college, and maybe to graduate school. We come out at the end of that education believing that certain things that we were taught are true. When we are in school, we learn (1) the facts and theories that are currently accepted by scientists and (2) how to think critically. Especially in graduate school there is a focus on learning how to think critically, how to analyze, and how to read scientific papers and decide for ourselves if they hold up or not. By the time we become proficient at critical thinking, we have already learned a lot of things that we have accepted as being true. Before we are in a position to critically analyze, we already have restricted vision. But what is the alternative? We have to start somewhere. If we realize this problem exists, we are in a better position to overcome it. That is the benefit of understanding that science has limits.

In the study of evolution and informed intervention, we may be considering only how to fit the data into our favorite theory, and not be willing to let science tell us whether parts of our theory of earth history could be wrong. Actually, it is scientifically valid for a person to be convinced that life was created or that life has evolved. That is not the problem (I defend this proposition later). All scientists work within the framework of some world view. But if we make ourselves aware of the work and the ideas of other people, it can help us avoid some bad mistakes as we utilize our world view to suggest testable hypotheses. We consider this problem in chapter 5.

Implications for the Scientific Process

The scientific process has limits, but these are not all bad. The tendency to hang onto known theories makes science somewhat conservative, but also keeps it from running after every crazy idea that is suggested. There are advantages for science to be conservative and to resist change as long as there is a mechanism to bring about change when it is needed. There is such a process, and we will get to that later.

But aren't scientists objective, impersonal, and unbiased as they let the data lead them to truth? Sir Francis Bacon thought so. He proposed a scientific methodology to describe how science works. According to Bacon, scientists must empty their minds of all preconceived ideas and just let the data lead them to truth. Bacon thought that we would have the most success if we followed that approach, but Bacon's philosophy of science never was realistic. Actually, we are all imperfect with the universal limitations of the human race. So what is the answer? Bacon's training and experience did not prepare him to find the answer. He studied law and became a chancellor under James I, but he was dismissed for taking bribes. He never was a scientist and didn't even associate with scientists. He learned about science from what he read—not scientific literature but literary works (Goodstein & Goodstein 1980). He revealed how naive his understanding of science was by stating that if he were given two years free from any responsibilities, he could pretty well wrap up what was left to be done in science. Unfortunately, he never did get his research grant, so we are still left at the task (Popper 1963).

According to his method, scientists who empty their minds of all preconceived ideas and theories and then collect data are objective and can't be misled. Twentieth-century philosophers have problems with Bacon's philosophy, and I think rightly so. Karl Popper, a prominent philosopher of our day, wrote "Science: Problems, Aims, and Responsibilities" (1963) in which he outlines his understanding of the scientific method. He refers to Bacon's theory as "Bacon's naive dogma." Popper explains the scientific process as follows:

Popper's scientific method

1. *We stumble over some problem.*

2. *We try to solve it by proposing some theory.*

Right here, Popper and Bacon part company. Bacon says we should eliminate all preconceived ideas or theories from our minds. Popper says the opposite; we start our solution by proposing some theory to resolve it. Think about Bacon's idea for a moment. How would we go about purging our minds of all preconceived ideas? Even if we were successful, a mind purged of all such theories

would be an empty mind, not merely unbiased. Popper says that Bacon is wrong and that we should start our solution by proposing some theory. Then, Popper suggests the third point:

3. *Learn from our mistakes,* especially those brought home to us by other scientists' discussion and criticism of our experiments.

Popper briefly summarizes his view of the scientific method as: (1) Problems, (2) Theories, and (3) Criticisms.

The Source of Scientific Objectivity

Look a little closer at what Popper means by criticism, as explained in his 1963 article, and how it relates to objectivity. If scientists are not all that objective, how does science make progress? Popper maintains that "the growth of knowledge and especially scientific knowledge consists in learning from our mistakes" (p. 965). However, we learn from our mistakes systematically, not randomly. We carefully conduct experiments and examine the results to find the mistakes in theorizing.

Popper states that "it would be a mistake to think that scientists are more 'objective' than other people. It is not the objectivity or the detachment of the individual scientist, but science itself" (p. 965). Scientific objectivity "consists solely in the critical approach; in the fact that if you are biased in favor of your pet theory, some of your friends and colleagues . . . will be eager to criticize you, that is to say, to refute your pet theories if they can" (p. 965). He maintains that it is this "friendly hostile cooperation of scientists, that is their readiness for mutual criticism," (p. 965) that makes for objectivity.

To put that in simpler words— you develop a theory, you try to test it, and you support it if you can. Someone who disagrees will criticize your results and your logic; it is this criticism that brings about the objectivity in science. This objectivity is sometimes evident at scientific meetings or in scientific journals— especially when two scientists present different theories to explain the same line of evidence. Sometimes they even call each other names. That part is not beneficial. The process works best if each one tries his or her best to be objective and to correct errors in his or her logic while learning from each other. Even if they are not always objective, many other scientists are observing and evaluating the arguments that are presented. If scientists are careless in their research, you can be sure that sooner or later someone else will detect their carelessness and publish it for all the world to see. In science, objectivity comes from group interaction.

Popper makes a statement that would sound very odd if it weren't put in this context. He says, "There is even something like a methodological justification for individual scientists to be dogmatic and biased" (p. 965). That may sound strange, but hear him out.

"Since the method of science is that of critical discussion, it is of great importance that the theories criticized should be tenaciously defended. For only in this way can we learn their real power; and only if criticism meets resistance can we learn the full force of a critical argument" (p. 965).

Even a good theory may not have a fair hearing if someone doesn't take hold of it and try hard to develop it.

Objectivity comes from group interaction, not from the individual. Any scientists who think they have it all together and don't have to listen to anyone else are probably not going to be effective contributors to science.

Relation of Science to Total Experience

Science does some things very well. Despite its limitations, science is still a very productive activity—a powerful way of improving our world or of approaching truth. Science is at its best when studying the characteristics of objects and processes that can be observed and quantified. When analyses of these data are combined with the critical discussions between scientists that improve our level of objectivity, science is a great tool for discovering truth.

But the contribution of science in some areas is more limited. Some things are too complex to study adequately. An example comes from the study of bird song. Poets write beautiful poems about how birds sing for joy in the spring. Then a cocky young scientist comes along and studies birds and says the poet is all wrong. The male's singing is an aggressive activity to advertise his territory and scare away potential intruders. Who is right? Is the bird singing for joy or not? The scientist has data and the poet has emotion, so the contest is one-sided. Perhaps the scientist should be a bit more humble. When we study human behavior, we can evaluate what is going on in someone's head because we have the same feelings and ways of thinking. How are we going to find out what emotion the bird feels inside its head that stimulates it to sing? We can observe that when the bird sings, the other males act as if they recognize it as a territorial claim. But that only describes the result of the singing. What is the emotion inside the bird's head that causes it to sing? Is he feeling aggressive, or is he feeling something we would call joy? I think

that sometimes scientists have to be realistic and say that we don't know the answer. Maybe the poet is right after all.

Another challenge is the study of "moral values." Humankind has not done very well at learning from our scientific endeavor or scholarly thinking what true moral values bring happiness to people. Perhaps the results of a study of different behaviors are too short term to weigh long-term consequences of these behaviors. Science should not be expected to tell us anything about moral values. I think that is why God told us some of the basic things we need to know about moral behavior.

How can we study beauty, music, and poetry scientifically? We can study the physics of the effect of sound waves of music on our ears, but we can't study the real essence of those phenomena and of human reaction to them with science. Science has little or nothing to say about beauty, poetry, music, or morality.

A Russian cosmonaut, years ago, made the comment that when he was in space he didn't see God anywhere. The obvious implication was that since he hadn't seen God, there must not be any God. But how far out did he go? How much of the universe did he see? In actuality, he didn't even get far from the earth, so his comment doesn't have any significance at all and was certainly not a meaningful scientific statement. We are restricted in space and in time; we observe only a tiny segment of human history and we can't go out and see God in heaven. Consequently, science has little to contribute to our understanding of theology.

Our scientific knowledge at any point is only a progress report along the road to understanding. If we see it in that context, we will be more realistic and better comprehend the meaning and role of science. One philosopher said:

> The old scientific ideal of episteme—of absolutely certain, demonstrable knowledge—has proved to be an idol. The demand for scientific objectivity makes it inevitable that every scientific statement must remain *tentative forever*. (Popper 1959)

If an idea is not tentative, it has become dogma, and science cannot function with dogma.

Scientific knowledge changes; theories have a life span. Someone has calculated that over the whole history of science, the average theory has a life span of three hundred years. Certainly now, during the last hundred years, since science moves much faster, that life span will be much shorter. We need to be ready to move on as science progresses with new data and theories.

Think of scientific ideas as arranged on a continuum from well-studied fields at one end of the continuum (e.g., the effects of gravitation) to fields at the other end (e.g., parts of molecular biology) in which science is challenging the frontiers of our knowledge. The fields of molecular biology and molecular genetics are very active disciplines, but major portions of those fields are just in their infancy. Our understanding will undergo many changes in those areas. It isn't realistic to put science into one box and either believe everything or doubt everything. Either one of these approaches would be the easy way out since they don't require thinking. There isn't a good way to avoid the need to think and evaluate, to critically analyze what we read, and to remind ourselves periodically that basic humanitarian factors and religious values are important complements to science.

(Further insights into the thinking of modern philosophers of science may be found in Feyerabend 1978, 1987; Frodeman 1995; Gale 1979; Laudan 1981; Medawar 1984; Moreland 1989; Oldroyd 1986; and Reichenbach 1968.)

Aspects of the History of Science

This chapter presents highlights of the history of science (Fig. 3.1) The process of scientific revolutions (chapter 4) and the origins of the theory of evolution and the philosophy of naturalism can be best understood if put in their historical context. Science in Mesopotamia, Egypt, and Asia Minor about 4,000 years ago did not much resemble modern science, but individuals were beginning to think about the structure of the universe. Thales (639-544

B.C.) thought the earth was flat and floated on water, but one of his pupils, Anaximander (c. 611-547 B.C.), described the earth as a sphere.

Greek Science

Beginning in the 5th century B.C., the most highly developed science was in Greece. Three famous representatives of this era were Socrates (470-399 B.C.), his student Plato (429- 347 B.C.), and Plato's student Aristotle (384-322 B.C.). They were interested

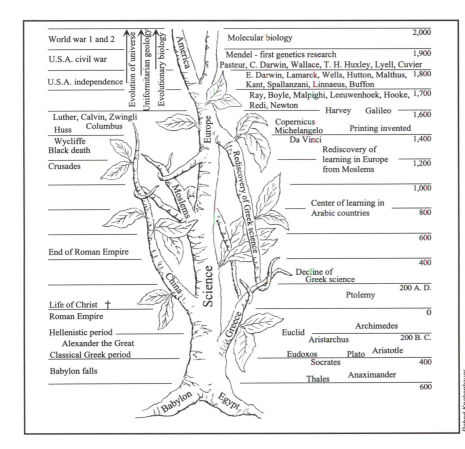

Figure 3.1
A brief summary of the history of science in its cultural, political, and religious contexts. Intertwining of branches represents flow of scientific information between cultures.

Robert Knabenbauer

both in human conduct and the physical world. Plato had no faith in the senses, which he felt were unreliable. He had faith only in the intellect and thought the mind could be trained to lead us to truth.

Aristotle, Plato's greatest pupil, rejected Plato's philosophy and tried to restore sense experience to the study of nature. Plato would think about how many teeth a horse should have, but Aristotle would open the horse's mouth and count them. Aristotle wrote in many disciplines, such as ethics, politics, biology, cosmology, and logic, and developed quite a coherent system of thought, though many of his ideas were wrong. His work was the inspiration for the sophisticated Greek science of the Hellenistic age. Unfortunately, many later scholars did not continue his careful inquiry; they looked to the old masters for truth. In the area of cosmology, Plato believed the planets moved in perfect circles (the perfect orbit). Scientists then thought the earth must be the center of the universe because of God's special concern for humankind. Eudoxos (409-356 B.C.) made the first mathematical model of planetary motion. In it the planets were carried on theoretical spheres carried by other spheres. This model could account for the observed phenomena of planetary motion. It was geocentric; that is, the earth is in the center of the universe. Aristotle further developed the geocentric model of cosmology; but instead of theoretical mathematical spheres, his spheres were hard, physically linked transparent spheres made of "crystalline." In the Middle Ages, this idea became dogma.

Not all ancient cosmologists were in complete agreement with the geocentric theory. Heraclides, a contemporary of Aristotle, suggested that the earth rotates on its axis. In a classic case of anticipating a future development, Aristarchus (310-230 B.C.) suggested that the sun and fixed stars are motionless and the earth and planets rotate around the sun, with the earth circling the sun once a year. He also suggested that the earth rotates on its axis. His ideas were not accepted. Instead, the geocentric theory was further developed and refined to account for new data. Ptolemy (A.D. 85-165), the last of the great Greek astronomers, wrote *The Almagest*, a comprehensive treatise on cosmology (Encyclopedia Britannica 1952). He believed in a geocentric cosmology and argued that the earth is stationary because, for example, if it rotated, objects would fall off and the birds couldn't keep up. These were reasonable arguments given the information available at the time.

A fundamental concept of this work was the reduction of the

apparent irregularities of planetary motion to mathematical law. For example, Mars, Jupiter, and Saturn rotate more slowly than Earth, and Earth overtakes them. Consequently, they appear to go backward (Fig. 3.2). Also, some planets (like Mars) vary in brightness because of the changing distance from Earth throughout the year. Ptolemy explained these observations with two devices. One is an eccentric, a sphere whose center is not Earth. Another is an epicycle, a small sphere that rotates around a point on the perimeter of a larger sphere, the deferent. These mechanisms could mathematically explain the data surprisingly accurately.

The Dark Ages

Greek science flourished until the Roman domination and then began to decline. It was almost dead by A.D. 200. Finally, Rome decayed, the Germanic barbarians overran Europe, and Greek culture largely disappeared. During the Middle Ages, the Moslems occupied large areas in the Middle East, Northern Africa, and parts of Europe. During this time, the centers of learning were in Arabic countries. These scholars learned from the Greeks, and from the highly developed science of China (Kneller 1978, p. 4-7), and then added their own contributions and became the keepers of European science.

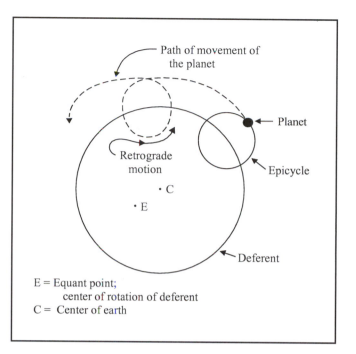

E = Equant point;
    center of rotation of deferent
C = Center of earth

Europe Rediscovers Its Past

Beginning in about the 12th century, Christian Europe began to rediscover its scientific heritage, along with the contributions of the Moslems and the Chinese. During the time of the Renaissance (1300-1650), many original Greek manuscripts were translated. Scientists in the Middle Ages did little experimentation. When Aristotle's ideas were finally rejected, it was more from the philosophers deciding that Aristotle's philosophy had logical inconsistencies in it than from empirical problems. The beginning of European technology, with inventions such as the printing press (1454), smelting methods, and magnetic compass (from China), began to transform society and to aid science.

In this way, Europe in the Middle Ages recaptured Greek

Figure 3.2
Diagram of mechanisms used in Ptolemaic astronomy to explain the movements of planets, including the retrograde motion of some planets.

thought, mastered it, and developed new skills and a new intellectual approach. By the mid 16th century, Europe was fully in possession of its intellectual history, and scientists began to think that the golden age for science was in the future. The way was prepared for modern science.

Relationship of the Church to Science

The Christian concept of a consistent, law-giving God who can be trusted provided the foundation for European science, but the Church made mistakes along the way. During the Middle Ages, the Church accepted Aristotle's ideas and other Greek thought, made them part of church dogma, and attempted to defend these ideas with isolated Bible texts. Scientists who proposed new ideas were persecuted. Oresme (1323-1382) discussed the theory that the earth rotated, but then he denied it because he thought the theory contradicted the Bible.

During this time, scholars tended to believe that any phenomena they could not explain was evidence of a direct, vitalistic action of God in nature. In other words, the direct involvement of God was invoked to explain the gaps in human explanations, creating a god-of-the-gaps. As natural mechanisms were found that would explain these phenomena, God was no longer needed as an explana-

tion and the god-of-the-gaps was pushed farther and farther away until science altogether dispensed with Him. For example, the flow of blood was thought to result from the vitalistic, mystical action of God in human bodies until William Harvey (1578-1657) demonstrated that the heart is a pump that moves it. This example is often cited as one of the most important events in the freeing of science from the shackles of theology; it was also a significant setback for the concept of creation.

Further Developments in Cosmology

Copernicus (1473-1543) wrote a book entitled *On the Revolutions of the Celestial Orbs* (Encyclopedia Britannica 1952) presenting his heliocentric theory. This was still based on the ptolemaic system, with crystalline spheres carrying the planets and with the outer sphere carrying the fixed stars (Fig. 3.3). The important feature of his theory is that the focus changed from the earth to the sun—with the sun in the center of the universe, the planets rotated around it.

Most scientists rejected his book. At the turn of the century (1500), few people were Copernicans. Science does not readily accept radically new ideas, and Copernicus' theory was contrary to the teachings of the Church. In fact, part of the data did not favor the Copernican system. The

Italian scientist Galileo Galilei (1564-1642) popularized the experimental method in science. He supported the Copernican heresy, and for this he was tried and convicted of heresy by the Church in 1633. Actually, the Church has been blamed for what began as a scientific dispute between the followers of two incompatible theories of the structure of the universe.

Spontaneous Generation

During the Middle Ages people believed that organisms arose spontaneously. Anyone could observe that mice would appear if a pile of rags was left in a corner and that maggots would materialize in meat without having come from anywhere. Also, microbes would appear spontaneously in nutrient broth. Even the scientists believed that these organisms developed spontaneously. To be sure, some doubted this theory, and their attempts to disprove it make a long and interesting chapter in science.

Between the 17th and 19th centuries, a series of experiments by Francesco Redi (1626-1697), Lazzaro Spallanzani (1729-1799), and Louis Pasteur (1822-1895) gradually wore down confidence in spontaneous generation. The spontaneous origin of maggots in meat was

refuted first; it took longer to show convincingly that microbes do not appear spontaneously in nutrient broth. An elegant set of experiments by Pasteur finally eroded the foundation for belief in spontaneous generation (Asimov 1964, p. 92). However, it wasn't long before the stage was set for the reappearance of a theory, in more modern form, of the spontaneous origin of life.

The Development of the Theory of Evolution

World View Before the 19th Century. John Ray lived at a time when there were many great scientists—Anthony van Leeuwenhoek, Marcello Malpighi, Robert Boyle, Robert Hooke, Sir Christopher Wren, and Isaac Newton. In 1690, Ray wrote a book entitled *The Wisdom of God Manifested in the Works of the Creation.* The philosophy of Ray's book, which gives us a glimpse of the thinking of his day, definitely did not contain any concept of evolution. He expressed the general belief that the universe and living things are stable

**Figure 3.3
Comparison of the geocentric theory and the heliocentric theory as understood by Copernicus.**

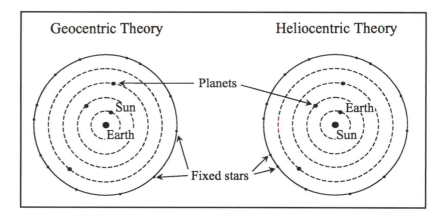

and unchanging. He stated: "The works created by God at first, and by him conserved to this day in the same state and condition in which they were first made." The earth was considered to have been made for humanity's benefit, and its structure adapted to human needs. Halley and Ray said the mountains were made to distill water for humankind and beasts, and were placed to make all of the continents inhabitable (in Greene 1959, p. 1-7).

Up to this time, people tended towards supernatural interpretations of even ordinary events and processes. Ray, Newton, and Boyle countered this notion, and tried to weld into a single philosophy two main concepts: (1) Nature is a "law-bound system of matter and motion" and (2) "nature is a habitation created for the use and edification of intelligent beings by an omnipotent, omniscient, and benevolent God." In this philosophy, God made the universe for humankind's benefit, but He created it to function according to a definite set of laws (Greene 1959, p. 1-13).

New World View Developed in the 19th Century. Not everyone was as eager as Ray and his peers to keep the two parts of his philosophy together. Some believed that if nature is a law-bound system of matter and motion, the possibility of creation is

ruled out. They developed completely mechanistic theories which did not in any way include the involvement of God in the history of the universe. In time, the principles of this mechanistic philosophy even were applied to the study of humans. There was a growing realization of the changes that occur in the seemingly permanent structures of nature and a greater willingness to think that living things have been changing also (Greene 1959).

Religion had become tied to a very static picture of the universe and ordinary events tended to have supernatural explanations. Science moved away from that toward a method of interpretation based on "actualism"— answering questions about the unknown by using only data on what can be actually observed in experiments or field observations. This meant that hypotheses about biological or geological history would be tested by comparison with processes that occur now. The pendulum swung to a completely naturalistic philosophy—one that would accept only theories and explanations that did not require any supernatural activity at any time in the past or present.

Another factor was natural theology (Wheeler 1975, p. 77-79). According to this philosophy, God made everything as it is, and every feature of nature was made to teach us something. If a squirrel was storing pine cones, one would not ask how that adapted the squirrel to survive in its environment, but what God wants to teach us by making the squirrel that way. Scientists could not accept this. One of the problems was that natural theology made God responsible for the bad things in nature as well as the good. Thinking people were turned away by the concept of a supposedly loving God who would make repulsive parasites to teach us something.

The first coherent theories in subjects like geology, paleontology, and biological change developed during this general rebellion against religion. Undoubtedly, it was necessary for the concept of a static universe to be rejected before those disciplines could prosper. The intellectual atmosphere of the times also had some influence on the nature of the specific theories that developed. Naturalistic thinking was beginning to dominate the intellectual world, and influential scholars in geology and biology were strongly influenced by it. Many scientists did believe in a creator God, but their ideas did not prevail as the majority view.

Development of Naturalistic Theories

The stars had been thought of as perfect and unchanging. Then astronomers discovered spots on the sun and craters on the moon and they realized that the heavens actually are changeable. The philosopher Immanuel Kant (1724-1804) and others devised a theory of the evolution of the universe through the operation of the laws of motion, beginning with uniformly dispersed matter (Greene 1959).

A similar revolution was taking place in geology. A greater recognition of the significance of earthquakes, volcanic eruptions, floods, and landslides aroused more interest in geology, but until the 1700s no coherent theory existed in geology. Some geologists believed the biblical flood was a reality that caused the geologic deposits. Another interpretation was that multiple creations and catastrophes have occurred and that Genesis only records the latest such cycle. Others argued that the Bible should not be used at all in interpreting geology.

The first to publish a comprehensive theory of geology was James Hutton (1726-1797). His book, *Theory of the Earth* (1795), was a completely uniformitarian explanation of geology (geological history explained by the same geological processes and natural laws observable today) with millions of years in earth history. However, he did say that the origin of the geological systems could not be studied because of a lack of data. He apparently believed God made the systems. Then Charles Lyell (1797-1875) wrote *Principles of Geology*, published in 1830-33, a further development of Hutton's ideas. Lyell's book was more readable than Hutton's and was widely influential. This book was very important to the rise of evolutionary thought, because without uniformitarian geology and its long span of time, the general theory of evolution could not have been viable.

Biological Evolution

For centuries, people thought that species were immutable (unchanging) since they were created by God. This dogma began to erode at least as early as the mid 1700s, when a trend toward accepting the possibility of natural change in organisms developed. Many individuals were involved in these changing ideas, but we consider here a few who contributed concepts that were later molded together into the theory of evolution proposed by Charles Darwin (Greene 1959). Some of these persons believed only in microevolution (changes within species), but others suggested larger-scale evolutionary changes.

Compte de Buffon (1707-1788) recognized the evidence for variability of organic forms. He suggested that organisms have

changed through the operation of a system of laws, without Divine action, to produce the great variety that we see in nature. He said that weaker species die out and he anticipated, at least partially, the concepts of natural selection and the struggle for survival. Wells (1757-1817) suggested that new forms arise by chance variations. He applied natural selection to humans. Lamarck (1744-1829) had a strictly materialistic view of nature. He had learned that change occurs in the geological structure of the earth, so he thought it likely that animals would also change since they depended on their environment. He postulated an evolutionary theory (called his development hypothesis) with evolution of new species and evolutionary progression from the simplest forms of life to humanity. He discussed the evolution of humankind explicitly.

His mechanism for this process was quite different from modern evolutionary thinking. He said that as animals and plants interact with their environment, changes are caused by (1) felt needs, (2) use and disuse, and (3) the inheritance of acquired characters. In other words, if an ancient proto-giraffe felt the need to reach higher to get more food, its neck would get longer because of its stretching to reach new heights. This acquired characteristic would be inherited by the next generation.

Erasmus Darwin (1731-1802), the grandfather of Charles Darwin, also proposed a theory of evolution. He was the first to support such a theory with facts from comparative anatomy, geology, botany, and zoology.

Thomas Robert Malthus (1766-1834) was not a biologist and probably had no idea that he would contribute to any theory of evolution. He was an economist who wrote *Essay on the Principle of Population* (1798), a study of the nature of the growth of human populations. Insights gained from reading his book laid the foundation for Charles Darwin's understanding of how many excess individual animals that are produced will not survive.

By 1818, these ideas were present in the scientific world, but they had not been put together in one coherent theory. Edward Blyth, a man about the same age as Charles Darwin, probably made a significant contribution to Darwin's understanding of natural selection, though Darwin never gave him any credit (Eiseley 1979). Blyth wrote articles on natural selection in *The Magazine of Natural History* in 1835 and 1837. "The leading tenets of Darwin's work—the struggle for existence, variation, natural selection and sexual selection—are all fully expressed in Blyth's paper of 1835" (Eiseley 1979, p. 55). However, Blyth was not an evolutionist; he viewed natural selection as a conserving rather than a creative force, maintaining kinds of animals by eliminating the weak individuals.

As we have noted, Charles Darwin (1809-1882) did not originate the idea of evolution; his contribution was integrating these different ideas into one convincing theory supported by a mass of data. Darwin's evolutionary mechanism, based on natural selection, was not generally accepted until decades later (Mayr 1996). However, his theory that the evolution of life forms through geologic time was quickly accepted by most of his scientific colleagues. Darwin convinced them that there was a way to explain biology within the same naturalistic philosophy that already held sway in the physical sciences. Darwin's victory was primarily philosophical—ridding biology of the need for reliance on any kind of supernatural intervention (Moreland 1989, p. 215-218; Numbers 1992, p. 5, 6).

A number of biologists in Darwin's era, including Linnaeus, had proposed that considerable change has occurred within the created groups of organisms. This concept could have retained belief in a Creator, while recognizing the evidence for biological change.

Darwin was unaware of this movement, and it was not in harmony with the prevailing intellectual trend toward naturalistic thinking (Landgren 1993).

Charles Darwin tried the study of medicine and theology before he took a trip around the world (1831-1836) on the *Beagle* as a gentleman guest of the captain. He read Lyell's book on the trip and made many observations and collections. He came back to England and studied his collections and also studied the variation in domestic animals. From these sources, he got the idea that selection was the cause of variation. From reading Malthus' book on population growth and recognizing the role of excess numbers of individuals, he saw how natural selection applied to natural populations.

In 1844, he wrote an essay on his theory but was too cautious to publish it. He was startled out of his caution when another biologist, Alfred Russel Wallace (1823-1913), developed the same theory. In 1858, papers by Darwin and Wallace were presented to the Linnaean society, and the next year Darwin's book *The Origin of Species* was published.

An interesting episode concerning the relationship between Darwin and Wallace was their difference of opinion over the origin of the human brain (Eiseley 1955; Gould 1980a, chap. 4). Darwin believed that humanity arose by the same gradual process of change that produced all other life forms. Darwin and his colleagues readily envisioned a natural progression from the apes to some of the primitive cultures which they believed to be only slightly superior to the apes, and finally to the superior races of western humanity. Wallace, in contrast to Darwin and the other great biologists of that time, had years of experience with the natives of the tropical regions, and he saw evidence that these "primitive" cultures were not mentally inferior. Wallace did not see evidence for an evolutionary progression in the human races, and he questioned why people in those simple cultures would have brains evolved so far advanced beyond what was needed for their survival. He also insisted that "artistic, mathematical, and musical abilities could not be explained on the basis of natural selection and the struggle for existence" (Eiseley 1955, p. 67). Wallace contended that there must have been divine influence in the origin of the human brain, a position to which Darwin strongly objected.

Darwin's work was the culmination of 200 years of developing ideas. It was important for his trend of thinking that at the time his suspicions were aroused that species could change, he had at his disposal the writings of men such as Lyell, Lamarck, and Erasmus Darwin; he was also subject to the strong trend toward naturalism in science (Greene 1959).

Darwin's theory had important theological implications. He could see no evidence of purpose in nature. Greene (1959, p. 336-337) explains Darwin this way:

> Here, indeed was agnosticism— an agnosticism which trusted in the power of science to discover the origin of stars and planets, mountains and species, morality and religion, but which to all the deepest questions of the human spirit returned an *Ignoro*, followed by an *Ignorabo*. . . . Certainly Darwin had done little to raise man's estimate of his own nature. The creature whom the Psalmist viewed as "little lower than the angels" Darwin showed to be but little higher than the brutes. If man were in fact descended from the animals, what reason was there to believe that his "better instincts" or his reason would prevail over his self-regarding instincts and aggressive passions?

Darwin seemed to be struggling with these implications. In his letter to Asa Gray, dated 3 April 1860, Darwin stated:

> I remember well the time when the thought of the eye made me cold all over, but I have got over this state of the complaint, and now small trifling particulars of structure often make me very uncomfortable. The sight of a feather in a peacock's tail, whenever I gaze at it, makes me

sick. (MacBeth 1971, p. 101) However, late in life Darwin said that unbelief crept over him so slowly that he felt no pain.

The first coherent theories in geology and much of biology developed at a time when the general attitude among learned people was to reject formal and restrictive religion. Thus, belief in creation finally was eroded also. Truth isn't weakened by honest inquiry. Even a Christian must recognize that it was not wrong for Darwin and others to ask hard questions. The Bible doesn't say that animal species have never changed or that the earth is the center of the universe. The Church insisted on holding these ideas anyway, and many scientists responded by throwing God entirely out of their interpretations of origins.

From Darwin to the Contemporary Scene

After the naturalistic theories of evolution and uniformitarian geology became the ruling paradigm, many people, including some scientists, still believed in creation, but they did not respond by using their understanding of creation to develop a competing paradigm.

The Bible predicts that near the end of time, people no longer will believe that "by God's word the heavens existed and the earth was formed" (2 Peter 3:5, NIV) or in the flood. That prediction certainly has come true in the 20th century as the intellectual community, in particular, has abandoned such beliefs. At the beginning of this century the general population was creationist, but the scientific community was not. Those who did believe in creation did very little to respond actively to this situation.

In succeeding decades, creationists became more active and attempted to understand how to deal with the data. One leader in this effort was a school teacher, George McCready Price. He had no training or field experience in geology, but he started reading the literature and critiquing the scientific theories of uniformitarian geology and evolution. He wrote several books including *Illogical Geology* (1906) and *The New Geology* (1923). He believed in a literal seven-day creation and a world-wide flood, and he rejected several basic geological concepts including glaciation and the idea that there is order in the fossil record. These were the key elements in the theory he developed.

Geological theory tells us that the stack of rock layers (the geological column) that contain the fossils was laid down layer after layer through millions of years of time (570 million years for the Phanerozoic rocks which contain most of the fossils). These fossils are in a particular sequence. For example, the lower layers of the fossil record (Cambrian) contain almost entirely invertebrates; dinosaurs and many other types of reptiles occur only in the middle third of the Phanerozoic rocks (the Mesozoic), and human fossils are found only at the very top, in the Pleistocene. This is explained as an evolutionary sequence; that is, no mammals are in the lowest layers because they had not evolved yet. Price said that this theory was not right, that there really is no reliable order to the fossils and that science has invented the order to fit the evolution theory. He maintained that the fossils occur in the expected order in some places, but not in other places.

Actually, the fossils do occur out of the expected order in a number of places in different parts of the world, and everyone recognizes that. The real point of contention was the explanation given for this observation. Geological theory says that the fossils are out of order because of overthrusts or mountain building (tectonic) activity that pushed older layers of rock up over the top of younger rocks. Price believed that overthrusts were just an invention to explain away the out-of-order fossils.

Price was influential among creationists at the time of the Scopes trial in 1925. Scopes, a Tennessee school teacher, was convicted of teaching evolution to the children, thus breaking a Tennessee law. This trial was the beginning of a protracted legal battle which eventually was resolved in the 1987 Supreme Court decision declaring it unconstitutional to require equal time for the presentation of the creation doctrine in public schools (Gould 1987-88).

Price later taught biology at Pacific Union College (PUC) in northern California. A student of Price's, Harold Clark, taught biology at PUC after Price moved on. Clark had learned Price's geological concepts and taught them as he learned them from Price. But Clark spent time in the field studying the rocks. From his study of the evidence, he became convinced that glaciation was more widespread at some time in the past and that the order in the fossil record is real. He developed the theory of ecological zonation to explain this in the context of a worldwide flood. According to this theory, a predictable sequence of fossils appears in the rocks; but rather than being a record of evolution, it is a record of preflood ecological zones being buried and preserved one after the other during a worldwide flood. George McCready Price could not agree with Clark's theory (Clark 1966), and this led him to make some

unfortunate accusations. Clark was a believer in the Bible, but he put the biblical concepts together with the geological data in a way that was different from Price's ideas, and Price could not accept that. Humans tend to have pet theories about the details beyond what the Bible says; and when those theories are questioned, they assume others are attacking the Bible. Obviously, the Bible does not say anything about Paleozoic rocks or Mesozoic reptiles. We can't equate our specific theories about such things with Bible truth.

Many individuals have been and now are involved in developing interventionist ideas, but the work of Price and Clark highlights some important themes in biblical creationist thinking. Meanwhile, a book written by John C. Whitcomb and Henry Morris (1961), *The Genesis Flood*, was apparently a very influential factor in convincing many people to accept flood (catastrophic) geology (Numbers 1992).

The Research Era for Interventionists

Only in about the last two decades have interventionists done any serious research using interventionist/catastrophic geology paradigms. The approach used in this work is based on the conviction that if we really believe that Genesis contains truth, we do not need to be afraid of data;

we don't need to be afraid to go out
and look at the rocks and fossils and
do real research. This concept is
developed in chapter 5.

So far we have discussed the nature and limit of science and some of the major features in the history of science. The process of replacing one theory or paradigm by another is explained in *The Structure of Scientific Revolutions* (Kuhn 1970), a book that has changed our understanding of scientific progress (Frodeman 1995). A paradigm is a major theory with broad explanatory value. Examples of paradigms are the theory of gravitation, the atomic theory, the evolution theory, and an alternative informed intervention theory.

Scientists choose one of the thousands of possible research projects within a given paradigm. A geologist may study the characteristics of a certain rock formation and the process by which it may have formed—working out the details within a paradigm. Right now, however, we are looking at the big picture—how paradigms come to be accepted or rejected.

Two quite different points of view on the nature of scientific progress are described by Kuhn. The first is the traditional way in which historians and philosophers of science have looked at the history of science. In the second, he describes what he believes is a better way of understanding the history of science.

The Traditional View of the History of Science

In the traditional view, science is just a stepwise accumulation of facts, one on top of the other. This continues again and again in a continuous chain of progress toward our modern scientific views. The historian of science who follows this approach tries to determine where, when, and by whom each specific fact, as recognized today, was discovered. The historian also tries to determine how we got rid of the myths, superstitions, and errors that prevented this fact from being discovered sooner (Kuhn 1970, p. 1-2). Implicit in this view is an assumption that whoever discovered this fact long ago was thinking the same way people do today. Looking back at the history of chemistry, one could easily assume that the chemist who discovered oxygen was thinking of the periodic chart as we know it. Upon discovering a new gas, he or she decided that it fit right up there in that spot on the chart.

Is this really the way progress was made? The discovery of oxygen serves as an example as we try to answer that question. Scientific textbooks often have a little bit of the history of scientific discoveries in them but, as Kuhn points out, their overly brief historical accounts can obscure the facts. One textbook (Brescia et al. 1974) says that "oxygen was first prepared by Joseph Priestley," and includes the method he used. It then says, "It remained for Antoine LaVoisier (1775 to 1777) to show the important role that oxygen plays in combustion and respiration" (p. 499). That description tells who and when, but it doesn't tell us much about the process of discovery. Perhaps we can forgive the author whose goal is to tell us about chemistry, not about the historical process. A chemistry text by Linus Pauling (1964) notes that LaVoisier advanced a new theory of combustion, hinting that some real changes in thinking occurred at that time.

That is about all the history we get in science textbooks. They assume, generally, that the scientists of another era were thinking as we do, and that the old ideas some of these scientists helped to replace were just superstition, not really science. However, that view doesn't seem to work. The old ways of thinking can't always be called superstitions and

myths. A more careful study reveals that those scientists of long ago often were using research methods just like those in use today. The people working on the geocentric theory believed the earth was the center of the universe, but they were collecting and interpreting data the same way we do now. The same scientific process in the past has led to completely different paradigms, incompatible with what scientists believe today. Out-of-date theories were not necessarily unscientific. They simply have been replaced by other scientific theories.

A New View of the History of Science

This brings us to Kuhn's new way of looking at scientific history. He suggests that significant progress is made through scientific revolutions in which an entire paradigm is replaced by another one. The main point that leads to a correct understanding of the history of science is that we must evaluate scientists' views and discoveries, not in comparison with our views, but in light of their own surroundings and the science of their time (Kuhn 1970, p. 3). We must evaluate Priestley's work in light of known facts and concepts of his time, not in comparison to our science today. Priestley and LaVoisier in the late 1700s were working within the phlogiston theory. Everything, according to this theory, has either caloric or phlogiston, one of which is lost when the substance burns. If it is a metal that burns, it loses phlogiston (which has a negative mass) and thus weight. Caloric, on the other hand, has a positive mass. So things that disintegrate and lose mass when burned (such as paper or wood) lose caloric rather then phlogiston.

Another old concept was that acidic substances contained something called the principle of acidity. Early scientists also thought that acids were molecules with little hooks on them; bases had little holes in them. Therefore, they said, they both tasted bad because the hooks pricked our taste buds and the holes had rough edges that scraped our taste buds. When acids and bases were put together, the hooks fit into the holes and they neutralized each other. This was part of the chemical theory Priestley and LaVoisier worked with. They knew nothing of our periodic chart of the elements or of oxidation reactions. When Priestley collected that new kind of gas, he called it air without its usual amount of phlogiston. LaVoisier did the same experiments. He said the new substance was an atomic principle of acidity and formed a gas only when that principle had united with caloric. That doesn't sound like anything we

learn in chemistry class today; it is an entirely different way of thinking. Priestley never comprehended what he had discovered. He didn't know he had discovered a new gas called oxygen, and he never accepted the oxygen theory of combustion.

LaVoisier approached these experiments from a different background. He had already done experiments which convinced him that something was wrong with the phlogiston theory. He was ready to question the very basis of chemical theory. He was convinced that burning objects absorb something from the atmosphere. Consequently, he was willing to recognize what the discovery of oxygen implied for chemical theory. He didn't just discover a new fact and fit it into existing theory; rather, his discovery led to the development of the oxygen theory of combustion—a new theory that led to the reformulation of chemistry and overthrew the phlogiston theory.

Progress didn't occur by adding one fact to another; rather, it came when one entire paradigm was replaced by another—a scientific revolution. This is an example of Kuhn's view of scientific progress; when we evaluate scientific discoveries in light of the thinking of their time, we find that scientists then were practicing the same kind of science we do now, even though the thinking is very different. In the process of research, scientists sometimes make discoveries that overthrow old theories. Kuhn says this is the primary form of scientific progress. He recognizes that facts often do add on to one another but, according to Kuhn, science really makes a big leap in progress when one theory is entirely replaced by another in a scientific revolution, and science works on within that new paradigm.

The old theory was not just superstition. In its time, the theory met all the criteria for a useful scientific theory. In fact, chemists working under the phlogiston theory didn't have the information necessary to lead them to the new theory. It was when chemists made the right discoveries, including the discovery of oxygen, that they were able to develop the new theory which we now take for granted.

Note, too, that the data did not dictate the theory. Within a short passage of time, two very different ways of interpreting the data of chemistry were used. True, the data make boundaries for our theories. But with the data available at any given time, there is likely room for a variety of scientific theories, like phlogiston and the alternative chemical theory. Which theory is accepted at a given time has a lot to do with sociology,

with the experience of the researchers, and with historical accidents as to what experiments were done and in what sequence.

SUMMARY
Old view of scientific history

1. Determine when and by whom each of the facts that we recognize was discovered.

2. Evaluate these ancient discoveries in light of modern knowledge.

3. Determine how we got rid of the errors and superstitions that impeded progress.

New view

1. Evaluate ancient ideas and discoveries in the light of the science of that time, not in comparison to modern science.

2. Recognize that ancient scientists may have been using the same scientific methods that we use. Out of date theories were not necessarily unscientific, simply because they have been discarded.

The Life Cycle of a Paradigm

Pre-paradigm Stage. A scientific revolution is part of the life cycle of a scientific discipline. The cycle starts with the beginning of a new scientific discipline. At this stage, no unified theory tells which facts are important and how to understand them, so the field of study is somewhat unorganized.

As one paradigm gains acceptance in the new discipline, more uniform thinking occurs. Which group of scientists wins out in this situation is not always determined by entirely objective factors. For example, the geology book by Lyell was very important. He was a good writer and this probably became an important factor. But as geologists look back at the discipline's beginnings now, they recognize that some of the core concepts of Lyell's thinking are wrong, even though he was successful at winning support for his theory over other points of view we now consider as more correct than his (Gould 1984). A new paradigm generally tackles only a few problems; but once it succeeds with those, it makes predictions in other areas that seem to show promise.

Normal Science. Finally, most of the people in a discipline think in similar terms; a mature field of science has developed. Normal science does not question or test the paradigm—it just accepts it as true and works within it. Kuhn (1970) calls this "normal science" because it is what scientists normally do. As he expresses it,

> Normal science seems an attempt to force nature into the preformed and relatively inflexible box that the paradigm supplies. No part of the aim of normal science is to call forth new sorts of phenomena. Indeed, those that do not fit the box are often not seen at

all. Instead, normal scientific research is directed to the articulation of those phenomena and theories that the paradigm already supplies. (p. 24)

For instance, people who work on atomic theory do not question whether it is true or not. They accept it and work out details within it. That is the inevitable result of science being focused on a particular paradigm. This may seem contrary to our expectation that science should be testing its theories all the time. Kuhn's point is that science does not normally do so. The testing comes over the long term, not at each step along the way. Actually, we can't always be questioning the foundation of our discipline. We must take some things for granted and work within those basic assumptions in order to make any progress. We trust that if the theory is wrong, the data sooner or later will reveal the error.

The paradigm defines which research will be productive and which will not. For instance, the Copernican (heliocentric) theory claimed that the earth is moving through space, around the sun, and, consequently, its geometric position relative to various stars should change through the year. (This is called parallax [Fig. 4.1].) However, if the geocentric theory is correct, there would be no such parallax. The heliocentric theory said that looking for stellar parallax would

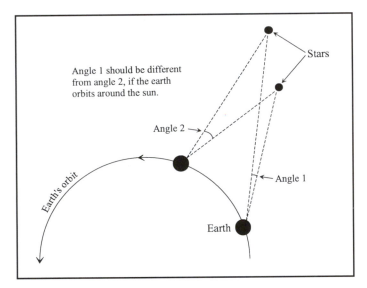

Angle 1 should be different from angle 2, if the earth orbits around the sun.

Stars

Angle 2 →

← Angle 1

Earth's orbit

Earth

Figure 4.1 Copernicus' theory predicted that parallax would be seen in relative star positions (shown in this figure), as measured at different points in earth's orbit. The geocentric theory said there would be no parallax, since the earth didn't move.

be a profitable line of research; the geocentric theory implied that it would be a waste of time. If you were working on your Ph.D. in Copernicus' day, would you have the courage to do your dissertation research looking for stellar parallax when the dominant theory said you would fail? Science is still that way. Different paradigms lead people in different directions as to what research they believe is worth doing.

Within normal science, one important factor that keeps scientists focused on the current paradigm is the education process. The scientists write textbooks and tell students which paradigm is correct. This helps to maintain a constructive unity in science, but it also makes it difficult for a competing paradigm to gain a fair hearing. If scientists within a dominant scientific paradigm reject a competing one on the grounds that scientists have all agreed on the truth

of the accepted paradigm, we need to ask whether that unanimity exists because the supporting evidence is so strong or because of the dominating influence of the well-entrenched paradigm.

The Crisis. The process of normal science works well until the paradigm reaches a crisis (Kuhn 1970). Research may have been going well, with expected results, but then the researchers gradually run into things that don't fit the paradigm. Their experiments don't come out as expected, and the paradigm runs into what we call anomalies—problems that persist and do not go away. When the data don't fit the theory, it can mean one of at least two things: Either something is wrong with the data-collection process, or a discovery is waiting to be made. And this discovery may indicate that a new paradigm is needed.

Several characteristics indicate a crisis period. There is a persistent failure to explain the anomaly; this leads to scientists' insecurity as to the ability of their science to explain the problem. This activates a proliferation of versions of the theory. Typically, there's an increased interest in the philosophy of science as researchers try to understand why this is happening to them (Kuhn 1970).

The crisis process can be observed in the history of some theories.

The geocentric theory explained the data very well. Its equations were good predictors of the movements of stars and planets. But, as the theory was developed and attempts were made to deal with the finer details, some problems became evident, and a crisis arose. In the face of problems, most scientists believe that they will be able to answer the questions, so they continue to work within the existing paradigm. Even when the paradigm is plagued with problems and insecurity, scientists do not abandon a paradigm that has worked well unless a better replacement is available (Kuhn 1970, chap. 8).

The Revolution. Finally, the revolution comes! One paradigm replaces another. A few creative individuals are convinced of the need for a new paradigm, so they propose one and try to develop it. No matter how good the idea is, it's important for the new paradigm to convince a few capable people who will do research to begin to build arguments in favor of it. If that doesn't happen, the new paradigm won't go any-where. It must win converts, as Kuhn says (chap. 12). "Converts" here is an interesting term. We usually don't think of science that way, but that subjective term is used here because at the time when two paradigms are beginning to be weighed one against another, the new paradigm isn't likely

to have much strong evidence to prove it right or wrong. It is more a matter of winning a few converts who think it is right and who are willing to try to develop it.

If the revolution is successful, the new paradigm will replace the old. This is neither an easy nor quick process. When the Copernican theory was proposed, a lot of people resisted it. Almost one hundred years went by before it had much strong support.

Several other paradigm revolutions illustrate this same process: the chemical revolution in which the old phlogiston theory was replaced; and the geological revolution when the theory of continental drift (the idea that the continents move) and plate tectonics became an important unifying concept. Another example in geology resulted from the discovery of turbidites—a rapid underwater sediment (mud, sand, etc.) flow which deposits a sedimentary layer (Hamblin & Christiansen 1995, p. 130-132). When turbidites were discovered, thousands of sedimentary deposits were reinterpreted as occur-ring in minutes instead of years. Such a big change in geologic under-standing has been called the turbidite revolution (Walker 1973).

Another example from the field of geology is the recent paradigm shift from uniformitarianism to what is called neocatastrophism. The geological paradigm developed by Hutton (1795) and Lyell (1830-33) was strictly uniformitarian. For example, streams erode mountains and layer sediment in lakes and valleys. According to Lyellian uniformitarian theory, these same processes produced the rocks slowly and gradually. In the last couple of decades, the data have forced a recognition that many geological processes occurred rapidly and catastrophically. Thus, Lyell's rigid version of uniformitarianism is being replaced by neocatastrophism.

A new paradigm is typically not just a modification of an existing one. Often it is not even compatible with the old paradigm. Putting the sun in the middle of the universe is one option, and putting the earth in the middle is another. One can't make a compromise between them; we must choose one or the other. A new paradigm succeeds with only a few problems; the old one has failed with only a few. A decision between the two competing ways of doing science must be made, and that decision at first is made less on past achievement of the paradigm than on promise of its success in the future.

> The man who embraces a new paradigm at an early stage often must do so in defiance of the evidence provided by problem solving. He must, that is, have faith that the new paradigm will succeed with the many large problems that confront it, knowing only that the old paradigm has failed with a few. A decision of that kind can only be made on faith. (Kuhn 1970, p. 158)

We usually think of faith in terms of religion; here, a type of faith also has a relation to science.

Criticisms of Kuhn's Philosophy

Kuhn has been criticized for appearing to say that change from one theory to another is not based on reason or evidence. That's not quite a fair criticism of the scientific revolution concept. Ultimately, the data will have their say. We have evidence now that Copernicus was right. Kuhn's ideas really apply when an old theory is running into difficulties and a new theory has been proposed, but the evidence is not adequate to say for sure which is correct. One example is the stellar parallax theory. The new heliocentric paradigm predicted it would be possible to see parallax when viewing stars from the earth. But, in fact, parallax could not be seen. We know now that the angles are so small that the researchers then did not have adequate instruments to measure them. Even at that time, some of these data seemed to say that Copernicus was wrong, and it wasn't easy to make a correct decision between the competing paradigms. At such times, decisions may be made on individual bases that don't even seem rational; in fact, strong evidence on which to make a decision probably isn't available in the crisis period. Unless a few capable, independent scientists have faith in the new paradigm, we will never know its potential for success.

There is always the possibility that a new paradigm is wrong, and the scientists who choose it take a risk. But if change is ever going to occur in science, some people must make uncertain decisions. After a revolution occurs, science moves into the normal science under the new paradigm and the change is complete.

Creativity and Conformity in Science

In a book called *The Essential Tension*, Kuhn (1977) discusses the tension between creativity and conformity in science. Normal science is driven by the conformists who accept the theory and work out the details. On the other hand, creativity arises with mavericks like Einstein and Copernicus who have their doubts about accepted theories and come up with new ideas. Kuhn feels that science needs both types. Without conformists, we wouldn't accumulate adequate data to discover that a new paradigm is needed. But every now and then, science needs mavericks—creative people who think new thoughts. An article in *The Scientist* (De Sousa 1989) says that scientists are becoming too much like chefs—they tend to follow a recipe for research rather than thinking creatively. Another *The Scientist* article (Raup 1986) says "New ideas are guilty until proven innocent" (18). This article urges scientists to try out new ideas. "Perhaps the only thing that saves science is the presence of mavericks in every generation." Science is a fascinating enterprise and has need of all kinds of people. When the United States was developing, it needed mavericks who were willing to brave the unknown wilderness, but it also needed the solid, stable people who would follow behind them and build the structure of the nation. Science is the same way.

5

The Paradigm of Naturalism and an Alternative

A Scientific Philosophy for the Study of Origins

The evolution theory is based on the philosophy of naturalism and does not consider any hypotheses that involve divine intervention in the history of the universe. Is it possible that an alternative philosophy could also be successful in guiding scientific research?

Many diverse areas of science today build on the common underlying paradigm of naturalism (or materialism). People in the Middle Ages were quite mystical in their thinking and commonly appealed to the supernatural to explain things they did not understand. Then a shift toward the philosophical position of naturalism began and an attempt was made to explain everything in nature through known natural laws. This philosophy is a key element for understanding the relationship between informed intervention and science. In a discussion on the issue of teaching creation in the public schools, I heard a prominent scientist state that even if creation were right, he would have to deny it to remain a scientist. To understand why a reputable scientist would make such a

statement, one must understand the role of naturalism in science. Naturalism has become part of the definition of science. "If there is one rule, one criterion that makes an idea scientific, it is that it *must* invoke naturalistic explanations for phenomena, and those explanations must be testable solely by the criteria of our five senses" (Eldredge 1982, p. 82, emphasis in original). Science cannot do experiments to test the supernatural. This concept is clear enough and is accepted by interventionists, but science has gone a step further and has decided to accept only theories which do not imply or require any supernatural activity at any time in history (Johnson 1991).

What basis is there for this concept? When we observe the world around us, we see that predictable natural law is in effect. Modern science has convinced most of us that God does not normally tinker with the universe, causing unexpected things to happen. The data are consistent with the proposal that He has established a set of laws, and the universe operates accordingly. Consequently, a scientist, including one who believes in God as Creator, can function on a day-to-day basis as a naturalistic scientist, and science has achieved much success by following this approach. However, some effective scientists acknowledge that God could have acted at times in history in ways which we would call miracles, such as creating the first living organisms. Science cannot test the concept of informed intervention in history, but it should not reject a theory just because it implies that an event may have happened that is outside of our testable hypotheses (Moreland 1994).

From the naturalistic point of view, one who believes in informed intervention cannot be a scientist. How can informed intervention, which by definition involves supernatural phenomena, be scientific? Can this seeming contradiction be resolved? We have discussed the characteristics of a good theory, and we have noted that evolution theory has these characteristics. Can there be any type of informed intervention theory that also has the same characteristics? I believe the answer is yes.

It is often implied that because interventionism originates from religion, it is unscientific. Does the source of a theory affect its validity? A theory is not scientific or unscientific because of its origin; it is scientifically useful if it can be tested.

If it cannot be tested, it is outside the realm of science. That concept remains valid, even though theory falsification is not always as easy as we would like.

Testable and Untestable Hypotheses

Some readers may conclude that the above explanation eliminates interventionism from the realm of science, since the hypothesis of informed intervention cannot be tested. But it is not that simple. There are testable aspects and other untestable features of both interventionism and naturalistic evolution. Scientists would generally agree that the hypothesis "God created life" (Table 5.1) cannot be tested by science. We cannot define an experiment or set of observations that potentially would falsify that hypothesis. This leaves us with the alternate hypothesis "Life was not created by God," which is more likely to be accepted as valid science.

What is our definition of a useful scientific theory? One that can be tested—susceptibility to testing makes it scientific. Now let us consider again the last hypothesis and challenge any reader to define an experiment or set of observations that potentially would falsify the hypothesis "Life was not created by God." Be careful with your logic as you devise a test. For example, to describe how a creator would design

Table 5.1
Testable and Non-Testable Hypotheses
(Evidence supporting the testable hypothesis does not demonstrate the truth of the corresponding non-testable hypothesis; it does allow it as a feasible possibility.)

Non-testable Hypotheses	Testable Hypotheses
God created life.	All living and fossil organisms fall into discrete groups without a series of evolutionary intermediates between major groups.
God did not create life.	Series of intermediate forms between major groups of organisms have existed in the past.
Vertebrates originated by evolution from the echinoderms. Echinoderms and vertebrates were both created by God.	The simplest vertebrate animals have more similarities to some echinoderms than to any other group of invertebrates.
God caused a global geological catastrophe.	Most individual rock formations formed quite rapidly and catastrophically.
God did not cause a global geological catastrophe.	Most individual rock formations formed over long ages of time. The Coconino Sandstone was deposited under water. The Coconino Sandstone was not deposited under water.

organisms and then show that organisms are not designed that way is not valid. How would we know how a creator would design life? The test must be more objective and independent of our own opinions.

The concepts "God created life" and "God did not create life" are equally untestable. Science should either (1) devise a valid experimental test for one or both of these hypotheses, or (2) not say that one is scientific and the other is not.

Even though both theistic and naturalistic paradigms include concepts that cannot be tested by science, it is possible to define hypotheses which describe results that should be discoverable in nature if one of these nontestable hypotheses

were true. The first requirement for making testable hypotheses is to leave out any consideration of whether a divine being or designer was or was not involved. What is left are questions about objective things that may be found in the rocks or in living organisms. For example, if at least the basic groups of life forms were created, series of evolutionary intermediates between these groups are unlikely to be found; but if these groups were all the result of evolution, it seems that a reasonable number of intermediate series would be found. Someone looking for an easy falsification of either of the two basic hypotheses will be disappointed. The evidence is complex and our understanding very incomplete; but, in principle, science ultimately should be able to test between these two descriptive hypotheses.

I propose that scientifically useful (testable) theories like some of those listed in Table 5.1 can originate from religious concepts. We cannot directly test whether God involved Himself in earth history; but if He did involve Himself in ways described in the Bible (creation and worldwide geological catastrophe), these events should have left some evidence in the natural world (for example, limited evidence for evolutionary intermediates and pervasive evidence for catastrophic geological action). The possible existence of such evidence can be investigated scientifically.

The Supernatural and the Laws of Nature

An important difference lies between saying that perhaps miracles have happened though science cannot tell us if they have or not, and saying that science denies that any miracles have ever happened, and will not accept any hypotheses that imply that miracles have happened. Consider, for example, the hypothesis that many phyla of organisms appeared on earth suddenly, independently of each other. The response that this may have happened but science can't test it is quite different from suggesting that science can't consider this hypothesis because it implies a mirac-

ulous origin of life forms. In practice, science generally takes the second view and will not allow for miracles even when they appear to be required by rigorous logic. This helps to explain the statement by our friend that even if creation were correct, to be a scientist he would have to deny it. This doesn't necessarily mean that he is a bigot. Evidently he sincerely believes that it is necessary to accept the naturalistic definition of science in order to be a good scientist. Is that the way it should be, or has the pendulum swung too far? Has it gone from one extreme (medieval pervasive supernaturalism) to another (strict naturalism)? I respect the right of others to believe that it is necessary to accept naturalism to be a scientist, but I will try to persuade them that strict naturalism is not the only paradigm that can lead to effective science.

Are miracles really capricious magic, or is there another way to understand the supernatural? Imagine that God wrote on microfiche all laws that govern the universe. In the year A.D. 1500, for example, scientists knew a small percentage of these laws (Fig. 5.1). Eventually, people learned more of them. By the late 1990s, people knew a larger proportion of the laws, but many still remain to be discovered. Imagine someone had invented a time machine that would allow us to bring to our day a person who had lived in A.D. 1500. We take him into a supermarket and the door opens by itself as we approach. We get into a car and turn a switch and the strange carriage roars and moves down the road. We go home and flip a little lever on the wall and the lights come on. By now, the poor fellow may flee in terror at these supernatural manifestations. Why would he think that? It's simply the difference between his thinking and ours; he is not familiar with the laws governing the operation of cars, electricity, etc. He thinks of these as supernatural but, in reality, he just does not understand them.

Another aspect of this same issue can be explained with another example. If I hold a book in the air and drop it, the law of gravity dictates that it will fall to the floor. We can try it a million times and the same thing always happens. However, since I am a mobile, reasoning being, I can decide to stick out my hand under the falling book so it doesn't fall to the floor. I have interjected an outside force into the system and changed the course of events, but I have not broken any laws. God could decide to interject an outside force into earth's balanced geological systems and change the course of events to bring on a catastrophe without breaking any laws of the universe.

The portion of the universal laws that we understand are called natural law. The things that God does which we do not understand, we call supernatural. To God, all the laws of the universe are a unified whole. They do not limit Him because He designed them to control the operation of the entire universe according to His plan. If this is true, someday He could explain to us how some of the laws currently beyond our understanding were used to perform what we call miracles, such as instantly creating life or turning water to wine. We still will not have the power to do many things that God can do, but we will see that they are not magic or capricious acts; they are part of the law-bound whole that God understands and uses to accomplish His purposes. God may use some of those laws only during the process of creation. He can make use of all of those laws, but we never will have the power to utilize some of them even if we do eventually understand them.

**Figure 5.1
Relationship between natural law and the "supernatural," in A.D 1500 and now.**

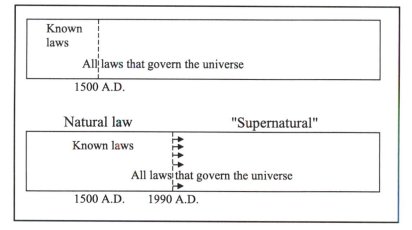

That is the difference between natural law and what we call supernatural.

This concept is fundamentally different from the "god-of-the-gaps" that gave way in the face of modern science. The old "god-of-the-gaps" existed because of our tendency to explain things that we couldn't understand (the "gaps" in our explanations) as the direct result of God's power. When science searched for the answer to one of those gaps, God no longer was needed to solve that problem; consequently, the more we learned, the less we needed God—or so it seemed. When William Harvey learned that the heart was a pump (a "machine" whose operation could be understood), and that the blood was not moved by the direct intervention of God, his new insight was not appreciated by some individuals, because it seemed to push God a little farther away. The faulty logic in the old "god of the gaps" concept implies that if we can understand how something works, God does not have any part in it. A further implication is that if God is involved in some process, that process does not function through nature's laws. That is no more defensible than to claim that since we understand how a computer works, there must not have been an intelligent being involved in its origin. I submit that God works through the laws that He has estab-

lished; when we learn how the heart works, we have not diminished God—we have just learned more about His laws and His magnificent inventions. There is much about the universe that we do not know. So we are unreasonable to assert that God cannot work outside the natural laws we know, because they are only a small part of the laws of the universe.

If this concept is sound, we're not being unscientific if we admit the possibility of miracles. All that's required is our willingness to admit there could be a Being in the universe powerful enough and knowledgeable enough to know and use all those laws. But even if we admit this, it is still true that historical accounts of miracles are something that science cannot test. But it is not unscientific to consider the possibility of such things happening.

Biases from Various Sources

Could a person's religious perspective cause a bias in his or her interpretation of scientific data? Certainly. Can a naturalistic philosophy bias a scientist's interpretation of data? Again, evidence seems to indicate that it can. Our research only answers the questions we are willing to ask; naturalism allows only certain questions to be asked. Consider the difference between the two questions in each of the pairs in Table 5.2.

Naturalism allows only question number 1; thus, answer 2a is ruled out of scientific consideration by strictly *a priori* considerations. Naturalism has a powerful biasing influence in science, in steering scientific thinking and, in many cases, deciding what conclusions are to be reached. Generally, this is not recognized.

When the discipline of geology was taking form in the 18th and 19th centuries, the geologists Hutton (1795) and Lyell (1830-1833) each wrote books in which they developed a paradigm of geology that rejected the catastrophic theory of their day and replaced it with a theory based on uniformitarian (the same natural laws have always been in operation) and gradualistic (always slow) processes over eons of time. Lyell's book was the more influential of the two and constricted geology to a very gradualistic, uniformitarian paradigm until the mid-20th century. A recent historical analysis of Lyell's work has reached the conclusion that the catastrophists in Lyell's day were the more unbiased scientists. Lyell took a culturally derived theory and imposed it upon the data (Gould 1984). Gould and others are not saying this because they agree with the biblical views of Lyell's colleagues, but because it is apparent that those colleagues were more careful observers than Lyell and did not let their religious views twist their interpretation of data.

Various authors have stated that Lyell's strictly gradualistic version of uniformitarianism is not needed—that it has been bad for geology because it has prevented geologists from considering any hypotheses involving catastrophic interpretations of the data (Gould 1965; Krynine 1956; Valentine 1966). These authors are not recommending a return to a

Table 5.2
Differences between a Naturalistic and a Non-naturalistic Philosophy

Questions	Responses
A Question 1: Which hypothesis is correct?	A. Naturalistic hypothesis A B. Naturalistic hypothesis B
Question 2: Which hypothesis is correct?	A. Naturalistic hypothesis A B. Naturalistic hypothesis B C. Life did not arise by a naturalistic process (this answer implies creation by an intelligent designer, but this cannot be part of the testable hypothesis, just as the concept of naturalism cannot be a testable part of an evolutionary hypothesis)
B Question 1: Which hypothesis is correct?	A. Gradualistic evolution of all life forms B. Evolution by punctuated equilibrium
Question 2: Which hypothesis is correct?	A. Gradualistic evolution of life forms B. Evolution by punctuated equilibrium C. Independent, non-evolutionary origin of major groups of organisms; evolution only within each of these groups.

Bible-based catastrophism; they're simply recognizing the evidence that many sedimentary deposits were catastrophic in nature. This has brought the discipline of geology to accept neocatastrophism, a naturalistic paradigm that explains the geologic record as developing over millions of years of time with many catastrophic events that left their mark on the rocks. For a long time, Lyell's paradigm prevented geologists from recognizing the evidence for these catastrophic processes. Now that Lyell's bias has been recognized and abandoned, the philosophy of naturalism does not prevent recognition of catastrophic processes.

Controlling Bias in Scientific Research

The problems a portion of Lyell's theory has caused in geology suggest that religion is not the only factor with the potential to bias one's interpretation of data. This problem is not an informed interventionism problem; it's a human problem everyone must be aware of and seek to overcome. Science has a method for dealing with this problem which will be effective for interventionists as well as others,

if we use it (Table 5.3).

This method is the peer-review system that helps to maintain quality in science, or one might call it the critical discussion in Popper's (1963) scientific method. The peer-review system cannot deal with philosophical questions like informed intervention. However, any time we can use this philosophy (or any other) to help us define a hypothesis and collect data from rocks, fossils, or living organisms to test that hypothesis, the research data and their interpretation can be subjected to the process outlined above.

Bias is best controlled by critical interaction between scientists of varying views. Peer review did not soften Lyell's rigid geological gradualism for over a century. Why? Peer review could have functioned better if scientists with different views had continued to dialogue, but the catastrophists ceased to be an influence in geology. As it was, Lyell's gradualistic uniformitarianism was the only paradigm in use. Years of accumulating data finally forced scientists to review Lyell's version of uniformitarianism and address foundational questions about catastrophism.

I believe science will be benefitted if it encourages scientists with a naturalistic orientation and interventionists who are research-oriented to be productive. Both groups are

---

Table 5.3
Components of the Scientific Method of Bias Control

1. Use good research design and careful data collection.
2. Discuss specific results with scientific colleagues and present papers at scientific meetings.
3. Submit papers for publication in refereed scientific journals (papers that are reviewed by several recognized peers before publication).

searching for truth, and neither has anything to fear from the other as long as both are (1) active in the scientific process and engaged in quality research, (2) honest with the data, and (3) taking an active part in the scientific community, publishing their work, attending meetings and presenting papers, and talking with their peers about their work. No quality control is quite as effective as knowing that when one presents a paper on his or her latest work, others, including some who disagree, will be ready to point out the mistakes that may have been overlooked. Also, scientists in each group are likely to recognize some types of data that the other might overlook.

Is There a Viable Alternative to Naturalism?

One should use caution when criticizing scientists who make naturalistic assumptions. Science has reason to take this approach. It has been very successful since the adoption of naturalism. But before we conclude that this success demonstrates the truth of the naturalistic assumption, we must look at the issues in more detail. The development of modern scientific thinking involved the adoption, as I interpret it, of several specific concepts:

1. Living things and physical phenomena are like machines in the sense that they are mechanisms that can be studied and understood.

2. On a day-to-day basis, natural processes are not dependent on the capricious whims of the spirits or the operation of magic.

3. The processes of nature follow predictable laws. By experimentation and observation, we can learn what these laws are.

4. Scientific hypotheses must be testable using only criteria accessible to our five senses.

5. Change has occurred in organisms and in the physical universe—neither are static. New species of animals and plants have arisen, and geologic structures change with time.

6. Science does not consider the possibility of any intervention in the history or functioning of the universe by higher power (naturalism).

Are these six items equally essential for the success of science? The first concept is an assumption that is crucial for science, the second and third items are assumptions that expand on the first, and the fourth item is an operational assumption. These four concepts constitute the breakthrough that launched science on the road to its modern success. The fifth is an empirical observation, and the recognition of this concept was also an important insight that opened up large vistas for research.

Some might say that naturalism follows inevitably if the first four concepts are true, but this is not necessarily correct logic. My car operates according to natural laws, and I find it interesting to study the natural processes that make it travel down the road. It is not necessary to assume a naturalistic origin for the car in order to successfully understand its operation. The question of design, or informed intervention in the car's history, only becomes an issue if I delve into the question of the car's origin. If I do, I need to ask myself if I am willing to consider the possibility that in the origin of the car the laws of nature had some assistance from an intelligent designer. That may sound like a silly question, but it's not silly if we have no record of the origin of cars or similar machines. Of course, such analogies have limits, and the car analogy breaks down because cars do not reproduce and have a mechanism to evolve, but it still helps to illustrate that as long as we accept the first four concepts, most of what science does would not be affected by whether or not we accept the sixth concept—naturalism. Only when we study the beginnings of life, or the history of life and the universe, does it become necessary for us to decide what to do with naturalism.

The scientific paradigm that includes naturalism has been successful, but is it the only potentially successful paradigm? We must compare naturalism here with an alternative, which we call partial naturalism (generally interchangeable with the term interventionism).

Naturalistic science only accepts hypotheses based on the uninterrupted operation of natural laws, understood today to explain biological or geological events and processes. One clarification needs to be made at this point. Even naturalistic science doesn't properly deny that God exists or that divine intervention could have happened. It just doesn't use the scientific process to study such things. Science can only investigate natural processes. Hence, hypotheses that require or imply the existence of any type of divine intervention in earth history at any time are not acceptable to science. However, naturalism is often consciously or unconsciously interpreted to include the idea that divine intervention is not true or is unscientific. In any case, the result is a strong bias against interventionist concepts.

Partial naturalism assumes that on a day-to-day basis the processes of nature do follow natural laws. Living things and physical processes are like "machines" in the sense that we can figure out how they work and what laws govern their structure and function. An interventionist scientist who subscribes to this paradigm can work and think like a naturalistic scientist with one exception: he or she does not rule out the possibility that an intelligent, superior being has, on rare occasions, intervened in biological or geological history, particularly in connection with the origin of life forms. He or she also would acknowledge that such interventions could have involved the use of the laws of nature that are far beyond the outer limits of current human knowledge.

Thaxton et al. (1984) have distinguished (a) operation science (study of recurring phenomena in the universe) from (b) origins science and conclude that intelligent intervention may have been involved in origins but should never be invoked in operation science. Science cannot test or define the nature of these possible interventions (they are in the realm of philosophy, not science), but it can recognize evidence that may point to the existence of discontinuities or unique events in history and can examine their plausibility. The philosophy presented here is based on the conviction that if such discontinuities occurred, it is better to recognize their existence than to ignore them.

One story tells of a man who was on his knees under a street light. A friend came by and asked what he was doing. He answered that he was looking for his keys. The friend helped search for some time and then asked, "Are you sure you lost them here?" "No," he answered, "but the light is better here." Science can, indeed, see better when studying observable natural processes, but is that sufficient reason for denying that any other events could have occurred?

A comparison of the tenets of the two philosophies further helps to clarify the relationships between naturalism and interventionism (Table 5.4). The set of assumptions labeled "partial naturalism" is a part of our definition of informed interventionism. One crucial difference exists between the thinking of a naturalistic scientist and an interventionist: the interventionist is unwilling to set up definitions that eject the Designer out of the universe without a fair trial. In any attempt to draw out the potential similarities between informed interventionists and others, one has to be candid about that difference.

Anyone who is not willing to accept assumption #6 under partial naturalism (Table 5.4) will no doubt reject much of the approach taken in the rest of this book. Assumption #6 does not specify what sort of intervention occurred—it just leaves the door open to ask seriously the second question in Tables 5.2 and 5.5. A commitment to naturalism, on the

66

Table 5.4	
Comparison between Naturalism and Partial Naturalism Philosophies	
Naturalism Tenets	Partial Naturalism Tenets
1. Living things and physical phenomena are like machines in the sense that they are mechanisms that can be studied and understood.	1. Living things and physical phenomena are like machines in the sense that they are mechanisms that can be studied and understood.
2. On a day-to-day basis, natural processes are not dependent on the capricious whims of the spirits or the operation of magic.	2. On a day-to-day basis, natural processes are not dependent on the capricious whims of the spirits or the operation of magic.
3. The processes of nature follow predictable laws. By experiment and observation, we can learn what these laws are.	3. The processes of nature follow predictable laws. By experiment and observation, we can learn what these laws are.
4. Scientific hypotheses must be testable using only criteria accessible to the five senses.	4. Scientific hypotheses must be testable using only criteria accessible to the five senses.
5. Change has occurred in organisms and in the physical universe—neither is static. New species of animals and plants have arisen, and geologic structures change with time.	5. Change has occurred in organisms and in the physical universe—neither is static. New species of animals and plants have arisen, and geologic structures change with time.
6. No intervention has been made by any higher power. Science does not consider any hypotheses that imply such intervention.	6. At certain times in history, an informed intervention may have occurred in geologic or biologic history, especially in connection with origins. Hypotheses are not to be shunned just because they imply the existence of such interventions.

other hand, does not allow question #2 to be asked because option 2c implies an interventionist origin of life forms (Table 5.2), or implies that not enough time has elapsed for an evolutionary origin of the life forms preserved in the geological column (Table 5.5).

Evaluating the Two Paradigms

As people within either of these paradigms evaluate the other paradigm, they have the tendency to do exactly what Kuhn (1970, p. 148) says will happen. The two paradigms have differences in the rules that they follow (#6, Table 5.4); and as a result, the practitioners of each approach end up talking past each other. The rules for doing science within naturalism

(items 1 - 6, Table 5.4) declare that partial naturalism/interventionism is, by definition (rule #6), unscientific. In contrast, the interventionist considers this rule to be merely an untested hypothesis that could never be demonstrated by scientific data and, in fact, has the potential to introduce serious biases into science. Lyell's geological gradualism restricted the range of hypotheses that could be considered, to the detriment of geology. Is it possible that naturalism has the same detrimental effect?

If the two groups sincerely wish to understand each other's thinking, followers of either paradigm must learn what it is like to think as those in the other paradigm think without

Table 5.5 Comparison between the Naturalist and Interventionist Philosophies	
Questions	Proposed Hypotheses
Question 1. Which hypothesis is correct?	A. Lyellian uniformitarianism, including geologic gradualism B. Neocatastrophism: catastrophic events in a naturalistic framework
Question 2. Which hypothesis is correct?	A. Lyellism uniformitarianism, including geologic gradualism B. Neocatastrophism: catastrophic events in a naturalistic framework C. Catastrophism involving a global geologic catastrophe a relatively short time ago that produced a significant portion of the geological column (with its implication of informed intervention in earth history)

being judgmental (Thaxton et al. 1984, p. 212). Only then will they be prepared to make a fair evaluation of the internal consistency of each paradigm and its success in dealing with the evidence.

In some cases, informed interventionism is judged more by naturalism's rules than by the data. For example, the criticism has been made that rivers, streams, flash floods, etc., could not deposit so much sediment in a few months or years. Of course, this criticism ignores the fact that the theory which puts all of this activity within such a short time does not rely on present-day water systems to do the work. It proposes that at one time there was a much more catastrophic water flow. The same also works in reverse. If interventionists want to understand the paradigm of naturalistic evolution and be prepared to critique it meaningfully, they must evaluate it by its own rules before trying to compare it with the interventionist paradigm.

If we admit the possibility of divine intervention in history, we may be accused of implying that earth history will be capricious and non-understandable—not amenable to scientific investigation. Here, we must point out, it is important to evaluate the paradigm's internal consistency using its own rules. In fact, if interventionism builds on the conviction that the Bible is a reliable communication from the Designer, it has a consistent and meaningful answer to this question. The God who intervened in history has taken the trouble to tell humankind about unusual events which would confuse the study of history if the events were left unknown.

Imagine a large dam built across a canyon backing up a lake as big as one of the Great Lakes. One day the dam gives way. The enormous rush of water erodes away all traces of the dam. As the water cascades through the valleys downstream, it erodes them into canyons many times larger than their original size. With time, all human memory of the dam and its destruction is lost. One ancient book tells the story, but arguments go on over the book's authenticity.

A geologist studying the canyons along the river rejects the validity of the old book and concludes that no natural process could have produced a flood that massive. She measures the flow of the river, and the amount of sediment it is carrying away, and calculates how long it took for the present river to carve the canyons. In time, additional data point to catastrophic processes in the canyons, but the geologist concludes that the indicated catastrophes were isolated floods with long time periods between them.

Another geologist is willing to consider seriously that the book may be reliable. He decides that if it is correct, the insights in the book will help to keep him from misinterpreting the data. Without the book and its story of such a unique event—totally different from the natural catastrophes that are part of our modern analogies—it would be difficult, if not impossible, for the geologist to have any hope of being able to think of the correct hypothesis for the origin of the canyons. More serious, he wouldn't even be aware of the problem.

If the book is correct, it provides a logically consistent approach to the problem: the flood was the consequence of an unusual event, someone told us about it, and this knowledge

gives us a trustworthy beginning point for developing specific hypotheses about the erosion processes. The central issue is our willingness to seriously consider that the book might be telling the truth. If those who think it is true conduct themselves as good scientists, science probably would be benefited more from maintaining a friendly dialogue than if it defines them out of science.

Interventionism can take many forms. The version of interventionism presented here concludes that the "old book" is a reality: the Designer communicated to us and evidence indicates the communication is reliable in describing the actual history of life. The communication is brief; it leaves many unanswered questions. But if it is a reliable account, the most productive approach will be to take it seriously and see what insights its concepts can give us in our research. Statements from the book cannot be used as evidence in science; but if those statements are true, we should be able to use some of them as a basis for defining hypotheses that lead to productive research. Several very general hypotheses that follow from this approach are listed in Table 5.6a; contrasting parallel hypotheses based on a naturalistic evolutionary paradigm are listed in Table 5.6b. Of course, one must remember that the "old book" also contains much material that cannot be addressed with the scientific process.

Research under the Philosophy of Interventionism

My experience indicates to me that interventionism, as defined above, is an effective framework for doing science. Let us consider several specific examples of research that have been done under this interventionist philosophy and published in peer-reviewed scientific journals.

1. *Yellowstone fossil forests.* In and adjacent to Yellowstone National Park, volcanic deposits contain a series of fossil forests, one above another, with upright stumps that appear to be in their original position of growth. If these forests containing some very large trees grew in their current position, one forest after another, a very long time would be required. Interventionists began studying these forests to determine whether there was an equally valid alternative interpretation. Their research has led to the development of the hypothesis that the fossil trees did not grow where they now are, but were transported to that location together with the sediments. Several lines of research, published in professional journals, now lend support to this hypothesis (Chadwick & Yamamoto 1984; Coffin 1976, 1983a, 1983b, 1987).

2. *The Coconino Sandstone trackway research.* The Coconino Sandstone is generally considered to be formed from a series of desert dunes. The only fossils it contains are trackways of invertebrates and of either amphibians or reptiles. When I began to study the fossil vertebrate trackways in this formation, I had doubts about the desert-dune origin of the tracks, initially for philosophical reasons, and set out to evaluate alternate hypotheses for formation of the tracks. So far, the data from my study of the tracks support the hypothesis that the fossil tracks were made underwater (Brand 1979, 1992, 1996; Brand and Tang 1991). Whether future research continues to support this hypothesis remains to be seen.

3. *The history and status of white-footed mice (genus* Peromyscus) *on several islands in the Gulf of California.* Alternative hypotheses for the status of these mice were: (1) the island mice were a separate species that had arisen from related mice on the mainland, *Peromyscus eremicus,* or (2) the island mice were still the same species as the mainland mice. In this case, interventionist theory does not automatically favor one over the other. The evidence supports the conclusion that the

---

Table 5.6a
General Hypotheses Derived from Christian Interventionism

1. There were independent, nonevolutionary origins of at least the major groups of organisms. The limits of these groups need to be determined from an analysis of the evidence.

2. Life has existed on earth for a short time, measured in thousands of years, and the rocks containing at least the Phanerozoic fossil record were formed during that time.

3. A very high level of catastrophism was involved in the formation of a significant portion of the Phanerozoic record.

Table 5.6b
Hypotheses Derived from a Naturalistic Evolutionary Paradigm

1. All life forms trace back to the natural origins of life from non-living material.

2. Life has been on earth for many millions of years, and the geologic record formed over this long time period.

island mice have become a separate species, apparently in response to isolation on the islands (Brand and Ryckman 1969). This, and a number of similar studies, demonstrates that an interventionist philosophy can be an effective stimulus for research on evolutionary processes without assuming that major groups of organisms arose by the process of evolution.

4. *Precambrian pollen in the Grand Canyon.* Some researchers contended that Precambrian rocks in the Grand Canyon contain fossilized Angiosperm (flowering plant) pollen, and that this is evidence against evolution (Angiosperm plants presumably did not evolve until long after the Precambrian era.) A claim as significant as this should be verified independently to be sure of its authenticity. Another interventionist repeated the research. His data indicated that these rocks do not contain fossil Angiosperm pollen. The original claim apparently resulted from contamination of the samples by modern pollen (Chadwick 1981).

5. *Human tracks in Cretaceous rocks.* Some interventionists have claimed that Cretaceous limestone by the Paluxy River in Texas contains fossil human tracks in association with dinosaur tracks. As with the Precambrian-pollen story, such a significant claim should be followed

up with extensive, careful study. The more significant the implications, the more rigorously the claim should be examined before proclaiming it as evidence for or against intervention or evolution. A restudy of the Paluxy River tracks convinced a number of interventionists that the tracks are not human (Neufeld 1975).

6. *Other fields.* In the medical sciences and areas of biology, chemistry, and physics that don't deal with evolution or history, a number of interventionists are doing high quality scientific research. Their philosophy does not in any way hinder them from effectively using the scientific process in their study of the workings of the natural world.

One danger we must avoid at all costs is the very human tendency to think that because we believe the Bible contains special insights, whatever ideas we develop based on this book are automatically right. George McCready Price (1906, 1923) provided an example of this problem. Even though the Bible says nothing about the ice age or the "out of order fossils," Price could not accept the possibility that his way of explaining the evidence pertaining to these might be wrong.

Research under the paradigm of interventionism (like any other research) does not automatically lead to correct conclusions but merely begins a search in a particular direction. After the search is begun, several different turns may be necessary before the theory satisfactorily explains the evidence and has predictive ability.

Examples:

1. *Yellowstone fossil forests.* Initial interventionist hypotheses were that the fossil trees were actually on the surface of a slope, that they did not go back into the hills in a vertical series of layers, or that there really were not many layers of forests. Research falsified these hypotheses, and led to a productive scientific hypothesis—that the fossils were transported with the sediments.

2. *Order of fossils in the rocks.* George McCready Price began with the hypothesis (he didn't see it as only a hypothesis) that the sequence of organisms in the fossil record was not predictable, that the organisms were buried randomly during the flood. His hypothesis has been proven false, but the research that proved his hypothesis as false led to another hypothesis—ecological zonation (Clark 1946). This hypothesis still needs much refinement before it adequately explains the fossil record. Whether it will stand in a modified form or be replaced by a different hypothesis remains to be seen.

3. *Coconino Sandstone trackway research.* My first hypothesis

concerning the vertebrate trackways in the Coconino Sandstone was that they formed in some type of wet sand environment (but not underwater). The data did not support this hypothesis. Further study suggested that the fossil tracks were most likely made while the animals were completely underwater. So far, the second hypothesis has strong support from continued study of the tracks.

In the long run, errors in the initial theory do not prevent truth from emerging, although beginning with the correct assumptions speeds the process. If catastrophic geologists after Lyell's time had continued to use their paradigm successfully in research, their work would have provided an influence to counterbalance Lyell's rigid gradualism. Had they done so, the turn to catastrophic interpretations could have occurred sooner.

A Need for Caution

At this point, we must consider another side of the issue. Even if catastrophic geologists use their theory effectively and make discoveries others have overlooked, their scientific research has limits. Science cannot demonstrate whether God was or was not involved in influencing geologic history. Even if research eventually demonstrates that the best explanation for the geologic column is rapid sedimentation of a major portion of the column in one short spurt of geologic activity, it only would make it reasonable to believe the flood story if confidence in Scripture leads one to do so. It would not prove, scientifically, that God caused a flood.

This principle can be further illustrated by considering a specific formation—the Coconino Sandstone—and by trying to decide what kind of evidence would tell if it was a flood deposit. Often, it is helpful to begin a specific project by trying to think of all possible hypotheses that could explain a particular phenomenon. Table 5.7 lists several representative hypotheses for the Coconino Sandstone.

A catastrophic geologist may predict that the correct hypothesis is

Water 4 (however, we cannot rule out Wind 4 without adequate evidence, since we don't know all that was going on during the flood). One must not go beyond the data when claiming support for such a conclusion. If compelling evidence indicates that the Coconino Sandstone was deposited underwater, can that evidence prove that the flood occurred? No, that evidence could be explained equally well by any of the water hypotheses. Evidence that can be explained by two or more hypotheses cannot say which hypothesis is more likely to be correct. We must seek evidence that fits one hypothesis and contradicts all the others.

If the evidence finally accumulates to indicate that the Coconino was deposited underwater very rapidly and that a significant portion of the geologic column was also deposited catastrophically, would it prove the biblical flood? No, but such data would eliminate all hypotheses except Water 3 and 4. What scientific evidence would prove which of these two hypotheses is correct? Science can never demonstrate that God was or was not involved in influencing earth history. The choice between hypotheses Water 3 and 4 always involves a strong element of faith. Catastrophic geologists cannot expect to prove that God caused a flood; but they can hope to

---

Table 5.7
Representative Hypotheses for the Deposition and Geological Context of a Cross-bedded Sandstone

Wind	1. Deposited by wind over hundreds or thousands of years in a desert.
	2. Deposited rapidly by wind during a period of unusually persistent high winds; the rest of the geologic column was formed over a period of millions of years.
	3. Much of the geologic column was deposited rapidly and catastrophically, and the Coconino Sandstone was deposited rapidly by wind. God was not involved, and this rapid deposition had nothing to do with a worldwide flood.
	4. Deposited very rapidly by wind during the early part of the biblical flood during a period of lowered water level and persistent high wind.
Water	1. Deposited over hundreds or thousands of years by water.
	2. Deposited rapidly in an area with persistent, relatively rapid water currents and a plentiful sand supply. The rest of the geologic column was formed over a period of millions of years.
	3. Most of the geologic column was deposited rapidly and catastrophically and the Coconino Sandstone was deposited rapidly by water. God was not involved; this rapid deposition has nothing to do with a worldwide flood.
	4. Deposited rapidly underwater by the persistent water currents during the biblical flood.

demonstrate that hypotheses based on the biblical flood account can stimulate productive research and produce superior explanations for geologic phenomena. As this process achieves success in verifying a reasonable number of the hypotheses that it generates, an open-minded person is more likely to conclude that it is not unreasonable to take that paradigm seriously.

Why Bother?

Maybe interventionism can be a basis for doing scientific research, but is that paradigm really needed? Geology did correct Lyell's mistake without any help from outside of naturalism; so why is informed intervention needed? Many bright and successful scientists are convinced that the theory of the evolution of life forms adequately explains the evidence. I can understand the rationale for their attitude and will defend their right to disagree with me. I also suggest that some dimensions to these issues often are overlooked. There are good reasons for taking seriously the possibility of informed intervention—not because there is proof for it or because it will answer all the questions, but because of a conviction that it has something important to offer science as well as religion. A clear discussion of the issues requires a differentiation between several

separate questions that are a part of the evaluation of interventionism vs. naturalism (Table 5.8).

The progress of the last two centuries tells us that the answer to question 1—Can good science occur within the rules of naturalism?— is yes. Whether or not we agree with the tenets of naturalism, one cannot say that naturalism is not an effective paradigm. For reasons that are spread throughout these pages, I argue that question 2—Can good science occur within the rules of informed intervention?—can also be answered "yes", although the demonstration of that potential is just beginning. Interventionism can produce good science, and many of the specific questions that can be addressed with testable hypotheses are essentially the same under the two paradigms. But some will differ, as illustrated by the examples in Table 5.9.

Questions 3 and 4—Can the concept of naturalism be tested? and Can the concept of informed intervention be tested? (Table 5.8)—are both answered no. Both naturalism and interventionism are based on non-testable assumptions; the decision between them is based on a philosophical choice. We consider the answer to questions

---

**Table 5.8
Comparative Evaluation Questions for Interventionism and Naturalism**

1. Can good science occur within the rules of naturalism?
2. Can good science occur within the rules of informed intervention?

3. Can the concept of naturalism be tested?
4. Can the concept of informed intervention be tested?

5. Does naturalistic evolution provide a sufficiently convincing explanation for the evidence (evaluated by its own rules)?
6. Does informed intervention provide a sufficiently convincing explanation for the evidence (evaluated by its own rules)?

7. Which of the two paradigms gives the more convincing explanation of the evidence? (An attempt at a valid answer to this question is possible only if one is willing to look honestly at the relation of each paradigm to the evidence without being judgmental of the rules of each paradigm.)

8. Which paradigm has more promise for effectively guiding scientific research in the future?

5, 6, and 7 in later chapters. For now, I suggest that at this time naturalism has better answers for some data and interventionism does better at interpreting other data. No doubt, some say that science has the answer to question 7—Which of the two paradigms gives the more convincing explanation of the evidence?—and naturalism is the clear winner. However, one could identify reasons for considering that answer premature. Ultimately, when more data are available, the evidence should point more clearly to a definite answer for question 7. The adherents of each paradigm have their own predictions as to which way the data will point. The answer to question 8—Which paradigm has more promise for effectively guiding scientific research in the future?—is largely based on philosophy, on a prediction determined by what each believes is the true history of life on this earth.

Attempts by some creationists to make naturalistic scientists look foolish are unfortunate and unrealistic. Naturalistic scientists are doing productive science. However, if proponents of naturalism wish to say that interventionism cannot be science, they need to devise credible scientific tests with the potential to falsify one or both of the hypotheses: "God created life" and "God did not create life."

One could argue that naturalism, properly defined, does not make either statement used in these hypotheses. Naturalism recognizes that science cannot address either hypothesis and asks only how life could have originated if it arose by purely mechanical means. If more people understood that most scientists consider naturalism this way and that most of them are comfortable with the thought that it is also intellectually credible to approach science from within a non-naturalistic philosophy, this book would not be necessary. However, many scientists think it is intellectually

---

Table 5.9
Comparison of Research Questions and Testable Hypotheses in Two Paradigms

Questions equally important in both paradigms

What physiological, anatomical, behavioral, or other mechanisms make each type of living organism well-adapted to its environment?

What are the genetic processes that control the changes in plants and animals?

What have been the phylogenetic pathways of change in living things and how have these changes adapted the organisms to their changing environments?

How and when were the fossils buried?

What were the geological processes that produced the geological column and the geological structure of the earth?

Questions that differ in the two paradigms

Naturalism	Interventionism
Asks by what processes life could evolve from non-living matter.	Predicts that life cannot arise without informed intervention and that abiogenesis research ultimately will fail.
Predicts that such research will not succeed because all life forms have arisen by evolution.	How much of the living world could rise by evolution? Are there aspects of the biosphere that are logically incompatible with a purely materialistic explanation?

unacceptable to consider seriously that God created life. But in the absence of experimental tests for these and similar hypotheses, the attempt to make interventionism, as defined here, outside of the realm of science is based strictly on an arbitrary *a priori* definition.

So, "why bother?" My answer is that interventionists do not ask people to try this approach if they do not see any reason to do so. Some of us actually believe that interventionist science ultimately will be more successful than naturalism because we believe that its basic tenets are closer to reality. This belief is based now on a philosophical choice and is criticized for being a religious choice; so it is. But the only religion worth having is one based on truth. If people believe their religion is truth and that it offers insights into earth history, they would be missing something important if they didn't use it for generating testable scientific hypotheses.

Thomas Kuhn (1970) pointed out that when a new paradigm is first suggested, only a few persons will think that it is worthwhile. The chance of success for the paradigm depends on those few people demonstrating that they can do effective research under it. I propose that Kuhn's general concept of scientific revolutions has many similarities with the naturalism/interventionism debate. The naturalistic paradigm has successfully guided science for a long time. The much newer paradigm based on informed intervention and catastrophic geology is being applied as a guide in selected cases of field and laboratory research. Evidence in these cases has been successful and is beginning to be developed as a competing paradigm.

Someone may think the revolution was back in Darwin's day when creationism was rejected. I suggest that the theories of evolution and uniformitarian geology developed in fields which, up to that time, were in a pre-paradigm state. The first cohesive paradigms developed in an intellectual atmosphere strongly favoring naturalism. Consequently, they were purely naturalistic. Now we can look carefully at the accumulated data, see strengths and weaknesses in the established paradigms, and propose competing paradigms. Research under this new interventionist paradigm is beginning to have an influence on the scientific evidence available in certain areas where the research has been concentrated.

This discussion doesn't imply that the scientific community is on the verge of a paradigm shift to interventionism. The relationship between the two origins paradigms has some interesting similarities, but also some important differences from other paradigm competitions. The shift to plate tectonics (the theory that explains drifting continents), for example, did not require anyone to reevaluate the scientific method. Plate tectonics and the previous paradigm were both compatible with a naturalistic, evolutionary explanation of earth history. In contrast, interventionism redefines the limits of the scientific endeavor and raises fundamental questions about the meaning of human life and its relationship to a higher power. Also, since the evidence needed to resolve the intervention/naturalistic-evolution debate is an order of magnitude more complex than in other recent paradigm competitions, it is unrealistic to think that a few key discoveries will win over the scientific community. A peaceful coexistence between the two philosophies is a more practical goal.

What Should Interventionists Be Doing?

A key point often brought up is that creationists, no matter what they may say, are not scientists. They are not doing research. Eldredge (1982, p. 83) stated that no creationist "has contributed a single article to any reputable scientific journal." Actually, a number of interventionists are active in research and scientific

publication; but in an atmosphere of unfriendly debate between the two views, interventionists often don't make their philosophical views known.

The approach that would be beneficial in the long run would be for interventionists to conduct themselves as genuine scientists and get actively involved in research. It is better to develop an alternate paradigm than to merely poke holes in someone else's theory. If interventionist efforts center around disproving the prevailing evolutionary paradigm, this question will raised: What do you have that is better?

A person's philosophy shouldn't matter as long as he or she does good science; that is the ideal. Both naturalists and interventionists spend too much time accusing each other. Why do we do this? We don't have to agree on everything in order to value each other's work. The ultimate test of any scientist is honesty in dealing with the data and the quality of research, not personal philosophy. For science simply to judge a person on his or her honesty and effectiveness in research should be enough. This would eliminate many battles over philosophical issues.

6

Faith and Science
What Is Their Relationship?

This chapter explores the relationship between faith and science. Science is often said to be based on evidence, and religion on faith. Just what is faith? How does it differ from scientific evidence? One definition of faith is confidence or belief which is not based on proof (Webster's unabridged dictionary). But, shouldn't faith have some evidence to support it? Would we want to build our philosophy of life upon something for which we had no supporting evidence? Some see faith as a leap in the dark, and perhaps that is a valid way to define the type of faith that is not based on any evidence. How much better it seems to have some evidence to give us confidence in an idea before we put our faith in it. Faith is that which takes us beyond the partial evidence which we have. I suggest that several potential lines of evidence can help us evaluate whether we should have faith in the reliability of the Bible.

The Reliability of the Bible

One type of evidence is prophecy. The Bible long ago predicted that certain things would happen. When they do, our confidence in biblical reliability is supported. As a graduate student, I remember feeling the need to evaluate some of my beliefs for myself. I took the book of Daniel, a world history book, and some other references and followed some of Daniel's predictions. The prophecy of four main world empires in the western world of ancient times included detailed information. I was fascinated to see how these predictions unfolded in world history. Prophecy, then, is a useful line of evidence, because through it we can check whether the events occurred as the prophecy declared.

We also can look at internal consistency in all the books of the Bible written over a period of more than a thousand years. Surely the consistent message they present would provide evidence for the reliability of the entire book.

Historical accuracy is another line of evidence that can be examined. In the ancient writings, secular kings wrote about the history of their nations. Their goal was not to give accurate information about previous rulers; they wanted to make themselves look good. We can compare the Bible with other ancient writings and with the known facts of history to see if the Bible is more reliable (i.e., if it presents accurate history). Nineteenth-century archaeologists believed that the Bible provided very inaccurate history. For example, the Bible talks about the Hittite empire as a mighty, influential empire in the Mediterranean region. An active program of archeological investigation did not find any Hittite cities. In many such cases, they thought the Bible stories were just fables and unhistorical legends. When much more digging was done, the capital of the Hittite empire was discovered. In the long run, the Bible turned out to be exactly right.

Another supposed error concerned Nineveh, an important city in Bible history. Again, archaeologists did not believe it existed until, at last, the ruins were found. In case after case, the critics were wrong and the Bible was right. Today, the Bible is recognized as containing accurate history even by some who do not accept it as a divinely inspired book.

Other lines of evidence farther afield from scientific thought are also important. One of these is the effect of Christianity on people. In considering any religion, we need to ask what it is like to live under that system. Here we can't produce proof, and we are aware that personal testimonials can sound convincing even if based on nothing. But if we are honest and careful, we can evaluate whether Christianity has made a positive difference in our lives.

From this discussion, we are aware of the areas of evidence that support the biblical paradigm. But we must remember that the appeal to external evidence has limits. Many concepts in the Bible can never be tested—consider the stories about Jesus and the miracles that He performed. We can compare other parts of the Bible with the evidence, however; and if the evidence fits, it increases our confidence in all of the Scriptures (Rice 1991, p. 198-199).

Science and Religion: Their Sources

One important difference between science and the Bible is the source of their information. The Bible claims that God has seen all of earth history, has taken the responsibility to communicate to us through the Bible, and He supports the trustworthiness of that communication. If the evidence has led us to have confidence in this claim, we have a strong reason to take the Christian paradigm as a unit—to accept it as a whole. The more confidence (faith) we come to have in the Person who is communicating to us, the more that faith carries us beyond what can be tested and gives us confidence in the parts of the paradigm we can't test. We must continue study of the Scriptures realizing that we don't always understand the sacred documents correctly, but knowing that God has taken the initiative to communicate with us.

In contrast, formulation of scientific theories is a very human process. There is no god who developed the scientific theory and has taken upon himself to communicate it to us. Science wouldn't want to maintain that the significant aspects of a theory or paradigm must be either all right or all wrong. It recognizes that it may be part right and part wrong.

The Biblical Contribution to Origins and Early History

Because faith is built on evidence, let us apply that concept more specifically. Does any evidence leads us to take seriously the first books of the Bible, including the creation story? If we did not have Genesis, chapters 1-11, science and the Bible would get along well. I would suggest that tangible evidence exists in the earliest books of the Bible for intelligent, well-informed communication from a source outside the human race.

Creation/Flood Myths and the Genesis Account

In addition to the book of Genesis, other stories are found in the ancient world about creation and the flood. These include *Enuma elish,* the *Atrahasis Epic,* and the *Gilgamesh Epic.* When these myths are compared with the Genesis account, many similar ideas appear. One of note is that a hero survives the flood. These parallel tales lead some scholars to the conclusion that the Bible account is borrowed from other sources.

Does the evidence really point to that conclusion? If we use the same methods to compare two politicians, Edward Kennedy and Ronald Reagan, we can find many similar motifs in their political philosophy. They both believe in democracy and hold other ideas in common. If we then follow the same logic that has been used in the study of creation-flood stories, we would reach the conclusion that these two politicians were in the same political mold. But there is a fundamental flaw in that logic—it only considers data that show similarities between the two persons or stories. That introduces a serious bias into the study. If we want to make a valid comparison, we must also look at differences and compare them with the similarities.

Hasel (1974), Wheeler (1974), and Shea (1984) have examined the creation/flood stories looking for differences as well as similarities and have found some interesting things. Genesis is monotheistic, in stark contrast to the other accounts. In

Genesis, humankind was made in God's image and the earth was made for humanity's benefit. In the Babylonian creation myth *(Enuma Elish)*, a battle is waged between the gods. Finally, the god Marduk killed the goddess Tiamat, split her body in half, and made the earth and heaven out of the two halves of her body. The god Ea then made human beings from the blood flowing from the primeval monster Kingu. In this account, the creation of life occurred after a struggle between the gods so that humanity could carry out the gods' unwanted tasks.

In the *Atra-hasis Epic,* the god Enlil forced the younger gods to dig rivers and canals. When they finally rebelled, the problem was solved by creating man to do the work. Humans were made from clay and the blood of a sacrificed god, We-ila (Shea 1984).

In these near-eastern creation stories, matter is the source of life and even the gods arise from physical matter. The principal activity is in the realm of the gods, and earthly events are merely reflections of events in the realm of the gods. In the Bible account, humans are beings with dignity created in the image of God and given dominion over the earth; God controls matter and is indepen-dent of it. In the Bible account, the activity is centered on the earth, not in the realm of the gods.

Genesis does not follow the religious themes of the other stories. Instead, it deliberately speaks out against the pagan religions of Moses' time (Hasel 1974). For example, the Genesis account doesn't give the sun and the moon names (they are called the greater and lesser lights). This may have been done to avoid giving them any measure of respect, since other cultures worshiped them. The Bible creation story is unique and does not follow the ideas present in the other concurrent creation stories. "Genesis reveals insights that run counter to the culture and thought patterns of the ancients. . . . A document so out of keeping with surrounding culture could hardly have been created by those cultures" (Wheeler 1974).

Important parallels between these various accounts are described by Shea (1984, 1991). The similarities support the conclusion that the dif-ferent accounts trace back to an actual series of events. The possibility that the biblical account is more accurate should be considered.

Discussions of creationism often claim that Genesis 1 and Genesis 2 give two different, conflicting accounts of creation. Shea (1978, 1989) and Hasel (1980c, p. 48) have analyzed the literary structure of these chapters and found strong evidence pointing to a unity in their structure that argues for a single author. Genesis 2 focuses the discussion on the creation of man and woman and expands on the brief account in chapter 1.

Abundant flood legends are found in many cultures (Roth 1990). The differences among them tell us that each one has gone through a different history. The similarities revolve around the idea of a catastrophic flood, often focusing on a hero who survives it. Is it realistic to think that local floods in many different countries could have impacted different cultures enough to account for all of these flood legends? The similarities suggest that they trace their origin to an actual significant event in the distant past that found its way into the legends of all these cultures and is recorded in the Bible. The unique, elegant biblical accounts of the creation and flood stand out from the other stories and deserve consideration of the possibility that these accounts have not experienced a loss of accuracy apparent in the legends.

Moses and Laws of Health

Moses wrote many fascinating things about health in the early books of the Bible approximately 3500 years ago. Science didn't begin to understand germs and molecular biology until the 19th century A.D. Louis Pasteur

(1822-1895) is credited with discovering bacteria that carry disease. Dr. Ignaz Semmelweis, a physician in Vienna in the 1840s, wondered if some dangerous element was possibly being carried from dead patients to living patients. He encountered strong resistance to his new requirement that physicians and interns wash their hands after performing autopsies on dead patients before going to examine living patients. But he was persistent and discovered that the death rate in his maternity ward dropped dramatically (McMillen 1984). His experience graphically illustrates the ignorance of humankind towards germs prior to the modern age.

Moses was educated in Egypt centuries ago. Egypt had a medical textbook, but included such medicines as snake oil, cow dung, and ground-up flies (McMillen 1984). If Moses, who was trained by the Egyptians, had written the Pentateuch (the first five books of the Bible) based on the knowledge of his day, we might expect to find many of these same remedies in the Bible. But what do we find? Moses told the people of Israel that if they would follow the rules they were told, God would not put upon them the diseases He put upon the Egyptians. (That may sound as though God made the Egyptians sick. I would suggest that God did not explain the germ theory to the

Israelites. He accepted responsibility without further explanation and just said, "If you do what I say, you will not get these diseases.")

A physician who has studied the health-related laws given to the Israelites has compared them with what we know today (McMillen 1984). The Israelites were told that anyone who touched a sick or dead person was to be kept out of camp for a period of time and was to go through certain routines of washing with running water. That rule doesn't make sense unless we understand quarantine, the practice of keeping people with a disease separate so they don't communicate the germs to the rest of the group. The Israelites were given many other rules which would be considered correct even today if we did not have modern medical equipment.

Could Moses have invented these health laws that just happened to be right? I don't have enough faith to believe it just happened that way by chance. In our universe, there usually is a cause-and-effect relationship. The instructions given in the early books of the Bible are not based on Egyptian remedies; however, they do include things that suggest some understanding of the germ theory which the people in Moses' day certainly did not know. This suggests that Moses had external help.

Somebody knew what was going on even if it was not at that time defined and described in medical and scientific terms.

Some argue that the "books of Moses" were not written by Moses, that they were written later. Even if that argument were correct, it wouldn't change the picture since the people living 2,000 years after Moses still didn't have a clue as to the real cause of disease.

Jacob's Sheep

One interesting Genesis (chapters 30-32) story concerns Jacob and his problem with his scheming father-in-law. Jacob took care of the sheep and agreed that his father-in-law would get all the pure white sheep while Jacob would get all the off-colored ones that were striped and spotted. Jacob thought he was very clever and could cause the sheep to have striped or spotted young. In the centuries before modern genetic research, people believed that if a female animal saw a striped object while she was breeding, it would affect her offspring and make them striped. Jacob cut a striped pattern into pieces of wood and put these objects in front of the female sheep at their drinking troughs during the breeding season. Jacob thought this would cause the females to have striped offspring.

This story is sometimes cited as

evidence that the Bible teaches erroneous ideas. Anybody who makes that claim didn't read far enough—the very intriguing part of the story is in Genesis 31. After Jacob had become quite successful with his sheep, he had a dream. Before we discuss the dream, let's consider some basics of the genetics of sheep coloration. Modern knowledge of genetics indicates that the unusual characteristics of Jacob's sheep are recessive traits. If a sheep receives a (recessive) gene for spots from one parent, and a (dominant) gene for white wool from the other parent, it will be pure white because the dominant gene "overrules" the recessive one. Even though Jacob's father-in-law took all of the off-colored sheep out of Jacob's initial flock, some individuals remaining with Jacob would have the recessive gene for non-white wool, although there would be no visible evidence of it on the sheep. Since the genes for plain white sheep were genetically dominant, Jacob should have received far fewer sheep than his father-in-law.

Jacob thought the sheep were bearing so many off-colored lambs because of his striped sticks. However, in his dream, God basically told him that he was not as clever as he thought. He was shown that the males that were mating with the females were striped and streaked.

Remember, though, that Jacob's father-in-law had taken away all the males that had any visible evidence of stripes or other recessive traits. As far as Jacob (or anyone else before the 19th century A.D.) knew, none of the sheep in Jacob's flock had these characteristics. How would anybody at that time know that the recessive genes for striped coloration were lurking inside of the males doing the mating? The Bible says that God showed him that the ones that were mating were striped and streaked. Someone might argue that we cannot demonstrate that God actually did speak to Jacob or give him that dream, but it really doesn't matter. The point is that somebody who wrote the story of the dream knew that something invisible was inside those seemingly pure white sheep that made them not all white. Somebody knew that 3000 years before Mendel did any of his genetics experiments (Nichol 1953, p. 395). That to me is evidence upon which we can base our faith. If God communicated to Moses about health laws and striped sheep, perhaps it is reasonable to believe He also might have communicated the other concepts found in Genesis.

How Should We Interpret the Bible?

The concept of informed intervention, in its most basic form, does not depend on the Bible or any other specific religious source. However, I am presenting here a version of informed intervention that is built on the biblical account. Consequently, our study of the relationship between faith and science must consider theological methodology. How should we interpret the Bible and determine its meaning (Hasel 1980c, 1985; Hyde 1974)? Are we justified in placing confidence in the Scriptures as a reliable communication from God? Do we believe that the Bible gives reliable information even when it addresses topics outside of theology, like science and history (Hasel 1980b, p. 62, 68)? These are crucial questions. We have noted some lines of evidence that point in that direction, but many modern theologians wouldn't agree for reasons that have to do with the history of ideas. The intellectual movement that produced the philosophy of naturalism in science had a parallel influence in theology (Hasel 1980c, p. 18-30). The various views on the nature of the Bible cluster around two diverse positions: the traditional Judeo-Christian view (uses the grammatical-historical method) and a naturalistic view (scientific theology, or encounter theology; uses the historical-critical method).

In the traditional Judeo-Christian view, God transmits information to the prophet. Then, with the guidance of the Holy Spirit, the prophet communicates this information in his or her own words. The words are the prophet's, but the concepts are from God. Therefore, we can trust them as God's true communication to us. Other parts of the Bible are historical records and other non-prophetic documents, but God through the Holy Spirit has somehow exercised quality control on all of this material.

The other major position had its ultimate origin during the Enlightenment, when theology as well as science came to rely less on authority, became more inductive, and denied the supernatural (Hasel 1980c, p. 18-30). In this view, the part that God plays was diminished. Humanity became more central in determining the content of the Bible (Barth 1936-1969; Schleiermacher 1821-1822). It is a human-centered theology comparable to naturalism in science. According to this theology, a prophet is impressed in some way to write out his or her thoughts, but God does not speak or communicate ideas to the prophet. The prophet may have an impressive encounter with God or may be inspired by thoughts about God, and then she or he communicates these feelings in the form of the stories in the Bible, but the ideas in those stories are his or her own. This approach interprets the Bible as a series of confessions of faith by its writers. The *a priori* denial of supernatural intervention in history (including the origin of the Bible) is exemplified by the theologian Bultmann (1960, p. 292) who said, "The continuum of historical happenings cannot be rent by the interference of supernatural, transcendent powers and that therefore there is no 'miracle' in this sense of the word." If we accept this position, we would likely see science, not the Bible, as our best source of truth, since the Bible only tells us that the writers had great faith in a "god." It does not contain communication of information from that god (another view doubts whether god exists at all).

Let's consider an example that compares these two theological methods. According to the Bible, Moses met with God on the mountain and received the Ten Commandments. The traditional view is that they are the actual words of God; consequently, they are as important for us as they were for Moses. In contrast, naturalistic theology says that Moses met with God, opened up to God, and was deeply impressed by this experience. He then went his way and wrote something that expressed what he felt in that experience. The result was the Ten Commandments; hence, they were not given by God. Under this interpretation, nothing is binding to us unless we have the same experience as the Bible writers.

There is a great difference between these two points of view and where they lead us. Even in more conservative denominations, people struggle over which of these approaches should govern church belief and practice. It is important that we think these things through and understand what we believe. When we find a fork in a road, we have to decide which way to turn. The two roads initially may not look very different, but they can lead to very different places.

In logic and in theology, we also encounter forks in the road; the two theological roads may lead to two very different conclusions. The traditional Judeo-Christian view is a God-centered view. God is the standard and the Bible is an authoritative document (Hasel 1980b). In the naturalistic approach, God is not the standard and the Bible is not authoritative. It is only another human book containing myths, legends, and other literature (Hasel 1980c, p. 28).

Once, a friend of mine observed that the key difference between religious conservatives and liberals is a matter of authority. The liberal says the Bible is not authoritative, while the conservative says it is. I responded that if the Bible is not authoritative, then the standard for all truth is a person's own mind. His response was, "That is true, but that is all we have." This illustrates very well the naturalistic approach to theology. In this point of view, science, not the Bible, brings us truth (even in religion), and the Bible is not authoritative for religious belief and practice.

A few years ago, a theologian told about his experience with his teachers in Europe. One, a prominent German theologian, was asked by his students what he thought about the resurrection of Jesus Christ. He avoided this question, but, when finally pinned down, said, "The fact is, Jesus' disciples were intelligent enough to know that there is no such thing as physical resurrection. Their stories of the resurrection as told in the Bible were included to convey the thought that He is always with us."

That response implies that religion is only an emotional experience, that it has no reliable information or inherent truth. The Bible writers wrote stories that in reality are only fairy tales to encourage us to have the same faith in God as the writers had. But do fairy tales help us to have confidence in God? What are we expected to have confidence in? If the Bible writers wrote a collection of stories that are false, are we supposed to be impressed?

The Bible writers repeatedly stated that God spoke to them. According to their own claims, they were not just inspired in an emotional sense; they were spoken to (Hasel 1980c, p. 30-37). If those claims are false, then these writers were nothing more than frauds. On the other hand, if their claim that the Bible is authoritative is true, we would be wise to take it seriously. Since God is infinitely more knowledgeable than human beings, the revelation of God in the Bible is a superior source of information. The Bible is not a scientific textbook in the sense of giving exhaustive scientific information, but where the Bible does give scientific information, that information is accurate (Schaeffer 1972, p. 35-36, 166). "Whenever biblical information impinges on matters of history, age of the earth, origins, etc.," as well as theology, it gives us trustworthy information (Hasel 1980b, p. 68). The choices that we make in interpreting the Bible are of great significance.

The Relationship Between the Bible and Science

Now let us look at the science-and-faith question from a different perspective. If we believe that the Bible does give reliable information in theology, history, and science which we should weigh carefully, how do science and the Bible relate to each other? If we compare the two and find things that don't seem to fit, must we accept science and reject the

Bible, or vice versa? Or is there a better way? This section explores the latter question, suggests some answers (largely after Brand 1985), and ends with illustrative case studies showing the proper relation between science and religion.

Biblical and scientific information originate through different processes that must be kept in mind as we consider the relationship between them. The Bible claims to be a body of information communicated to us by the God who has participated in the history and workings of our planet and of life. This communication is in a book completed nearly 2,000 years ago and written in Hebrew and Greek. Our exegetive task is to see past the language and cultural differences expressed in the Bible and to understand its message. Then we have to decide if we are willing to trust the biblical message. Careful study of the culture and usage of words and expressions in Bible times helps us to correctly understand the Bible (Hasel 1980c, p. 42-65).

Because the Bible claims full inspiration by the same God for all portions of Scripture, the message it contains is a unity. Thus, one portion of Scripture can be better understood by comparing it to other portions that deal with the same subject—the Protestant Reformation principle of Scripture as its own interpreter. This position is the one adopted here.

Science, in contrast, is an ongoing, open-ended human search for understanding of the physical universe. It utilizes observation, experiment, and analysis to test the validity of human ideas and to help us think of new hypotheses. Science does not claim but, in fact, vigorously rejects the notion that any of its conclusions has divine authority. The Bible claims authority; science inspires confidence by its success, but does not claim "authority"—its claims are always subject to revision when required by new data.

Science is a slow process. It has many human limitations, but it still is a very effective way of discovering truth. We often do not have enough data to be certain of the correct scientific explanation or theory, but even then the data help to eliminate some of the incorrect theories. Accumulating new data enables scientists to develop new theories that they had not thought of before. These new theories may be stepping stones to even better theories, or they may stand the test of time and turn out to be correct (Fig. 6.1). For example, prior to 1950, sedimentary rocks composed of coarse-grained, graded beds (Figure 6.2) were believed to have been deposited slowly in shallow water. For instance, the Pliocene (a relatively recent geolog-

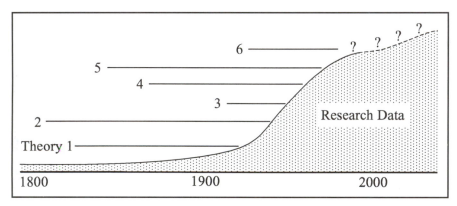

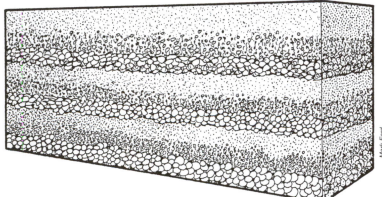

Figure 6.1
**A diagrammatic representa-
tion of the relationship
between theories and data.
In this and in Figures 6.3,
6.6, and 6.7, the height of
the stippled area at any
given date represents the
amount of data available at
that time. Horizontal lines
represent the life span of
various theories. A theory's
life span ends by "collision"
with accumulating evidence
that contradicts the theory,
or by radical alteration (a
scientific revolution represented by a vertical line)
into a new theory which is
not contradicted by the
available evidence.**

Figure 6.2
**A cross section through
three graded sedimentary
beds. In each bed, the
larger particles are at the
bottom and the smaller
particles at the top.**

Mark Ford

ical time period) rocks in the Ventura Basin, near Ventura, California, consist of hundreds of graded beds. Evidence indicated that it took several years to deposit each layer in shallow water (Eaton 1929). Then in 1950, a published paper reported the discovery of a previously unknown phenomenon—turbidity currents (Kuenen and Migliorini 1950). Turbidity currents are rapid under-water mudflows that can deposit a layer of sediment over a large area. The layers produced by turbidity currents are called turbidites, and they are graded beds.

Turbidity currents provided an even more satisfactory explanation for the graded beds in the Ventura

Basin, and the entire sequence of layers was reinterpreted as a series of turbidites (Natland and Kuenen 1951). Each graded bed was now understood to have been deposited in minutes rather than years, and in deeper water. This change in theory (Fig. 6.3) was brought about by the accumulation of new data and the discovery of previously unknown processes.

Many such changes have oc-curred in the history of science, and, undoubtedly, many more will occur as new discoveries are made, some of which will be related to phenomena we have not yet dreamed of. Science is always a progress report on the road to truth; it is not final, absolute truth. In contrast, the Bible claims to deal with propositional truth origi-nating with the God who has seen all and understands all of earth history and all natural laws. Each scientist must decide how much confidence to place in the Bible, and to what extent science can "correct" the Bible.

Some of the many possible approaches to the relationship between science and Bible-oriented religion are illustrated by the partial list in Table 6.1. Models 1 and 5 represent the easiest ways to make a decision. They are essentially all-or-nothing approaches and do not require much careful thought on questions of the relationship between science and faith. I don't believe either position realistically comes to grips with the problem.

Model 2, keeping science and religious faith separate, is a popular model and superficially seems attractive. It even may work for a scientist whose field of inquiry does not require much thought about the history of life on earth. However, what do Bible-believing advocates of this model do when they encounter a biblical statement that contradicts the conclusions of science? When faced with such a contradiction, Christian scientists no longer can keep the two sources in separate compartments. Then, even though they may not realize it or may even deny it, they move from model 2 to one of the other models. Consequently, model 2 has failed at the very point where we need a model to help direct our search for truth. A number of different models can work equally well in areas where science and the Bible do not conflict. It is when conflict arises that the relationship between the two sources of information becomes significant. Model 2 merely avoids the issue or pretends that it does not exist, which, in my opinion, renders this model unworthy

of further discussion.

Many authors strongly disagree with this conclusion. They maintain that science and religion should be kept separate, and/or that they do not conflict even in theories of origin— they simply deal with different aspects of these questions. Careful study of their approach convinces me that they are in fact working within model 1, not 2, and that their approach assumes that science provides facts and the Bible only provides inspirational material or some vague spiritual meaning.

The most fruitful approach to the study of origins and of earth history, I believe, is found between models 3 and 4, which take both the Bible and science seriously. Furthermore, I believe that one of the most crucial features of either model is its definition of the steps to be taken in resolving conflicts that arise between our interpretation of revelation and our interpretation of scientific data. The remainder of this chapter proposes an approach to resolving such conflicts.

Table 6.1
Several of the Possible Relationships Between Science and the Bible
(Loosely adapted from Watts 1976.)

1. Science is the only reliable source of information. The Bible may contain inspirational religious concepts, but these are only relative and allegorical. The Bible is not a source of reliable facts. The person who accepts this view reinterprets or disclaims anything in the Bible that conflicts with current scientific interpretations.

2. Science and religious faith should be kept separate. The Bible is taken more seriously than in model 1, but science and biblical faith are kept in two separate compartments, and no attempt is made to relate one to the other.

3. The dualist recognizes a type of authority in both the Bible and science, and takes both sources seriously in the search for truth. Conflict between the two arises only because of human limitations in the scientific process and/or in our understanding of the Bible.

4. Science and the Bible are both taken seriously, but the Bible is granted a higher level of authority than science.

5. Only the Bible is accepted as reliable. This extreme view tends to reject all of science as a tool of the devil, designed by him to destroy faith.

Figure 6.3
A diagrammatic representation of the change from the shallow-water theory of graded-bed deposition to the turbidite theory. This change occurred through a scientific revolution stimulated by the accumulation of new data.

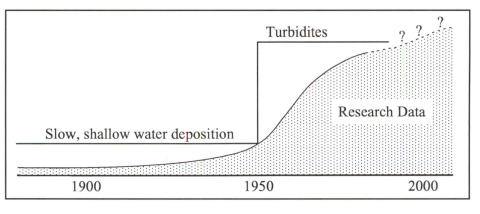

Science and Revelation: A Working Relationship

Within Christianity, many different attitudes are held toward the authority of the Scriptures. This study is built on the conviction that many lines of evidence indicate that the Bible writers speak for a loving and all-knowing God who can be trusted, and in whose prophetic and historical messages we can have confidence. If this is true, ultimately no conflict will remain between science and revelation when we correctly understand both. Within such a framework, an effective working relationship between science and revelation can result if we utilize the following process:

1. The accumulating data from scientific research continue to suggest new ideas or hypotheses that we might not have thought of if the research had not been done. Science sometimes challenges us to examine our beliefs more closely.

2. When a new idea involves a subject concerning which the Bible speaks, we must examine all relevant biblical passages, comparing Scripture with Scripture, using the Bible as its own interpreter. In doing so, it is important to make use of all the latest information that helps us to reach a correct understanding of the original meaning of the words used in the biblical manuscripts. In this way, we attempt to understand exactly what the Bible does or does not say about our new idea. Is the idea compatible with the Bible or not? Do the relevant Bible statements say what we think they say or are we incorrectly reading something between the lines?

3. Next, we can make one of the following decisions or an appropriate variation of one of them:

a. It is evident that revelation does not speak to this issue at all and does not help us in our research.

b. The revelation addresses this topic but does not condemn the new idea. No biblical reason indicates we shouldn't accept it as a valid possibility. We then can proceed with scientific research to rigorously test it. This research may give us more confidence in the idea, or it may lead to better hypotheses which also need to be compared with the Scriptures.

c. Our study indicates that revelation clearly contradicts the new scientific idea, thus challenging our scientific conclusions and telling us to go back and do some more research because something is wrong with our interpretation of the data.

If we follow this process, the Bible is maintained as the standard for religious doctrines and for areas for which the Bible makes claims in natural history; yet science and the Bible continue to shed light on each other. Science suggests ideas that may help us to recognize that we have been reading some preconceived ideas into the Bible. In other cases, the Bible can help us to recognize incorrect scientific theories so we can turn our efforts toward developing more accurate interpretations of the data. This can be an on-going feedback process in the interface between science and religion that challenges us to dig deeper in both areas (Fig. 6.4).

At this point we must remind ourselves not to let our religious views twist our interpretation of scientific data (see chapter 5). A Christian does not need to fear good data. We may indeed struggle with seeming conflicts because of limits in our available data and our interpretations, but ultimately genuine truth will not contradict itself.

Still we must ask how science can be an open-ended and open-

minded search for truth if we adopt the view that "whenever biblical information impinges on matters of history, age of the earth, origins, etc., the data observed must be interpreted and reconstructed in view of this superior divine revelation which is supremely embodied in the Bible" (Hasel 1980b, p. 68). Would we reject a scientific idea on scriptural grounds alone? The answer requires a correct understanding of the domains in Fig. 6.4. The processes occurring in the scientific and religious domains are different and cannot be interchanged. Scientific experiments are not a basis for testing divinely inspired scriptural statements; science does not test its conclusions by linguistic analysis and "comparing Scripture with Scripture." The interaction between them occurs in the thinking process called here "the interface."

This can be illustrated with a study of a (hypothesized) rock forma-

Figure 6.4
An approach to the relationship between science and religion that provides constructive interaction between them, without inappropriate interference of one with the other.

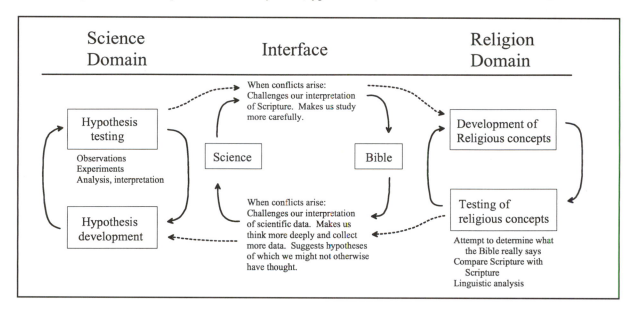

tion, the Redbluff Formation, with its abundant fossils. A careful scientific study of the Redbluff Formation would conclude that "the scientific data indicate at least a 10-million-year time for the accumulation of this formation, but this time period is not correct because the Bible contradicts that conclusion." Such a statement is not scientific and, perhaps, isn't even a good religious statement. It is a confusing statement! Another approach is to conclude that "the scientific data currently available are most consistent with a 10-million-year period of deposition for the Redbluff Formation (scientific domain), but my study of Scripture (religion domain) leads me to predict (interface) that additional geological discoveries await us that will indicate a rapid, catastrophic origin for the Redbluff." That is an entirely valid, honest statement. It cannot be criticized for improperly mixing science and religion. The honest, probing attitude indicated by that statement, if

combined with the scientific quality-control process (chapter 5), could stimulate a more careful geological restudy of the Redbluff Formation as well as more careful study of Scripture that might otherwise not have been done. In the meantime, if we truly have confidence in God's communication, we will be comfortable living with unanswered questions.

I concluded above that keeping science and religion separate is not a valid approach. That conclusion can now be refined to include the concepts in Fig. 6.4. There is a procedural sense in which science and religion are separate. The two use different methods. The second of the two statements about the Redbluff Formation illustrates the sense in which science and religion must be kept "separate," or at least not be confused. The interface (Fig. 6.4) allows interaction between science and religion without confusion. Now Fig. 6.5 illustrates two ways in which

Figure 6.5
Two ineffective ways to try to keep science and religion separate: (A) Keep the two in separate "compartments" and not try to analyze how they interact. (B) Science determines facts and religion provides spiritual meaning. In this approach science actually becomes the standard for evaluating religious concepts.

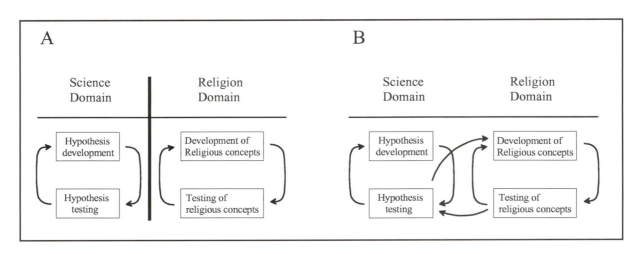

some individuals try to keep science and religion separate. Method A suffers the problems discussed earlier—it cannot deal with questions of origins without being schizophrenic. Method B is the same as model 1 in Table 6.1; it does not actually keep science and religion separate, but tests Bible statements by external, scientific criteria. The interface in Fig. 6.4 is the key to an honest and productive interaction between science and religion; it is the secret for granting science a constructive degree of autonomy and placing "reason in the service of faith," while not giving it "mastery over faith" (Rice 1991, p. 198). This approach to the relation between science and faith is not just a theoretical idea. Some of us have been using it for years and find it both effective and practical.

Examples

The following examples illustrate the application of this approach to current conflicts between science and religion and to some past conflicts which probably could have been avoided if the individuals involved had followed this same approach.

1. *The Copernican revolution in astronomy.* Before the Middle Ages, scientists developed the geocentric theory and supported it with volumes of observational data (Kuhn 1957; Encyclopedia Britannica 1952). As

the Christian church developed, the geocentric theory became incorporated into church dogma to the point that a challenge to the geocentric theory was considered a challenge to the Scriptures and to the Church itself. Copernicus introduced a radical new idea, the heliocentric theory. If the Church, instead of persecuting the advocates of the heliocentric theory, had studied the Bible carefully to see what it actually says about the theory, a serious mistake could have been avoided. The Bible does not address itself to the issue of whether the earth rotates around the sun or vice versa. An attempt to support the geocentric theory from the Bible can only be done if one resorts to arguments akin to saying that 20th-century scientists must believe in the geocentric theory because they speak of the sun rising and setting. Careful Bible study could have indicated that the heliocentric theory is not unbiblical. Consequently, science could explore this issue without antagonism from the Church. Of course, hindsight helps us to see these issues more clearly, but this example illustrates the goal of the approach outlined above.

2. *The theory of evolution.* Previous to the 19th century, people believed animal and plant species do not change. This also became part of Church dogma. It was assumed that the Genesis-creation account

supported this very static concept of nature, referred to as "fixity of species." Charles Darwin and his contemporaries saw evidence that animals and plants change and started another conflict between science and Christian faith. Because of the complexity of the evolution issue, let's break the conflict into two parts: (a) organisms do change, resulting in variations within created groups, and (b) the major groups of animals originated by evolution and not by creation.

(A) *Microevolution and speciation.* If Darwin had studied the Bible carefully, he surely could have concluded that the Bible says nothing against the possibility that changes have occurred within the created groups of plants and animals (Coffin 1983c, p. 18-20), including the production of new types of organisms to at least the species and generic level. In fact, an interventionist must believe either that some changes have occurred or that God designed and made even the destructive things in nature. However, Darwin didn't reexamine his Bible. He concluded that since his evidence invalidated what he believed to be the biblical creation account, he had to explain the origin of all living things by some mechanism other than creation. This brings us to the second part of the evolution theory.

(B) *Evolution of the major groups of organisms.* Darwin's theory proposes that even the major groups of living things arose by evolution from a common ancestor. If Charles Darwin had examined his Bible and compared it with his theory, he would have found that although the Bible doesn't say anything against microevolution and speciation, it clearly states that the major groups of both plants and animals (including fish, birds, reptiles, mammals, human beings, and flowering plants [fruit trees]) were created by the end of creation week. This is definitely not compatible with part of his evolution theory. If Darwin had been willing and had followed the approach outlined here, he could have developed a theory which included creation of the groups of living things with limited evolutionary changes occurring within the created groups. Such a theory would be consistent with Scripture and with the scientific data. It could have been an excellent example of the Bible and science shedding light on each other.

3. *Geology.* Part of the Christian Church has been in conflict with geologists for over a century, but we will look at this issue from the perspective of the 20th century. As we compare the biblical account of origins with scientific theories requiring many millions of years for

the evolution of earth life, how can we best approach truth? We should follow the same process outlined above. Science has proposed a theory that the fossil-bearing geologic deposits have accumulated over hundreds of millions of years. We then examine what the inspired writings have to say about this issue. We find that, in contrast to the absence of significant revealed information on astronomy or microevolution, the Bible states that life was created in six days (Genesis 1; Hasel 1994), and the chronogenealogies in Genesis 5 and 11 imply that creation occurred a relatively short time ago (Hasel 1980a, 1980b). These statements are compatible only with the conclusion that life on earth (and thus also the rocks containing fossils) has only been in existence for a short time. We also find the story of a worldwide flood significant enough to cover the highest mountains (Genesis 15). I conclude that the Bible indicates that current geological theory, in certain respects, is an incorrect interpretation of the data. Our task is to go back to the research lab and develop a more correct theory, allowing revealed information to open our minds to new possibilities that can be tested against the data.

How does one deal with data such as radiometric dating that does not appear to harmonize with the biblical view of earth history? I

propose that some new fundamental scientific principles are yet to be discovered that will explain these data. Consider the following two propositions: (a) There are no significant principles to be discovered in this field; the data are mostly being interpreted correctly (Fig. 6.6). (b) There are principles to be discovered that will lead to significant reinterpretations of data (Fig. 6.7), just as occurred with turbidites.

We must now ask whether we have data that allows us to test between propositions (a) and (b) to determine whether the radiometric dating theory is comparable to theories of graded-bed deposition after the discovery of turbidites or before. If science could do that, we would have the key to answering many difficult questions, but science cannot test between (a) and (b). We would have to go into the past and observe what really happened, or go into the future and see what data will become available, or talk to someone who actually has done one or the other. The Bible writers claim to have that type of information, but science does not. Consequently, science cannot test between (a) and (b).

Since we cannot prove which is correct, should we assume that (a) is correct if there is no definite evidence for (b)? Science would normally take this approach, but we must remember that this is only a practical working approach, not a method for determining truth. A scientist must push ahead with the most successful theory available, trusting that the data eventually will tell if the theory is wrong. A Christian may want to keep an open mind to the possibility that current scientific interpretations are not correct. Scientists, ideally, choose the interpretation that is supported by the weight of available evidence. Interventionists do the same, except that on some issues their confidence in Scripture convinces them that there must be significant discoveries yet to be made that will outweigh the evidence available at this time.

The history of science does not support the notion that a well-developed theory is true if at a given time there is little or no convincing evidence against it. Before the

discovery of turbidites, good evidence indicated that the then-current theory was correct. Even as some problems began to appear, scientists did not have a better explanation until turbidites were discovered. A Christian who is convinced that God's revelations are trustworthy is led to believe that, in the radiometric dating of fossil-bearing rocks, some more important discoveries are yet to be made of equal or greater significance than the discovery of turbidites.

A decision in favor of the current scientific interpretation of radiometric dates of fossiliferous rocks or a decision against that interpretation are both made on faith. A person who places greater confidence in current scientific theories than in revelation will likely conclude that radiometric dates as currently interpreted are accurate. However, a person whose faith in divine revelation is stronger than his or her faith in current scientific theories will be convinced that radiometric dates of fossiliferous deposits are not being interpreted correctly. If one goes a step farther and uses the scientific method to develop and test new theories to explain radiometric phenomena and other data, scientific progress can result from our search for harmony between science and revelation.

Figure 6.6
Hypothetical history of radiometric dating theory if no major changes occur in the future of this theory.

Figure 6.7
Hypothetical history of radiometric dating theory if future data accumulation necessitates a major change in the theory.

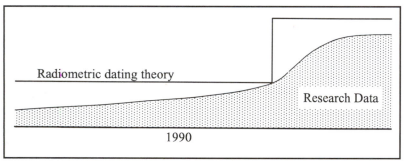

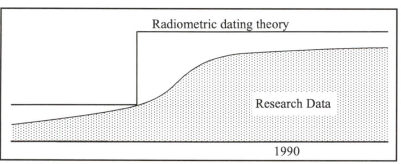

The Origin of Life 7

A vast complex of fundamental biochemical characteristics are shared by virtually all life forms today, and any theory of origins must explain this common theme of life in addition to how and why life began. The following components of life, at least, must be present for a biological entity to survive and produce more of its own kind: proteins, DNA and/or RNA (nucleic acids), membranes, enzymes (to catalyze biochemical reactions), ribosomes (or the equivalent, for producing proteins), energy source and method of processing energy, and a method of replication.

Naturalistic evolution proposes that life originated through abiogenesis (molecular evolution), the production of organic molecules and, ultimately, life from non-living material on the primitive earth. The evidence for abiogenesis and the problems that it faces have been well presented by Thaxton et al. (1984) and Bradley and Thaxton (1994). The following account draws heavily from their analysis.

The theory of abiogenesis deals with the atmosphere and other conditions on the primitive earth and four steps in the origin of life. These steps are (1) the production of simple organic molecules such as amino acids and nucleic acids and their accumulation in a "primeval soup," (2) the wide-scale polymerization (linking together) of these molecules to form biological macromolecules (proteins, DNA, or RNA), (3) the formation of protocells to hold the macromolecules together in a working unit, and (4) the development of true cells.

The Primitive Atmosphere: Conditions Necessary for Abiogenesis
Abiogenesis could only occur if the earth's primitive atmosphere was without free atmospheric (molecular) oxygen. Organic molecules exposed to free oxygen are quickly decomposed by oxidation. Our current atmosphere has abundant carbon dioxide, molecular oxygen, water, and nitrogen. Abiogenesis clearly could not occur in this atmosphere. The ideal early atmosphere would be strongly reducing, composed of carbon monoxide, carbon dioxide, ammonia, nitrogen, methane, and water vapor. An energy source would

be needed to generate chemical reactions in the atmosphere, producing biological molecules as the first step toward the origin of life. Possible sources of this energy include ultraviolet light, shock waves from thunder, electrical energy from lightning, and geothermal heat.

The hypothesis of a primitive, reducing atmosphere developed because a reducing atmosphere is needed for life to evolve on the early earth. If life can only begin in a reducing atmosphere, then a naturalistic paradigm must conclude that the primitive earth had one. A problem with this hypothesis is that there is no convincing evidence for the existence of a reducing atmosphere. If the earth's oldest rocks contained compounds that could indicate, with reasonable certainty, that the rocks were formed under a reducing atmosphere or under an oxidizing atmosphere, that would be very helpful. As yet, no agreement on the interpretation of the evidence has been reached and the mineral evidence doesn't point convincingly to an oxidizing or a reducing atmosphere.

Observations made in recent space exploration indicate that a cloud of hydrogen gas is escaping from the earth because ultraviolet photolysis in our atmosphere splits water into hydrogen and oxygen. The hydrogen escapes from the earth and

the oxygen accumulates in the atmosphere. Present information indicates that the earth would have had an oxidizing atmosphere early in its history because of this process, but no agreement has been made on how much oxygen would have been in the early atmosphere. The level of oxygen in the early atmosphere is a problem without a solution for abiogenesis. In the presence of oxygen, many crucial organic molecules would not form; if they did form, they would be quickly broken down. On the other hand, without a sufficient amount of oxygen to form an ozone layer in the atmosphere, there would have been no shield to block ultraviolet radiation, and ultraviolet rays would break down most organic molecules in the air or in the ocean.

In spite of these difficulties, the theory of abiogenesis must assume that the earth did have a reducing atmosphere or tackle the difficult problem of producing a life form different from the biochemistry that forms life today, and then transform it to the modern biochemistry currently found in living things.

Origin of Life Experiments: Synthesis of Simple Organic Molecules

The theory of abiogenesis proposes that fatty acids, amino acids (the building blocks of proteins), sugars, and the bases (adenine, guanine, etc.) found in nucleic acid (nucleic acids are DNA and RNA) formed in the atmosphere and settled into the ocean to form a dilute soup which, perhaps, thickened by concentration in smaller pools or lagoons. Numerous experiments in the last 40 years based on the abiogenesis theory have attempted to reproduce the simplest organic molecules under conditions simulating the earth's early reducing atmosphere. The evolution of the first live cell is presumed to have taken many millions of years, but these experiments are based on the assumption that it is valid to separate individual chemical reactions in the laboratory in order to shorten the time necessary to achieve results.

These experiments, pioneered by Miller and Urey (e.g., Miller 1953; Miller and Urey 1959), used closed glass chambers containing an artificial reducing atmosphere and electric sparks as an energy source to cause chemical reactions (Fig. 7.1). Other researchers have used the same system or modifications of it with various energy sources. These experiments have yielded a variety of organic molecules, as predicted by the abiogenesis theory, including 19 of the 20 amino acids found in

proteins; sugars including glucose, ribose, and deoxyribose; all five heterocyclic bases found in nucleic acids; and many non-biological molecules. These results aren't too surprising since the correct conditions were chosen that would produce them. The researchers believed they had reproduced the beginning steps in the origin of life. However, many problems remain to be solved before that conclusion is warranted.

More recent thinking seems to favor an early atmosphere that was not so strongly reducing. It would contain carbon dioxide, nitrogen, and water, but not methane or ammonia. Abiogenesis experiments done with this type of atmosphere yield smaller quantities and less diversity of organic molecules than experiments in the strongly reducing atmosphere.

The experiments produce not

**Figure 7.1
Apparatus for classical origin of life experiments (after Keeton and Gould 1986).**

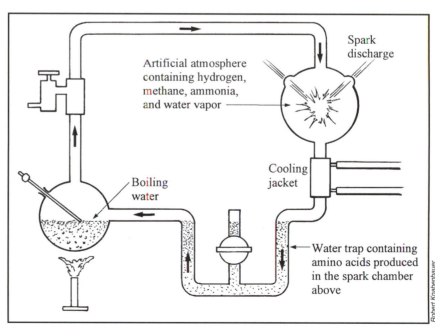

Artificial atmosphere containing hydrogen, methane, ammonia, and water vapor

Spark discharge

Cooling jacket

Boiling water

Water trap containing amino acids produced in the spark chamber above

Robert Knabenbauer

only biologically significant molecules, but many others as well, including amino acids that do not occur in biological proteins. Consequently, many of the complex molecules forming naturally from them would not be biologically useful proteins. Also, any proteins or nucleic acids that did form would be very likely to react with formaldehyde or other chemicals to produce compounds not suitable for incorporation into a biological system. Sugar and amino acids combine to form a non-biological compound. This would eliminate many molecules from involvement in subsequent biological synthesis.

The sources that energize the synthesis of amino acids and other molecules also break down those same molecules, and biological molecules break down much more readily than they form. In other words, ultraviolet radiation and other energy would be predominantly destructive. This is a significant problem for abiogenesis. Even molecules that fall into the ocean would not be safe as ultraviolet rays reach tens of meters below the surface and ocean currents would be sufficient to bring molecules to the surface occasionally where they would be subject to destruction. The result is that biological molecules would survive only in the "primeval

soup" for a short time, and the soup would have been very dilute. The concentration of amino acids has been estimated to have been about 10^{-7} to 10^{-12} molar, which is as dilute as modern ocean water in the North Atlantic (10^{-7} M).

In the experiments, this problem is surmounted by using a trap to catch and hold the molecules. This makes the experimental conditions unrealistic because, under natural conditions, a trap to accumulate the products doesn't seem plausible. Perhaps the dilute soup could flow into pools, possibly near a volcanic vent, to heat the water and evaporate it. If more water periodically flowed into the pool, the organic compounds could be concentrated. However, the necessary geological conditions in this hypothesis are not very realistic. In addition, that process would concentrate both the desired biological materials and the destructive organic compounds, thus accelerating both destructive as well as constructive reactions. Because of these problems working in concert under natural conditions, any primeval soup that realistically can be envisioned would have been too dilute for polymerization of macromolecules to occur. What would be needed to make the system work is a mechanism to sort out the biologically useful molecules (including only L-amino acids) from all the others. So far, no such mechanism is known.

The severe problems discussed above argue against the existence of an adequate primeval soup. But since it would be necessary to have that primeval soup for the next step in abiogenesis to occur, we discuss the next step, polymerization, as if there were sufficient evidence that the primeval soup did exist.

Formation of Macromolecules by Polymerization

The next step in the process is the combination of simple organic molecules into larger molecules, or macromolecules, by polymerization. The amino acids would join together in chains to form proteins; the fatty acids would form lipids and, eventually, membranes; and the appropriate bases and sugars would combine with phosphates to yield RNA and DNA.

Sydney Fox, from the University of Miami, assumed that some of the organic soup would splash onto warm volcanic rock, the volcano would dry up the water, and reactions in the resulting concentrated soup would produce complex molecules. He simulated this process in the laboratory by heating a mixture of pure amino acids and driving off the water as steam. This process produced polymers containing as many as 200 amino acids. These experiments are highly unnatural, since the required

geological conditions are unlikely and the process doesn't work unless it starts with a mixture of pure amino acids. No natural process is known that would generate a mixture of pure amino acids without the help of a chemist. An equally serious problem is that the experiment produced random amino acid sequences held together with predominantly β, γ, and ε peptide bonds, containing approximately equal numbers of D- and L- amino acids. Such a polymer has little resemblance to biological proteins, which use only α peptide bonds and only L-amino acids.

Other experiments using different energy sources and more likely conditions have produced small polymers. Some use layered clays to catalyze the polymerization reactions. The reactants are adsorbed on the clay which concentrates and protects them from reacting with water. This type of reaction produces polymers of up to 50 units, but only if it starts with energy-rich aminoacyl adenylates rather than amino acids. It is clear that this is an unrealistic starting point for such experiments.

Forming DNA in abiogenesis experiments seems to be even more difficult than making proteins. Nucleotides link together under experimental conditions, but do not form a helical DNA molecule. The formation of a helical structure requires that the sugars that are part of the DNA be attached by specific 3'-5' links rather than the 2'-5' links predominant in abiogenesis experiments.

In summary, abiogenesis experiments have had considerable success in synthesizing amino acids but consistently fail to synthesize protein or DNA. This is not surprising when we consider how simple amino acids are in comparison with protein or DNA.

Protocells

The next step in the synthesis of life (assuming the problems of forming the primeval soup and of synthesizing proteins and DNA can be solved) is the formation of a protocell structure to bridge the gap from macromolecules to true cells. Sydney Fox's experiments produced small concentrations of polypeptides (not really proteins) which he called proteinoids. When solutions of proteinoids cool, they form small, round structures called microspheres, with outer membranes, that grow and divide. Microspheres also form in some Miller-Urey-type experiments, and lipids have been used to form microsphere-like structures as another protocell type. However, none of these "protocells" contains an energy-utilizing system, nucleic acid or genetic code, enzymes, or reproduction system, and their "membranes" don't carry out the functions of biological membranes.

They grow and divide like soap bubbles, by purely physical forces. Their resemblance to true cells is very superficial, and they would have a short life in a natural setting.

The First Living Cells

If a way could be found to make the primeval soup, if there were reactions that could produce proteins and DNA, and if a suitable protocell structure were to form to hold them together, the correct macromolecules would then have to be combined in precisely the correct structure to produce a living, metabolically active system. Any protocell that formed under natural conditions would have to escape destruction as its biochemical complexity increased in exactly the right way to produce a primitive cell capable of sustaining itself by transforming and utilizing energy, growing, and replicating. The process of natural selection would not assist the production of this first cell. Natural selection cannot operate until a reproducing cell is present so that the feedback process of natural selection can eliminate the less fit individuals and thus determine the characteristics that will be present in the genes of the next generation. Consequently, if the first cell formed by abiogenesis, it would have to happen essentially by chance, rather than by any form of natural selection.

Does the Second Law of Thermodynamics Make Evolution Impossible?

The second law of thermodynamics states that energy naturally moves from a more-organized state to a less-organized state. A common creationist argument is that the second law makes not only abiogenesis impossible but also the evolution of increasing complexity. That may seem like an attractive argument, but it is often misapplied.

A living system could only escape the implications of the second law and evolve by increasing complexity if there is:

1. an open system (input of energy into the system—on earth the input of energy is from the sun)

2. an adequate amount of energy (yes, there is plenty of energy)

3. an energy conversion system to allow directed utilization of that energy (photosynthesis & mitochondria in living things)

4. a system to control the energy conversion.

Although our earth is an open system, receiving energy from the sun, complex biological energy conversion and control systems (items 3 and 4) are needed before that solar energy can be put to use in abiogenesis. Those systems don't appear to have been available on the early earth before life was present. This, then, is the most significant reason why the origin of life is a problem for naturalistic philosophy—along with the problem of the origin of biological information.

The Origin of Information in the Cell

The feature that distinguishes living from non-living systems is not order but complexity. Many inanimate structures, such as crystals, have precise order. Crystals are composed of atoms in orderly, spatial arrangements—repetitive or periodic sequences of components. In contrast, the sequence of units in proteins and nucleic acids is not at all repetitive or periodic, but the units occur in complex, non-repetitive arrangements. Just as a sentence makes sense only if the words are in a specific order, so the amino acids must be in a specific order for a protein to be functional. Proteins and nucleic acids are not only non-repetitive; they are arranged in a sequence that contains the information necessary for the construction and functioning of the entire living system. These concepts are summarized by Thaxton et al. (1984).

1. An ordered (periodic) and therefore specified arrangement:

   THE END   THE END
   THE END   THE END

   Example: nylon, or a crystal.

2. A complex (aperiodic) unspecified arrangement:

AGDCBFE   GBAFED
ACEDFGB

Example: Random polymers
(polypeptides).

3. A complex (aperiodic) specified
    arrangement:

    THIS SEQUENCE OF
    LETTERS CONTAINS A
    MESSAGE!

    Example: DNA, protein.

    (Thaxton et al. 1984, used by
    permission)

Any theory of the origin of life
must resolve the critical question of
the origin of biological information.
The DNA in a cell is like a comprehensive instruction book with all the
instructions for the reproduction and
functioning of an organism, including
instructions for the correct sequence
of amino acids in each protein.
Biological cells have the machinery
to read and carry out those instructions. How did the information coded
in the sequence of nucleotides in
DNA get there?

Proteins are very large molecules
which contain the correct sequence of
amino acids to cause them to fold into
the specific three-dimensional shape
needed for the peculiar biochemical
task of each protein. However,
without instructions to direct the
synthesis of these proteins, amino
acids can hook together in any combination. In a cell, the instructions are
present in the DNA and in the

messenger RNA on the ribosomes;
but without such instructions and the
machinery to carry them out, the
amino acids will link up in random
order, producing generally useless
molecules. The same is true for the
sequence of nucleotides in RNA and
DNA. The nucleotides can link
together in any order and must have a
preexisting pattern to put them
together in a biologically useful
sequence. The origin of this biological information is the fundamental
problem for abiogenesis. The genetic
code contains all the information
needed for life, stored in the DNA.
The underlying physical and chemical
laws do not contain that information.
Each new organism receives the
information from its parents, but
where did the first organism get the
information?

We can illustrate the nature of
biological information further with a
modification of one of Dawkins'
(1986) analogies, comparing a living
system with a computer. If you wish
to write a book, you may purchase a
computer to assist with the writing.
You then have the computer hardware
on your desk, with its transistors,
wires, and logic circuits. You have
all of the complex machinery, but that
is not your book. It won't even help
to write your book without one other
thing: software.

Software is information—a

sequence of instructions put together by an intelligent person who knows what is needed to make the computer do what it should do. If we compare our bodies with the computer, the hardware is comparable to the cellular machinery and the biochemical reactions that our cells can perform. I call them hardware because their function is predictable, based on natural laws. If particular biochemical reagents are put together, an informed person can predict what will happen, either inside the body or in a laboratory. That is the hardware controlled by natural laws. But life has another very important component: software, the information content of DNA, RNA, and proteins. If we put together the appropriate compounds containing hydrogen, oxygen, carbon, sulfur, and nitrogen in the right situation, we can predict that amino-acid molecules are likely to be formed. This is the biological hardware which is formed by predictable reactions. However, if we put together many amino acids in a suitable situation, outside of a cell, they may link together to form proteins; but natural law cannot predict what sequence the amino acids will link up in. They can link up in any random order, unless some intervening outside influence puts them in the sequence needed to make a functioning organic system.

Where does this intervening outside influence come from? Of course, in the cell the intervening influence is the DNA and RNA which control the protein fabrication mechanism. But how did the original life get that information into the DNA? Natural laws do not contain the information to specify the sequence of nucleotides in the DNA. It could not happen by a process of natural selection, because, until a living entity contains DNA with the instructions to direct the production of all that is necessary for it to support itself and reproduce, the process of mutation cannot function to stimulate evolutionary changes.

Various theories attempt to provide a more likely mechanism for abiogenesis. Some say life started with proteins, and others think it started with RNA. One theory suggests that clay templates influenced the organization of the first life forms, and another (Nicolis & Prigogine 1977) makes use of the fact that in some physical systems that are far from equilibrium, ordering may appear spontaneously. An example of the latter is the vortex that may appear as water drains out of a bathtub.

Some mechanisms that have been proposed may increase the rate of biochemical reactions, but they do not have any potential to provide a means of specifying the information: the sequence of subunits in proteins or nucleic acids. They do not distinguish between order and complexity and do not have a way to generate the information in biological macromolecules.

Some suggest that there might indeed be inherent self-ordering mechanisms in matter that facilitate the origin of life. Such mechanisms that operate at a simple physical level are in no way comparable to the proposed concept of self-ordering mechanisms in living things. These mechanisms would have to sort out the biologically useful organic molecules to favor the effective formation of macromolecules and cause proteins and DNA to form with biologically appropriate information content. If such mechanisms were found, their presence would not help to provide a naturalistic explanation for the origin of life. They would merely push the challenge back one step farther, to explain how it came to be that matter contains the innate ability to specify the needed sequences of biological information in DNA for making such an incredibly complex and improbable entity as a living cell.

How was the first living, reproducing organism assembled without the aid of natural selection? Discussions of this topic come down to the question of the probability that if enough simple molecules existed in the primeval soup for enough time, the correct combination of molecules, with the right information content, could have occurred at least once to give life a start. Many calculations of the probability of such an event have been made and published. I will not make a new one. Abiogenesis probably cannot be proven to be impossible, but it is clear that the probability of such an event is extremely small.

A broader question is of greater significance: Is it even possible for the random combining of chemicals to produce successive levels of biochemical complexity, escaping destruction at each stage, until a living organism is produced? The probability of impossible events in reality is equal to zero. Consequently, calculating probabilities has no meaning until some experimental evidence provides reasons to take seriously the theorized process of abiogenesis.

Try as it may, naturalistic abiogenesis cannot escape the important role of chance in the origin of life. Whichever version of the theory of abiogenesis one prefers, one ultimately must resort to an argument summarized by Richard Dawkins in *The Blind Watchmaker* (1986): "What is the largest single event of sheer naked coincidence, sheer unadulterated miraculous luck that we are allowed to get away with in our theories and still say that we have a satisfactory explanation of life?" Dawkins was expressing his faith, and nothing more. Where else in science would that kind of thinking be tolerated? Nowhere! So why does science accept it here? How is it different from the interventionist's reliance on divine action in the beginning of life? Is one less scientific than the other?

It is impossible to fully understand how science deals with questions of origins unless we understand the dominant role that the assumption of naturalism plays in scientific thinking today (Johnson 1991). The explanation of the origin of life is critical to the philosophical debate. Abiogenesis is clearly one of the weakest links in naturalistic theories of origins; but if it is admitted that the origin of life requires informed intervention, naturalism has been dealt a death blow. Consequently, for naturalism to survive, the theory of abiogenesis must be maintained, no matter what the evidence. If one admitted that naturalistic theories cannot adequately explain the origin of life, and informed intervention might be necessary in this case, then the only remaining question is, What was the

nature and boundary of the intervention? Or, What are the limits of the evolution process? That question is incompatible with the very principle of strict naturalism as science understands it today. If naturalism is accepted, then one must believe in some form of biochemical evolution, which means one must believe in this "sheer unadulterated miraculous luck." In other areas, where science is studying processes that can be observed and experimentally tested, that type of thinking is never accepted.

How Should Science Deal With the Origin of Life?

When no hard evidence exists for events so far in the past, science has serious handicaps, but it can explore possible ways that the hypothesized processes could have occurred and examine their plausibility (Thaxton et al. 1984). Ruling out unrealistic possibilities is more feasible than determining which hypothesis is correct, especially on a difficult topic like the origin of life.

If a person says, "I choose to assume that life originated by naturalistic processes, and I am going to use the scientific method to determine what is the most likely process involved in that event," I have no argument. In fact, I will defend anyone's right to choose that approach, even though I may be convinced that the effort will not succeed.

Many individuals go a step farther and state that any approach other than naturalism is not intellectually or scientifically valid. De Duve (1995, p. 428) states: "It is now generally agreed that if life arose spontaneously by natural processes—a necessary assumption if we wish to remain within the realm of science—it must have arisen fairly quickly. . . ." When this type of logic is used, some additional principles need to be brought into the discussion. When abiogenesis comes down to "miraculous luck", what fundamental difference is there between choosing to believe in the origin of life by naturalistic means in spite of the lack of supporting evidence and choosing to believe in informed intervention? Is science an open-minded search for truth or a closed process that accepts only certain answers irrespective of the evidence or the lack of evidence?

Both theories are based on faith in a particular philosophy. Adherents of both views have reason to choose their philosophy, but neither can be verified or refuted by science. When discussing microevolution, macroevolution, and the fossil record, evidence is abundant, though it may not always be conclusive. What evidence can be found in rocks to demonstrate

whether or not the original life forms evolved from non-living matter without any informed assistance? Can we be honest enough to say "science does not have an answer for that question"?

No scientist has observed the history of the world. When we consider ultimate questions about origins, it is likely that any answer will have aspects that are difficult to accept or understand. Scientists wonder what has gone wrong when public opinion surveys indicate that most people still believe in a creator. Perhaps the public would take science more seriously if the scientific community were not so dogmatic on such a question as the origin of life, which is really just a philosophical choice.

I will hazard the prediction that when we look back on the 20th century from, let's say, the 23rd century, our knowledge of biochemistry and of the complexity of life will have advanced to the point that the theory that life could originate without informed intervention will be seen as an area of naivete in 20th-century thinking. The basic concept of abiogenesis originated before we had a sophisticated understanding of the cell. Each new discovery in molecular biology makes the challenge to the theory of abiogenesis more serious. This is not a repeat of the god-of-the-gaps phenomenon; it is the opposite. Two hundred years ago, the action of God was invoked to explain things not otherwise understood. As more information accumulated, it became clear that the problem could be solved by the action of natural law. Today's advances in biochemistry are not reducing the problems for abiogenesis. The more information accumulates on the nature of life, the more it indicates that natural law does not have the answer to the origin of life.

A few scientists conclude that biochemical evolution is unlikely to have happened on our earth, that it must have happened elsewhere. The Nobel Prize-winning scientist Francis Crick (of Watson and Crick fame) has advocated the theory of directed panspermia (Crick 1981; Crick and Orgel 1973). This theory proposes that the first life forms evolved somewhere else in the universe, were brought here, and then proceeded to evolve into many forms of life. Is this a scientifically satisfying option? For all practical purposes, it appears to be another nontestable hypothesis. It is one way to salvage the philosophy of naturalism—to face up to the improbability of abiogenesis on planet earth but still work within the rules of naturalism. Others take a different approach, such as de Duve (1995) who concludes: ". . . life is an obligatory manifestation of matter, bound to arise where conditions are appropriate." This conclusion is based on his confidence in the naturalistic assumption, not on finding solutions for the problems that confront the theory of abiogenesis.

To summarize, what principle should be the core of our paradigm of origins? One option is the assumption of naturalism. If we accept that paradigm, it requires belief in biochemical evolution—we must believe that chance had a very important role in at least the early stages of life's origin. The other option, informed intervention, puts more credence in cause and effect. If we accept that concept and make it our guiding principle, chance does not have a central role in the causation process. In the paradigm of informed intervention, if we see complex information in biological systems, we recognize the probability that someone, somewhere invented that information and knew how to put it into living organisms.

This is foreign to the thinking of many scientists today. But why should science not be open minded enough to allow it as an option? Part of the reason is the common belief that a non-naturalistic philosophy is incompatible with the scientific method. This does not have to be the case. We can think in different ways but use the same scientific process in seeking to understand our universe; both philosophies can be compatible with the scientific process. The only difference is whether we are willing to accept the possibility that there could be a Being in the universe with the knowledge and ability to put together the first living things, and whether we are willing to admit, if necessary, that some questions in the naturalistic paradigm cannot, as yet, be answered.

LIFE —AN ANALOGY
(Modified from Dawkins, 1986)

A summary of critical issues in understanding the origin of life

Hardware: biochemical reactions that are predictable on the basis of natural laws.

Software: information content in DNA, RNA, and proteins. The sequences of nucleotides or amino acids are not determined by any known laws, but are random, unless some intervening outside influence puts them in the particular sequence needed to make a functioning organic system.

What is the intervening influence?

1. Chance. "Sheer unadulterated miraculous luck" (Dawkins 1986).

2. Cause and effect. Every effect has a cause; chance does not have a central role in the causation process. This principle may require the recognition of the possibility of informed intervention at some point in the process of origins.

Microevolution and Speciation

8

The belief of the Middle Ages that animals and plants did not change (fixity of species) was replaced by Darwin's theory of evolution, first published in 1859. Darwin's theory was developed before the beginning of such fields as genetics and cell and molecular biology. The accumulation of new data (Mayr 1996) has made some modifications in Darwin's original theory. Let us consider the current understanding of evolution theory.

The theory can be divided conveniently into microevolution, speciation, and megaevolution (Fig. 8.1). Microevolution refers to relatively small evolutionary changes within the species of organisms. Speciation is the development of a new species. Megaevolution, a term defined by Simpson (1953a) but not commonly used, refers to evolutionary change which produces major groups of organisms including new families and any taxonomic category above the family. Macroevolution is a term more commonly used, but variation in the definition of that term limits its usefulness in this book. A common definition of macroevolution, as used

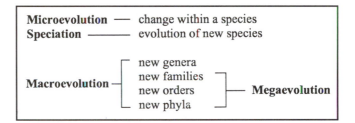

in scientific literature, is evolution above the species level (Ridley 1993). Some interventionists define it differently, which leads to confusion. Consequently, in most contexts, the term megaevolution is more useful than macroevolution in our discussion.

If several species of mice evolve from an ancestral mouse, the changes are generally in color, size, proportions of appendages in relation to body size, behavior, habitat preference, and other minor features. All of these mice are homeothermic (warm-

Figure 8.1
Speciation within lizards and within mice compared with megaevolution--evolution of major groups from a common ancestor. Each animal symbol represents one species. Microevolutionary changes occur within each species.

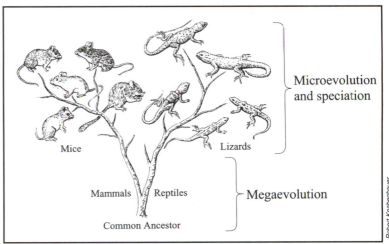

Robert Knabenbauer

blooded), have hair and milk glands, and bear live young. For them to evolve from one species of mouse would not require new structures and possibly no new genes. This is microevolution and speciation. However, if mice and other mammals evolve from a reptile ancestor, it would require the evolution of major anatomical and physiological features that did not exist in the ancestor and complexes of new genes to code for the structure and embryological development of these new features (Fig. 8.1). Examples are the structures and the endocrine control mechanism for the development and birth of live young, milk glands to nourish them, a larger, more complex brain, and the mechanism to maintain the mammals' higher metabolism and warm-blooded condition. This magnitude of change is megaevolution.

Microevolution

Today, both evolutionists and many interventionists recognize that microevolutionary changes occur. Many of the processes involved in microevolution can be observed or are supported by evidence that is circumstantial, but abundant.

Excess Individuals Are Produced. Almost all animals produce many more eggs or young than would be necessary for a constant population size. Female field mice of a partic-

ular species produce an average of four litters per year, with four young per litter. If their offspring live long enough to have one full reproductive season, the offspring of just one original pair after 20 years would number 2.59×10^{18} mice. If we stood them all side by side on the earth, they would form a pile 17,280 miles high over the entire land surface. If you look out the window you will notice there aren't that many mice around. Animal population sizes, on average, are stable, which means that most offspring either don't live long or don't successfully reproduce. The mouse example would be insignificant in comparison with such other animals as some insects or fish that produce hundreds or thousands of eggs per female each year.

Individuals Are Not Alike. Even though the 17,280 mile stack of mice are all of one species, some variation is evident in their characteristics: differences in size, color, behavior, reproductive potential, alertness, etc. New variation arises through the processes of mutation and genetic recombination. Mutations are changes in the hereditary material, the genes, caused by various kinds of radiation (e.g., x-rays, cosmic radiation, radiation from nuclear reactions), by some chemicals, or by factors within the cell. If the mutation is not lethal, it may be passed on to offspring and, perhaps, spread through a population of animals. Figure 8.2 illustrates a few of the numerous mutations that have been produced in fruit flies in the laboratory. Most mutations are harmful; some are not.

The process of recombination increases the number of different combinations of characteristics within a population of animals. Recombination is the rearrangement of the genetic material occurring during sexual reproduction. It is analogous to shuffling a deck of cards. If a female mouse with a short tail, short ears, and light color mates with a male with a long tail, long ears, and dark color, the offspring may show all combinations of these characteristics. The variations we observe in domestic animals indicate the amount of genetic variability that can occur through the process of mutation and recombination (Fig. 8.3).

Natural Selection. Mutation and recombination are essentially random processes. The cause of the mutation is blind to the needs of an animal. Which combinations of characteristics actually appear as the result of recombination is also the result of chance. However, another factor

has been important in the development of breeds of domestic animals. If an animal breeder notices an individual with a highly desirable combination of characteristics, he or she doesn't allow chance to determine the contribution of this individual in producing the next generation. The breeder makes this desirable animal

Figure 8.2
A few of the numerous mutations in fruit flies (genus *Drosophila*) that have been produced in the laboratory (after Villee 1977).

Figure 8.3
A few of the many varieties of domestic animals. The Rock Dove is a wild species. All of the other varieties of pigeons, chickens, and dogs shown here have been produced by selective breeding (after Clark 1979; Moore 1964).

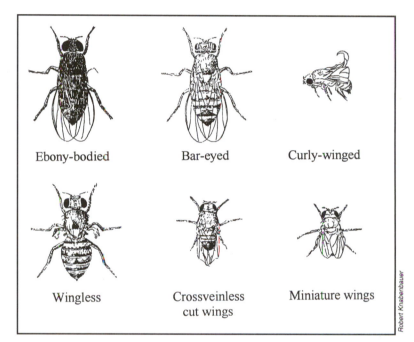

Ebony-bodied Bar-eyed Curly-winged

Wingless Crossveinless cut wings Miniature wings

Robert Knabenbauer

Rock Dove ——— Domestic pigeon breeds ———

Chickens

St. Bernard Pekingese Fox terrier Bulldog

Robert Knabenbauer

an important part of the breeding stock to assure that its characteristics are passed on to as many offspring as possible. Selectively breeding only animals with the features we want has made it possible to produce faster horses, collie dogs with longer muzzles, cows that produce more milk, and a breed of show chickens with 12-foot-long tail feathers! The short legs of dachshunds, flat muzzles of bulldogs, curly hair of poodles, and tumbling flight of some show pigeons (actually a nervous disorder) are examples of mutations that would probably not survive in nature but have been preserved through selective breeding.

Darwin and others wondered if there might be natural processes that would result in selective breeding. Indeed, we do find that some individuals have a much greater natural likelihood of surviving and producing offspring. This process, called natural selection, is defined as "differential reproduction of genetically diverse organisms" (Avers 1989, p. 213). Those individuals with characteristics best adapted to their environment have the best chance of surviving and successfully reproducing.

Wolves and caribou inhabit the same Alaskan valleys. Wolves like to eat caribou, but a wolf can capture only those that are sick, slow, or unalert. Even a very young caribou with normal health and vigor can outrun a wolf. The Eskimos have a saying: "The wolf keeps the caribou strong." This is natural selection in action. The wolves' ability to catch only the weaker caribou selectively eliminates those individuals from the reproductive population.

Another interesting example of natural selection is commonly described in evolution textbooks and general biology texts. The peppered moth (*Biston betularia*) of England spends the day resting on tree trunks or branches. Years ago their normally speckled gray color camouflaged them well on lichen-covered bark (Fig 8.4). A black mutant form remained rare because its color made it conspicuous and easy prey for insect-eating birds. However, the picture changed during the industrial revolution. In industrialized areas, the formerly harmful black mutation became beneficial because the black moths were better camouflaged on soot-covered trees. Birds easily could see the normal speckled moths on the sooty trees, so they became the rare form while the black mutant form became dominant. Selection pressure now favored the black mutant rather than the gray speckled form. This case study actually is not as straightforward as pictured in most textbooks (Mettler et al. 1988, p. 150-155), but it does illustrate the effect of natural selection in changing environments.

The operation of natural selection usually is not as dramatic as a race between a caribou and a wolf. The results of natural selection are expressed most precisely as changes in gene frequency. Genes occur in different forms called alleles. For example, in a gene that affects eye color, some individuals may have the allele for blue eyes; others have the allele for brown eyes; and others have both (in this case, since brown is dominant, their eyes are brown). Each individual in a species has a different combination of gene alleles in its chromosomes that determine its characteristics. If any factor (selection pressure) makes individuals with one particular characteristic more likely to survive and successfully reproduce, the allele for this characteristic becomes more common in the population.

Now we are ready to put together the major components of the micro-evolution process. In a given species of animal or plant, an excess number of offspring are produced and many or indeed most of them die before reproducing. Since there is also

variation in the characteristics of these offspring, resulting from mutation and recombination, some have combinations of characteristics that give them a better chance of surviving than others. That same variation also leads to differences in the number of offspring produced by the successful breeders. Hence, the individuals whose characteristics enable them to survive and produce the most offspring will make the greatest contribution to the genetic makeup of the next generation. This is natural selection.

Many complexities in the evolution theory are evident beyond those covered here. For example, the

Figure 8.4
Two color variations of the peppered moth on a clean tree trunk and a soot-covered trunk (after Stebbins 1971).

116

Process of Microevolution

1. Overpopulation—more offspring are produced than can survive.

2. Variation—no two offspring are ever exactly alike because of mutation and recombination.

3. Natural selection (survival of the fittest)—those individuals with variations that give an advantage in competition are more likely to survive and reproduce.

4. Inheritance of fitness—variations giving an advantage are passed on to offspring.

genetic makeup of a species is influenced not only by natural selection but also by random shifts in gene frequency called genetic drift. Another influence, the founder effect, occurs when evolution of a new species begins with a small population consisting of individuals that do not represent the average of the ancestral population. For example, if individuals who are large for this species move into a new environment and start a new population, their offspring will retain this feature of large size and it will be a characteristic of the new species. When a small population becomes isolated, influences like the founder effect and genetic drift may be significant factors in molding the characteristics of the resulting species. Several recent books provide a more complete discussion of evolution theory (Avers 1989; Futuyma 1986; Grant 1991; Maynard Smith 1989; Mettler et al. 1988; and Ridley 1993).

Is Natural Selection a Circular Concept?

Natural selection sometimes has been criticized as involving circular reasoning. According to this criticism, evolution theory states that the fittest will survive, and it defines fitness as those who survive. This leads to the conclusion that those who survive do survive. Is evolution theory so shallow? One argument against that

conclusion (Kitcher 1982, p. 55-60) states that the concept of fitness is not circular because mathematical population geneticists can define fitness in precise, quantitative terms. I agree that the circular reasoning criticism does not stand up, but for another reason. Fitness, as defined in population genetics, is a mathematical term describing the likelihood that a particular gene allele will spread in the population. Thus, it is based essentially on survival and, in a strict sense, is circular. Its purpose is merely to allow quantitative analysis of the spread of genes in animal or plant populations, not to demonstrate that the concepts of natural selection and fitness are meaningful. Stopping here however, misrepresents the topic. Population genetics is based on the conviction that there are objective reasons why some traits are more likely to survive. It is not difficult to understand that moths with better camouflage are more likely to be overlooked by predators, that rabbits that can run faster escape more predators, or that insects with a gene giving them resistance to an insecticide have a better chance to survive.

Natural selection and the resulting differences in fitness are a reality, but relationships between animals and the selection pressures that affect them are complex. It is difficult to make the study of these factors quantitative and predictive. Precise analysis of the factors that determine, in any given natural situation, which characters have increased fitness is challenging but it's not based on circular reasoning.

Abundant evidence shows that the process of natural selection occurs (Endler 1986; Weiner 1995). But, how much change can be produced by the processes of mutation, recombination, and natural selection? This is considered in chapter 10. Here, let's look at the process by which microevolution is related to the development of new species.

Speciation

Evolution theory proposes that evolution not only causes black moths to become more common than grey moths, but under the right circumstances also produces new species. Biologists define a species as a population or group of populations of animals that interbreed among themselves but do not breed with other populations (Mayr 1970). The many breeds of domestic dogs look very different, yet they freely interbreed. If you doubt that, let your prize registered female pet run the streets for a while! By definition, this makes all domestic dogs members of one species. On the other hand, many similar species of wild animals live side by side in nature, with no evi-

dence of any hybrids appearing. The differences between these species may be small, but they are consistent, and they include features that prevent them from interbreeding. The development of new species is believed to occur through the processes of geographic isolation, adaptation to new environments, and the development of reproductive isolation.

Geographic Isolation. Many differences of opinion arise about the details of the speciation process (e.g., Gibbons 1996; Morell 1996); but according to the concept of speciation that has the best supporting evidence, two populations of animals first become geographically separated before speciation occurs. For example, if chipmunks live on two mountain ranges and also through the forests between the two ranges, they remain as one species. Even though the chipmunks on one mountain range may look a little different from those on the other range, the interbreeding throughout the species causes enough mixing and sharing of genes, or gene flow, to prevent them from separating into two distinct species (Fig. 8.5). However, if a strip of desert lies between the mountains and the chipmunks do not enter the desert, they are geographically isolated. The two groups have no opportunity to interbreed, and thus no gene flow exists between them.

Process of Speciation

1. Populations become geographically isolated from each other.

2. Each population becomes adapted to its own environment, through natural selection.

3. The populations become different from each other in some feature of their structure or behavior that prevents them from interbreeding (reproductive isolation).

Adaptation and Reproductive Isolation. If the environments on the two mountain ranges are different, natural selection along with genetic drift may cause the two groups of chipmunks to become different also. If their differences prevent them from interbreeding, they have become new species.

A species of salamander (*Ensatina eschscholtzi*) in California illustrates an incipient stage in the development of a new species. *Ensatina* is found in the mountains all the way around California's central valley (Fig. 8.6). They interbreed all through their long range except where the Sierra Nevada range meets the coast range in Southern California. There they do not interbreed.

A variety of mechanisms produces this reproductive isolation. In some cases, the species are so genetically different that even if they do mate, they can produce only infertile offspring (like the mule) or perhaps no offspring at all. Often reproductive isolation mechanisms

are more subtle. Some species that may be able to cross and produce viable, fertile hybrids in the laboratory do not hybridize in nature because of differences in habitat or behavior. For example, in some cases, two species of chipmunks live on the same mountain range, but one species lives in low-elevation, Pinyon Pine forests and the other lives only in high-elevation, Lodgepole Pine forests. Consequently, they have no opportunity to interbreed.

Two species of fruit flies live in the same areas and breed at the same time of year, but one species limits its breeding to the morning hours and the other breeds only in the evening. In many animals, reproductive isolation is maintained by their courtship rituals which are unique to each species. For example, part of the courtship of songbirds, frogs, toads, and some insects is the courtship song or call given by the males. The song is different for each species, and the females respond only to the song of their own species.

Figure 8.5
Geographic ranges of chipmunks, (a) without geographic isolation and (b) with geographic isolation.

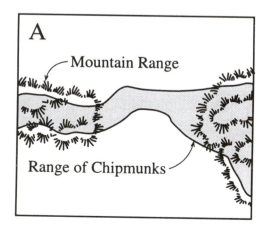

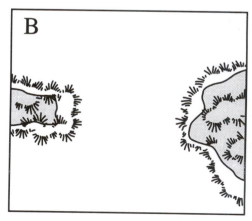

Carole Stanton

Punctuated Equilibrium

In his theory, Charles Darwin proposed that evolutionary change occurs gradually, at a slow and fairly even pace. The many small changes that occur gradually in the process of microevolution, over very long periods of time, add up and generate the larger changes that produce new species, families, etc. This gradualistic evolution that Darwin insisted on was something not even his contemporaries were sure they wanted to uphold. However, Darwin's gradualism became dogma for a long time. Evolutionary scientists today know much more than Darwin did, since fields such as genetics and molecular biology had their beginnings after Darwin's day. In the 1930s and 1940s, the Neodarwinian Synthesis was developed, a modern version of evolution theory based on gradualistic thinking (Mayr 1996).

A new theory proposed by Eldredge and Gould (1972) was called punctuated equilibrium. This theory proposes that microevolution occurs slowly and, perhaps, much as described by the Neodarwinian Synthesis, but speciation occurs rapidly, and generally very little change occurs until the next speciation event (Fig. 8.7). The proposed reason for this is that speciation is most likely to occur in small populations, peripheral to the main population. In the main population, occupying a large geographic area, there is enough gene flow to prevent

**Figure 8.6
Distribution of subspecies of salamander (*Ensatina eschscholtzi*) in California (after Eaton 1970).**

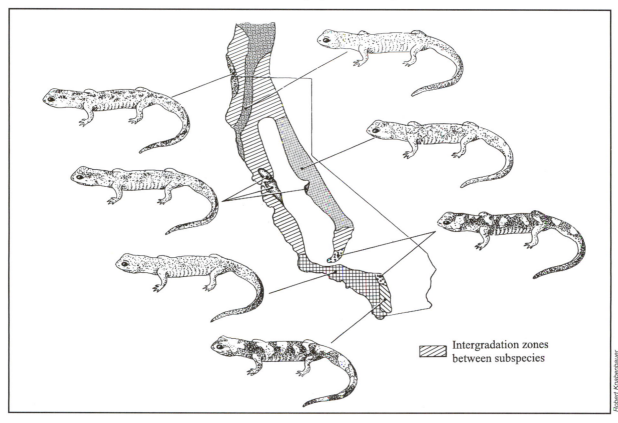

Intergradation zones between subspecies

much change. But when a small population becomes isolated, perhaps in a slightly different habitat, change occurs quickly. Some scientists are beginning to doubt that the microevolutionary process extrapolated over time is adequate to produce more significant changes. They suggest that larger scale evolution must involve a different mechanism than microevolution and that it happens rapidly (Ridley 1993, p. 523-525).

Most scientists conclude that there is no question that evolution occurred; the only question is by which naturalistic process or mechanism it occurred. Plenty of questions and lively discussions debate that issue. On the other hand, Kurt Wise (1989) developed a creationist version of punctuated equilibrium, something we'll discuss later.

Figure 8.7 Phylogenetic trees showing the difference between gradualism and punctuated equilibrium.

Gradualistic Neo-Darwinism Macroevolution occurs through the gradual accumulation, over a long period, of all the changes produced by microevolution. Macroevolution is just an extrapolation of the microevolution process.

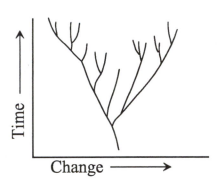

Punctuated Equilibrium Microevolution occurs slowly, as described by the Neo-Darwinian synthesis. Speciation occurs rapidly, often with very little change between speciation events.

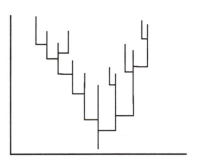

Can a Creationist Believe the Evolution Process?

Charles Darwin saw abundant evidence for microevolutionary changes and speciation in animals and plants. This led him to reject the rigid creationism of his time. The interventionist of today believes Darwin's mistake and that of some of his contemporaries was in equating belief in creation with a belief in the fixity of species. Several lines of reasoning lead us to reject the idea that all species were created as they now exist. The variation we observe in domestic animals tells us that the genetic system is capable of considerable change. Selective breeding has produced dogs ranging from Pekingese to Saint Bernards, chickens with 12-foot-long tail feathers, and horses varying from the impressive Clydesdale and other working breeds to a dog-sized miniature. This evidence, by itself, does not demonstrate that the same thing would happen in nature, but it does show that the genetic potential for microevolution and speciation is present.

The interventionist also must explain another type of evidence— the origin of parasites and other destructive forces in nature. Many parasites are highly modified in their anatomy and physiology for their dependence on parasitism as a way of life. The idea that a benevolent God would create these repulsive, destructive things in nature greatly bothered Charles Darwin, and rightly so. The old concept of the fixity of species made God responsible for everything in nature, both good and bad. A more consistent interventionist approach suggests that God designed nature to operate harmoniously and that some features of the biological world have developed through evolution since creation. This concept is developed further in chapters 11 and 12.

When Darwin visited the Galapagos Islands, he found that the finches and the giant tortoises were somewhat different on each island (Fig. 8.8). This (and numerous cases like it) led him to wonder if God really made a different species on each island or if each might have developed by evolution. This is a question that still must be answered. Of the 22 species of chipmunks in the United States, for example, 13 appear in California. Most of these are or nearly are restricted to California. The differences between them (Fig. 8.9) are quite small, involving variations in color patterns, size, behavior, ecology, and bone proportions. Some have white tips on their tail hairs, and others have yellow tips; some have bright and contrasting stripes, while others are less contrasting; their chipping calls are different enough

that, after some practice, one can identify them by their calls alone; and some live in open forest, while some prefer dense brush or forest with considerable brush and logs. Certainly the differences between these chipmunk species do not seem as great as the differences between many breeds of dogs, but since the different chipmunks do not interbreed, they are different species.

We also find that each species has its own geographic range (Fig. 8.10). *Eutamias sonomae* occurs only in the chaparral brush of northwestern California. *E. panamintinus* is found only in the semi-desert Pinyon Pine forest east of the Sierra Nevada Mountains, and *E. alpinus* is limited to rocky mountain meadows above the 9,000-foot elevation in the Sierra Nevada. Did God make these chipmunk species and put them where they are? Certainly He could have done so, but the evidence seems to

Figure 8.8
Several species of Darwin's finches and giant tortoises from the Galapagos Islands (after Stebbins 1971).

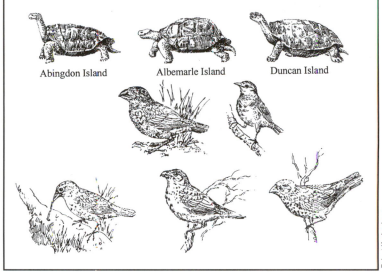

Abingdon Island   Albemarle Island   Duncan Island

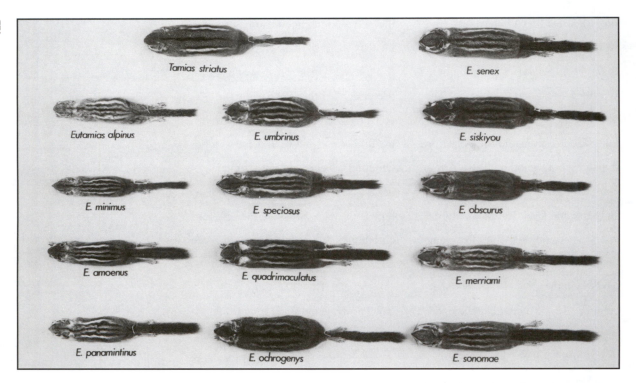

Tamias striatus

E. senex

Eutamias alpinus

E. umbrinus

E. siskiyou

E. minimus

E. speciosus

E. obscurus

E. amoenus

E. quadrimaculatus

E. merriami

E. panamintinus

E. ochrogenys

E. sonomae

Figure 8.9
The 13 species of
chipmunks from California,
and the eastern chipmunk,
Tamias striatus.

indicate that He didn't do it that way. It's more likely He made animals with the potential for great genetic variability: the ability to adapt, through microevolution and speciation, to new habitats and climatic changes they would encounter after they were created. This is reinforced even more if we take seriously the possibility of a worldwide flood and recognize that the mountain ranges and climatic conditions that determine chipmunk distribution didn't even exist in their present form until after the flood. Perhaps the original chipmunks spread through Asia (one species does exist there) and into North America where groups of chipmunks colonized many different areas and adapted to the local conditions to produce the 22 species. When one species, such as the ancestral chipmunk species, gives rise to several new species as different populations adapt to different ecological niches, the process is called adaptive radiation.

The word "evolution" means change. Good evidence indicates this genetic process of evolution (or some variation of it) does occur and produces new varieties and new species. Of the many similar examples we could examine, let's look briefly at just one—the meadow mice or voles. These little, short-eared mice are worldwide and live predominantly in grassy areas in systems of tunnels they chew through the vegetation. The most famous voles are the lemmings in the Arctic. You may have seen them by the thousands in a movie, jumping over a cliff (or were they pushed?) into the ocean. A few of the many species of voles in the genus *Microtus* are shown in Figure 8.11. They are all quite similar—as similar as the species of chipmunks. Further investigation reveals a number of genera of voles not much different from *Microtus* (Fig. 8.12). They are classified in different genera because each has certain characteristics consistently different from *Microtus* and from each other, but these differences are still relatively minor. They include variations in the cusp patterns on the grinding surfaces of the teeth, differences in the characteristics of toes and claws, and minor differences in the proportions of anatomical features. It does not seem inconceivable that all of these genera devel-

oped from one created ancestor. Even the muskrat and the round-tailed muskrat are in the same sub-family as the voles. They are different mainly in size and in a few adaptations for life in the water (Fig. 8.13). Could they be from the same created ancestor as the voles? Perhaps so.

But Didn't Moses Say . . .

Some still may raise the objection that the Bible says God created the animals as they are now. Where does it say that? The only Bible statements that might be interpreted that way are the declarations in the creation account stating that the newly created animals were to reproduce after their own kind (Coffin 1983c, p. 18-20).

First of all, one cannot demon-

Figure 8.10 Geographic ranges of chipmunks in California (after Hall 1981; Johnson 1943).

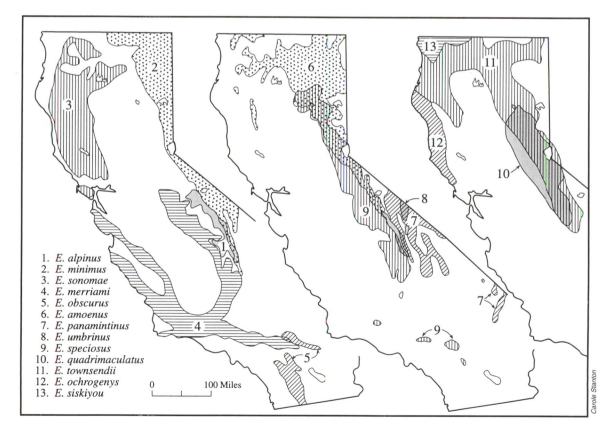

1. *E. alpinus*
2. *E. minimus*
3. *E. sonomae*
4. *E. merriami*
5. *E. obscurus*
6. *E. amoenus*
7. *E. panamintinus*
8. *E. umbrinus*
9. *E. speciosus*
10. *E. quadrimaculatus*
11. *E. townsendii*
12. *E. ochrogenys*
13. *E. siskiyou*

0   100 Miles

Carole Stanton

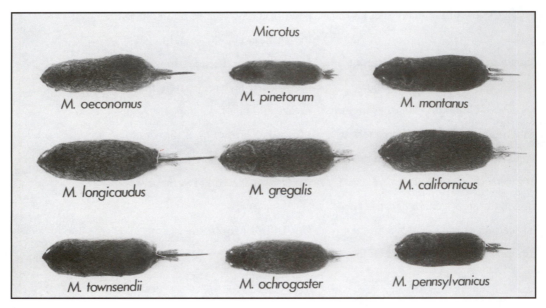

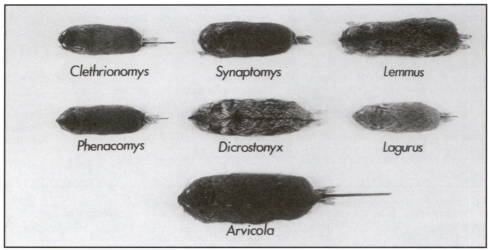

Figure 8.11 Several species of voles in the genus *Microtus*

Figure 8.12 Several genera of voles. The genera *Lemmus* and *Dicrostonyx* are lemmings from the arctic region.

strate that the phrase "after his kind" was intended as a technical genetic statement meaning that every species would be unchanged. It more likely indicated that offspring would be similar to their parents. Also, the phrase "after his kind" is used only once in connection with the order to multiply (Gen. 1:11-12). The rest of the time it is used in connection with the statement that something was created. The original Hebrew phrase can be translated in more than one way. Some modern English translations use the more easily understood statement "God made the various kinds of wild beasts of the earth" (Gen. 1:25, The Bible, An American Translation), rather than the somewhat awkward "God made the beasts of the earth after his kind" (Gen. 1:25, KJV).

The fact that the major groups of organisms were present at the end of creation week, including supposedly highly evolved types like flowering plants (fruit trees) and human beings, indicates that megaevolution is not compatible with biblical interventionism.

Genesis does not seem to have anything to say against microevolution and, perhaps, even some macroevolution, at least to the development of new genera. The scientific evidence is strong in favor of microevolution and speciation; the Bible does not speak against them. Interventionists today have no reason to doubt their validity. They are incorporated as a part of "informed intervention theory." The theory of how microevolution and speciation occur is, in many ways, the same for interventionists and naturalistic evolutionists; some exceptions are discussed in chapter 12.

One can only wonder what would have happened in biology during the last century if Darwin had read his Bible more carefully and learned that the Bible doesn't rule out the evolution of new species. If he had developed a theory of evolution within the limits of the created groups, would science have been as successful as it has been? I see no reason why not.

Interventionists and other scientists can agree on microevolution, speciation, and some macroevolution; thus research in these areas would be unaffected by the researcher's philosophical preferences. The interven-

tionist disagrees on the question of megaevolution and proposes limits to the changes that evolution can produce. This suggests that some types of current research are not useful. In their place one can ask, "What are the limits of evolutionary change?" "What were the limits of the original independent groups?" The naturalistic evolution theory does not ask such questions. It assumes that all plant and animal groups could have arisen by evolution.

The limits of evolutionary change are not easy to define—the uncertainty we encounter in the study of things that happened in the more distant past. Still, it is a question worth trying to answer. The Bible does not give much specific information to help us determine how much evolutionary change has occurred since creation. On this topic, like many others, the Bible only gives the important principles to guide our thinking and leaves the details to

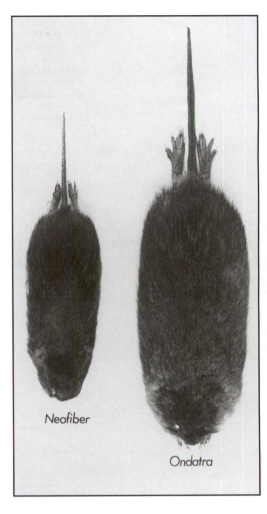

Neofiber

Ondatra

Figure 8.13
Relatives of the voles, the round-tailed muskrat (*Neofiber alleni*) and the muskrat *Ondatra zibethicus*).

challenge the curiosity.

Some claim that if we accept microevolution, we have no reason to question megaevolution—the evolution of major groups of organisms. Is that true? If we accept microevolution, does that lead to acceptance of the evolution of everything? Not necessarily. My reasons are discussed in chapter 10.

9

The Case for Megaevolution

Naturalistic theory and interventionist theory differ most significantly on the question of the origin of major groups of organisms. Evolution to the level of a new class or phylum (megaevolution) would require that many new genes and new structures evolve. If one accepts the naturalistic assumption, that assumption dictates that megaevolution has occurred and has produced all of the living world. On the other hand, interventionists ask, "What are the natural limits to the evolution process? How much change can evolution actually accomplish?" Here I summarize the evidence and present as strong a case as possible for megaevolution. In chapter 10, we'll go back over the same evidence and present the case for the alternate interpretation. In the process, we search for some critical questions that have the potential to differentiate between the two theories.

In evaluating the data, we attempt to determine into which of the following categories each type of evidence fits:

1. Data compatible with both theories are of no help in determining which theory is correct.

2. Data that are compatible with one theory but contradict the other provide support for the theory with which the data are compatible. The more data in favor of one theory, the more confidence we can have in that theory.

The strength of each line of evidence must be evaluated separately. If, in comparing these two paradigms, we conclude, for example, that since evidence A and B fit megaevolution best, evidence C should be explained by megaevolution, this can be circular reasoning. If evidence C cannot stand by itself, it is irrelevant to the debate.

Megaevolution

The theory of megaevolution states that over the billions of years of earth history, evolutionary processes have produced all the existing and extinct kinds of plants and animals from the first single-celled ancestors. These changes occur by the processes of microevolution and speciation. Such changes accumulate through the ages to produce organisms different enough so biologists call them different families, orders, or phyla. A number of lines of evidence support the concept that the diversity of life has resulted from megaevolution.

Embryology

In the 19th century, scientists noted that the embryos of different groups of vertebrates were much more similar than the adults of these groups. This led to the theory that ontogeny (embryological develop-ment) recapitulates phylogeny (evolu-tionary history); the embryo repeats its evolutionary history (Fig. 9.1). This idea, as originally proposed by Ernst Haeckel, does not hold up to modern genetic evidence (Gould 1977, p. 202-204), but some of Haeckel's observations are still relevant and form part of the modern understanding of the relationship between ontogeny and phylogeny. This modern theory of recapitulation recognizes that an embryo does not necessarily resemble the adults of its ancestors; but in its early stages, it resembles the embryonic stages of its ancestors because of evolutionary descent. The early embryonic stages of the different classes of vertebrates are very similar; but as they grow, they develop unique adult features (see Gould 1977 or Ridley 1993, p. 537-551, for other complexities in the ontogeny-phylogeny relationship).

This same concept can be seen in the embryological development of the mammalian heart and kidney. The heart in a mammalian embryo goes through a developmental sequence similar to its evolutionary progres-sion, from a primitive two-chambered state in the young embryo to the fully developed four-chambered mammal

**Figure 9.1
Comparison of various types
of embryos, as used by
Haeckel to support his
theory of recapitulation
(after Coffin 1983c).**

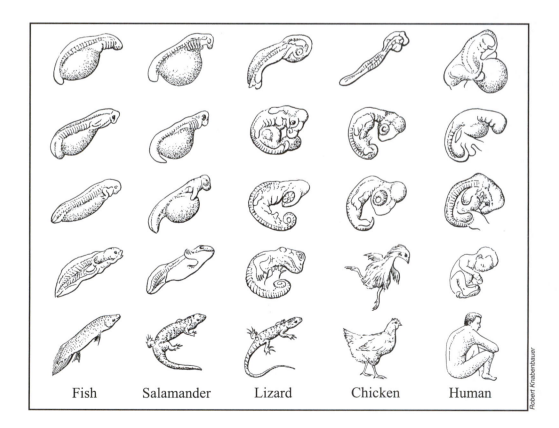

| Fish | Salamander | Lizard | Chicken | Human |

heart. A young mammalian embryo has a very simple kidney, similar to the hypothetical ancestral vertebrate kidney. It increases in complexity until it resembles the simple kidney of a hagfish.

When the complex adult (metanephric) mammal kidney completes its growth and is ready to function, the simple (ancestral) kidney atrophies and disappears. Thus, it appears as if the kidney and heart repeat their evolutionary history in their embryological development.

Futuyma (1983, p. 48-49) discusses additional embryological evidence for evolution. Some aquatic salamanders have gills and fins for life underwater, but terrestrial salamanders develop entirely within the egg with gills and fins they never use and which are lost before the salamanders hatch (Fig. 9.2). This seems more like an evolutionary remnant than a wise design.

The lower part of reptile back legs consists of the tibia and fibula and tarsal (ankle) bones which articulate with the metatarsals in the foot (Fig. 9.3). In the legs of birds, the tarsal bones apparently are fused to the lower end of the tibia. This combined structure is called the tibiotarsus. The fibula is vestigial, consisting only of a short bone along the

upper part of the tibiotarsus. Hampe (1960) devised an ingenious experiment in which a thin sheet of mica was put between the tibia and fibula in a young chick embryo. The fibula then grew down to the ankle, and the tarsals developed as separate bones, as in reptiles. This seems to indicate that birds still have the genes for the "reptile" bones; but in a normal bird embryo, the tibia somehow inhibits the development of the fibula. When the fibula doesn't contact the ankle, the tarsals don't develop either.

Figure 9.2
Three salamander life cycles: (A) species with gills and tail fin retained into an aquatic adult life; (B) a species with an aquatic larva that loses its gills and fin in the transition to a terrestrial adult form; (C) a fully terrestrial type that loses its gills and fin when it hatches from the egg.

Figure 9.3
(A) Reptile and (B) bird leg bones, and (C) bird leg bones that resulted from the experimental separation of the tibia and fibula (after Futuyma 1983).

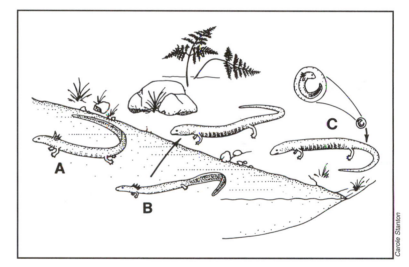

Carole Stanton

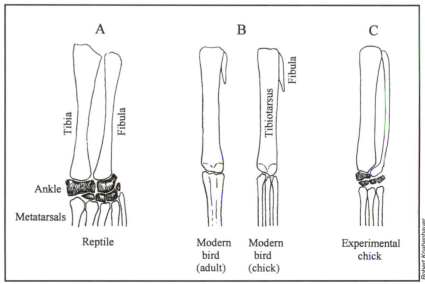

Robert Knabenbauer

An experiment by Kollar and Fisher (1980) yields a similar result. They laid tissue from a mouse embryo over the jaw tissue of a chicken embryo. The chicken jaw developed teeth, complete with enamel. Kollar and Fisher concluded that when birds evolved from reptiles they did not lose the genes for making enameled teeth. Changes in embryologic development blocked the production of teeth in birds, but the genes for teeth are present though quiescent.

Vestigial Organs

Vestigial structures are remnants of an animal's evolutionary history. If animals are changing and evolving new structures, some old structures no longer needed will slowly disappear. During this process, a remnant or vestige of the original structure may still remain. Several organs fit the criteria of vestigial features (Fig. 9.4).

The human appendix is a vestige that often poses a problem. It gets diseased and has to be removed. Another vestige is the caudal vertebrae, a remnant of a tail. Humans don't have a tail, but a short bony structure exists that is homologous to the tail of other mammals. Sometimes a human baby will actually have a short external tail (Hamilton & Mossman 1972, p. 432). Humans even have a remnant of segmentation in the abdominal muscles. Many invertebrates are segmented animals—especially worms and arthropods whose bodies are partially divided into many segments with muscles present in each segment. Some of this segmentation remains in vertebrates and is evident in the abdominal muscles of humans. Even though humans do not have hair covering their bodies as do other mammals, vestiges of hair are on parts of the human body. Most mammals have muscles that move their ears to get the best reception of the sounds they hear. We have the same muscles connected to our ears even though we can't turn our ears and have no real need for these ear muscles. Some vertebrates have a third eyelid that can be brought

Figure 9.4
Several vestigial organs in humans and vestigial hind limbs in a whale (after Villee 1977).

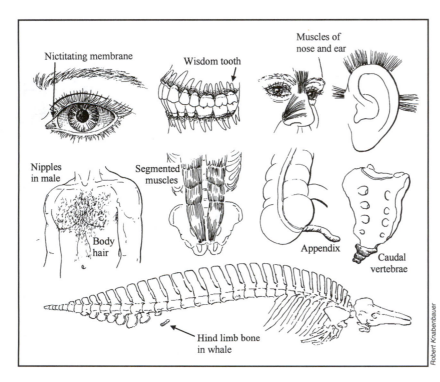

Nictitating membrane
Wisdom tooth
Muscles of nose and ear
Nipples in male
Segmented muscles
Body hair
Appendix
Caudal vertebrae
Hind limb bone in whale

Robert Knabenbauer

across the eye to protect it. Humans don't have that third eyelid, but they do have a small vestige of it, the nictitating membrane in the corner of the eye. Third molars or "wisdom teeth" are often a problem for humans, and sometimes they don't fit and have to be taken out. Humans have canine teeth which are still somewhat pointed, but they are not large enough to serve the original purpose of the long canines in many other mammals. These are all vestiges of things that apparently we don't need anymore.

Whales have front flippers and tail flukes but no hind limbs. Whales evolved from other mammals that did have hind limbs. In the process of evolution, the hind limbs disappeared except for two little bones embedded in the flesh, vestiges, apparently, of hind limbs (Ridley 1993, p. 49-50).

A number of examples at the microevolution level can illustrate the reality of the development of vestigial structures and show how the vestiges described above must have developed. We point to blind cave salamanders with vestiges of eyes, flightless birds with vestigial wings, and flightless beetles with useless wings sealed under their fused wing covers (Futuyma 1983, p. 48). All of these vestigial structures are evidence of evolution from other animals that needed those structures.

Hierarchical Nature of Life and the Ascending Scale of Complexity

All animals share essentially the same basic biochemical functions; but when we compare features of physiology and anatomy, we can arrange the animal groups in an evolutionary scale of complexity (Fig. 9.5). Protozoa are composed of only one cell and can be described as acellular. Sponges are multi-celled but don't have separate germ layers. Flatworms added separate germ layers, and roundworms were the first to have a complete digestive tract. Fish were the first to have an internal skeleton, amphibians were the first tetrapods or four-legged animals, reptiles added a completely terrestrial life cycle, mammals and birds became warm blooded, and mammals bear live young. Each group added important

**Figure 9.5
Principal animal phyla arranged in the ascending scale of complexity.**

	Multicelled	Germ layers	Complete digestive tract	Circulatory system	External shell or skeleton	Internal skeleton	Complete terrestrial life cycle	Warm blooded	Bear placental live young
Mammals	x	x	x	x		x	x	x	x
Birds	x	x	x	x		x	x	x	
Reptiles	x	x	x	x		x	x		
Amphibians	x	x	x	x		x			
Fish	x	x	x	x		x			
Snails	x	x	x	x	x				
Insects	x	x	x	x	x				
Earthworms	x	x	x	x					
Starfish	x	x	x	x					
Roundworms	x	x	x						
Flatworms	x	x							
Jellyfish	x								
Sponges	x								
Protozoa									

features as life "climbed" the evolutionary scale.

The evolution of plants and animals occurred by a series of sequential, splitting events. For example, mammals split off from reptiles; then mammals and reptiles each split to produce various orders. The mammalian order Carnivora split into families, including cats, dogs, and bears. After that, the dog family split into wolves, jackals, and foxes. The result of this process is a hierarchical arrangement of living things in groups nested within groups (Fig. 9.6). Objects that did not descend from common ancestors, like minerals, cannot be arranged that way (Futuyma 1983, p. 53). If life had been created by an intelligent Designer, we would expect more of a continuum of types of organisms, not a hierarchical arrangement.

Homology

Homology is a key line of evidence used to determine evolutionary

relations between organisms and in developing phylogenies—theories of the evolutionary pathways by which these organisms arose (Ridley 1993, p. 50-52). Let's consider two ways of defining homology and related terms. The definitions commonly used are already an interpretation, so we use a functional definition first and then introduce the standard (or interpretive) definition later.

Homology: parts of different organisms that may serve different functions but have the same internal structure and develop from the same embryological pathways.

Analogy: parts that serve the same function but have different internal structure and develop along different embryological pathways.

The principle of homology can be illustrated by front limb structure of four kinds of mammals (Fig. 9.7). A human hand and arm are adapted for fine manipulations, a seal's flipper is designed for swimming, a bat's wing for flying, and a dog's leg for fast running but not for delicate maneuvers. The front limbs look different and have different functions; but in their internal anatomy, they have the same basic features. All have the same bones: a shoulder blade; a humerus, radius, and ulna; and the wrist and hand bones. Proportions of the bones

**Figure 9.6
An example of the
hierarchical arrangement
of life**

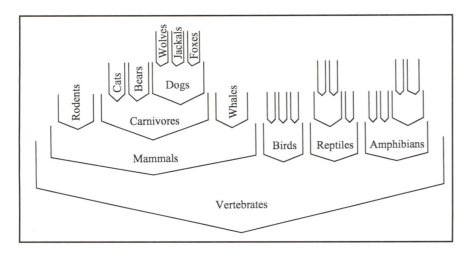

are different, but the muscle attachments and articulations are the same. In the bat, the radius is reduced, or vestigial. Even the "hand" has the same bones in these four very different limbs. A bat's wing has the same bones as a human hand, and the wing is supported by four fingers with very elongated finger bones. This is the meaning of homology: functions may be different, but the internal structure is the same.

Mammals have these homologies because the four types of front limbs evolved from a common ancestor that had the basic bone arrangement found in them. They inherited the bone structure from the common ancestor and evolved modifications to adapt the limb to the needs of each. In contrast, when different animal groups have analogous structures, such as wings, the animals didn't evolve from a common ancestor that had wings. Each group independently evolved wings to serve the same purpose; and because they evolved independently, they have different structural features.

The concept of analogy can be illustrated by four different kinds of wings: butterfly, bird, bat, and pterosaur (a flying reptile, Fig. 9.8). In bird wings, the finger bones are quite reduced and feathers make the main flight surface. In a pterosaur

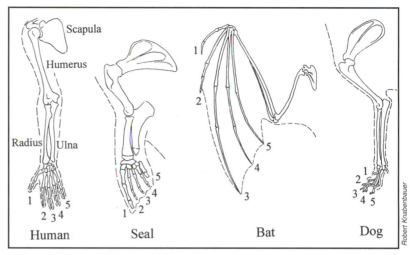

wing, the fourth finger alone supports the wing membrane. Insect wings have no bones at all. Externally these wings are superficially alike; yet internally they are very different, so they are analogous.

The term convergence is closely related to analogy. Animal lineages having different ancestry have become more similar because of similar needs. Their structure has converged toward a common pattern (at least superficially) as they have evolved independently of each other.

Figure 9.7
Homologous limb bones in four kinds of mammals (after Dunbar 1961).

Figure 9.8
Analogous structures— the wings of a butterfly, bird, bat, and pterosaur (after Moody 1962).

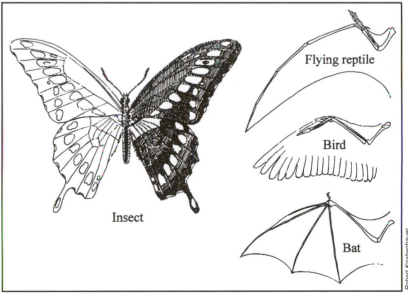

The same principles of homology and analogy also apply at the level of physiology or biochemistry. Cytochrome c is a molecule found in virtually all living things, and amino-acid sequences in cytochrome c have been studied in a wide variety of organisms from humans and donkeys to chickens and castor beans (Mettler et al. 1988, p. 37-41). Between humans and monkeys, only one amino acid is different; but between yeast and humans, 45 differences are found in the sequence of amino acids (Fig.9.9). If life has evolved, we would expect the differences to increase as we compare organisms farther apart on the scale, and that is what we find. As evolution progressed from the yeast, mutations in the cytochrome c molecule would increase, as in other parts of the organism, and the cytochrome c would become more changed as life evolved. In general, the data fit this expectation, although the change is not very smooth.

From this information, one can develop phylogenetic trees based on cytochrome c (Fig. 9.10). The amount of homology determines how close together different groups are on the tree. Notice that the different groups of mammals end up together, roughly as we would expect. The other relationships on this tree also are at least approximately what one would expect if life had evolved.

This study of biochemical homology can be applied in a very quantitative manner at various taxonomic levels. This method is being used extensively for research on the evolutionary relationships of groups of plants and animals. One paper (Miyamoto & Goodman 1986) uses biochemical data to analyze homologies and relationships between mammal orders (Fig. 9.11). The numbers next to the branches of the tree indicate the minimum number of amino-acid changes needed to evolve from one group to another. This tree is similar to the one that would result from using morphological data.

Phylogenetic trees also can be based on comparison of DNA from different organisms, and this method

Figure 9.9 A diagram showing the number of amino-acid differences in cytochrome c obtained from different species of animals, plants, and microorganisms (data from Villee 1977).

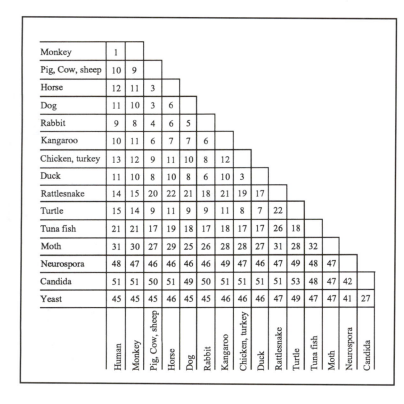

	Human	Monkey	Pig, Cow, sheep	Horse	Dog	Rabbit	Kangaroo	Chicken, turkey	Duck	Rattlesnake	Turtle	Tuna fish	Moth	Neurospora	Candida
Monkey	1														
Pig, Cow, sheep	10	9													
Horse	12	11	3												
Dog	11	10	3	6											
Rabbit	9	8	4	6	5										
Kangaroo	10	11	6	7	7	6									
Chicken, turkey	13	12	9	11	10	8	12								
Duck	11	10	8	10	8	6	10	3							
Rattlesnake	14	15	20	22	21	18	21	19	17						
Turtle	15	14	9	11	9	9	11	8	7	22					
Tuna fish	21	21	17	19	18	17	18	17	17	26	18				
Moth	31	30	27	29	25	26	28	28	27	31	28	32			
Neurospora	48	47	46	46	46	46	49	47	46	47	49	48	47		
Candida	51	51	50	51	49	50	51	51	51	51	53	48	47	42	
Yeast	45	45	45	46	45	45	46	46	46	47	49	47	47	41	27

is being widely used. The interesting thing is that if we make a tree based on bone structures, one based on amino-acid sequences, and another based on DNA, they generally are similar. The interpretation of these data is that homologies show evolution from common ancestors. Increasing divergence in characteristics indicates increasing distance from the common ancestor. Homologies are the prime evidence used in developing phylogenetic trees.

With this background, let's look at the interpretive definitions of homology and analogy. The functional definitions used above are not usually used. The more common definitions, which I call interpretive definitions, are interpretations of the data based on evolution theory.

Homology: the correspondence of features in different organisms due to inheritance from a common ancestor.

Analogy: features that are superficially alike but have evolved independently (a type of homoplasy—a non-homologous similarity) (Wiley et al. 1991, p. 9-14).

Mistakes and Imperfect Designs as Evidence of History

The study of evolution is in part the study of how organisms have adapted

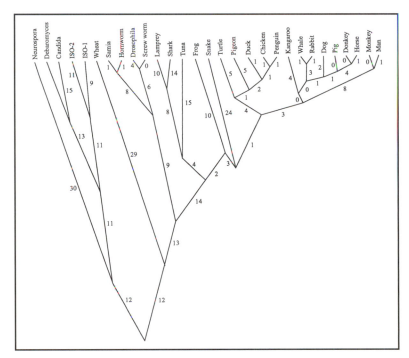

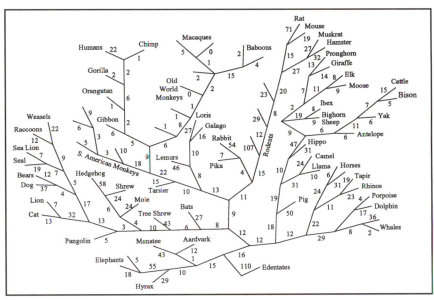

to their environment. But perfect adaptations or "ideal design is a lousy argument for evolution, for it mimics the postulated action of an omnipotent creator" (Gould 1980a, chap. 1, 2). Adaptations that seem illogical or suboptimal are better indications of evolutionary history.

A few years ago, I bought an old house and proceeded to remodel it. In

Figure 9.10
Phylogeny of vertebrates, based on the structure of the cytochrome c molecule (after Mettler et al. 1988).

Figure 9.11
A phylogenetic tree of the eutherian mammals (includes all mammals except marsupials and monotremes), based on study of amino acids. Numbers indicate nucleotide replacements needed to account for the observed amino-acid differences (after Miyamoto & Goodman 1986).

my crawling about in the attic and in the crawl space under the house, I encountered many interesting things. The heavy beams and pillars supporting the floor explained why the wood floor was not squeaky in spite of the house's age, and the water pipes all connected into a logical system. Other features were more intriguing. These included a set of concrete steps under the house and another set buried in the ground outside the house, and a main sewer line that exited the house on the side opposite the sewer connection and then went halfway around the outside of the house to its destination. Sections of sturdy foundation under the house looked like exterior wall foundations, but they didn't support anything except the middle of a bedroom floor (which eased my concern about the weight of our water bed).

It soon became evident that these odd features could not be explained by logic or by the structural needs of a house; they could be explained only by history. The house had been through a series of remodelings and additions by previous owners. The unusual features were historical remnants of those events and no longer relevant to the current structural needs of the house. The extra foundations were under exterior walls before the bedrooms were enlarged with new foundations and new walls. The old steps indicated the positions of exterior doorways at early stages in the home's history. The circuitous sewer line was explained by the existence of an abandoned septic tank at the place where the sewer line came out of the house. I began to feel like an archeologist as I pieced together the history of the house (Fig. 9.12) on the basis of these and other historical remnants while my family thought I was under the house working hard. In the process of adding on to the house, I left a few historical remnants of my own. Thus, if the next owner is of a curious disposition, he will have the material

**Figure 9.12
Sequence of additions to a
house, reconstructed from
the historical remnants of
this series of events.**

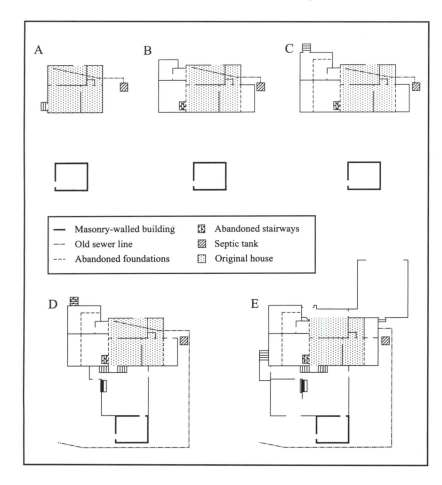

for many happy hours of archeological investigation, but he also will have new difficulties because my work destroyed some of the evidence.

This story is exactly analogous to the study of evolutionary history using suboptimal adaptations or odd structures as evidence for historical, evolutionary events. Vestigial structures do not have a functional explanation; they are remnants of evolutionary history. Since life has a history, the types of adaptations that can develop in any given organism depend on the raw material that history has provided. For example, when bats evolved, they could not develop wings like insects or birds because their immediate ancestors already had the typical mammalian hand structure. So bats were constrained to develop a wing that was a modification of that mammalian hand structure. If an intelligent Creator had designed life, why would a bat's wing not be uniquely and optimally designed for its purpose instead of being a mere modification of a terrestrial mammal's front limb? This is always the way it is: the structure of every organism consists of adaptations of existing characters of the group that it evolved from rather than showing the originality and creativity that we would expect from a Creator (Futuyma 1983, p. 62).

This principle is illustrated nowhere better than in the panda's thumb (Ewer 1973, p. 21-23, 138; Gould 1980a). The giant panda eats only bamboo which it dexterously handles between its thumb and other fingers. The thumb, however, is not an ordinary thumb. It is a sixth "finger" that is really an elongated radial sesamoid bone in its wrist. The muscles present in other mammals have been modified to serve the panda's novel thumb (Fig. 9.13). Other members of the bear family do not have an opposable thumb and, consequently, the panda did not have the raw materials to readily evolve a dexterous thumb like some other mammals have. Instead, it developed, from the already somewhat enlarged sesamoid bone that other bears have, an unusual thumb that adequately meets its needs. The panda also has an enlarged sesamoid bone on the other side of its front foot. The muscle attachments suggest that this bone also may be mobile (Ewer 1973, p. 21-23), though it has not been

Figure 9.13
The structure of the panda's foot, with its unique thumb on the left side (after Ewer 1973 and Gould 1980a).

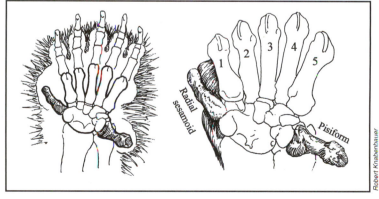

Robert Knabenbauer

studied as much as the radial sesamoid.

Another type of suboptimal feature is the struggle, destruction, and cruelty so evident in nature, instead of the harmony that an intelligent Creator would be expected to produce. Some animals seem poorly adapted, such as the lemmings and locusts which have no adaptation to prevent overpopulation. Their populations periodically experience uncontrolled expansion with devastating results to themselves and their habitat (Futuyma 1983, p. 127).

Biogeography

Among Darwin's most important lines of evidence were the patterns of geographic distribution of plants and animals, and the agreement between biogeographic distribution and presumed evolutionary history. The distribution of plants and (especially) animals matches the pattern that we would expect to see if each group originated at a particular geographic location and spread from there, adapting to the ecological conditions encountered. The historical explanation of such oddities as abandoned stairways and pandas' thumbs also applies to the oddities of animal distribution.

Very few types of animals are widely distributed over the earth in their preferred habitat. Instead, the animal groups found in each geographic region have evolved species to fill the habitats in that region (Fig. 9.14). Moles of the family Talpidae live underground in burrows and eat worms and other small animals. They are common in North America, Europe, and Asia. In Africa, the same niche is occupied by a different family of moles, the golden moles of the family Chryso-chloridae. In Australia, moles look similar to the others but are marsupials unrelated to them. Many other examples could be applied to this principle. In the Galapagos Islands, a group of finches (Darwin's) evolved into an insect-eating species, some seed-eaters, and a woodpecker. In other parts of the world, those same niches are filled by birds in families different from Darwin's finches. Oceanic islands, like the Galapagos, only have animals that would be able to cross great expanses of ocean (Futuyma 1983, p. 50-51). If life was created, why wouldn't the Creator put giraffes on an island or two?

South America has a complex of about 11 families of rodents (sometimes called the hystricomorph or hystricognath rodents) with common skeletal features indicating that they are closely related to each other. But they don't share these features with other rodent families on other continents (Wilson & Reeder

1993, p. 771-805; Corbet & Hill 1991, p. 201-207). Apparently, the South American rodents originated there and radiated to fill the many ecological niches occupied on other continents by other families of rodents. Almost all of the mammals in Australia are marsupials. These have radiated to fill the ecological niches occupied on other continents by non-marsupials. "The only rational—that is, scientific—explanation for such patterns must be that species were not distributed over the face of the earth by the Creator but had originated in different places and had dispersed from there" (Futuyma 1983, p. 51).

A Developing Synthesis for Megaevolution Processes

Within the last two decades, considerable progress has been made in our understanding of the processes that generate large evolutionary changes, including the origin of novel body plans (new phyla). Those processes center around changes in regulatory genes and alteration of growth processes during embryological development (see Alberch 1985; Avers 1989; Gould 1977; McKinney & McNamara 1991; Valentine

1992; Valentine & Campbell 1975; Valentine & Erwin 1987).

The genetic material contains structural genes that produce specific proteins and regulatory genes that control the activation of structural genes. These determine when, in what cells, and for how long each structural gene produces its unique protein. It has been recognized that to produce major evolutionary changes merely by a succession of mutations in struc-

Figure 9.14
Ecological equivalents on four continents. The same ecological niche is often filled on different continents by unrelated animals. The animals on each row are ecological equivalents.

North America	Europe	Africa	Australia
Mole Talpidae	Mole Talpidae	Golden mole Chrysochloridae	Marsupial mole
Kangaroo rat Heteromyidae	Jerboa Dipodidae	Gerbil Muridae	Kultarr Marsupial
Flying squirrel Sciuridae, *Glaucomys*	Flying squirrel Sciuridae, *Pteromys*	Scaly tailed squirrel Anomaluridae	Gliding possum Marsupial
Rabbit Leporidae	Rabbit Leporidae	Rabbit Leporidae	Bandicoot Marsupial
Wolf Canidae	Wolf Canidae	African hunting dog Canidae	Marsupial wolf
Deer Cervidae	Deer Cervidae	Antelope Bovidae	Kangaroo Marsupial

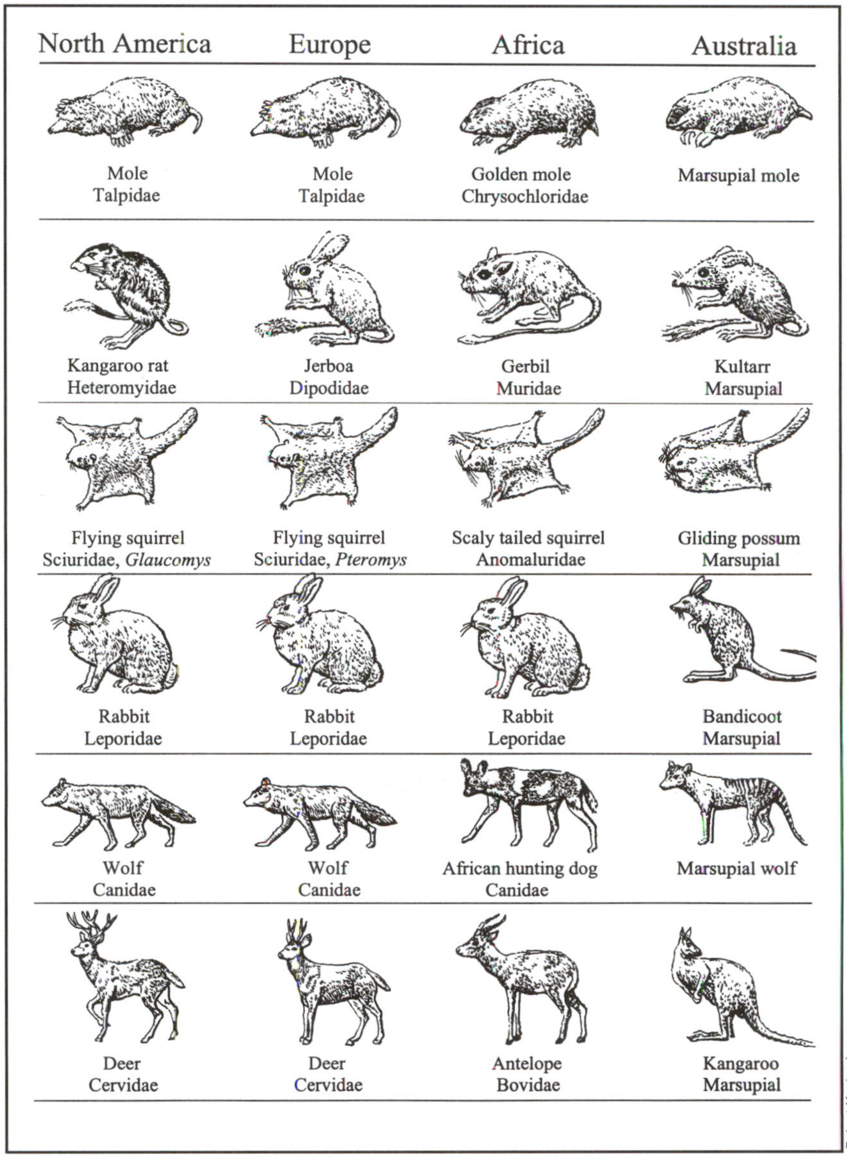

Robert Knabenbauer

tural genes would be a painfully slow and unlikely process. A different process has been suggested that relies more on changes in regulatory genes. The first step in the process would be the evolution of a great variety of structural genes through the action of gene duplication, mutation, and natural selection. When living systems had evolved a sufficiently diverse array of structural genes, novel body plans would result from changes in regulatory gene systems, altering the patterns of activation of structural genes. New body plans would be primarily just new combinations of features that were already present and, consequently, the establishment of these new body plans (new phyla) could proceed rapidly in relation to geologic time (but still over thousands to millions of years).

Regulatory changes can be particularly effective if they alter the pattern of embryological development. A minimal amount of genetic change in the timing of developmental events (heterochrony) might result in significant morphological evolution. Accelerating or retarding the time of reproductive maturity relative to physical growth can cause quite different effects depending on the direction of the change. For example, speeding up maturation relative to physical growth can result in paedomorphosis, which is the retention of juvenile characteristics in the adult. If this results in adults with small body size, it is called progenesis; and if the adult is at least as large as its ancestral form but retains juvenile features into the adult stage, it is neoteny. Some salamanders have gills as larvae but not in the adult form. Other, neotenic species retain the gills as adults (Fig. 9.2). Humans are neotenic in relation to apes (Fig. 9.15). Skull proportions are similar in juvenile humans and apes, but only humans retain the short face and relatively large cranium and brain as adults.

Timing of embryonic events apparently controls the stripe pattern in some zebras. The stripes on the lower back of the zebra *Equus burchelli* are widely and irregularly spaced. This results because the back part of the embryo grows faster than the rest of the embryo after the stripe pattern is estab-

Figure 9.15 Growth of a chimpanzee skull and a human skull. The fetal skulls are very similar, and a baby chimpanzee face can look very similar to an adult human face (after Gould 1977).

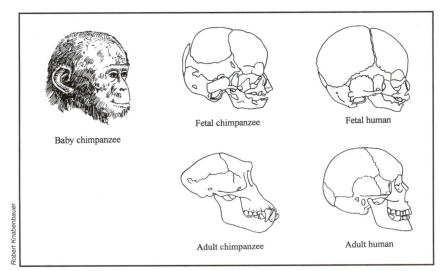

Baby chimpanzee

Fetal chimpanzee

Fetal human

Adult chimpanzee

Adult human

Robert Knabenbauer

lished. The stripe pattern in *Equus grevyi* is not established until that differential growth is completed. Consequently, the stripes in the adult of this species are more equally spaced (Fig. 9.16) (Mettler et al. 1988, p. 16-18).

Allometry, or differential growth, can explain the differences, for example, between several species of fossil titanotheres (Fig. 9.17). The change from one species to another is simply increased overall size and proportionally faster growth of the horn and certain other facial features. These examples illustrate how small genetic changes can produce significant morphological evolution when selection pressures favor these changes.

worms and molluscs, at some point as we go farther down in the fossil record they should become more similar and finally merge into a common ancestor through a series of evolutionary connecting links). The Grand Canyon is an elegant example of the series of layers of sedimentary rocks that cover a significant portion of our continent. These layered rocks formed when sand, mud, or other sediments were washed into a basin by water, primarily, or carried by wind, and were deposited one layer on top of another (Hamblin & Christiansen 1995, p. 121-127). This stack of layers of rock is the geologic column, and its sequence of fossil deposits is referred to as the fossil record.

Figure 9.16
Embryonic development and stripe patterns of the zebras *Equus burchelli* and *Equus grevyi* (after Futuyma 1986).

Figure 9.17
Four species of fossil titanotheres showing allometric growth. The horns and the distance between the eye and the back of the skull grow faster than the overall size of the head as indicated by differences in lengths of the arrows (after Futuyma 1986).

Fossil Record

To really settle a question about the past, we need historical evidence. The fossil record is the most direct historical evidence available. Evolution theory implies certain expectations about the fossil record. For example: Simple creatures should occur first (lower) in the rocks; more highly evolved groups should occur farther up.

Ideally, one expects to find series of links connecting different groups of organisms (e.g., if we compare fossil

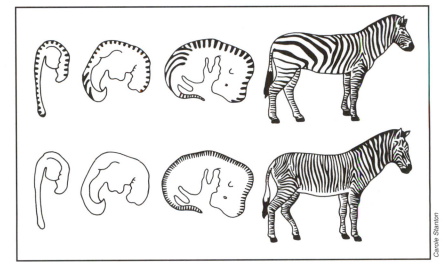

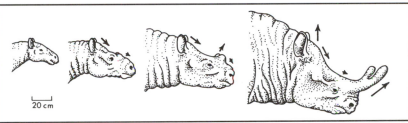

20 cm

There are basic rules for interpreting this rock record. Since the layers are formed by the process described above, those on the bottom must have been deposited first. The result is a time sequence from oldest on the bottom to youngest at the top. This is true no matter how much or how little time we think has elapsed during the formation of the geologic column with its fossils. This fossil record (Benton 1993) has the potential to provide convincing evidence of whether megaevolution has occurred.

The oldest rocks on earth are Precambrian rocks. In the Grand Canyon area, Precambrian rocks are exposed only in the very bottom of the canyon. The only fossils found in most of the Precambrian rocks are single-celled organisms, but near the top of the Precambrian layers are fossils of more complex animals (Clarkson 1993, p. 57-63). The portion of the geologic column above the Precambrian is called the Phanerozoic. This part of the column contains abundant fossils. The Phanerozoic rocks are divided into three portions: the Paleozoic (the lowest portion), the Mesozoic, and the Cenozoic (the highest portion) which contains the most recently deposited rocks. The lowest part of the Paleozoic contains only invertebrate fossils (Clarkson 1993). Higher in the fossil record, different groups

appear in a sequence. The first vertebrates to appear as fossils are the fish, then amphibians, and finally reptiles including the dinosaurs. They have yielded fascinating insights into the biology of this unique group, but scientists still argue over whether the dinosaurs were warm or cold blooded (Barrick & Showers 1995; Fischman 1995). The last groups to appear are the mammals and birds (Carroll 1988; Prothero & Schoch 1994). Within these groups the different orders, families, etc., also appear in an evolutionary sequence. Most of the familiar mammal groups that we see today do not appear as fossils until lower or mid Cenozoic. Human beings appear first at the very top in the Pleistocene (Fig. 9.18).

Clearly, a sequence in the order of appearance of different groups of animals occurs in the fossil record. This pattern also holds true at lower taxonomic levels (genus and species). This part of the evolutionary expectation is fulfilled quite well. The invertebrate animals appear first, and the more structurally complex types appear at successively later periods. There is also an ever-increasing percentage of extinct groups as one goes farther back in the fossil record (Fig 9.18). The groups of animals and plants that live today are common as fossils in the Pleistocene and upper Tertiary, but farther down in the record are more ancient groups that died out and were replaced by modern groups, showing the process of evolution through time.

What about the second expectation for connecting links between groups? Darwin recognized that the fossil record did not show much evidence of connecting links. He thought that as much more fossil collecting was done over time, these links would be found. In the 130 years since Darwin's prediction, many fossils have been collected and

Figure 9.18
Stratigraphic distribution of major groups of animals in the fossil record (figs. by author, based on Benton 1993), showing distribution of extant and extinct forms, and the stratigraphic ranges of dinosaur families.

****Flowering plant data from Harland (1967), since Benton (1993) did not include these data for flowering plants.**

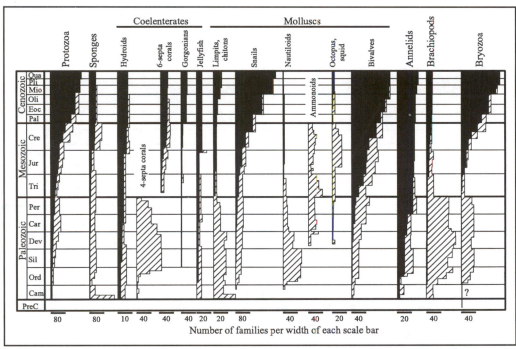

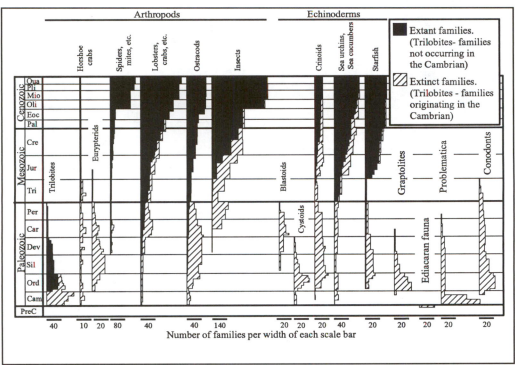

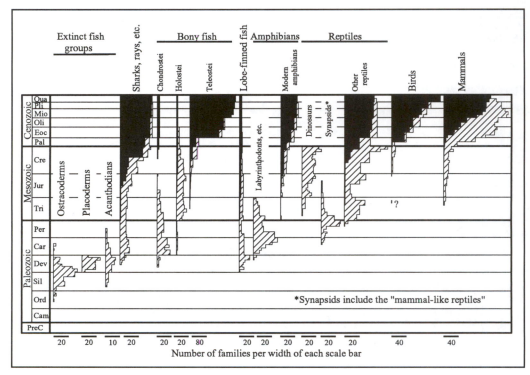

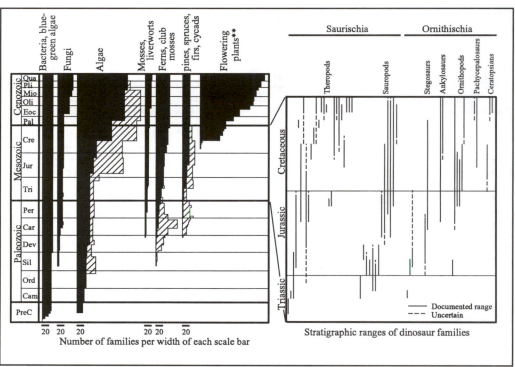

Stratigraphic ranges of dinosaur families

greatly increase our understanding of the fossil record. This improved data base still suggests that, for most animals and plants, the fossil record does not contain connecting links between types. In most cases, some features of the fossil process apparently haven't allowed the series of connecting links to be preserved.

The major groups (phyla) of invertebrates first appear in the lowest Paleozoic and are distributed through the fossil record without links between the groups. The major groups of vertebrates do not appear as early in the record, and the vertebrate classes appear in the record in a logical evolutionary sequence (Prothero & Schoch 1994). The vertebrate record, in many cases, does not contain convincing series of evolutionary links between orders or classes. There are exceptions such as *Archaeopteryx*, which, essentially, had a reptile skeleton, feathers, and could fly (Ostrom 1994) (Fig. 9.19). The early mammals and mammal-like reptiles form a good evolutionary sequence from reptiles to mammals with many different species at various stages of the process (Hopson 1994) (Fig. 9.20). Also, the first amphibians are remarkably similar in many features to their ancestral group, the rhipidistian fishes (Fig. 9.21). Both have the unique labyrinthodont tooth structure, a large notochordal canal through the floor of the braincase (not found in other tetrapods), and other common features. Some early fossil whales are found with small hind limbs (Berta

1994; Gingerich et al. 1994; Novacek 1994; Thewissen et al. 1994; Trefil 1991); the fossil horses form a classic evolutionary sequence (MacFadden 1992) (Fig. 9.22); and hominid fossils (humans and "ape men") form a sequence with increasing brain size (Mettler et al. 1988, p. 305) (Fig. 9.23).

In spite of these notable exceptions, the general picture is that no fossil connecting links occur between most groups of animals. In plants, the lack of connecting links is perhaps even more striking. This is well recognized today by science. What is the reason for this lack of intermediate forms? Increased awareness of

Figure 9.19
The skeletons and the arrangement of wing feathers for *Archaeopteryx* and a modern bird (after Carroll 1988).

Figure 9.20
The reptile *Thrinaxodon*, a part of the line of reptiles that led to the mammals (after Carroll 1988).

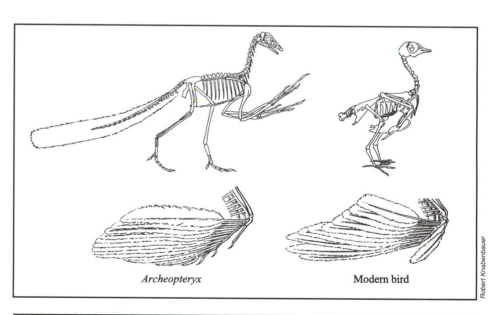

Archeopteryx   Modern bird

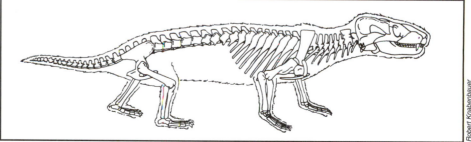

Robert Knabenbauer

Figure 9.21
The Rhipidistian fish
***Eusthenopteron* compared to**
the primitive amphibian
***Ichthyostega* (after Carroll**
1988).

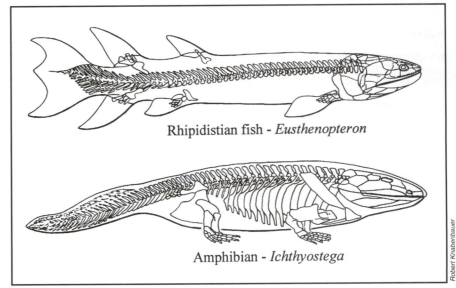

Rhipidistian fish - *Eusthenopteron*

Amphibian - *Ichthyostega*

Figure 9.22
The evolution of horses
(after McFadden 1992).

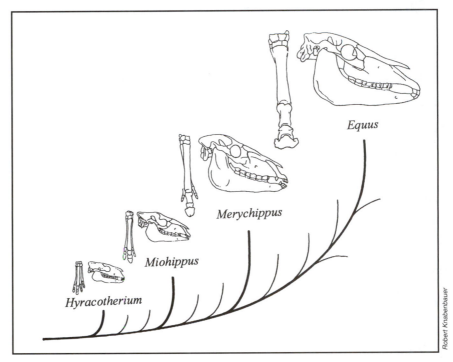

Equus

Merychippus

Miohippus

Hyracotherium

the lack of connecting links has led to lively discussions within evolutionary science in the search for the answer to that question. When the data do not occur as a paradigm expects, it can sometimes stimulate more careful research and thought.

The evolution theory as proposed by Charles Darwin maintained that evolutionary change occurs gradually, at a slow and fairly even pace. The many small changes that occur in the process of microevolution, over very long periods of time, add up and generate the larger changes that produce new species, families, etc. Today, most recognize that Darwin's gradualistic concept of evolution is not adequate to explain the evidence. The theory of punctuated equilibrium

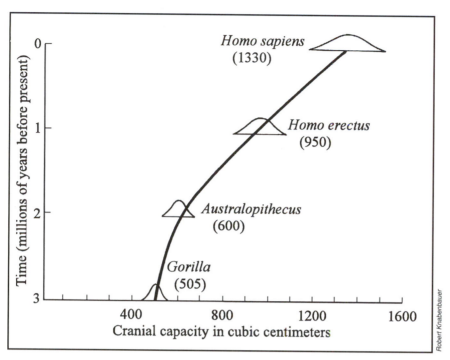

Robert Knabenbauer

(Eldredge & Gould 1972) recognizes that new species are not likely to evolve in large, widespread populations but in small, isolated populations at the edges of the species range. Rapid speciation in these small populations has much less chance of being preserved in the fossil record than the many individuals representing the status quo in the main population. As a result, new species generally appear suddenly in the fossil record, and very little change occurs between speciation events (Kerr 1995b).

The evolution of new groups of land animals occurs in upland environments where fossils are not likely to be preserved. This fact also works against the preservation of connecting links as fossils. The incompleteness of the geological record is another factor that reduces the probability that intermediates will be preserved. Fossilization is a rare event and any given population of animals has a very small chance of being preserved as fossils. If evolution of new body plans (new phyla) and of orders and classes within those phyla occurs quite rapidly, the sequences of intermediates likely would not be preserved, and we are fortunate to have even a few good sequences of intermediate forms.

Convergence of Lines of Evidence

All of the lines of evidence we have considered plus the radiometric dates (to be discussed later) that indicate the great age of the fossils point to the evolution of life through hundreds of millions of years. The fact that a few basic concepts contained in the

theory of evolution can explain so
many lines of evidence is a strong
argument for megaevolution.

The Case for Informed Intervention   10

We have examined the evidence for megaevolution—the evolutionary origin of groups of plants and animals that are different enough to be placed in separate families, orders, classes, and phyla. Is it possible that the same evidence might fit the idea of informed intervention followed by evolution below the megaevolution level? Could it be that there might be limits to the evolution process (Lester & Bohlin 1989)?

The way we deal with this subject is important. Creationists, perhaps beginning with George McCready Price, have developed some bad habits when speaking on the subject of evolution. Some have a tendency to be sarcastic and to talk down to evolutionists. Scientists are portrayed sometimes as being very stupid to believe in evolution. That approach is neither true nor constructive. Evolution is not a theory to laugh at. One who is knowledgeable about the data can make a good case for it. We also can make a good case for an alternate point of view, but we are talking about things that are complex, that happened a long time ago, and, thus, neither paradigm can

expect to have proof. A line of evidence may seem to point strongly in one direction, yet another good explanation may fit as well. In many lines of evidence, parallels appear in what both interventionism and megaevolution would expect to see in the data. This makes the search for definitive answers more arduous than we might think.

Theoretically, we suggest that several groups of people believe in megaevolution. Interventionists sometimes talk as if all non-interventionists want to deliberately push God out of the way. Probably some are in that category, but many do not think that way at all. Some are Christians and, to some degree, are interventionists, but they're not sure what to do with the evidence. Others have been trained to believe in a naturalistic evolution and are not aware of another viable alternative. Others have looked at both theories and have decided that megaevolution is the correct one. Many intelligent, thoughtful people believe that life has come about through the evolution process. Nothing is ever gained by making fun of others who have different beliefs on these issues. We each carefully must evaluate these philosophical questions, and then deal politely and respectfully with those who disagree with us. Can a Christian do less than that? Let us reconsider the lines of evidence that were discussed in chapter 9 and explore how the informed intervention theory can handle the data. The emphasis is not to prove informed intervention. First, we must attempt to develop an internally consistent interventionist theory and then evaluate the strength of the evidence for the theory.

Embryology

Ernst Haeckel proposed that a vertebrate embryo repeats its evolutionary history as it matures (Fig. 9.1). In reality, the early embryonic stages do not look as similar as Haeckel pictured them. The more realistic modern version of the theory suggests that an embryo in its early stages is like the early embryonic stages of its ancestor. As it develops, it gradually becomes less like the ancestral form and acquires the characteristic features of its own species.

Another logical explanation is consistent with that same data. Most vertebrates have an elongated body with a head on one end, usually a tail on the other, and four limbs on the four "corners" of the body. As all of these animals develop from a one-

celled egg to a fully formed juvenile, it is not surprising that many similarities appear between them in the early stages. The embryo develops the basic body plan first; the unique features of the individual organism appear later in ontogeny. Similarly, a home builder builds the foundation first (homes that look very different when complete can have similar foundations) and adds the unique features of the home later. An engineer attempting to design the developmental stages of all these organisms would very possibly find that it is most efficient to follow a basic plan for all and add special features later in the process, as needed for each animal. Other problems also challenge the theory that ontogeny repeats evolutionary history (Wise 1994).

Non-interventionist scientists recognize that the developmental stages of the mammalian heart and kidney are not historical remnants that provide evidence for evolution (Romer 1962). I included the argument above because it is still encountered in some fairly recent college textbooks. Think of yourself as a bioengineer whose task is to devise the chemical distribution system for an embryo as it develops from the one-celled stage to a complete mammal. The mature mammalian heart and kidney are complex structures that require some time to be fabricated as the embryo grows. But the embryo can't wait that long to circulate blood, distribute nutrients to the tissues, and eliminate metabolic wastes. How would you solve this problem? Life's engineer has devised an intricate and complex solution. The heart begins as a simple structure that can develop and begin functioning quickly. As it grows, it gradually transforms into the four-chambered state and is fully functional during the entire process. The kidney follows a slightly different path. A simple kidney develops quickly and handles waste disposal while the more complex metanephric kidney is developing. When the more complex kidney is ready to begin functioning, the simpler initial kidney disappears. Romer (1962) recognized that the successive kidneys in the embryo are needed for functional reasons; they have nothing to do with evolution. It appears that the mammalian heart and kidney would need to develop approximately this way, whether we evolved or were created, and thus the embryology of these organs tells us nothing for or against evolution or intervention.

It appears that salamanders (Fig. 9.2) have the genetic program to produce the equipment for an aquatic life, which they lose when they leave the water, and heterochronic alteration of the timing of this process determines when they lose their aquatic adaptations. A species that won't be living in the water may keep the gills only when in the egg. Why isn't the development of their gills aborted entirely? Perhaps the gills are used for gas exchange while in the egg, or, perhaps, it is more biologically efficient to maintain the option of having gills to allow the possibility of adapting to changing conditions. In summary, gills that persist only while in the egg may be a true vestige of evolutionary changes occurring since the creation because of adaptation to environmental stresses, or perhaps the short-lived gills have a function that, as yet, is not well understood.

The experiments that demonstrated that birds still have the genes to produce "reptile" leg bones give intriguing insight into developmental processes (Fig. 9.3). It seems very unlikely that an unused assemblage of genes for producing reptile bones would remain intact in birds for over 100 million years without serious mutational damage to those unneeded genes. It seems more plausible that birds and reptiles have a common set of "instructions" for making legs and that regulatory genes control the specific application of these for making the structure appropriate for each animal. The experiments by Hampe (1960) and also the induction of teeth in chick embryos by Kollar and Fisher (1980) appear to say this is the case. But why? The only reason for arguing this as evidence against informed intervention is to suggest a Creator would use a more efficient design. A very weak argument, indeed, until we understand genetic code and embryological processes enough to accurately evaluate the efficiency of various approaches to designing organisms. Hampe's and Kollar and Fisher's experiments may be revealing that living systems contain more genetic information than is evident and that regulatory genes are being used to control the operation of a set of basic instructions.

Vestigial Organs

Vestigial structures are the presumed leftovers from our evolutionary past (Fig. 9.4). At the turn of the century, a long list was compiled of vestigial organs in mammals (Wiedershiem 1895). The list was considered convincing evidence for megaevolution. Over 80 items were on the list which included the thyroid, thymus, and pituitary glands; the olfactory lobe of the brain; and the middle ear. Now we know that these structures are vital for life and for our sense of hearing and smell. At the time the list was compiled, no one knew what functions they had. Researchers believed them to be vestiges from an

ancestral form that needed them. As physiologists have studied, the list has shrunk. The logic used in this line of evidence must be analyzed carefully. If we don't know the function for something, it becomes a candidate for a vestigial organ. The weakness in that approach is that the more we know, the greater the chance that we will learn of useful functions for these supposedly vestigial organs.

Several structures still appear in textbooks as vestigial organs. As we review them, keep in mind that an organ qualifies as vestigial only if it can be demonstrated that it has no function (and it is difficult or impossible to prove a negative argument). Or, if the function or the form of an organ is altered from its form in presumed ancestors, it could still be claimed that the modified organ is an evolutionary vestige. However, before accepting this as evidence for evolutionary origin of the altered structure, we need to ask if there are any feasible alternate explanations. It is easy to propose a hypothesis to explain something. It is altogether another matter to demonstrate that it is the correct hypothesis and all alternate hypotheses are wrong.

The human appendix was once routinely removed by physicians, since it seemed useless and often caused trouble. Now it is known to be part of the immune system. We do have a disease problem with the appendix, and when it gets infected, it must be removed. However, one is better off with an appendix.

Are the fused caudal vertebrae useless? Actually, this small structure has a very important function as an attachment point for the muscles that allow us to stand upright (and to provide padding when we sit down). No way can it be considered vestigial. The embryological pathway that makes a tail in other mammals is used in us to produce an important structure. Did this happen through evolution, or was it so engineered by an informed Designer? What evidence would answer that question? Not the evidence from embryology or from these "vestigial organs"—some other type of evidence is needed. The external "tail" that, in rare cases, is present on a human newborn is a small, boneless structure, not equivalent to the tails of other vertebrates (O'Rahilly & Muller 1992, p. 63).

The segmented muscles on the abdomen are important for bending our body and for maintaining the tone of the abdominal wall. Whether this muscle arrangement came from a primitive ancestor is strictly conjecture, not evidence for or against evolution or intervention.

Why do humans have hair on their bodies? Is it vestigial, or did a designing engineer intend it? The answers are a matter of opinion that depend on what assumptions we make, not evidence that should be used to choose a theory. The canine teeth in humans are a little more pointed than other teeth. Some may also prefer to consider this a vestige, but it is far from a compelling argument for or against anything.

Why do men have nipples? That's a valid question, but to call these vestigial is a bit strange considering the logic behind the concept "vestigial." To call them vestigial would be to say that men evolved from women. Male nipples are not relevant to the question of origins.

The hind limbs of a whale are isolated bones buried in the tissue, but with a definite function. They are the attachment point for muscles in the reproductive system. Interventionists can argue that the Designer modified the genetic instructions for hind limbs to make these structures serve their unique function.

In these examples, the vestigial-structures argument is not as convincing as it might appear at first glance. In fact, one can question whether any of them can be called truly vestigial. Even if we think they are, we may be calling them vestigial simply because we don't yet know their function. This line of evidence does not point clearly to either theory and should not be used as support.

154

The nictitating membrane in humans does not function as a third eyelid; it occurs in connection with the tear ducts. Its function is not entirely clear, but to declare it nonfunctional is probably premature.

Why are muscles attached to our ears? Some wish to call them genuine vestiges, or say they give shape to our head or support the ears. More information is needed before deciding.

The third molars can be a problem in humans when not enough room is in the jaw for them. This could be explained readily if humans were once larger than they are now, or had heavier jaws because of differences in diet. They appear to be truly vestigial: vestiges of teeth needed by humans as they were originally designed, but are not needed now.

Many cases of truly vestigial structures have resulted from microevolutionary changes within created groups of organisms. Some salamander populations have lived in complete darkness in caves so long that no selection pressure was needed to eliminate individuals with ineffective eyes; thus mutations have made them blind. Some populations of birds have lost the ability to fly, even though they still have small front limbs. These flightless birds live primarily on islands where there are no predators. Without the need to fly to escape from predators, apparently

there was no disadvantage for some of these birds if mutations reduced their powers of flight. In fact, flightlessness can be an advantage. In recent hurricanes, most flying birds were blown out to sea from some of the Pacific islands (David Cowles, personal communication).

Some beetles have become nonflying, not by losing their wings, but by mutations that fused the wing covers and made the wings nonfunctional. It seems likely that additional mutations might eventually eliminate the useless wings. In fact, the energy saved from not growing these wings would be an advantage to the beetles. Why haven't all beetles lost their wings by this process? If flight is vital to a species (and it evidently is for most beetle species), a mutation that reduces the ability to fly reduces or eliminates the chances for that individual to survive and reproduce.

In summary, many presumed vestiges actually do have functions and are not truly vestigial. Some are questionable and can be given various interpretations; and some are true vestigial structures resulting from evolution (mostly microevolution) since the creation.

Hierarchical Nature of Life, and the Ascending Scale of Complexity
Is the ascending scale of complexity (Fig. 9.5) evidence for megaevolution? It may not be, since another

potential explanation exists for the same data. In any complex assemblage of things showing great diversity with different combinations of features, be they machines or animals, one can arrange them in a sequence from simple to complex. Does this imply an evolutionary sequence? Actually, the ecology of our world is extremely complex. It needs a great diversity of organisms to fill the many ecological niches so the intricate system will work. All the "advanced" features in mammals make them unsuited to fill the niche of a sponge. A creature with the suite of characteristics found in sponges is needed to fill that. One can arrange this great diversity of organisms in a sequence with those having a simpler organization at one end of the list and the most structurally complex organisms at the other. This "ascending scale of complexity" is only a description of nature. We must have a different type of evidence to tell us if the diversity came about by evolution or by informed intervention. The order in which these organisms appear as fossils is a part of the picture that is discussed later in connection with the fossil record.

The hierarchical arrangement of life illustrated in Fig. 9.6 has been used by Futuyma (1983) and others as evidence that life must have evolved. They believe that if life were created,

the characteristics of different organisms would be arranged chaotically or in a continuum, not in the hierarchy of nested groups evident in nature. If we think of that concept as a hypothesis, how could it be tested? Actually, to state how a Creator would do things and then show that nature is or is not designed that way is an empty argument. Such conjecture depends on the unlikely assumption that we can decide what the Creator would be like and how He would function. The nature of life is empirical evidence that if life were created, the Creator used a hierarchical plan with a nested system of basic designs that were modified to meet the needs of each subgroup. There is no evident reason why such a hierarchical system would not be effective. The hierarchical nature of life is consistent with both megaevolution and interventionist theories. It is not evidence for or against either theory.

Homology

How did the limb bones of those four mammals (the human, seal, bat, and dog in Fig. 9.7) develop the way they did? An engineer devising different kinds of machines wouldn't start from scratch for every machine. The data indicate that if an intelligent Creator designed the limb system for vertebrates, He developed a flexible general plan which could be adapted for the lifestyle of each animal. The result is a series of homologies from the work of a common Designer who created all of these animals in an organized fashion.

The same concept applies to analogies. Different kinds of wings (Fig. 9.8) are analogous because the Designer gave different kinds of organisms some of the same abilities. He made insects with a body plan different from mammals and birds, but some representatives of each group were made to fly. Because of their different underlying structural organization, their flight mechanisms are analogous, not homologous.

What do we do with homologies in the details of physiology and biochemistry? Is our ability to arrange cytochrome c molecules in a logical phylogenetic sequence from bacteria to humans good evidence for mega-evolution? There are different degrees of relationship and of similarity between various animals. Apes are structurally more similar to humans than to fish. This descriptive reality of nature makes it possible to draw phylogenetic trees, since those trees are based on degrees of similarity or difference in animal or plant characters. How did organisms get that way? Why are phylogenetic trees based on morphology similar to trees based on biochemistry? Is it because of megaevolution or could another

alternative be considered?

Anatomy is not independent of biochemistry. Creatures similar anatomically are likely to be similar physiologically. Those similar in physiology are, in general, likely to be similar in biochemistry, whether they evolved or were designed. The data show that nature is not organized in a chaotic fashion. In general, close integration exists between various aspects of living systems. However, within any given morphological plan, a certain degree of biochemical flexi-bility is also likely. When major groups of animals are compared, the degree of congruence between morphology and biochemistry exists for primarily functional, rather than evolutionary, reasons. Consequently, it is not surprising when anatomical and biochemical data produce similar phylogenetic trees. Whether these trees should always coincide needs to be determined by inspection of the data as research proceeds.

One assumption that is made in phylogenetic analysis is that the differences in the sequence of amino acids in some proteins indicate evolu-tionary distance between the groups, rather than being primarily the result of differences in functional require-ments of the organisms. Is this a correct assumption? Or, are the cytochrome c molecules (Figs. 9.9 and 9.10), for example, different in various animals for functional reasons? Denton (1985) presents the cytochrome c data in a way that raises some interesting questions. Starting at the upper left corner of Fig. 10.1 and moving across to the right, the number of differences in the amino acid sequence increases, as would be expected in an evolutionary sequence. However, the number of differences between the bacterium *Rhodospirillum rubrum* and all other groups is astonishingly similar.

Why would such a consistent evolutionary distance occur here from all of these other groups? The same phenomenon is seen in the yeasts which are close to being the same distance from all other groups, and the same applies in each group outlined in heavy lines. The data in Fig. 10.1 and 10.2 show that all of the organisms analyzed fall into discrete groups, and each group is essentially constant in its number of amino-acid differences from all other groups above it on the chart. Why, for example, would the evolutionary distance between bacteria and horses be the same as the evolutionary distance between bacteria and insects?

Figure 10.1
The cytochromes percentage of sequence difference matrix (after Denton 1985; data from Dayhoff 1972).

	Horse	Dog	Kangaroo	Penguin	Pekin duck	Pigeon	Snapping turtle	Tuna	Bonita	Carp	Lamprey	Screw-worm fly	Silkworm moth	Tobacco horn-worm moth	Castor	Sunflower	Wheat	Candida krusei	Debaryomyces kloeckeri	Baker's yeast	Rhodospirillum rubrum C2
Horse		6	7	12	10	11	11	18	17	13	15	20	27	26	40	41	41	46	40	42	64
Dog	6		7	10	8	9	9	17	16	11	13	19	23	23	38	39	39	45	38	41	65
Kangaroo	7	7		10	10	11	11	17	17	13	16	22	26	26	38	39	42	46	41	42	66
Penquin	12	10	10		3	4	8	17	17	14	18	22	25	25	38	39	41	45	40	40	64
Pekin duck	10	8	10	3		3	7	16	16	13	17	20	25	25	38	39	41	45	40	41	64
Pigeon	11	9	11	4	3		8	17	17	14	18	21	25	24	38	39	41	45	40	41	64
Turtle	11	9	11	8	7	8		17	16	13	18	22	26	27	38	39	41	47	42	44	64
Tuna	18	17	17	17	16	17	17		2	8	18	22	30	28	42	43	44	43	42	43	65
Bonita	17	16	17	17	16	17	16	2		7	18	23	31	29	41	41	42	42	41	41	64
Carp	13	11	13	14	13	14	13	8	7		12	20	25	24	41	41	42	45	39	42	64
Lamprey	15	13	16	18	17	18	18	18	18	12		26	30	31	45	44	46	50	43	45	66
Screw-worm	20	19	22	22	20	21	22	22	23	20	26		13	11	40	40	40	43	39	44	66
Silkworm	27	23	26	25	25	25	26	30	31	25	30	13		5	40	40	40	43	39	44	65
Horn-worm	26	23	26	25	25	24	27	28	29	24	31	11	5		39	40	38	42	39	42	64
Castor	40	38	38	40	38	38	38	42	41	41	45	40	40	39		10	12	45	43	42	66
Sunflower	41	39	39	41	39	39	39	43	41	41	44	40	40	40	10		13	47	44	43	67
Wheat	41	39	42	41	41	41	41	44	42	42	46	40	40	38	12	13		45	41	42	66
C. krusei	46	45	46	45	45	45	47	43	42	45	50	43	43	42	45	47	45		23	25	72
D. kloekeri	40	38	41	40	40	40	42	42	41	39	43	39	39	39	43	44	41	23		27	67
Baker's yeast	42	41	42	40	41	41	44	43	41	42	45	42	44	42	42	43	42	25	27		69
R. rubrum C2	64	65	66	64	64	64	64	65	64	64	66	64	65	64	66	67	66	72	67	69	

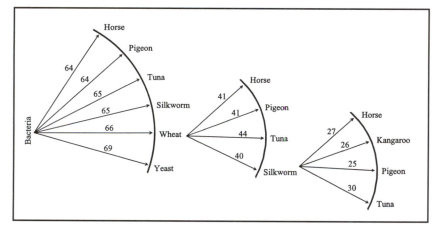

Figure 10.2
The genetic distance between bacterial cytochrome and other organisms is nearly equal; the same relationship is also true for wheat and for silkworm, with organisms above them on the phylogenetic scale (after Denton 1985).

One answer might be the existence of a molecular clock, a constant rate of mutation in the cytochrome c molecule that has maintained the same amount of difference between bacteria and all modern organisms, irrespective of how long ago they diverged on their phylogenetic tree. One problem with that explanation is that, since the number of generations per unit time is vastly different for different organisms, the rate of change of a given molecule should not be the same in these different groups (Denton 1985). The mutation rate per generation in higher organisms is about the same for many genes. Since the length of a generation is measured in minutes in microorganisms, in weeks for some insects, and a year or much more for higher animals and plants, what clock mechanism would generate the mathematically precise relationships in Fig. 10.1? Clock hypotheses based on genetic drift or on natural selection both face great difficulties. It is not

clear that a viable clock mechanism could overcome these difficulties (Denton 1985, p. 294-306). Several reviews of Denton's book have been published (Eldredge 1986; Landau 1990; Spieth 1987; Woodward 1988), but none have many specific criticisms. Unpublished criticisms of Denton's molecular arguments point out that the mutation rate is correlated with time, not generations; thus the data in Fig. 10.1 are exactly what megaevolution theory would predict.

An alternate, interventionist hypothesis is that the cytochrome c molecules in various groups of organisms are different (and always have been different) for functional reasons. Not enough mutations have occurred in these molecules to blur the distinct groupings evident in Fig. 10.1. Even if Denton's critics are right, this interventionist interpretation is still a valid alternative explanation of the data. If we do not base our conclusions on the *a priori* assumption of megaevolution, all the data really tell us is that the organisms fall into nested groups without any indication of intermediates or overlapping of groups, and without indicating ancestor/descendant relationships. The evidence can be explained by a separate creation for each group of organisms represented in the cytochrome c data.

A close correspondence doesn't always appear between phylogenetic trees from morphological and biochemical data. Cytochrome c is the textbook example, and even it has viable alternate explanations, as described above. Some phylogenetic trees based on biochemical data (e.g., Fig. 9.11) match fairly well with morphological data, but in other cases biochemical data yield phylogenetic trees that don't correspond so well with morphology or with trees based on different biochemical data.

Christian Schwabe (1986) discussed several incongruencies in molecular data, not in a discussion of evolution vs. creation, but in an evaluation of various lines of evidence within the naturalistic evolution theory. He stated: "It seems disconcerting that many exceptions exist to the orderly progression of species as determined by molecular homologies; so many in fact that I think the exception, the quirks, may carry the more important message." He compared several lines of evidence regarding the evolutionary divergence of cartilaginous fish (sharks, skates, and rays) from mammals. Each branching point on his diagrams (Fig. 10.3) shows the amount of time in

millions of years since the ancestors of the cartilaginous fish diverged from the ancestors of the mammals, according to one particular line of evidence. The fossil data say that the cartilaginous fish originated 400 million years ago, and the mammals originated about 100 million years ago. Comparing the relaxin A proteins from these two groups indicates that the mammals and fish originated at the same time, about 100 million years ago. Another protein, relaxin B, indicates that they originated at the same time and that it was over 400 million years ago. These three lines of data point to very different conclusions and don't provide a clear picture for developing a phylogenetic tree. One explanation might be that the two relaxins have mutated at different speeds. Is that a testable hypothesis or an *ad hoc* explanation to make the data fit? Interventionism is not the only theory that contains both nontestable and testable elements. It is important not

Figure 10.3
Time of evolutionary divergence of mammals and cartilaginous fishes, based on paleontological data, relaxin A and relaxin B (after Schwabe 1986).

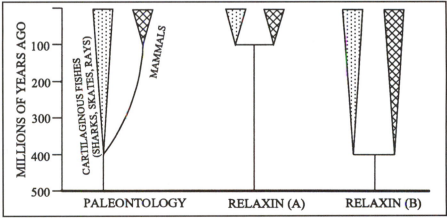

to confuse the testable and nontestable ideas and to be honest about the difference between them.

Relaxin is a molecule that widens the birth canal in organisms that bear live young. A table of percentage homologies of relaxin molecules in various animals (Table 10.1) reveals that shark relaxin, for example, is no more different from pig relaxin than pig relaxin is from human relaxin— even though it would appear that mammals and sharks should have evolved relaxin independently. Shark relaxin widens the birth canal of mice and guinea pigs, acting "specifically on structures that developed only millions of years later in different species" (Schwabe 1986). In the same paper, Schwabe lists several proteins with specific functions in higher vertebrates that also seem to occur in some invertebrates or even in plants. The head activator enzyme occurs in hydra, rat intestines, and in the human hypothalamus, and "has an identical sequence regardless of source. In the hydra, it causes regeneration of a

severed head while its function in humans is unknown but presumably different."

Schwabe didn't conclude that we should turn to interventionism for the answer to these problems. He frankly was facing some difficulties and evaluating the options within naturalistic explanations. Some scientists have summarized this type of data by saying that convergence is everywhere (Patterson 1981, unpublished). The data don't point to a consistent conclusion. There must be features which are really convergent or analogous rather than homologous, and thus the data don't always give a clear picture of phylogeny.

Schwabe (1985, 1986) was convinced that the evidence favors polyphyletic origin of life forms (each group evolved independently; the groups did not come from common ancestors). However, he makes the assumption of naturalism and, consequently, is led to the conclusion that since so many lines of evolutionarily independent organisms exist, life must evolve very easily and must have evolved many times. He has no actual evidence for that. A person who believes that the evidence indicates polyphyletic origins of animal groups and also accepts the naturalistic assumption must reach the conclusion that Schwabe reached. Interventionism's answer for this

Table 10.1
Percentage of Homology Between Relaxins From Various Species

	Human 1	Human 2	Pig	Rat	Sand . . shark	Spiny . . shark	Skate
Human 1	—	77	46	46	46	45	34
Human 2	77	—	46	46	48	50	35
Pig	46	46	—	54	50	52	31
Rat	46	46	54	—	37	41	25
Sandtiger shark	46	48	50	37	—	75	42
Spiny dogfish shark	45	50	52	41	75	—	48
Skate	34	35	31	25	42	48	—

evidence is that the different animal groups were designed independently; megaevolution did not occur.

Gorr and Kleinschmidt (1993) point out that most land vertebrates have adult and juvenile versions of hemoglobin; fish, on the other hand, have only one type. Gorr and Kleinschmidt propose that vertebrate juvenile hemoglobin descended from fish hemoglobin, and vertebrate adult hemoglobin evolved later from a duplication of the juvenile hemoglobin gene. Based on this proposal, they decided that the correct evolutionary relationship should be based on the similarity between fish hemoglobin and frog juvenile hemoglobin, not adult frog hemoglobin. An alternate, interventionist hypothesis could be that land vertebrates have adult hemoglobin functionally suited to an air-breathing existence, while fish and juvenile land vertebrates have similar hemoglobins because fish and unborn land vertebrates both live in a basically aquatic environment.

It is important to remember that even an interventionist recognizes that microevolution and a certain amount of macroevolution does occur. Consequently, when we consider phylogenetic trees at the level of at least species or genera, part or most of the observed differences that appear in these trees are due to

genuine evolutionary change. Anyone, interventionist or non-interventionist, can use these lines of evidence to determine patterns of evolution of subspecies and species and some higher categories.

The interventionist theory states that as we go up the taxonomic scale from species to genera to families and orders, at some point homology does not result from evolution—it is a part of the original design. An interventionist goal is to find definite evidence of where that point is and what the upper boundary of evolutionary change is. Keep in mind that finding that point will not be simple because both the evolution process and intelligent design might produce a similar pattern.

Perhaps in some cases, we see evidence of the dividing line. When DNA hybridization is used to make phylogenetic evaluations, it is most effective at indicating groupings of species. At higher taxonomic levels, the data is much harder to interpret (Gibson 1987). Perhaps this is a reflection of what the interventionist predicts, that evolution was going only at the lower taxonomic levels (genus, species, etc.) and that above this we see only a reflection of the original design rather than evolution.

From the interventionist theory, we can derive interpretive definitions of homology and analogy. These definitions are interpretations of the data. They are based on the assumption that the informed intervention theory is correct, just as the former set of definitions are interpretations of the data based on the assumption that the evolution theory is correct.

Homology: Correspondence of features in different organisms at higher taxonomic levels is due to the same basic structural plan in both organisms. In lower taxonomic categories, homologies result from correspondence of features in organisms due to evolution—inheritance from a common ancestor.

Analogy: Correspondence of features in organisms that are not closely related because these features were designed for similar functions. In lower taxonomic categories, analogies are features that are superficially alike but which have evolved independently.

Note that at lower taxonomic levels, both interventionists and naturalistic evolutionists are using the same definitions of homology and analogy; at higher levels, they use different definitions. It is true that the scientific process would be simpler if we stayed with only one set of definitions, either the design or the evolution definitions, at all taxonomic levels. This discussion makes the assumption, however, that science should be a search for true answers,

whether or not they are simple. Another way to look at it is that the interventionist is asking a question that many other scientists are not asking: Is there a limit to the extent of evolutionary change that has occurred?

The Process of Phylogenetic Analysis

Now let's look more closely at the process that is used in developing phylogenetic trees. We can collect evidence on the characteristics of organisms and construct phylogenetic trees (e.g., Fig. 9.11). Does that tell us that those trees are necessarily real and that megaevolution does occur?

The process used in constructing phylogenetic trees begins with the collection of data on the characteristics of the groups being studied. If we study the relationships between several orders of mammals, we compare many characters of these orders, perhaps beginning with tooth and skeletal anatomy to determine which orders have canine teeth and which have a complete postorbital bar behind their eyes. Many additional characters would be added. Then we tell the computer to compare these groups, to determine the similarities (homologies) between them, and to generate phylogenetic trees. Determining which characteristics are primitive (ancestral) and which are derived is called polarization. This is usually accomplished by including an outgroup in the analysis for comparison. The outgroup is a group that is closely related to but is outside of the groups that are being studied. For example, a study of the orders of mammals might use reptiles as an outgroup. The mammalian order with the fewest differences from the outgroup is considered the most primitive order, closest to the common ancestor of the mammals. (For further information on different approaches to phylogenetic analysis, see Hillis & Moritz 1990; Mettler et al. 1988, p. 31-47; Wiley et al. 1991.)

From a given data set, many different trees can be produced. For example, compare the trees in Fig. 10.4. The branch pattern in A indicates that organisms 1 and 2 are very similar and that they branched off from their common ancestor not long ago. Organisms 3 and 4 also are similar; so both groups (1 & 2, and 3 & 4) had a common ancestor much farther back in time. Tree B indicates that organisms 1 and 2 are similar, and that 3 and 4 are more distantly related. Tree C says that 1, 2, and 3 are closely related, but they share an ancestor only distantly with 4. Which tree is the best hypothesis of relationships for these animals? In making such decisions, we use the principle of parsimony, which means that we accept the trees that provide the

simplest explanation and require the least number of evolutionary steps. A parsimonious tree doesn't require evolution to reinvent structures independently many times.

After several phylogenetic trees have been produced from our data, two levels of questions arise which we might want the computer to address:

1. If these groups of organisms have evolved from a common ancestor, which of these trees is the most likely pathway for that evolution?

2. Are any of these trees correct? Or, is it more likely that these animal or plant groups did not have a common ancestor?

Question 1 assumes the organisms evolved. We ask only which is the most likely tree. Question 2 asks whether independent origins (which implies informed intervention), plus limited evolution within the polyphyletic groups better fits the evidence, or whether unlimited megaevolution does. It is important to understand that science asks only question 1. Science does not ask the second, broader question. Question 1 is like a multiple-choice quiz that asks "Which of these options (which

Figure 10.4
A-C Three alternative phylogenetic trees for four animal taxa.

D An unrooted tree (indicates relationships, but does not indicate which are ancestral and which are descendent groups).

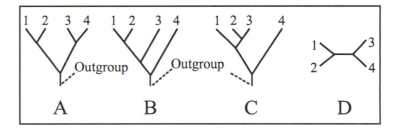

A   B   C   D

phylogenetic tree) is most likely correct?" The answer "none of the above" is not acceptable.

The process gives us a tree no matter what the reality is in the history of life. The computer analyzing the characters and generating trees has been given no instructions that allow it to ask the second question. When we first put the data into the computer, it does not produce a tree; it has no way to determine which one of the groups is the ancestor or closer to the ancestor. It can only produce an unrooted tree, showing which groups are more similar (D in Fig. 10.4). An outgroup must be added before it can produce a tree. However, we have no reason to introduce an outgroup unless we first assume evolution of the two groups from a common ancestor. A study of mammals, using reptiles as the outgroup, is based on the assumption that they both evolved from a common ancestor. If we make that assumption, then the computer looks for the order of mammals with the most characters in common with the outgroup. Now the computer makes that mammalian group the root of the tree that it can construct. It cannot even construct a tree unless the researcher first makes the assumption of megaevolution by adding an outgroup. This is the basic reason this process is not even capable of asking

the second question. Phylogenetic trees don't pop out of the data; they come from massaging the data with evolutionary theory.

Does this tell us that this process is a waste of time? No, not at all. Even the interventionist uses it to study microevolution and speciation and for examining the very real evolutionary changes that have occurred within major groups of organisms. Also, if a person chooses to make the assumption of megaevolution, it is logically consistent to use this method to determine the most likely phylogenetic tree for the animals he or she is studying, even for higher taxonomic categories. The important thing to remember is that this process is capable of answering only question 1; it cannot even address question 2.

If we carry our logic one step further, we find that the ability to use the process described above to produce phylogenetic trees is not evidence in favor of either megaevolution or microevolution. A process that is logically meaningful only if we assume that evolution is true cannot be used to test whether evolution is true. That would be circular reasoning. Also, the fact that this process cannot prove evolution is not evidence for intervention. It simply reflects the limits in the ability of humanity to analyze the ancient past.

Some other type of evidence is needed to answer the bigger questions of where we and our fellow organisms on earth came from. Colin Patterson, a prominent vertebrate paleontologist and evolutionist in England, made some interesting statements in a public lecture. No obvious evidence suggests that he favors interventionism, but he stated that he has "experienced a shift from evolution as knowledge to evolution as faith" (Patterson 1981, unpublished). Perhaps this honest attitude is appropriate for all as we study what happened in the past, whether we favor intervention or megaevolution.

Now let's consider another side of the limitations in the process of generating phylogenies. Phylogenetic trees are based on homologies, but homology by itself cannot demonstrate evolution or intervention. Homology has two potential explanations: evolution from a common ancestor and design by a common designer. Which is correct? If homologies were the only evidence we had, we would have to say we don't know which is correct.

If we collect data from fossils and living animals and make the assumption of megaevolution, it is possible to draw phylogenetic trees. For any complex assemblage of organisms (or even machines), it is possible to draw a phylogenetic tree

based on homologies. Are the trees true? Looking at a very general tree of the animals (Fig. 10.5A), we note that those sharing more homologies in common are closer together on the tree. Does that show that they evolved? If we use the same process to analyze a group of wheeled vehicles, we can draw a tree based on homologous mechanical principles (Fig. 10.5B). Nobody would say that the vehicles evolved. Homologous features can arise by another route— intelligent design. Such analogies never should be pushed too far. This one illustrates only one point: homology, in itself, cannot demonstrate evolution. If we ask only question 1: "Which is the most likely phylogenetic tree?", it is essential to rely on homologies to answer that question. That is perfectly legitimate.

Figures 10.5 A, B Phylogenetic trees for animals and wheeled vehicles.

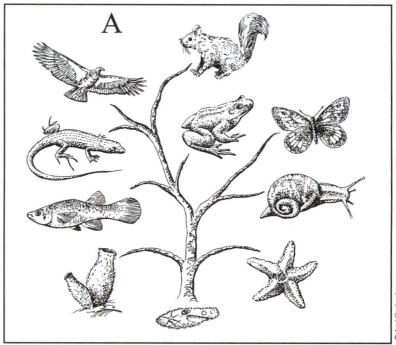

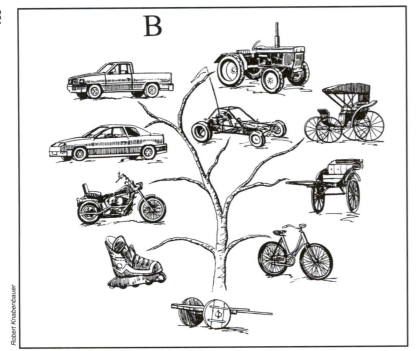

But, if we are asking question 2: "Did they evolve or did they not?", then homologies cannot answer the question. They don't have the potential ever to do so.

Mistakes and Imperfect Designs as Evidence of History

An animal perfectly adapted to its environment can be explained as the result of natural selection or as perfect design by the Creator. Imperfections, suboptimal adaptations, or outright mistakes seem to point more strongly to an evolutionary explanation. Therefore, one must have objective criteria for determining if the adaptation is indeed suboptimal. Is the panda's thumb suboptimal? Is there evidence that the panda has difficulty accomplishing the tasks that require use of its thumb? If not, what objective reason do we have for calling it suboptimal? How could we determine if a Creator would use such a whimsical design (Wise 1994)? The use of the panda's thumb (Fig. 9.13) as a scientific argument against interventionism is valid only if we have objective data to support the hypothesis that a Creator would not use such a design; otherwise, it is only a philosophical argument. The data show us that if there is a Creator, He used a hierarchical design for life. How can we be sure that He would not use the genetic patterns of other bears to fashion a thumb for the panda, rather than interjecting a feature from some other animal into the bear's already cohesive genetic system? Or could it be that the DNA was created with sufficient information to allow such a structure to originate after bears were created?

Futuyma (1983, p. 199) concludes that it is strange that an omniscient creator would make a bat's wing by just stretching out four fingers of the same type of hand that other mammals have. This argument has meaning only if he is implying that the bat's wing is suboptimal. That argument is even more unconvincing for bats than for pandas. Bats are able to achieve incredible feats of flying acrobatics with their hand-like wings. Slow-motion movies of a bat using its wing, as we would use a hand, to catch moths and transfer them to its mouth while in flight without interfering with the effectiveness of flight, makes it difficult to believe the argument that the design of a bat's wing is suboptimal. It's even more unbelievable because evidence documents bats locating, pursuing, catching, and eating two consecutive insects on the wing within one second!

The opinion that a hierarchical system of design that uses a basic plan for each group and modifying it for the needs of each member of the group is not creative or original is simply a subjective, personal opinion. One could just as logically argue that making a bat with such incredibly effective flying skills and a dog's foot from the same basic structural plan is very creative indeed. The panda's thumb and the bat's wing are not objective evidence for or against evolution or intervention.

Other types of suboptimal features are fundamentally different in nature than the panda's thumb. Consider, for example, the lemmings' and locusts' inability to control their population size (Futuyma 1983, p. 127). It is hard to justify this feature as a good design. The struggle, cruelty, and destruction in nature bothers most of us, no matter what our philosophical views. The version of interventionism that takes the Bible seriously has an internally consistent answer for this problem. The Designer gave enough information to keep us from being confused by this evidence. Life was created in a perfect state, but the rebellion of the human race introduced degenerative forces into other parts of nature as well. The earth is no longer an ideal habitation. Organisms have adapted through natural selection to changed conditions, and many of these adaptations are far less than ideal. The concept of creation and subsequent rebellion can't be studied by scientific methods; but the processes of change that have occurred after those events can be analyzed with the scientific process.

Biogeography

Since animals and plants first were created, there has been a complex series of changes in their distribution on the earth. During this time evolutionary change has been occurring within the original independent groups. The species of finches and tortoises on the Galapagos Islands, and the honeycreepers and hundreds of species of fruit flies in Hawaii have evolved as they colonized one island after another. No giraffes are found on islands because the animals and plants got there by natural means. God did not necessarily put the species where they are now. A large part of the biogeographic data has the same explanation in intervention theory as in megaevolution theory.

Some of the large scale biogeographic patterns are in a different category, however. Why are almost all Australian mammals marsupials with ecological equivalents to wolves, mice, rabbits, moles, etc.? Why are 11 closely related families of rodents found only in South America (Corbet & Hill 1991; Wilson & Reeder 1993)? Why do continents (i.e., South America and Australia) that are the farthest and most inaccessible from the landing place of the biblical ark have the largest number of unique groups of mammals and birds? These are challenging puzzles for the interventionist theory. Whether or not there is an effective solution depends on certain assumptions about the history of life since the intervention. Suggested solutions are best introduced after further discussion of the geological evidence, so we return to this question in chapter 16.

Evolution of New Structures and Body Plans—Is It Possible?

Can natural processes produce significant evolutionary advance? If one takes the naturalistic point of view, the answer is "obviously they can." Mammals don't occur in the fossil record until the Mesozoic rocks, so they must have evolved. This is one approach to the answer. But do we have any genetic evidence from the study of animals and plants today to indicate that major biological innovation can occur through evolution? In a laboratory, we can initiate mutations and observe some microevolutionary changes. Microevolutionary processes also can be observed or strongly inferred in nature (e.g., Endler 1986). Do we have real evidence that large-scale changes (megaevolution) also occur, or do we just assume that they occur if given enough time?

Here each line of evidence must be evaluated alone. No matter how convinced one may be by the sequence of types of fossils in the rocks, it is circular reasoning to argue that because of the fossil sequence, megaevolution must have happened and must be genetically possible. The possibility remains that the fossil sequence might have some other explanation. The evidence for the biological possibility of megaevolution needs to stand alone and not depend on the fossils to shore it up. Further, the statement that an alternate explanation for the fossil record may be possible does not, in itself, give evidence against megaevolution or for intervention. It is simply a statement urging us to keep an open mind and a willingness to subject each argument to rigorous scrutiny.

Could megaevolution produce

different body plans and complex structures? The eyes of vertebrates are fantastically complex. Octopuses have eyes that rival the vertebrate eye for complexity. Vertebrates and octopuses obviously did not get their eyes from a common ancestor with complex eyes (Gould 1994). Could the processes of genetic change have brought about the evolution of either or both of these eyes from an ancestor that did not have complex eyes?

One can find animals with eyes of many different levels of complexity and line them up in a sequence of increasing complexity (Dawkins 1986). The question remains: Do we actually have evidence that they could and did arise by evolution, or is that an untested assumption? Arthropods have a skeleton on the outside with joints that bend. Humans have an internal skeleton. Does current knowledge of genetics give us any reason to believe that these different body plans could arise by the process of evolution?

Agriculturalists have made much progress in their attempts to improve food crops. Careful, selective breeding has increased production. Wheat with small heads has given rise to domestic wheat with much larger heads. The same is true of corn and other crops. Small, sweet wild strawberries have become large domestic berries. Evidence also

shows that intensive selection for a trait cannot continue indefinitely. The amount of change levels off and reaches a plateau indicating the limit of the organism's genetic potential (Mettler et al. 1988, p. 184-186). So the genetic process that we know doesn't produce unlimited change. Does this have a wider application in evolution theory? Are there limits to natural evolutionary change?

Perhaps mutations have occurred in these plants through the ages and, by intensive selective breeding, we have "used up" the genetic variability of the species. We may have to wait millions of years before more beneficial mutations can occur. Mutations accumulate as a new variation in the population, and only then can we select again for more increases in production (Fig. 10.6). Will the occasional beneficial mutations actually build up the genetic potential for increased productivity, or is this a false hope? Will significant numbers of potentially beneficial mutations accumulate, or in the long run is mutation actually a destructive process that must by held in check by

Figure 10.6
Increase in plant production that levels off as genetic limits are reached. Dotted line is hypothesized increase that would be possible after an additional time period for more accumulation of mutations.

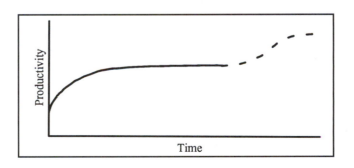

natural selection? The evidence for evolutionary innovation consists mainly of such data as the development of resistance to insecticides, adaptation of bacteria to new culture media, or new enzymes produced by laboratory organisms.

An article, "How the Slot Machine Led Biologists Astray," was written by a biochemist (not an interventionist) who examined the evidence that new enzymes have been produced in organisms by mutation and selection in the laboratory (Opadia-Kadima 1987). He examined the literature and recorded the total number of new enzymes that had been reported in that literature at that time—two. These two enzymes had been reported by two different laboratories. In actuality, they were the same enzyme. What is the chance that they would appear in different labs independently? Even more interesting, they had appeared independently in 30 different strains of bacteria. That seems unlikely. In fact, this presumed new enzyme appeared whenever certain combinations of nutrients were in the culture medium. This indicates that it wasn't a new enzyme. The genetic potential to produce this enzyme was already there and was activated when the conditions were right. If this is all one can find in the literature, where is the evidence that mutation and selection

can produce new enzymes? Are other examples of new features arising in organisms also actually explainable by a similar process—activation of potential that was part of the organism's original gene pool?

The fundamental hypothesis of megaevolution is that natural selection is a creative process, generating new genes, new structures, and, ultimately, new body plans. Modern evolutionary theory incorporates many new concepts into its understanding of the process. Mutations in regulatory genes and altering developmental processes are expected to have much greater effects than point mutations in structural genes. Processes like heterochrony, neoteny, and allometric growth seem to be accurate descriptions of differences in developmental patterns in at least some animals (see chapter 9). Interventionist theory proposes that these patterns were built into the organization of the genetic system by informed intervention and subsequent variation occurs within these patterns. In interventionist theory, one doesn't have to reject the possibility that such processes may have been involved in producing, for example, neotenic salamanders, the zebra's stripe patterns, and even titanotheres and horses (Fig. 9.2, 9.16, 9.17, 9.22). All of these probably could occur even without the production of any new genes. They only used variation and rearrangement of the genetic material. The presumed neotenic nature of the human skull (Fig. 9.15) can be explained as a designed difference in the regulatory genes of humans and apes, maintaining fairly constant proportions of the skull in humans during development but growing a more projecting muzzle and other skull differences in adult chimps.

When it comes to generating new genes, new complexes of structural and regulatory genes, and new body plans, heterochrony and other genetic mechanisms don't change the fact that in naturalistic theories all new genetic information can enter the genome only through mutations. One usually can answer that natural selection is not a chance process; it selects beneficial features and rejects detrimental ones. This is true, but selection can act only on the raw material that mutation provides for it, and mutation is a random process in the sense that it does not know the needs of the organism.

Recombination doesn't help to answer the question in the long run either. It is true that mutations generate new variation by altering existing genes or introducing new alleles. But that doesn't demonstrate that the same process can produce structural genes that did not exist before or alter them systematically to the point where they

acquire a new function. Such a process would have to produce additional genes to recognize and regulate the functioning of the new structural genes and repeat the process for all the new genes needed to code for some new structure or body plan that did not exist before. This is the major challenge faced by naturalistic megaevolution theory. This problem is magnified by the need for evolution to invent all of the essential, interdependent parts of some biological structures (Behe 1996).

An alternate hypothesis is that mutation, as a process generating random changes in the DNA, only produces increasing chaos if not held in check by selection. It is incapable of any truly creative role. This hypothesis is explored further in chapter 12. Hypotheses such as these should be testable as science advances in its understanding of the molecular processes behind the biological changes observed in the laboratory. An additional research emphasis suggested by interventionism is the evaluation of biochemical and other systematic evidence that could indicate the probable boundaries of the original, independently created groups.

Fossil Record

Much of the evidence examined here can be interpreted in different ways and still be logically consistent; it can fit either theory. We need a historical record to tell us what happened. Only two types of sources even claim to be such a historical record. The first consists of written accounts that claim to give a record of the history of life. But if we want to evaluate what science can tell us about history, we need to look at the other source—the fossil record. This record is the line of scientific evidence that, theoretically, could settle the question between the two theories. The interventionist theory implies the following expectations from the fossil record: First, complex creatures could occur as low in the rocks as simple creatures. There wouldn't necessarily be a sequence of ascending complexity. If a group of organisms does not occur in the lowest rocks, it would be for some reason other than that the group had not yet evolved. Second, a series of evolutionary connecting links are not expected in the fossil record.

Precambrian fossils are not as abundant as fossils in younger rocks, but they do form a sequence. The earliest fossils are single-celled prokaryotes, and then single-celled eukaryotes appear. Fossils of complex animals are concentrated near the top of the Precambrian (the Ediacaran fauna) (Clarkson 1993, p. 55-63). They are multi-celled animals, but they are not considered ancestral to the Cambrian animals (Gould 1989a;

Seilacher 1984). They are a unique, extinct assemblage of animals with no clear ties to other groups. One recent paper even suggested that they may be lichens (Retallack 1994).

The fossil record (Fig. 9.18) from the Cambrian through the Cenozoic is called the Phanerozoic—the age of abundant life—for good reason. At the beginning of the Cambrian, so many groups of animals suddenly appear as fossils that a distinct break comes to view in the record. This striking diversity of organisms (Gould 1995), includes a number of groups of animals that have since gone extinct (Benton 1993). Even the first vertebrate animals may occur in the Cambrian (Repetski 1978). Almost all of the phyla of invertebrate animals which have a fossil record occur early in the Cambrian, including the familiar sea creatures such as sponges, molluscs, trilobites, and starfish. This sudden appearance of so many modern phylum and additional extinct phyla in the early Cambrian without obvious ancestors is referred to as the Cambrian explosion. This striking feature of the fossil record is a challenge to explain without informed intervention (Wise 1994). Interventionist theory proposes that the Cambrian explosion is not a record of the first appearance of life, but the first burials during a catastrophe.

Does the evidence indicate these earliest fossils were more primitive in the sense of being more crudely constructed or more simple? No. For example, trilobites are unique animals found only in the Paleozoic, but they have compound eyes, complex legs, and other features showing they are like arthropods of today (Clarkson 1993, p.342-362). The first arthropods are not underdeveloped or crudely put together. Other groups show that the basic features of the phyla appear at the beginning of the record. Megaevolution theory recognizes that the first fossils in these phyla already had the basic body plan that the same phyla have today. A mollusc is a mollusc all the way through the fossil record. The term "primitive" in evolution theory does not mean crude—it just refers to animals or structures that appear early in the record.

Phylogenetic trees in many texts and popular books show a complete tree all the way back to the beginning of life. Trees that show which parts are supported by fossil evidence and which parts are hypothetical are more interesting. Such trees show that the evolutionary connections between virtually all phyla and almost all classes are only theoretical. Non-interventionist scientists are aware of this. Charles Darwin identified this as the greatest weakness in his theory. He believed the intermediates would

be found. However, most of the thousands of fossils that are found fall within the existing groups. As more fossils are found it becomes more clear that the gaps between major groups of organisms are real, and sequences of intermediates are not likely to be found. This evidence has caused evolutionary theorists to look for new ways to explain the evolution of major groups consistent with the reality of the lack of fossil intermediates.

The plant fossil record is also very striking for its lack of intermediates. This evidence fits the expectations of the informed intervention paradigm. The groups of plants appear rather suddenly in the rocks without links to ancestors. Various groups of flowering plants that appear in the Cretaceous rocks are similar to those that exist now. No record has been found of their evolution.

Mammals have the best fossil record of the vertebrates. But for most orders, no fossils document evolution from presumed ancestors. However, the vertebrates contain the principal exceptions to the general lack of intermediates.

The Mesozoic rocks hold series of organisms that can be interpreted as a good evolutionary sequence from reptiles to mammals (Hopson 1994). The therapsid reptiles (Fig. 9.20), sometimes called the mammal-like reptiles, have clearly reptilian skeletons. Reptiles, including the therapsids, have some bones that mammals don't have. They also have only one middle ear bone rather than the three that mammals have. The articular bone in the reptile lower jaw articulates with the quadrate bone; in mammals, the dentary bone composes the lower jaw and articulates with the squamosal.

In other ways, the therapsids are not typical reptiles. Their legs are positioned upright under their body like mammals, but unlike other Permian reptiles. Their skulls have several features that are mammal-like—a secondary palate separating the mouth from the nasal opening, teeth that resemble mammal incisors, canines and cheek teeth, and a lower jaw composed mostly of the dentary with the other bones reduced. In the Triassic deposits, several groups simultaneously show more mammal-like traits. A few types seem to have remnants of the reptile articular-quadrate jaw joint and an incipient dentary-squamosal joint (Carroll 1988, ch. 17; Lillegraven et al. 1979).

The mammal-like features in the therapsids are morphological traits related to an active life style with a high metabolic rate requiring a higher food intake than other reptiles. Some have speculated that the therapsids were warm-blooded. The first

mammal fossils are found in the Triassic. Some seem to have a combination of characteristics making the choice to call them reptiles or mammals arbitrary (Carroll 1988; Lillegraven et al. 1979). The existence of a group of reptiles with features of anatomy and physiology parallel to the mammals' active life style is not a problem for interventionist theory, but the confusing group of Triassic fossils with apparently intermediate structures is a challenge.

The other famous intermediate is *Archaeopteryx*, the early fossil that looks like a good link between reptiles and birds (Fig. 9.19). *Archaeopteryx* is not the equivalent of the complex group of therapsids. It is just one species with several structural features that are different from other birds. Its bones are not light and hollow like birds, its tail has a long bony skeleton, it has teeth, and it has claws on three digits of its wing. However, it is fully feathered, has well-developed wings, and apparently could fly (Feduccia & Tordoff 1979; Olson & Feduccia 1979). The existence of *Archaeopteryx* and a Jurassic-beaked bird with some of the same skeletal features (Hou et al. 1995) does not help to explain the difficult problem of evolving the power of flight. They are a unique type of creature, perhaps related to other birds in the same way that monotremes (duck-billed platypus and spiny echidna) are related to the other mammals. Monotremes are mammals that have some bones normally found in reptiles but not in mammals, and they lay eggs. Since monotremes still live, we can study their soft tissues and verify that they are indeed mammals and are not suitable evolutionary ancestors to the other mammals. *Archaeopteryx* no longer live, so it's impossible to be sure of their true relation to the other birds. I prefer to consider various alternatives for the explanation of these important fossils, although I could not prove that they aren't ancestral birds.

The first amphibians have many skull features in common with the rhipidistian fishes, but no intermediate forms exist to help solve the problem of bridging the huge structural gap between fish with fins and amphibians like *Ichthyostega* with a fully terrestrial limb structure (Fig. 9.21). Controversies continue over whether the rhipidistians are actually the ancestors of the amphibians or whether the amphibians came from some other group of fishes (Gorr & Kleinschmidt 1993). The available evidence can't tell us if the similarities between early amphibians and rhipidistian fish resulted from evolution or from common design elements used in two differing groups.

The fossil whales with small hind limbs are different from living whales. This difference can be interpreted as just another type of whale and doesn't indicate whether whales evolved or were created. Certainly, a greater variety of whales lived in the past, and the presence of some whales with hind limbs removes one obstacle for megaevolution theory. Perhaps, originally, a diversity of created whale body styles was extant, and those with hind limbs have gone extinct. It still needs to be explained why those with limbs came first in the fossil record.

Some hominids look like intermediates between apes and humans (Fig. 9.23). One interpretation is that humans evolved from apes through these intermediates. Other hypotheses also are worth investigating. Perhaps Neanderthal man and even *Homo erectus* were degenerate forms of humans, while Australopithecus was another form of ape (see Lubenow 1992 for an analysis of human fossils).

These groups that seem like good intermediates are one of the strong points in favor of megaevolution. However, most of them have other plausible interpretations with the most difficult one being the mammal-like reptiles. If megaevolution of animals and plants occurred, it is puzzling why almost all of those major groups appear in the record fully formed with no evolutionary connecting links preserved—that so few contenders for good series of intermediates between major groups can be found.

When we consider the overall stratigraphic distribution of the fossils, many groups do not go all the way down through the fossil record (Fig. 9.18). Fossils in the Precambrian are mostly one-celled organisms. The invertebrates enter the record next, and later on the fish appear, then amphibians and reptiles, and, lastly, birds and mammals. In that sense, a sequence of ascending complexity seems plausible. The mammals do not appear in the record until the Mesozoic; our familiar modern orders are not found as fossils until the Eocene; and few modern species appear before the Pleistocene. There is a definite order in which major groups of vertebrates appear in the record. This feature needs an explanation. Informed intervention theory, as defined in this volume, says that mammals were in existence at the time the Paleozoic fossils were being buried. The mammals were not buried at that time for some reason other than not yet having evolved.

The vertebrate fossil record is a mixed bag for the interventionist theory. The megaevolution theory has accepted the challenge of seeking a new mechanism of macroevolution that will explain the scarcity of fossil intermediates. The challenge for the informed intervention paradigm is to find an alternate explanation for the apparent intermediates, for the sequence of fossils in the rocks, for the increasing percentage of extinct groups lower in the fossil record, and for the large-scale patterns in the biogeographic data. This, and not the biological evidence, is the major challenge for interventionist theories. For now, I simply propose that an alternate mechanism exists for distributing most of the fossils in the sequence in which they occur. The sequence represents something other than an evolutionary sequence; it is more related to sorting and burial processes during catastrophic events. That topic occupies the last chapters of this book.

Some groups of vertebrates have more complex skeletons than others. Some have more bones in the skull, for example, but the more complex skeletons of vertebrates are closer to the bottom, not the top of the fossil record (Fig. 10.7). A definite trend shows a reduction in the number of bones—simplification of the skeleton as we go up the fossil record from bony fish to mammals. Both megaevolution and intervention theories can suggest plausible reasons why mammals would have simpler skeletons than fish or Paleozoic amphibians. But how did fish get such complex skeletons in the first place? Intervention theory can give an answer to that question, but I predict that naturalistic theories will have increasing problems with questions like that as our understanding of life increases (Fig. 10.7).

The Convergence of Different Lines of Evidence

Darwin was much too optimistic in his belief that many lines of evidence pointed to an evolutionary origin of all life forms. Much of his evidence has other plausible interpretations and can point to informed intervention as a strong contender.

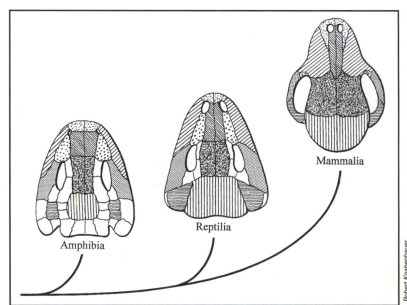

Robert Knabenbauer

**Figure 10.7
Skulls of several vertebrate groups, showing progressive simplification of the skull bones (after Moody 1962).**

Both naturalistic megaevolution and informed intervention have difficulty with some evidence. The following chart is my analysis of these lines of evidence:

Evidence Favoring Intervention	Neutral Evidence	Evidence Favoring Naturalistic Life Origin and Megaevolution
Lack of fossil intermediates between major groups	Microevolution	Biogeography - large scale distribution patterns
The problem of originating life from non-living matter	Speciation	Sequence of vertebrate fossils in fossil record
The problem of originating new body plans	Embryology	Reptile/mammal fossil intermediates
	Vestigial organs	
	Hierarchical nature of life	
	Diverse levels of biological complexity	
	Homology	
	"Suboptimal" adaptations	
	Biogeography (most)	
	Archaeopteryx	
	Fossil man	
	Fossil whales	
	Fish/amphibian "transition" Heterochrony, paedomorphosis, and allometry Regulatory gene evolution	

Conclusion

How does this relate to what is really happening in science? Thousands of scientists are doing evolution research. How can all this science be so successful if the basic biological concepts in the study of megaevolution are not on a more solid foundation? I find this interesting to think about as I attend annual meetings of organizations such as the American Society of Mammalogists or the Geological Society of America. Most of the scientists at these meetings would reject interventionism, and most would probably assume that interventionists could not be scientists. Yet, my personal estimate is that 80-90% of the research reported could be done by any interventionist trained in the same area because most of what is being studied is microevolution, speciation, and the aspects of macroevolution that interventionists also believe are the real evolution processes that have occurred. The same is true for most aspects of earth science, especially those areas that lend themselves to experimental research or comparison with modern processes. These topics of science lend themselves to collecting good data and effectively testing hypotheses, irrespective of personal philosophy.

A large part of what is happening in evolutionary science as a whole is primarily study of evolution at lower taxonomic levels, and that is not in conflict with informed intervention. Even at that level the interventionist may propose different explanations for some lines of evidence, but those differences can be analyzed with normal scientific methods. The study of megaevolution is where interventionists disagree in a fundamental way with other scientists, and megaevolution is all about events that are presumed to have happened in the distant past and consequently can never be a precise, testable science with the same level of confidence as many other areas.

Megaevolution is also the area in which evolutionary science is searching for better mechanisms. Interventionists should have no interest in preventing anyone from trying to develop a new theory of megaevolutionary mechanisms. But intervention theory suggests that no theory of megaevolution will ever work adequately, because the origin of basic new types of organisms won't happen without informed intervention by an intelligent Designer. Consequently, interventionists also suggest that perhaps it would be scientifically productive for at least some scientists to ask the question, "Are there limits to the evolution process, and what are they?", rather than for everyone to ask only "What is the mechanism of megaevolution?"

**TWO THEORIES OF
BIOLOGICAL ORIGINS**

Naturalistic Evolutionary Origin	**Informed Intervention, Followed by Evolution Within Created Groups**
1. Origin of life by molecular evolution	1. Origin of life and of major groups of plants and animals, by creation

2. Microevolution—evolutionary change at the population level within the species
  a. Excess individuals produced
  b. Variation, from mutations and recombination
  c. Natural selection
	2. Microevolution within species
	  a. Excess individuals produced
	  b. Variation, from mutations and recombination
	  c. Natural selection

3. Speciation—the evolution of new species
  a. Geographic isolation of populations
  b. Populations each adapt to their environments, by the process of microevolution
  c. Reproductive isolation
	3. Speciation—the evolution of new species within created groups
	  a. Geographic isolation of populations
	  b. Populations each adapt to their environments, by the process of microevolution
	  c. Reproductive isolation

4. Macroevolution (including megaevolution) above the species level. Origin of new genera, families, classes, phyla, and kingdoms: all life forms developed by evolution	4. Limited macroevolution above the species level, within created groups; origin of at least new genera, and in some cases even origin of higher categories (for example, some parasites)

Sociobiology: The Evolution Theory's Answer to Altruistic Behavior * 11

The theory of sociobiology, the application of evolutionary theory to the study of behavior, developed as science searched for a more adequate evolutionary explanation for all forms of animal and human social behavior. In chapter 8, we discussed the process by which mutation, recombination, and natural selection can introduce a trait into a population. For example, a variation in color could make an animal better camouflaged. If the individuals with the new color live longer, the new color variant would become more common. The impact on the next generation is determined entirely by how many offspring are produced that have the new color gene. The ability of organisms to reproduce successfully is described by the term "fitness." The individuals that produce the most reproductively successful offspring have the highest evolutionary fitness.

One can see how this works with morphological features, such as selection between color variations (improving camouflage), between individuals that differ in size or strength (ability to secure food and defend against enemies), or in speed (ability to escape). Could the same process be involved in explaining evolutionary changes in behavior? Could it explain why some species have monogamous mating systems and some are promiscuous, or why some species rely more on sound communication and some focus on chemical communication? Ewer (1968, p. *x*) summarized the challenge with his statement that "unless the mechanisms which produce the behavior are explicable in terms of natural selection working in the orthodox manner, we will be forced to postulate special creation or some unknown mystical-magical process." In many cases, convincing microevolutionary explanations for the origins of behaviors could be given. A problem remains, however, in attempting to explain altruistic behavior. An altruistic act is any behavior that benefits another individual at the expense of or risk to the one performing the behavior. Strictly Darwinian reasoning seems to

* The Sociobiological material presented in this chapter is from L. R. Brand and R. C. Carter, 1992. Sociobiology: The evolution theory's answer to altruistic behavior. Origins 19:54-71.

predict that an individual animal would compete to survive rather than act selflessly toward other individuals, especially if that act may put its own fitness into jeopardy.

A ground squirrel that gives an alarm call when a hawk appears warns others to hide, but it also draws attention to itself and may even increase the chances that it will be the one caught by the hawk. In evolutionary terms, a squirrel that is prone to give alarm calls may be decreasing its own fitness because it is decreasing the probability that it will live to reproduce. A squirrel whose genes predispose it to cheat, by benefiting from the alarm calls of others but not giving calls itself, would appear to be the one with the best chances of reproductive success, and thus have the highest fitness.

Some species of birds, such as the Florida Scrub Jay or the African bee eaters, have nests that are cared for by the parents with the assistance of one or more other adult "helpers at the nest." Why would one of these helpers decrease its own fitness to help other birds raise their young rather than raising young that carry its own genes?

Many who accept some form of creation by God consider the creation of humanity and morality to have been a separate and special act from other acts of creation. Therefore, an interventionist is tempted to simply dismiss any proposed evolutionary mechanisms for explaining altruistic behaviors. However, even interventionists must explain why evolutionary processes after the creation event have not eliminated altruistic behaviors. The question regarding altruism in animals remains essentially the same for everyone, no matter what philosophy we start from.

Sociobiology: A Proposed Answer to Altruism

In 1975, Harvard entomology professor Dr. Edward O. Wilson published *Sociobiology: The New Synthesis* (see also Wilson 1980a). He developed a new paradigm which he defined as "the systematic study of the biological basis of all social behavior, . . . a branch of evolutionary biology and particularly of modern population biology" (p. 4). This paradigm stimulated a considerable amount of controversy, but much of it has been generally accepted.

In *Sociobiology*, Dr. Wilson claims to have solved the problem of altruism. A cornerstone of sociobiology theory is the concept of inclusive fitness which refers to the rate at which an animal's own offspring and its close relatives' offspring are successfully reared and reproduce. While fitness is an animal's rate of success in passing its genes to its own offspring, inclusive fitness is its rate of success in passing its genes directly to its own offspring and indirectly to the offspring of its close relatives, because its relatives have many of those same genes. Two sisters share, on the average, 50% of their genes in common. If one sister helps the other to successfully raise her offspring to reproductive age, she assists in the passing on of many genes that she shares with her nephews and nieces, thus increasing her inclusive fitness.

Sociobiology theory predicts that, because of this sharing of genes between relatives, altruistic behavior should exist only in situations in which the "altruistic" individual would actually increase its inclusive fitness by that behavior. Biologist J. B. S. Haldane is reputed to have once said that he would lay down his life for two brothers or eight cousins. The reason for this is that, on the average, brothers share half of their genes; first cousins share one eighth of their genes. If Haldane died for one brother (thus eliminating his own chance to reproduce), his brother could only pass on half as many of J. B. S. Haldane's genes as J. B. S. himself could have done. However, if he died to save two brothers he would, statistically speaking, come out even (Fisher 1991).

If we apply this to our alarm-calling squirrels, sociobiology theory predicts that squirrels should be most likely to give alarm calls when they are surrounded by many close relatives. Hence, the squirrels that are helped by the calls share many genes with the caller, thus increasing the caller's inclusive fitness. Research has shown this is true. When young ground squirrels mature, the males disperse to distant places before they settle down and choose a territory. Young females don't disperse. They set up territories near home. Consequently, females have many close relatives living near them, but males do not. Just as the theory predicts, it is the females who give the alarm calls. When a female calls, many of the squirrels who are helped are relatives who share her genes. Even if she is caught by the predator, her relatives who run for cover will pass on her genes that caused her to give the alarm call (Holmes & Sherman 1983; Sherman 1977).

Natural selection in this situation is called kin selection. Favorable traits are shared by close relatives, and a family that helps its members survive will have more reproductive success than other families. Their behavioral traits are the ones that will become more common.

The processes of mutation and kin selection and their effects on

184

inclusive fitness are the elements of the mechanism by which sociobiology proposes to explain the origin of altruism and of all other social behavior. Sociobiology theory says that the entire focus of life is reproductive success; animals are "sex machines" (Anderson 1982) whose function is to pass on favorable genes that will improve the inclusive fitness of their offspring.

The evolution process has no room for unselfish actions that help a non-kin at the expense of the one performing the action. Thus, one corollary of sociobiology theory is that there is no such thing as truly altruistic behavior. Some apparent exceptions to this are explained as "reciprocal altruism"—you scratch my back and I'll scratch yours.

For example, olive baboon males solicit help from an unrelated male in an aggressive interaction against a third male. It often occurs that on another occasion the roles are reversed, and the original solicitor helps the same partner who is now the solicitor (Packer 1977; see also Trivers 1971).

Can sociobiology explain the helpers at the nest? Kin selection would predict that a bird nest has non-parent adult helpers only when the helpers' inclusive fitness is higher from helping relatives than from trying to raise their own young.

Research has confirmed that this prediction is correct (Fisher 1991; Krebs and Davies 1987, p. 270-276), and that the helpers are close relatives, usually offspring from a previous season. These helpers cannot secure territories of their own or are too inexperienced to be very successful in raising their own young. Until they are ready to do so, their inclusive fitness will be higher if they help raise their relatives who share many of their genes.

Behavioral Strategies

As animals compete with each other for resources such as food, living space, or mates, various behavioral strategies could be employed. The application of sociobiology theory suggests ways to predict which strategy will be most effective in different situations. For example, two competitors could simply fight, with the winner of the fight taking the resource. They could employ some type of conventional strategy (symbolic battle), like a stereotyped arm-wrestling match, that indicates which animal is stronger or more aggressive without the risk of anyone getting hurt. Game theory and the principles of sociobiology can be used to predict the benefits of each strategy (Krebs and Davies 1987, p. 134-160). Natural selection, in general, is expected to favor conventional strategies over all out "war" in animal conflicts (Maynard Smith and Price 1973). Many examples of this can be seen in nature (Eibl-Eibesfeldt 1975, p. 349-360). Male rattlesnakes wrestle each other, and the winner is the one that can pin the other's head to the ground with his own body. Lava lizards "battle" by hitting each other with their tails, and marine iguanas by butting heads together and pushing each other backward. Deer and antelopes have potentially lethal antlers or horns, but when the males battle over mates they do not try to impale each other. They butt their heads together and wrestle in ways that usually do not cause serious damage (Eibl-Eibesfeldt 1975, p. 349, 353-359; Wallace 1973, p. 221-229). Animals also commonly communicate the nature of their aggressive state to other individuals of their species apparently to allow the other individual to respond appropriately, thus reducing the amount of fighting (Drickamer and Vessey 1992, p. 211, 220, 237-255; Marler and Hamilton 1967).

Research under the guidance of sociobiology theory has led ethologists to recognize the role of some animal behaviors previously thought to be only bizarre abnormalities. For instance, a male African lion sometimes kills all the babies in his pride. This happens when a battle

between males occurs and the ruler of the pride is deposed. The new dominant male generally kills all of the young, the offspring of his deposed rival. Consequently, he is able to mate and produce his own offspring much more quickly than if the females were occupied with offspring of his former rival (Bertram 1975). Such infanticide is also known to occur in Hanaman langurs, mountain gorillas, chimpanzees, African wild dogs, and rodents (Fisher 1991; Hrdy 1974, 1977a, 1977b).

Implications for Human Behavior

Sociobiology has become the prevailing synthesis in the study of animal behavior and has been very successful. Apparently, sociobiological reasoning frequently provides useful and testable scientific predictions in animal-behavior studies. What are its implications for human behavior?

The basic claim of sociobiology is that human behavioral traits are not a result of special creation; they have developed through evolution from non-human ancestors. Increased inclusive fitness is gained by increased reproduction by oneself or one's close relatives. Consequently, according to sociobiology, reproductive success is the dominant factor determining human behavioral tendencies. Though we may think that we are rational, moral beings, our behavior is more programmed than we think it is. In other words, "sociobiologists contend, we were designed to be reproduction machines" (Anderson 1982, p. 74).

Many Christians believe that humankind has been given a set of moral rules for sexual behavior. These rules tell us what is right or beneficial and what is wrong and should be avoided simply because it is damaging to human relationships or is harmful to ourselves or others. Sociobiology says there are no morally right or wrong behaviors; our behavior is the result of the selection pressures that have created us. Anderson (1982) summarized the concept this way:

> The type of man who leaves the most descendants is the one who cuts his reproductive costs on all sides, by keeping a close watch on his mate and making sure he has no rivals; supporting his mate, if it seems that all her children were sired by him; and mating with other females—additional wives, single women, other men's wives—whenever a safe opportunity arises. (p. 77)

Sociobiology: An Alternative to Religion

In sociobiology theory, right or wrong behavior doesn't exist in a moral sense, only different behavioral strategies with effects on inclusive fitness. Sociobiology could be said to be the naturalistic answer to Christianity's

value system. "Wilson openly challenges Christian faith by offering a substitute belief system based upon scientific materialism" (Rothrock and Rothrock 1987, p. 87). Wilson believes that humanity has an innate tendency toward religious belief because, in the past, it conferred an adaptive advantage. He also believes that the content of religious belief is false, that we should replace it with a more correct mythology (Rothrock and Rothrock 1987). "This mythopoeic drive (i.e., the tendency toward religious belief) can be harnessed to learning and the rational search for human progress if we finally concede that scientific materialism is itself a mythology defined in the noble sense" (Wilson 1978, p. 208). He urges us to "make no mistake about the power of scientific materialism. It presents the human mind with an alternative mythology that until now has always, point for point in zones of conflict, defeated traditional religion" (p. 200).

Wilson does not deny that religion and moralism have value. He believes they can encourage reciprocally altruistic behavior by discouraging cheating. But he believes that moral values should be determined by science, which offers the "possibility of explaining traditional religion by the mechanistic models of evolutionary biology. . . . If religion, including the dogmatic secular ideologies, can be systematically analyzed and explained as a product of the brain's evolution, its power as an external source of morality will be gone forever" (p. 208). Wilson feels our ideas of sexual morality should be more liberal. He bases this conclusion on a survey of the behavior of our presumed nonhuman ancestors and on his convictions that Christianity's moral laws did not come from God. These opinions apparently are based on his conclusion that with continuing research "we will see with increasing clarity that the biological god does not exist and scientific materialism provides the more nearly correct perception of the human condition" (Wilson 1980b, p. 430).

Is Sociobiology Real?

To what extent are the proponents of sociobiology correct? To address this question, several different concepts can be isolated and considered.

1. *The proposed naturalistic origin of the higher groups of organisms, including the origin of humanity and the human brain.* Sociobiology theory, as proposed by Wilson, is built on the assumption of the naturalistic evolutionary descent of all organisms from a common ancestor. Sociobiology does not provide evidence for that evolutionary descent, however. It merely assumes the naturalistic evolutionary origin of animals and develops hypotheses and explanations for behavioral change based on that assumption.

2. *Kin selection and the evolution of behavior, at the level of species or genera of animals.* The alarm-calling female ground squirrels, the bird helpers at the nest, and a host of other examples certainly fit the theory very well. Whether future research will continue to support it remains to be seen. But with mutations causing random damage to the genes that influence behavior, it does seem very likely that behaviors not supported by some type of selection process eventually would be weakened or eliminated.

3. *Kin selection and its genetic influence on human behavior.* Aside from the question of whether humankind is the result of evolution, one can ask whether human behavior is controlled by genes, as claimed by sociobiology, or determined mostly by culture (i.e., learned rather than inherited). This debate has raged ever since (and before) sociobiology was introduced. Wilson (1975) actually does recognize that culture is an important component of human behavior, but he maintains that other important themes of primate behavior also are present in humans by inheritance. Others disagree. This group includes scientists who believe

Wilson's sociobiology goes too far in presuming biological determinism. Perhaps the most widely known person who challenges biological determinism is Stephen J. Gould, a colleague of Wilson's at Harvard. Gould praised most of Wilson's sociobiology, but he rejected what he saw as biological determinism in humans. He and others argue that there is no evidence for specific genes that determine human behavior and believe the theory of such genes is not testable (Fisher 1991).

Some others carry the concept of genetic control of human behavior farther than Wilson does (e.g., Anderson 1982; Barash 1979; Bellis and Baker 1990; Nalley et al. 1982). One must recognize that evidence does exist for genetic control of behavior in non-human animals (e.g., Bentley and Hoy 1972; Berthold and Querner 1981; Brandes 1991; Hirsch and McGuire 1982; Kyriacou 1990; Plomin et al. 1990; Provost 1991; Ricker and Hirsch 1988; Roubertoux and Carlier 1988). Consequently, even though much of human behavior seems to be modifiable by culture, the possibility that significant genetic control of behavioral tendencies exists in humans needs to be considered. If such control exists, the strong possibility, perhaps certainty, follows that mutations could alter that behavior. With random genetic damage of genes occurring, it would be difficult to escape the conclusion that some human behaviors can be altered or eliminated by mutations and would be subject to the processes of natural selection, including kin selection. Does that mean that socio-biological explanations of human behavior are correct? What does that say about morality?

Concepts of right and wrong for Christians are understood as a moral code given to humanity. The Ten Commandments and the teachings of Christ have provided a standard for human behavior. Clearly, humans do not follow that standard very well. Perhaps they have fallen so far from their original created condition because mutations have affected their behavior. Perhaps both humans and non-human animals were created with well-balanced behaviors as well as morphologies that since have undergone generations of change driven by mutations, recombination, and natural selection. As a result, part of human character reflects this change, and that has emphasized the selfish side of human nature. The view presented here differs from current evolutionary thinking in proposing that the basic process of kin selection and its effect on inclusive fitness has operated only within humans and within other created groups of organisms. It has not carried behaviors from one such group to another, since these groups have not evolved from common ancestors (this concept is developed further in chapter 12). Christians also accept by faith (and by reasoning which is at least logical, even though not scientifically testable) that humankind is not biologically destined but has a measure of free will to seek the ability from God to act in ways that are truly altruistic and not just the result of gene modification and biological determination.

Does genuine altruism exist in humans? Observations of human behavior makes it difficult to believe that some behavior is not truly altruistic, because abundant human altruism can be documented (Monroe 1996).

An Interventionist Theory of Natural Selection and Biological Change Within Limits

12

This chapter compares the naturalistic theory of the origin of diversity with a theory of limited genetic change after the major groups of organisms were brought into being by informed intervention. This presentation is simply a progress report and does not claim to answer all questions. The theory will no doubt change as more data are gathered. It will be fascinating to see how the accumulating data will affect our theories in the years to come.*

The theories of microevolution and speciation as presented here, in many respects, are not significantly different from currently accepted theories except for some basic points. However, this theory has a different starting point for life and implies a very different history of life. In each section, understanding of the naturalistic theory briefly is summarized, and an interventionist alternative is then presented. To be fair to the authors of papers cited here, I wish to emphasize that most of them would not support the basic premise of this

chapter. They are cited only for specific ideas or data, and I believe my reinterpretation is not inconsistent with the data cited.

Origin and Direction of Evolutionary Change

Naturalistic Evolution. According to naturalistic evolution theory, as structurally complex organisms evolved from simple ancestral life forms, all new genes or new information ultimately arose by mutation and recombination. Mutations occur randomly and most are deleterious and lower the individual's fitness or adaptation to its environment (Cain 1989, Maynard Smith 1989). New combinations of the genetic material are formed during sexual reproduction. Natural selection eliminates the deleterious mutations and preserves the available combinations that are best adapted in the organism's environment for maximizing successful reproductive effort (Endler 1986; Weiner 1995).

Within each taxon, evolution progresses from the ancestral state

* This chapter is based on the material presented in L. R. Brand and L. J. Gibson, 1993. An interventionist theory of natural selection and biological change within limits. Origins 20:60-82.

toward forms with more derived characteristics in their external appearance, as well as in their anatomy, physiology, behavior, and ecological adaptations. At lower taxonomic levels (within a species, genus, or family), these derived characteristics would not necessarily be more complex. But at some level in the evolution process, structures and physiological systems were evolving that did not exist before.

Interventionism. According to the interventionist theory, at the creation of life on earth, representatives of all major extant and extinct groups of plants and animals were present. Within each taxon, the earliest forms were at least as complex, although not necessarily as specialized, as any modern-day representatives of that group in their external appearance, anatomy, physiology, behavior, and ecological adaptations. In these early populations, the amount of genetic information and the potential for genetic diversity per species may have been at the highest level it has ever reached. The high point of the complexity of life on earth was at the very beginning.

Complexity in plants and animals was the result of intelligent design. Organisms were designed with a genetic system which possessed the capacity for generating genetic variability that would permit them to adapt physiologically to changing conditions and to produce new species that would be variations on existing themes. At first, this process did not involve the primarily destructive element of random mutations. It utilized the potential for variability built into the genetic system. The first populations of the original species were not all alike—considerable variation was evident in their characteristics—and they probably had a genetic system capable of generating additional diversity when needed by producing new alleles or by switching on stored, unexpressed genes.

As time went on, environmental changes occurred that increased the mutation rate. Radiation and other mechanisms began to produce random genetic damage, and/or a decrease appeared in the efficiency of the gene replication and repair mechanism. Since mutations are mostly deleterious, the damage must be controlled to prevent life from going extinct. Natural selection has been the agent which has eliminated the less fit individuals and assured that, on average, those which reproduce are the healthiest and best adapted to the environment in which they live.

Within each group of organisms, the origin of new morphological or behavioral variation has involved two basic components. First is adaptation to changing conditions by production of new alleles for existing genes and selection for those alleles best suited to the environment by the generally accepted process of microevolution.

An example of this type of adaptation to the environment is the development of dark pelage by a rodent living on dark soil (Dodson and Dodson 1985, p. 194). Another example is the behavioral adaptation of marmots to differences in climate (Barash 1974). Marmots have adapted to alpine areas with short summers (thus a short growing season) by being social, non-aggressive, and colonial, which facilitates a long parent-young relationship. The young take two years to reach sexual maturity. In milder, low-elevation climates, young marmots reach sexual maturity in one summer and establish their own territory. This reduced parent-young interaction apparently has allowed them to be more aggressive and territorial. This adaptation process does not necessarily involve either increase or decrease in complexity, nor the evolution of new genes or structures. Perhaps it could involve the turning on and off of genes by environmental signals. Thus, new characteristics might be caused by formerly inactive genes.

A second component of variation is the tendency toward loss of genetic information in organisms since their origin. Examples are loss of flight by some birds and insects, and loss of sight by cave organisms. We argue that organisms today are, on the whole, less complex and less adaptable, and interactions between organisms in ecosystems are less finely tuned than at the beginning of life on earth. In most cases, natural selection tends to slow down the loss of information by eliminating defective individuals, unless the environment allows or favors the genetic loss. However, this may sometimes be only an apparent loss from genes being turned off or suppressed, as illustrated by Hampe's experiments (Hampe 1960) and implied by data reviewed by Gould (1994).

Loss of Genetic Information

Naturalistic Evolution. Since most mutations are harmful, the potential is real for effective loss of genetic information unless natural selection is able to eliminate damaging mutations. An animal species has a certain amount of genetic material, some of which is absolutely vital for survival. Another portion of the genetic information is optional, including behavioral and physical traits that the species can lose (or turn off) and still be viable (Carson 1975) (Figure 12.1). Which features fall in this category will be influenced by the environment.

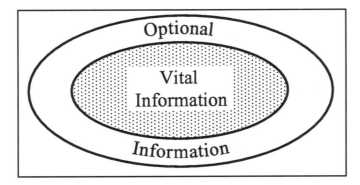

Optional

Vital
Information

Information

**Figure 12.1
A representation of the total
genome of a species and
the core of vital genetic
information necessary
for life.**

Loss of flight would probably doom most birds to extinction. However, on an island with no predators, losing the ability of flight might not be a problem and could even be an advantage in a tropical storm that can blow flying birds out to sea. A number of species of flightless birds are known and most of these inhabit islands (Diamond 1981). In this situation, flight is optional, illustrating how a certain amount of genetic loss is possible. Other examples of genetic loss are blind cave salamanders and parasites that lack a digestive system.

Where have parasites such as tapeworms come from? Their origin apparently involves the loss of much genetic information as they degenerated from a free-living state. Tapeworms do not have some organs that similar, non-parasitic worms have. They don't have a digestive tract; they are essentially a highly developed reproductive system that lives in the intestine of their host. All the nourishment they need is absorbed through their skin. In this situation, the tapeworm doesn't need

a digestive tract; all it needs is a way to reproduce itself and maintain its location. If ancestral tapeworms with normal digestive tracts mutated, the loss of those tracts would not have been disadvantageous because of the nutrients available from the host. In such situations an organism can lose much more than is possible in other environments and still be viable. These degenerate parasites exemplify change by loss of information.

Interventionism. Interventionist theory accepts the explanations given above for flightless birds, cave salamanders, and parasites. What was the purpose for creating tapeworms and other parasites? It seems more likely that these parasites reached their present form through degeneration—loss of genetic information leading to dependence on parasitism.

The interventionist theory presented here also proposes that loss of genetic information has been involved not only in extreme cases but has been a subtle, pervasive part of the genetic change in animals and plants since their original creation. The following example of possible loss of information is probably more typical than the type of loss experienced by some parasites or by blind salamanders. William Dilger studied the behavior of African lovebirds of the genus *Agapornis*, which are in the parrot family (Dilger 1960, 1962). He arranged the species of lovebirds in an evolutionary sequence. At one end is a species that does not have the specialized features of some other lovebirds; it is very plainly colored, has a simple courtship ritual, and makes a crude nest. The species at the other end of the family tree has beautiful, colorful birds, carries on a more complex courtship, and builds elaborate, covered nests.

The usual interpretation of such a sequence is that the plain lovebird, with fewer unique characteristics, was near the beginning of the family tree. The more specialized one was the most highly evolved. But how can we be so sure that the changes didn't go the other direction? The initial assumption is that these lovebirds have evolved from other, related types of birds. If so, one can assume that the species with the least specialized lovebird characters is closest to the base of the lovebird evolutionary tree.

If we do not assume that all creatures have evolved progressively (in this instance, from another kind of bird), we also can consider the option that their evolution went the other way, starting with the most unique lovebird behavior and bright colors. Since the origin of those lovebirds, some species have lost varying amounts of genetic information, depending on the selection pressures to which each has been exposed.

What has been lost are some of the optional features not required for a viable lovebird. The result of the above-postulated process of genetic loss is that, while the number of species of lovebirds has increased, the tendency is still toward loss of information. Many species are highly specialized and live only in a narrowly defined ecological niche.

Naturalistic evolution theory recognizes that groups of organisms may become divided into many species, each adapted to a specific niche. This specialization may be accompanied by loss of features or abilities that are needed by more generalist species. Hinegardner (1976) indicates that species with lower amounts of DNA tend to be more specialized. However, exceptions to this trend occur. Perhaps this indicates that genes are turned off, not lost. The theory considered here proposes a similar concept, except that the process started with a rich array of created life forms. Since the original creation of organisms, populations that were originally adaptable with a high level of genetic information have often become highly specialized, possibly with less functional genetic information per species. During this process, many taxa also have divided into numerous species, each being specialized. Division of the original groups into the many specialized species of today is not just the latest minor episode in the history of life, but a major part of the change that has occurred since life began on this earth. Figure 12.2 illustrates the basic differences between the two theories.

Natural Selection

Naturalistic Evolution. The naturalistic theory of evolutionary change begins with the random raw materials provided by mutation and recombination. Natural selection is the key process that rises above the randomness of mutation and selects the appropriate features to improve the adaptations of organisms. Most mutations are harmful, but natural selection is effective in eliminating most destructive mutations and preserving beneficial ones. Consequently, the net effect is upwards, towards improved adaptation to the environment, and, ultimately, the production of new genes, new adaptations, and even new organ systems (Figure 12.3A).

Interventionism. Both naturalistic evolution and informed intervention recognize natural selection as an important factor in the microevolution process, but the specific role of natural selection differs in the two theories. This interventionist theory recognizes the same forces but suggests that the balance of forces is different. Edward Blyth anticipated Charles Darwin's theory of natural

Figure 12.2 Comparison of the implications of the two theories of origins. The lower phylogenetic tree shows increased complexity through time. The upper tree (for the same organisms) shows independent origins of major groups, followed by speciation and some decrease of complexity through time.

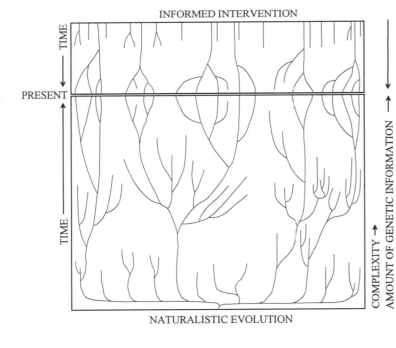

Figure 12.3 The balance of natural forces according to (A) naturalistic theory and (B) interventionist theory.

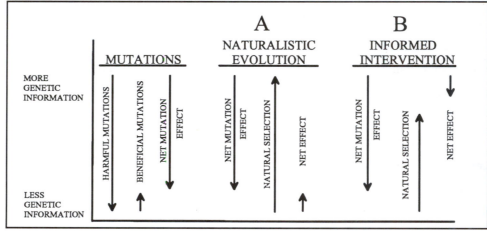

selection, but Blyth was not an evolutionist. He viewed natural selection as a conserving force, maintaining the species by eliminating the weak individuals (Eiseley 1979). Lester and Bohlin (1989) have suggested that Blyth was more correct than Darwin and that evolutionary change occurs only within limits. Interventionism suggests that mutation and natural selection are not able to produce an increase in complexity by generating new genes and organs. They are able only to change animals within the constraints of their original genetic potential and to slow down the slide toward oblivion which would occur if the accumulation of harmful mutations were not held in check. Natural selection is nearly able to offset most of the deleterious effects of mutation, but the net evolutionary change is slightly downward (Figure 12.3B). Natural selection acts as a brake to eliminate many individuals weakened by mutations and thus slows down the destructive forces that can come from mutation.

This theory of natural selection is actually not a new or radical idea. It does not seem to go against the data that are available, even though Ridley (1993, p. 508) claims that "no one seriously doubts that the microevolutionary processes . . . [described earlier in his book] are fundamentally responsible for all evolution in the history of life." He does not provide convincing genetic evidence that the proposed mechanism can accomplish the task. Some other non-interventionist scientists question whether natural selection can actually do some of the things that the Neodarwinian synthesis maintains that it does (Arthur 1984, ch. 4; Bakker 1985; John and Miklos 1988, p. 336; Løvtrup 1987, ch. 12). They are not suggesting that animals were created, but that the traditional process of point mutation and natural selection is not the process that generates significant evolutionary change. Interventionist theory recognizes that natural selection is a significant force but suggests that it is not able to generate significant new structures, and that no other evolutionary mechanism can do so.

Evolution Rate

Naturalistic Evolution. All new variability is ultimately the result of random mutations. Reshuffling of the genetic material provides many new combinations of traits for natural selection to act on, but the raw material is only provided by mutation. The cause of the mutations is blind to the needs of the organism, and most mutations are deleterious. It seems that some factors, such as mutator genes or environmental conditions, can control rates of mutation, but evolutionary rates are usually very low. Significant morphological change and megaevolution require a great amount of time.

Interventionism. Even though interventionists are often thought of as anti-evolutionists, the fact is that young-earth interventionists believe in a far more effective and rapid process of morphological change than non-interventionists. They have a shorter time period for the evolution of a large number of species and genera of organisms. Is that realistic? First of all, the major taxa were in existence from the beginning. All that is needed is a process of diversification within each major taxon. The interventionist theory does not depend on new structural and biochemical traits evolving through mutation and natural selection. Rather, change comes from a sorting out of genetic potential that already was present, from some loss of information, and from differential gene expression. Net evolutionary change has been downward or toward loss of information. Thus, the evolution process has not been dependent upon uncommon beneficial mutations. It utilizes the high level of genetic information that was a part of the original design. When the influence of the environment permits additional change by loss (or turning off) of information, the numerous deleterious mutations

whose effects are otherwise held in check by natural selection also speed the process of biological change. Thus, expected rates of genetic change would be much higher than predicted by the naturalistic theory.

According to the theory presented here, much of our current taxonomic diversity has been the result of limited evolutionary change after a worldwide catastrophe. The original groups of plants and animals have diversified into multitudes of species as they adapted to fill specific niches in the changed conditions after the catastrophe. If we consider such conditions and compare them with factors that are known to favor rapid genetic change, we find that they would be ideally favorable for rapid change. Let's consider these.

1. *An abundance of potential unoccupied niches to which organisms could adapt.* Animals that have successfully colonized islands have often developed a large number of species. Examples of this are the fruit flies and honeycreepers of Hawaii, and the Darwin's Finches of the Galapagos Islands. Apparently this speciation is facilitated by open niches and the resulting lack of competition (Ford 1964, ch. 2).

2. *Before the development of mature, balanced ecosystems, population dynamics would be unstable.* This situation would result in

flush/crash population dynamics: populations of animals expand, with all genotypes surviving, until they use up their food supply or until expanding predator populations catch up with them. The resulting population crashes produce the population bottlenecks (a time with few individuals in the population) favorable to speciation. Those individuals best adapted to particular niches have the best chance to survive the crash. Several, or many, species could be created simultaneously by a series of such cycles (Carson 1975; Mettler et al. 1988, p. 295).

3. *Rapid geologic and environmental changes would favor the separation of organisms into isolated populations, facilitating speciation* (Mayr 1970). This might have been particularly important for aquatic organisms, plants, and terrestrial invertebrates, which would likely have survived the global catastrophe in many scattered, isolated pockets. As the animals moved out over an empty world after the catastrophe, almost limitless opportunities would open up to occupy available new niches and speciate. In this situation, ecosystems initially would have been simple and relatively unstable. Until mature ecosystems developed, many population fluctuations would likely occur. These, along with rapid geologic changes in the recovery period after the catastrophe, would divide animals into smaller populations. The result would be a potential for very rapid rates of biological change after the global catastrophe (perhaps the most favorable situation for speciation we could imagine). The rate of change would slow down as environments and population dynamics stabilized, available niches were filled with increasingly specialized species, and ecosystems became more complex and balanced.

The overall implication of this theory is that evolution within the potential of the genetic system can be very rapid when conditions are favorable. Most of the modern (Holocene) species of animals evolved during the first few hundreds or thousands of years after the global catastrophe. Although it is commonly assumed that speciation takes hundreds of thousands or millions of years, even in modern times, introductions of monkeys, birds, copepods, and moths to new geographic areas has produced change equivalent to new subspecies or species in time spans of 30 to 1,000 years (Ashton, Flinn, and Griffiths 1979 [green monkeys]; Baker 1987 [mynas]; Johnson 1953 [copepod]; Johnston and Selander 1964 [house sparrows]; Zimmerman 1960 [moths]). Experimental studies show that rapid change can occur in animals introduced into a new environment (Morell 1997; Reznick et al. 1997).

Evidence shows that population bottlenecks usually reduce genetic variability (although usually only rare alleles are lost). This is a possible challenge for the theory of post-catastrophe evolution because of the expected loss of genetic variability in those species with small numbers of individuals surviving the catastrophe. This leads to the suggestion that some mechanisms must exist that rapidly increase genetic variability after a population bottleneck. Observations of much higher genetic variability than expected, after experimental or natural bottlenecks, provide some evidence for the existence of such mechanisms (Carson and Wisotzkey 1989; Dessauer et al. 1992; Mettler et al. 1988, p. 296; Terzian and Biemont 1988). Evidence shows that environmental or genetic stress produces genetic instability with increased rates of recombination and mutation resulting from movable elements (jumping genes—that move from one place to another on the chromosomes) (Fontdevila 1992; Parsons 1987, 1988). Movable elements seem to produce most spontaneous mutations in Drosophila (Langridge 1987) and in other eukaryotes (Reanna 1985). They have been implicated also in transferring genetic information from one type of organism to another, even

from one kingdom to another (Amabile-Cuevas and Chicurel 1993). Some have even suggested that environmental stress can "induce" mutations which will be beneficial to the organism, although that is highly controversial (Cairns et al. 1988; Lenski and Mittler 1993; Moffatt 1989; Revkin 1989).

An extension of this hypothesis suggests that the original genetic systems contained pre-programmed options susceptible to environmental induction. Perhaps organisms were originally designed with a mechanism for increasing genetic variability to meet changing conditions. These mechanisms may have suffered, after that time, from mutational damage and no longer are as effective or reliable. Movable elements may originally have made only regulated movements between specific sites on the chromosomes. Some such movements are still quite specific, but mutational changes in the system may have reduced their specificity.

Regulatory Genes and Heterochrony in Evolution

Naturalistic Evolution. Advances have been made by conventional evolutionary theory in understanding processes which can generate significant change with a minimum of genetic innovation. These processes (discussed in chapters 9 and 10) center around changes in regulatory genes and alteration of growth processes during embryological development. Examples were given that illustrate the theory of how small genetic changes over long periods of time can produce significant morphological evolution.

Interventionism. According to interventionist theory, the above-described processes of regulatory gene mutations and heterochrony would not produce new body plans or other major changes. But in lower taxonomic levels (within a family, for example), they would perhaps help to explain how a significant amount of change could occur rapidly. The original array of structural and regulatory genes for each body plan did not arise by mutation and natural selection; they were invented by intelligent design. The mechanisms described above are part of the process for introducing variations within each body plan for the purpose of permitting species to adapt to changes in their environment. The gene-switching model of Oster and Alberch (1982) also suggests how morphological change could occur by switching from one embryological "program" to another with each program leading to a different morphology. Other mechanisms beyond the scope of this book have also been proposed.

The growth of reptile leg bones (Hampe 1960) and enameled teeth

(Kollar and Fisher 1980) can be experimentally induced in chick embryos, and a gene involved in the embryological development of eyes has been found to be homologous in insects, squid, and vertebrates (Gould 1994). These data suggest that an animal's genes contain the information for making a wide variety of structures, and regulatory genes control their use. If this concept is so, it opens up interesting possibilities. For example, an original species of squirrel could have contained in its genes the information needed to produce several different species or even genera of squirrels, thus facilitating microevolution and speciation.

Mutations in insects have caused legs to grow on the head in place of antennae (Lodish et al. 1995, p. 581). This did not occur by many mutations methodically changing the antenna, step by step, into a leg. Insects apparently have a set of genes with instructions for making antennae, another set of instructions for making legs, and a regulatory gene "switch" to indicate if a particular structure should be a leg or an antenna. The regulatory gene can mutate and put legs on the head. This example suggests many interesting possibilities for variability that could have been built into the genetic system, facilitating rapid change in response to changing environments. For example, could horses have a regulatory "switch" that determines whether their legs each develop with one prominent toe with its single hoof, or whether three toes develop approximately equally? If so, and if other regulatory genes control size, teeth morphology, etc., then the evolution of horses may have been a fairly simple genetic process.

Figure 12.4 compares two concepts of evolutionary change. In classical evolution theory (Fig. 12.4A), a complex series of mutations, mostly in structural genes, changes the genetic potential (the information contained in the genome) of the species. Figure 12.4B illustrates a theory of evolution in which an organism has a broad genetic potential, and evolutionary change occurs by changes in which parts of that potential are expressed in different populations. In an interventionist theory, this broad potential was created and provides the basis for subsequent change. It also determines the limits of potential change for that group of organisms.

This could also explain why individual groups of organisms differ so much in their genetic variability. If specimens of each species of cat, from house cats to lions, were shaved and placed side by side, most of them would be very similar in structure. The difference would be mostly in size. In contrast, the dog family exhibits an amazing variety of body styles. The squirrel family offers another example. All the species of chipmunks are extremely similar in structure, and even in their chromosomes, whereas the ground squirrels differ considerably. These contrasting levels of variability in different groups may have been designed from the beginning.

Another result of this concept is that when geneticists learn enough about the genetic system, including the regulatory genes, it may be possible to alter a relatively few regulatory genes in an animal and make a very different type of animal, perhaps even resembling a hybrid between two families or classes of animal. This capability could create ethical dilemmas that dwarf our current problems.

Sociobiology

A naturalistic theory of evolution must be able to explain the origin of all animal behavior, and sociobiology claims to provide the mechanism to

**Figure 12.4
(A) Diagrammatic representation of change in the
genetic potential of a
species resulting from
evolution, as understood by
classical evolutionary
theory.**

**(B) Diagrammatic represen-
tation of evolutionary
change if the genome
contains the information for
much more potential variation. In this case evolution
results in a different portion
of the genetic information
(already present in the
genome) being expressed. In
an interventionist theory,
this broad genetic potential
was created and provides
the basis for subsequent
change.**

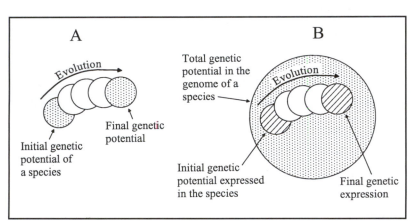

accomplish this. Chapter 11 discussed sociobiology, its success in explaining many aspects of animal behavior, and its implications for human biology. Alternative explanations for the data in this field are discussed below.

Naturalistic Evolution. Sociobiology theory claims that the behavior of animals is biologically determined (i.e., genetically controlled) and that its evolution has been governed by the incessant evolutionary competition between genes. Complex behaviors have evolved from simple maintenance routines such as preening, eating, defense, and other routine behavior. These behaviors became elaborated into more complex behaviors with new functions. Complex social behavior, including seemingly "altruistic" behavior, has evolved only as this behavior resulted in increased inclusive fitness through kin selection. Thus, no truly altruistic behavior exists; behavior that appears altruistic evolved only because it serves the interests of the "selfish genes" and increases the potential of these genes to be passed on to more offspring.

Interventionism. According to interventionist theory, the original animals had the greatest level of complexity in their behavior, and the interspecific and intraspecific interactions between organisms were the most finely tuned and harmonious at

the beginning of life on Earth. Potential conflicts between animals over the division of territory and other resources were originally settled by non-damaging conventional displays like those still common in a number of animals. Examples include the male rattlesnake wrestling matches and the lizard tail lashing or head butting "battles" (Eibl-Eibesfeldt 1975, p. 349-360). True altruistic behavior may have been much more common. Perhaps, originally, subadult animals commonly assisted their parents in raising the next brood or litter. Population-control mechanisms were also much more finely tuned than at present. Behavioral mechanisms for maintaining a stable ecological balance were built into the animals' genetic makeup as part of an ecological system that originated through intelligent design rather than chance.

The instinctive behavioral mechanisms which prevented damaging conflict were not originally subject to random mutational changes. Because of adequate protection from mutational damage, individuals with these behavioral mechanisms would not be subject to unfavorable competition from individuals who would benefit from "cheating." With the introduction of random mutations, these behavioral mechanisms began to break down.

Natural selection and, especially, kin selection have acted to slow this breakdown. The altruistic behaviors which have survived the negative effects of mutation are primarily those that have been preserved by kin selection and increase the inclusive fitness of the organism. When mutations began to cause the loss of some of the original created behavior patterns, natural selection would determine whether the original type or the mutated type would become most common. If mutations in a female bird removed the original pattern of helping her parents raise their young and she built her own nest, she would likely produce more young in her lifetime than others who began reproducing later (this is the same result that would be expected by naturalistic theory). As a consequence, the "non-helper genome" would become more common and eventually replace the "helpers." On the other hand, in some situations the genes for "altruistic" behaviors are favored by kin selection. Consequently, they continue to be common in the population. The Florida Scrub Jay lives in a situation in which the young are not likely to reproduce successfully the first year. Consequently, their inclusive fitness is increased if they help their parents raise young which share many genes that they also have. (Krebs and Davies 1987, p. 270- 276; Fisher

1991). Thus, kin selection favors retention of the "altruistic" behavior in this environment.

An intelligent and benevolent Designer could choose to invent an ecological system with a balance of nature based on harmony rather than on competition. In contrast, mutation and natural selection have no ability to look at the "big picture" and see what is best for the overall ecological balance. Natural selection is strictly shortsighted—it favors any change that increases successful reproduction. The ultimate result of the rule of natural selection is the competitive, vicious side of nature.

Conclusion

This interventionist theory has a number of implications for the genetic system, along with suggestions for future research. An obvious implication is that with adequate genetic variability and changing environments, morphological change and speciation can occur rapidly—even orders of magnitude faster than is commonly believed. Animal populations that are well adapted to their environment would not be expected to change, but rapid evolution within limits is seen as the normal expectation under some environmental conditions.

We propose that evolutionary change has occurred only within definite limits, but the limits are not at the species level. Because of the subjectivity involved in defining higher categories in different animal groups, it is not possible to define the limits of the original groups of animals and plants in terms of a specific taxonomic level such as family or genus. Preliminary analysis suggests that almost all modern species, probably most modern genera, and perhaps some families have resulted from modifications of the originally created species.

Frank Marsh (1941, 1976) proposed that a created group be defined as a taxonomic rank called the "basic type" or "baramin" which would include all individuals or species that are able to hybridize. Scherer (1993) has edited a volume summarizing the available hybridization data and 14 basic types that seem to emerge from these data, if we accept Marsh's proposal. These basic types are at the tribe, subfamily, or family levels. Some representative examples of these basic types are the family Canidae (dogs, wolves, foxes, jackals; 15 genera and 34 species), the family Equidae (horses; 6 species), the family Anatidae (ducks, geese, and swans; 148 species), the subfamily Estrildidae (Estrildid Finches; 49 genera and 131 species), and the family Phasianidae (quail, turkeys, pheasants; 34 genera and 203

species). Hybridization data are available for only a small portion of the animal and plant families, and much more research could be done.

These changes involved mutations and natural selection, loss (or turning off) of some genetic information, and adaptation to changing environments. Probably, changes in regulatory genes have been an important factor making rapid change possible, since small genetic changes produce relatively large phenotypic effects. Could even the series of titanotheres and horses have resulted from these processes?

Naturalistic theory proposes that existing structural genes accumulated through the action of mutation, recombination, and natural selection. The process is believed to have been facilitated by duplication of genes producing excess genetic material that could then be modified by mutations and eventually become new genes coded for new proteins. Much of the genetic material in organisms consists of "silent DNA" with no known function. Part of this DNA contains pseudogenes which appear to be copies of known genes, but with mistakes in them (Gibson 1994). Pseudogenes and other silent DNA are usually interpreted as duplicated genes that can evolve into new genes.

It is being recognized now that more of the "junk DNA" is functional than previously had been thought (Nowak 1994; Reynaud et al. 1989). We think that this trend will continue, and it will be found that much more DNA is involved in regulation than is currently recognized. Clearly, a vast complex of genes is needed to regulate when and where each protein will be made and in what quantity, the development of each different organ and its growth and integration with other organs, the functioning of the tremendously complex biochemical systems in each cell, as well as controlling such things as how long your fingers will be. There are many more regulatory genes than structural genes, and we predict that, in most organisms, the amount of DNA needed for these genes is much greater than presently recognized.

However, we cannot rule out the likelihood that in some cases mutations may have produced extra copies of genes. For example, it is puzzling why the amount of DNA per organism varies by two orders of magnitude in fish and in insects, and by three orders of magnitude in algae and in angiosperms (John & Miklos 1988, p. 150).

The most important difference between this interventionist theory and megaevolution theory is the ultimate source of the genetic potential present in organisms (Fig. 12.4B). Is it actually possible for complexes

of structural and regulatory genes to originate through mutation, recombination, and natural selection? This requires that the duplicated DNA gradually accumulate beneficial changes that can be selected, and that this process can produce a new gene with a new function. Is it possible for this to occur with no intelligent input, producing not only a new structural gene but also the complex of regulatory genes that recognize and control it? I predict that the answer is no.

Some have proposed that the evolution of resistance to insecticides and new enzymes appearing in laboratory cultures of bacteria, are examples of this process. As our understanding of the details of the genetic material improves, along with more effective techniques for analyzing it, it should become possible to test the theory that mutation and natural selection can produce new genes. And are those actually new enzymes that appear in bacteria cultures or just the activation of genetic potential that was already there but not in use (or used at a low level) before the environment was changed (Opadia-Kadima 1987)?

Research should focus on determining the exact genetic information in organisms used in the research described above so it will be known whether new genes actually appear by the hypothesized process. Perhaps it would also be possible to induce sufficiently accelerated mutation rates to attempt to duplicate the gene-evolution process in the laboratory. Efforts also are being made to develop computer simulations of genetic systems (Maynard Smith 1992). As our understanding of genetic mechanisms improves, perhaps the sophistication of such models could become adequate to test realistically theories of gene evolution.

We propose that any process of genetic change which depends on mutations as the ultimate source of new information tends to produce disorder and will never construct any new gene complexes. Until that prediction can be falsified, the theory of naturalistic megaevolution of higher categories from a common ancestor stands on a weak and shaky foundation.

The evidence suggests that quite a bit of speciation and morphological change has occurred. The reinterpretation of evolutionary genetics presented here is proposed as a step toward understanding the process of change that brought life from the original created state to its present adaptation to modern conditions. We propose that these genetic mechanisms are adequate only to diversify and adapt life from the original created taxa. They cannot produce an increase in the complexity of life. The evidence for a genetic mechanism adequate to produce increased complexity and new body plans is far from compelling.

The most direct source of evidence to test between megaevolution and informed intervention comes from the fossil record. The vertical stratigraphic sequence of fossils from one-celled prokaryotic (cells with no nucleus) organisms in the Precambrian to eukaryotes (cells with a nucleus), invertebrates, fish, amphibians, reptiles, mammals, birds, and, finally, humans, and the associated questions of geologic time with its support from radiometric dating are the real challenges that face interventionists. Consequently, we now turn our attention to geology and the fossil record.

Let's compare two alternate theories of earth history. One is conventional geology. The other, catastrophic geology, is quite different from the multiple-catastrophe theories of the 19th century. It also is not the same as the neocatastrophism that is characteristic of conventional geology today (neocatastrophism—catastrophic geological processes have occurred, but over millions of years). The following comparison of conventional geology (neocatastrophism) and modern catastrophic geology includes comments on the four meanings of uniformitarianism as analyzed by Gould (1984) to illustrate how a catastrophist geologist thinks. For further reading on these topics, consult recent textbooks of physical geology (e.g., Hamblin and Christiansen 1995; Monroe and Wicander 1992, 1995; Press and Siever 1986), historical geology (e.g., Cooper et al. 1990; Stanley 1986, 1993; Wicander and Monroe 1989), sedimentology (e.g., Fritz and Moore 1988; Prothero and Schwab 1996), stratigraphy (Prothero 1990), or structural geology (Hatcher 1995).

Theories of Earth History

Conventional Geology. Geological processes, generally like those observable today, have operated over a time period of several billion years to produce the earth's geological features (Harland et al. 1989). Life has been on the earth during much of its history. The Phanerozoic rocks have formed during the last 570 million years, and the fossil record is a record of the evolution and extinction of life forms through this time and before. Modern geological theory is a modification of Lyell's uniformitarian views and recognizes that Lyell was partly wrong. The term "uniformitarianism," as used by Lyell, actually includes four different concepts. These four aspects of uniformitarianism are defined in Table 13.1, with comments on their applicability to modern geological theory (from Gould 1984).

Catastrophic Geology. The Phanerozoic record was formed during a few thousand years, and much of it during a worldwide geological catastrophe. The major taxonomic groups of animals and plants arose before that event through independent origins (by informed intervention—which is not a testable part of the theory). Much of the fossil record consists of remains of these organisms that were buried in a sequence resulting from the order of events during and after (and maybe before) the worldwide catastrophe rather than from an evolutionary sequence. After the catastrophe, geological processes gradually slowed to the rates more observable today, and significant fossil deposits formed as a result of the progressively less catastrophic events during this time. A significant part of the Cenozoic fossil record, formed after the global catastrophe, includes evolutionary sequences of organisms within the individual created groups. Whether or not the basic structure of the earth and the lower portions of the geological column (e.g., the Precambrian) had a recent origin or has been here for billions of years is a separate question to be dealt with later. Table 13.1 presents my catastrophic geology interpretations of the four aspects of uniformitarianism.

Can Catastrophic Geology Theories Be Tested?

The catastrophic geologist proposes that, at some time in the past, a disturbance in the earth's crust temporarily disrupted the normal relationships between land and water bodies, initiating a period of rapid geologic activity on a worldwide scale. This period of rapid erosion and sedimentation produced a significant portion of the geological column. The geological and geophysical processes occurring during that event determined the characteristics of the rock formations formed at that time and the distribution of fossils in the rocks, and influenced the distribution of radioactive elements in those minerals used in radiometric dating.

A catastrophic theory expressed in this form is a simple descriptive statement. It says nothing about the untestable question of whether God was involved in initiating this geologic event. It does not attempt to explain any process or event that may have operated outside the known laws of geology, chemistry, or physics. This descriptive theory can be used as a basis for defining specific hypotheses concerning the sedimentary processes and the amount of time involved in depositing individual formations or in shaping the earth's landforms. These hypotheses can be tested in the same way that any geologist tests hypotheses.

Table 13.1
Comparison of the Principles of Conventional and Catastrophic Geology and Their Relationship to the Four Concepts in Lyrell's Uniformitarianism (quotations from Gould 1984)

Conventional Geology	Catastrophic Geology
The uniformity of law. The laws of nature have always been the same. "This is an *a priori* assumption made in order to practice science."	*The uniformity of law.* The laws of nature have always been the same. This *a priori* assumption is accepted, but with the recognition that significant portions of natural law may not yet be understood. This testable, descriptive theory about geological processes and rates differs from the majority scientific view in one important aspect: catastrophist theory does not reject a hypothesis just because it implies events in the past (such as informed intervention) that science cannot deal with. If a hypothesis has some testable portions, those fall within the domain of science.
The uniformity of process. "Whenever possible, explain past results" (or past geological events) "as the outcome of causes that are still operating on the earth. Do not invent causes with no modern analogues when present causes can render the observed results." This "is another *a priori* methodological assumption shared by all scientists and not a statement about the empirical world."	*The uniformity of process.* Whenever possible, explain past geological events as the outcome of causes that are still operating on the earth. Do not invent causes with no modern analogies when present causes can render the observed results. This *a priori* methodological assumption is also accepted. Whether the initiation of a worldwide catastrophe was the result of informed intervention is non-testable and outside the domain of science. However, the geological processes occurring before, during and after such an event are assumed to have operated according to known or potentially knowable laws of nature. This catastrophist theory differs from the conventional view only in predicting that when the evidence is all in, it will require more catastrophic explanations for large portions of the geologic record than our modern analogies, and much more catastrophic than even the neocatastrophist views of modern geology.
Rates of geological processes are not always uniform. Modern geology is abandoning the rigid gradualism of Lyell, which insisted that geological processes always acted at a slow, gradual rate. Whether or not any particular rock formation formed slowly or catastrophically must be tested by the evidence, not assumed. This more analytical attitude does not deny the accepted belief that earth history, overall, has covered several billion years.	*Rates of geological processes are not always uniform.* Catastrophist geology theory agrees that whether or not any particular rock formation formed slowly or catastrophically must be tested by the evidence, not assumed.
Nonuniformity of conditions during earth history. Modern geology also does not accept Lyell's original concept that geological and biological processes have always been in a dynamic steady state, cycling endlessly with no direction. The concept of uniformity of conditions can be tested, and the evidence is believed to indicate that there has been an evolutionary progression of life through the ages, and a progression in the development of landforms, plate tectonics, etc.	*Nonuniformity of conditions during earth history.* The concept of uniformity of conditions throughout earth history can be tested; and conditions in the past, when much of the fossil record accumulated, were very different from conditions on the earth today—more different than majority scientific views would expect. The geologic record is the result of a specific sequence of events beginning before the creation of life and leading up to the present day.

Two geologists could be doing research on the same rock formation, perhaps one of the Paleozoic formations in the Grand Canyon. One geologist believes that the formation must have taken a long time—thousands or millions of years—to be deposited. The other geologist believes the formation was deposited far more quickly. They both look for the same general types of data as they study the rocks. Each must analyze his or her data, as well as other published data, and interpret their meaning. When they disagree, each geologist analyzes the other's work and his or her own work and each tries to determine what additional data are needed to clarify the issue. If each is doing good work, the findings will be published in a scientific journal so others can benefit from the work. In time, as more data accumulate, more conflicts will be resolved and the total body of data will favor one explanation. It will point to rapid deposition, very slow deposition, or something in between.

If we are completely fair with the data, eventually the data will tell us which theory is true (unless our inability to go back in time and directly observe what happened limits the data too much). All geologists will use the same observational and experimental procedures in their research. But one primary difference arises in the research approach of catastrophic geologists and other geologists: the catastrophic geologist is confident that when "the data are all in," they will indicate that much of the geologic column was deposited in a short time. A conventional geologist is more likely to have confidence that the data eventually will indicate that all of the geologic column was deposited very slowly or in rapid spurts with long periods of time between. Many would say the data already are conclusive and have disproved the catastrophic theory. However, the catastrophic geologist notes with interest the recent definite trend toward catastrophism that is evident in geology (Ager 1981; Albritton 1989; Berggren and Van Couvering 1984; Huggett 1990).

A number of lines of evidence still challenge the catastrophic theory. Discrepancies between a theory and the available data can arise in at least two different ways: (1) either the theory is wrong or (2) important discoveries are waiting for the diligent researchers who use the theory to guide their research. Interventionists/catastrophic geologists recognize that if their theory is true, significant phenomena have yet to be discovered. Does interventionism stifle research, as some have suggested? Some approaches to interventionism may. But if interventionism is understood correctly and if its predictions of new phenomena waiting to be discovered are taken seriously, it could be a stimulus for vigorous new approaches to research. The scientist who uses the Bible as a source of ideas for developing hypotheses should be able to operate as a successful researcher and, I believe, even have an advantage in generating successful hypotheses. We will review the basic concepts of physical and historical geology and compare how the two theories deal with this evidence.

Types of Rocks

Different geologic processes produce different types of rock and influence the types of minerals that compose the rock (Hamblin and Christiansen 1995, ch. 4-7; Monroe and Wicander 1992, ch. 3-8). Table 13.2 presents the principle types of rocks which, like all rocks, are not specific to any theory. This, basically, is descriptive data and forms a part of the foundation for any geological theory.

Rate of Sediment Accumulation

The average thickness of the sediments on all of the continents is approximately 1,500 meters, and in some places it is much thicker. How long does it take to deposit such sediments? The answer depends on how we look at history or, more

specifically, our theory of geological history. Some may answer that radiometric dating provides an accurate, unambiguous answer. Radiometric dating is considered in the next chapter; but for now, let's examine the evidence in the sediments, independent of dating methods.

Imagine a small river running through a narrow canyon. Recall the story in an earlier chapter of a large reservoir behind a dam. The dam was broken and the suddenly escaping water carried away the remainder of the dam. In a few hours, it enlarged the canyon to several times its original size. Two hundred years later, all memory of the dam and the flood has vanished and a geologist comes to the area. He studies the canyon and measures the amount of sediment in the valley below the canyon, the flow of water in the river, and the sediment load carried by the river. He determines how much sediment is carried out of the canyon in a year. He uses those data to calculate how long it took the river to carve the canyon to its present size and deposit the resulting sediment in the valley.

His estimate of the length of time to carve the canyon would be incorrect, because he was unaware that for a brief but terrifying time the amount of water flow was vastly greater than he observed. From this example, we can derive a simple principle: little

Table 13.2
The Principle Types of Rocks

1. Igneous rocks

Form as molten magma cools to form rock. Examples: granite and volcanic lava. The highest parts of some mountain ranges are formed primarily of granite. A mass of granitic rock also underlies each continent.
Fossil content: uncommon in igneous rock, since hot magma would normally destroy any organisms. Exceptions occur when lava or volcanic ash surround an organism and preserve them. In rare cases, fossils occur in granite.

2. Sedimentary rocks

Form by a four-step process. Older rocks break down to form sediments, such as sand, mud, or pebbles, which are then eroded from upland areas by wind or water. The water or wind transports the sediment to basins where it is deposited in layers (Fig. 13.1). If it is exposed to the right conditions after being deposited, the sediment becomes cemented or compacted into sedimentary rock. Rivers carry sediment until they slow down enough for the sediment to settle out of the water and form layers. This is often a cyclical process— sediments become rocks which yield sediments to form other rocks. The four steps make sedimentary rock: erosion, transport, deposition, and cementation. However, the sedimentary layers do not always become indurated (hardened) into solid rock because the sediments may be in a situation that does not provide the favorable conditions to cement or compact them together.

Fossil content: animals or plants are often buried in the sedimentary layers, so the majority of fossils are found in sedimentary rocks. Even volcanic ash, which has an igneous origin, often is deposited as sedimentary layers. These layers of ash are effective agents for preserving fossils.

When sediments originally are deposited, they usually are horizontal (there are some exceptions) or at least approximately so (law of original horizontality). After they are deposited, they may be tilted by processes that are discussed later.

Representative types of sedimentary rocks are classified by the size of the grains or particles that compose them: shale and siltstone—very small grains; sandstone - larger, sand sized particles; conglomerate—a mixture of fine particles (sand or mud) and larger pebbles rounded by transport in flowing water; breccia—mixture containing angular (not rounded by water transport) pebbles or rocks; and limestone— principally calcium carbonate, in the form of the mineral calcite ($CaCO_3$) precipitated out of ocean water or alkaline rivers, streams, or lakes. Some limestones are an accumulation of the calcium carbonate shells or skeletons of organisms such as corals or molluscs.

3. Metamorphic rocks

Form when rocks are subjected to sufficient heat and/or pressure (perhaps by burial under additional rocks) and chemical changes to alter them into a different type of rock. These altered rocks are called metamorphic rocks.
Fossil content: any fossils are generally destroyed in the process of metamorphism.

water—much time; much water— little time. Thus, if a flood of water on a worldwide scale caused much of the deposition of sedimentary rock, it could have formed much more quickly than what we have observed in modern geological processes. This is obviously an oversimplification of the complex geological principles involved in shaping our earth. It should not be applied uncritically, but it's one way to begin defining the difference between the two theories of geological history (Fig. 13.2).

We have observed the earth's geological processes for only a short time—represented by the solid line in Fig. 13.2. Conventional theory assumes this line approximately extrapolates into the past. Variations in the rate of sedimentation and catastrophic events have happened along the way; but over the long haul, the average rate has been about the same. However, catastrophic geology makes a very different conclusion. Catastrophic theory concludes that in the not-too-distant past, the relative stability of the earth's structure was disrupted, causing a great deal of rapid geological activity over a short time—indicated in the theoretical curve (Fig. 13.2). This activity didn't stop suddenly; it gradually slowed down to the rate of change observed on the earth today. Notice that a transition of perhaps a few hundred or

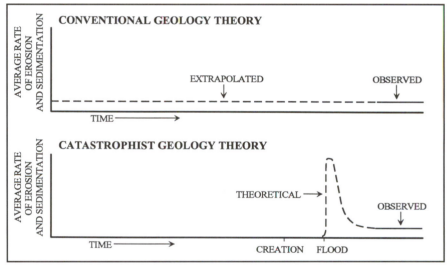

thousand years occurred while the earth was gradually returning to a stable condition. Geological study of the earth, as we know it, has been done since that time.

The processes of rock formation are the same in both of these theories, but the amount of time for the formation of the Phanerozoic rocks, according to the conventional theory (little water—much time) was 570 million years. In catastrophic geology theory (much water—little time), it was only thousands of years and a significant amount of the geologic record accumulated in one year. Do the sediments themselves give any clues to evaluate these two theories?

Sediment can be deposited much faster today than it appears to have accumulated in the geological record (Sadler 1981). Sedimentation rate was measured in meters of sediment per thousand years over different time spans (Fig. 13.3). The sedimentation rate measured for one minute during a flash flood is extremely high; it can be more than one million meters per thousand years. In other words, if a

Figure13.1
A sequence of sedimentary rock formations in the Grand Canyon.

Figure 13.2
A major difference between the two geological theories is in the magnitude of water action on the earth in the past (average rate of erosion and sedimentation) and the resulting amount of time involved in shaping the geological structure of the earth.

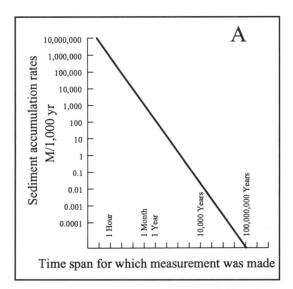

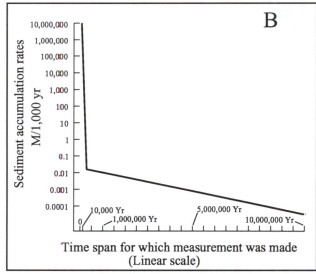

Figure 13.3
Relationship between
sedimentation rates and
time span over which the
measurements were taken.
(A) A graph of the average
sedimentation rates from
Sadler (1981) on the same
log/log scale that he used.
(B) A graph of the same
data, but with time plotted
on a linear scale.

flash flood continued steadily at its peak flow rate for a thousand years, it would deposit sediment one million meters thick. If the measurement is averaged over a few hours, the rate may be lower because flood water doesn't flow continuously at peak rates. A rate measured over a month is significantly lower yet because the flood occurs only part of that time. A measurement taken over several years is probably the most realistic because it reflects the changes in sedimentation through the seasons, and

averages that for several yearly cycles. Such rates actually can be measured today.

Rates of sediment accumulation over significantly longer time spans must be determined in a different way—by measuring the thickness of sediment between two radiometrically dated layers. If we assume that the radiometric dates are correct, the amount of time for the accumulation of this sediment and a rate in meters per thousand years can be calculated.

Sedimentation rates measured from the rocks and dependent on radiometric dating methods are tremendously lower than modern sedimentation rates. Fig. 13.3 indicates that the longer the time span over which sedimentation is measured, the slower the rate of sedimentation. Fig. 13.3A is plotted on a log/log scale. The same data plotted with a log/linear scale (Fig. 13.3B) more clearly reveals that sedimentation rates today are extremely rapid in comparison with the ancient sedimentation rates measured from the rocks. If we carry that logic one step further, it says (1) sedimentation occurred at a much slower rate in the past (an unlikely hypothesis), (2) much of the ancient sediment originally laid down has not been preserved in the record, or (3) the geological time scale is not correct.

The average sedimentation rate measured over a period of one year is approximately 100 meters per thousand years. Rates measured over a time span of a million years average about 0.01 meters per thousand years. One geologist, commenting on these figures, states that "invariably we find that the rock record requires only a small fraction, usually 1 to 10 percent, of the available time, even if we take account of all possible breaks in the sequence . . . the universality and especially the magnitude of the shortfall are startling." He is not giving this evidence in support of a catastrophic theory. He suggests that the data are best explained by many cycles of sedimentation and then erosion of most of that sediment before the next sedimentation begins, although he recognizes that field evidence for those proposed erosional breaks generally are not detectable. (Remember, he is addressing the shortage of sediment that remains after the detectable erosional breaks are accounted for).

Before anyone assumes that this shortage of sediment proves catastrophic geology, we must recognize that if modern sedimentation rates would produce the Phanerozoic rocks in 1 to 10 percent of the time usually assigned to that interval, it would still take 5.7 to 57 million years. Clearly, that's not long enough for the process of megaevolution, but it is much too long for the catastrophic geology time scale. Let's consider another factor. Catastrophic geology does not propose that sedimentation during the worldwide catastrophe was occurring at modern rates, but that it was far more rapid. Fig. 13.4 compares the predictions of the two theories with modern rates, assuming for the moment the following conditions during a world-wide catastrophic flood:

1. All Paleozoic and Mesozoic sediments were deposited during the flood. Cenozoic sediments were deposited postflood.

2. Almost all of the deposited sediment has been preserved in the geologic column. These were not extensive cycles of deposition and erosion.

3. The flood sediments (Paleozoic and Mesozoic) average about 700 meters thick on the continents.

4. During the flood, the volume and speed of flowing water were sufficient to deposit, on the average, the same rate of sediment as an average modern flash flood.

Standard geologic theory

Figure 13.4
A comparison of the expected time to deposit the geologic record from the base of the Cambrian through the Mesozoic, according to two geologic theories and according to modern deposition rates.

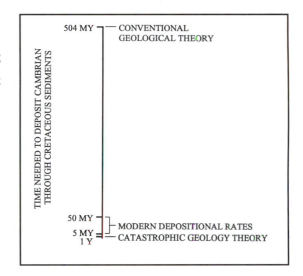

accepts 504 million years as the approximate time interval for the Paleozoic and Mesozoic. The time required by modern depositional rates for those sediments would be only 1 to 10 percent of that, or five to 50 million years. However, that estimate is already adjusted for known erosional breaks in the geological record presumed to represent the passage of time (thousands to millions of years) during which no sediment was preserved. If we simply compare deposition rates from the graph in Sadler's (1981) paper, the average deposition rate in a modern flash flood, measured over one hour, is one million meters of sediment per thousand years (one thousand meters per year). This rate is 100 million times the average rate measured over one million years (0.01 meters per thousand years). Consequently, if the flood water only equaled a modern flash flood continuously covering all the earth, it would take 8.4 months to deposit the existing Cambrian through Mesozoic sediments (Fig. 13.4). Other more challenging factors need to be understood also (e.g., the rate of cooling of igneous intrusions into the sedimentary rocks). That is discussed in chapter 14.

In some places, the sediments are much thicker than 700 meters. In northern Arizona and southern Utah, a section of Paleozoic and Mesozoic sediment is approximately 3,000 m (Strahler 1987, p.159, 279). To deposit this in one year would require flood water three times deeper or flowing 1.7 times faster (sediment-carrying capacity of water varies as the square of its flow rate) than the rate used in the calculation above. This is still well below the maximum flow rate for modern flash floods.

The assumptions used in these calculations are only rough approximations, but they illustrate one of the differences between catastrophic theory and conventional geological theory. In actuality, it is probably more realistic to assume that the water was deeper and was not flowing at a constant rate all the time, but these calculations suggest the possibility that such a flood could deposit the existing thickness of sediments.

Depositional Environments

Geologists also attempt to determine what environment a sedimentary rock was originally deposited in—such as a deep ocean basin, lake, river valley, or desert. They study geological processes in modern environments where sediments are being deposited and compare the characteristics of modern sediments with those of the rocks (Fritz and Moore 1988; Monroe and Wicander 1992, ch. 6, 7, p. 15-20). Since this method is the only one we have access to, it is used by all geologists. A catastrophic geologist probably is more conscious of the limitations of these analogues.

If geological processes in the past occurred on a more catastrophic scale than we observe today, our modern analogues may not be adequate to explain part of the geologic data. As long as we are aware of this limitation, modern analogues can be used in research by scientists of any philosophical orientation. Ultimately, the data should point everyone to the same conclusion, but different philosophical approaches may make different predictions as to what that conclusion will be.

When we compare modern analogues with the rocks, we try to interpret where the sediment was deposited, where it came from, and how it was transported to its site of deposition. The principal types of data that help in reconstructing sedimentary environments are sediment texture, sedimentary structures, facies relationships, mineralogy, and fossil types.

Sediment texture includes grain size, shape, and orientation. The grains may be oriented randomly or in a particular plane by the water current or wind that transports them. Sedimentary structures

are features like cross-beds or parallel bedding. Fig. 13.5 summarizes these features and what they indicate about the environment in which the sediment was transported and deposited (Fritz and Moore 1988, ch. 5).

Facies relationships are the horizontal spatial relationships between different types of sediment deposited adjacent to each other during the same period of time. Figure 13.6 shows a unit composed of sand (sandstone) in one area and mud (shale) in another area, interfingering

Figure 13.5
Summary of the relationship between sediment texture (grain size), sedimentary structures, and the depth and velocity of water flow that produces those features (after Reinick and Singh 1980).

Figure 13.6
Facies relationships in a sedimentary unit showing a transition from shallower-water to deeper-water environment (after Hamblin and Christiansen 1995).

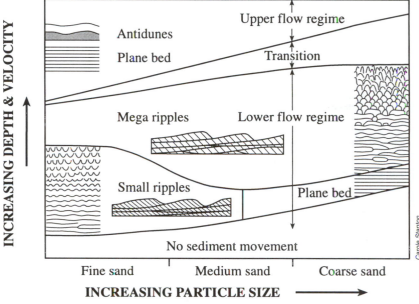

Carole Stanton

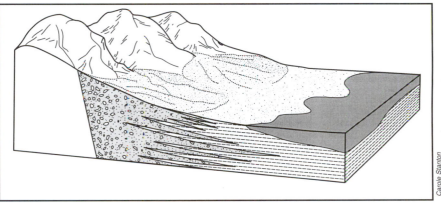

Carole Stanton

where they meet. This resembles deposits that form just offshore in a body of water. Sand is deposited near the shore, and mud is deposited at the same time, but farther offshore. The sandstone and shale are two different facies of the same formation. Many other facies can provide clues to the conditions under which the sediment was deposited.

The types of minerals found in sediments may be important indicators of the depositional environment. For example, sediment containing calcite was deposited in a marine or alkaline lake environment. Dolomite is similar to limestone but forms in hypersaline water—water with higher salt content than normal sea water.

The types of fossils in the rock tell much about the depositional environment as long as we are very careful in interpreting the data. Rock containing marine fossils suggests that the sediment was deposited in the ocean, and an interpretation of the original environment can be constructed (Fig. 13.7). Fossils of terrestrial mammals suggest that the rock was formed in an environment such as a stream bed, a lake (animals could be washed into the lake or even into the ocean), or a floodplain. However, we would need additional evidence, including some detailed characteristics of the sediments and the fossil assemblage, to provide clues to the exact environment.

The Green River Formation in Wyoming includes many fossil fish in association with fossil horse bones (Breithaupt 1990; Grande 1984). In what environment were they deposited? This example illustrates one problem that complicates the interpretation of depositional environments and paleoecology. Probably most fossils (especially vertebrates) were not buried where they lived. They were transported by water and then buried. If organisms from different environments got mixed together while being transported (and apparently this has often happened), the result would be a confusing picture to interpret. In the case of the fish and horses, it is helpful to ask whether it is more likely for a few horse bones to be washed into a lake or for

Figure 13.7
A reconstruction of an Ordovician sea-bottom scene, based on an assemblage of fossils, including trilobites, snails, corals, seaweeds, and straight-shelled nautiloid cephalopods (after Moore 1958).

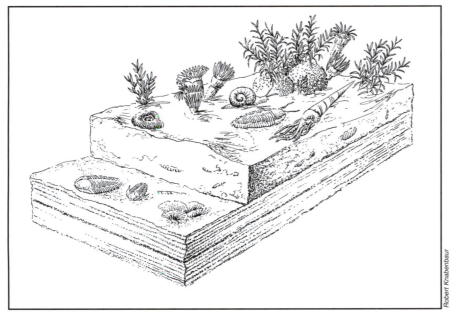

Robert Knabenbaur

millions of fish to be washed onto the prairie? The type of sediment containing the fossils also provides important clues to the environment. In other cases, the history of the various parts of the fossil accumulation may be more difficult to determine.

Fig. 13.8 illustrates some sedimentary environments. A geologist tries to determine which of these environments (or others) is the most likely interpretation of the sedimentary deposit. A catastrophic geologist reaches many of the same general conclusions. Even during a worldwide catastrophe, many of the same processes would still occur. No doubt fluvial (flowing water—rivers and streams) processes (Fig. 13.8A) would occur in some areas, and deep- and shallow-water marine deposition (Fig. 13.8B) would be elsewhere. The catastrophic geologist is aware that these processes in the geological record might have occurred at faster rates and on a larger geographic scale than is observed in most modern analogues and with little or no time between episodes of sedimentation.

Interpretation of Depositional Environments

Several examples of rock formations in the western United States illustrate

Figure 13.8
(A) Details of depositional environments involving fluvial processes—flowing water in rivers, streams, and floodplains. (B) Continental and marine depositional environments (after Hamblin and Christiansen 1995).

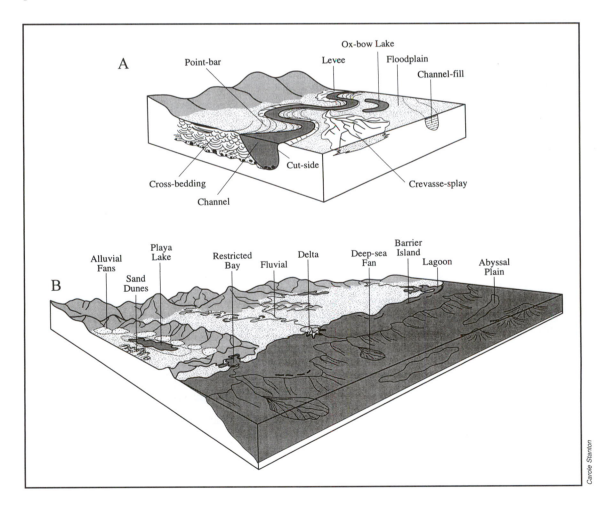

Carole Stanton

the process of interpreting depositional environments. The Green River Formation, covering large areas in Wyoming, Utah, and Colorado, contains very thick sequences of thin layers of shale and tens of thousands of extremely well-preserved fish fossils. This shale contains oil, but so far the commercial process of extracting oil is not cost effective. One story tells of a settler in Colorado who built a log cabin with a fireplace made of the abundant rock on his ranch. He didn't know that the rock was oil shale and would burn; so the first time he built a fire in his fireplace, the house burned down.

The geographical distribution of the Green River sediments, the relationships of the sediments to adjacent facies, the types of sediment, the kinds of fossil fish, and the mineralogy of the sediments indicate that the area was once a series of large lakes. At times, fresh water filled the lake, and at other times, salt water or even hypersaline (higher salt content than the ocean) lakes occurred (Buchheim 1994a and b; Grande and Buchheim 1994). Areas that would have been the middle of the lake reveal large fossil fish; baby fossil fish are found along the ancient lake shore line, along with fossil cattails, insects, and other organisms that would be expected to live along the shore. Some areas have evidence that

rivers were flowing into the lake. Thus many indications show that it was a lake with the animals living in normal ecological relationships. That is how most geologists would interpret it. But since this deposit is in the Eocene, the upper part of the geological column, a catastrophic geologist is likely to conclude that this was indeed a lake that existed during the time after the worldwide catastrophe. He or she would predict that when we understand all of the evidence, it would indicate that the lake was filled in to form the Green River Formation in a much shorter time frame than usually is believed.

The second example concerns the Shinarump Conglomerate, a formation that averages about 50 feet thick and covers more than 100,000 square miles in Utah and neighboring states. This formation is composed of sand and rounded pebbles like those found in stream beds. It looks like a stream deposit. The usual interpretation suggests that a network of braided streams flowed over this area for a long period of time. The stream beds of a braided system frequently change. Some think that as the streams migrated, they gradually covered the entire area with stream deposits (Dubiel 1994). A catastrophic geologist compares this deposit to modern analogues and is sensitive to indications that it may not match a modern depositional environment. For example, is there any place in the world today where streams are depositing sand and conglomerate of quite uniform thickness like this over an area of 100,000 square miles or even close to that? Not one that we know of. Streams make deposits that meander through a valley, but they don't create uniform deposits over thousands of square miles. Explaining this as a catastrophic event over a large area in a fairly short time seems more realistic.

The third example is a type of facies relationship that occurs in many places. Fig. 13.6 shows a cross section in which a sandstone and a shale facies are meeting and interfingering with each other like a series of tongue-and-groove joints. This is a common relationship between adjacent facies. It is generally interpreted that these deposits were formed in an area where, through time, the sea level fluctuated. As the sediments accumulated over the whole area, the sea level relative to the ground surface fluctuated, and thus the shore line moved back and forth across the area. When the sea level was lower, the shore line and the sand deposits were farther to the right. When the sea level was higher, the shore line was farther to the left and the sand was deposited only at the left side—as seen in the diagram.

During a large scale flood, the shorelines might fluctuate as the water moves about. The catastrophic interpretation could be the same as that given above, except that the process occurred more rapidly.

Another interesting possibility could be considered based on experiments in a sedimentation tank. It's very speculative but it doesn't hurt us to stretch our vision once in a while. When sediment accumulates under water near the shore, portions of it may break loose and slide into the water. The sediment mixes with the water to form a dense layer of turbid water which then flows rapidly down the slope. The heavier mixture of mud and water forms a unit, called a density current, and flows downslope under the lighter water above. As the density current flows, it deposits a layer called a turbidite. Other types of sediment or debris flows also produce underwater deposits. In a sedimentation tank in the laboratory, this process produced interesting deposits of interfingering sediments. A hill of sand was made in the water-filled tank before the experiment, and a large amount of mud was stirred up and suspended in the water. Then a density current was produced by releasing a container of fine sand into the water at the top of the hill. This current flowed into the muddy water and deposited a turbidite.

Meanwhile, as the mud settled out of the water, it produced a "mud gradient." The mud was densest at the bottom and was less dense farther up in the water. As the density current swept down the hill, it deposited the sand turbidite along the bottom until it reached the point where the settling mud was denser than the turbidite. At that point, the density current cut right into the muddy water above the denser mud layer and settled on top of it. The mud in the water continued to settle. When another container of sand was released later, its density current cut into the mud a little higher. A series of these episodes would result in a mud deposit interfingering with the sand layers (Fig. 13.9) (Chadwick, personal communication). Obviously, many interfingering sedimentary deposits are not turbidites, but perhaps a similar process produced some of them.

Sometimes "outrageous hypotheses" (Davis 1926) should not be rejected just because they are new. When studying past events, it is especially important to keep our minds open to new possibilities. A process like the turbidite experiment could be significant in a large-scale catastrophic process. However, whether it actually occurred must be evaluated by careful examination of the rocks, not by jumping to conclusions just because it fits our theory.

Overall Pattern of Depositional Environments

Catastrophic geology theory suggests that much sediment was deposited underwater. If so, why haven't geologists found evidence of it? Or have they? A series of maps (Dott and Prothero 1994) presents an interpretation of how much of North America was under water at successive geological periods (Fig. 13.10, Parts 1-6). These scientists don't interpret the maps as pointing to a worldwide flood, but the evidence reveals an interesting picture. They were made by examining the sediments for evidence that would indicate if they were deposited under water or in some other depositional environment.

In the Cambrian, virtually all of

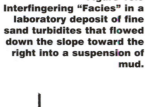

Figure 13.9 Interfingering "Facies" in a laboratory deposit of fine sand turbidites that flowed down the slope toward the right into a suspension of mud.

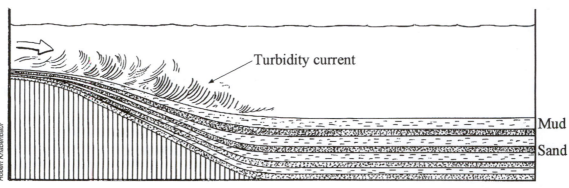

Turbidity current

Mud

Sand

Robert Knabenbaur

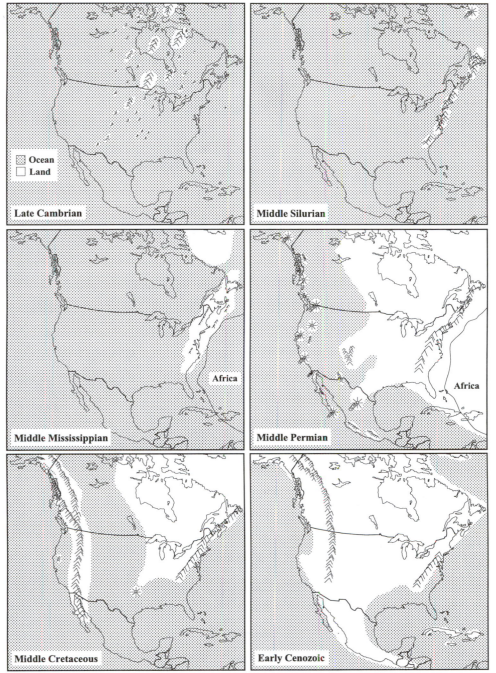

Figure 13.10
Parts 1-6
Maps of North America during successive geologic periods (showing approximately every other period). Shaded areas have been interpreted as being under water at the time those sediments were deposited (after Dott and Prothero 1994). Paleoenvironmental interpretation of eastern Canada (the Canadian shield) is very speculative since it has almost no post-Precambrian sediment.

North America except eastern Canada shows evidence that it was underwater. Eastern Canada is known as the Canadian shield. It has almost no sediments younger than Precambrian. Consequently, on all of these maps, the presence or absence of water over the area is a guess. The Cambrian evidence is consistent with the possibility that much or all of North America was under water. The maps show successive stages through the geologic column from the older rocks to the most recent. As time passed, the amount of land covered by water seems to have fluctuated.

In Late Jurassic and Cretaceous, the water again covered a larger area. During the Cenozoic, evidence of terrestrial environments increases, indicating that the oceans had receded and more of North America appeared to be above water—more like the continent as we know it. However, even these sediments and their terrestrial fossils were almost all deposited by water. During the Pleistocene, a lot of water was locked up in ice and, therefore, ocean levels were lower with more land than now appears.

The evidence indicates that the earth (if North America is representative of the rest of the planet) was covered largely by water sometime in the past. Is this proof of Noah's flood? While it seems to fit what a catastrophic theory would predict, we must avoid that word "proof." Other theories of earth history also can account for these data, but it is fair to say that geologists of different philosophical backgrounds agree that much larger areas of our continents were covered with water at times in the past.

Mountain Building and Landscape Development

We have discussed how different types of rock are formed and how sediments usually are deposited in generally horizontal layers. However, the layers don't always stay that way. Mountains rise up, tilting and folding the layers of sediment (Hamblin and Christiansen 1995, ch. 8, 22; Hatcher 1995, ch. 8-16; Monroe and Wicander 1992, ch. 14); then erosion carves the landscape that we are more familiar with (Hamblin and Christiansen 1995, ch. 13; Monroe and Wicander 1992, ch. 6, 16).

Uplift. Several processes can produce mountains (Fig. 13.11): (1) Folding - folded mountains; (2)

Figure 13.11 Cross sections through several types of mountains.

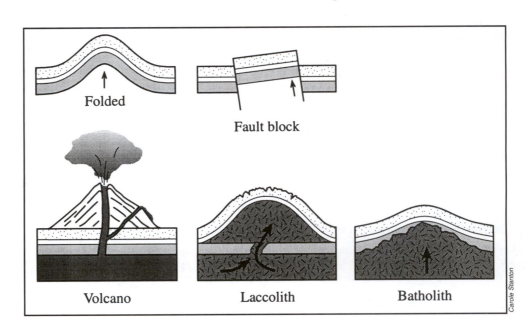

Folded

Fault block

Volcano

Laccolith

Batholith

Carole Stanton

Faulting - fault-block mountains; (3) Volcanism - volcanic mountains; (4) Intrusion - batholiths and laccoliths. Folded mountains arise by pressures in the earth that uplift and fold sediments into permanent wavelike structures. Fault-block mountains form when a section or block of the earth's crust moves up or down along a fault. Volcanoes form mountains composed of the magma that comes up through breaks in the earth's crust as lava flows, or as volcanic ash blows up into the air and drops down to form a volcanic cone. If the magma simply pushes up between two rock layers and does not break through the surface, it may produce a blister-like intrusion called a laccolith. A batholith is an intruded rock mass that has pushed up everything above it to form a mountain. In reality, mountains are often a combination of these processes. For example, the Sierra Nevada Mountains in California are composed of a number of batholiths that have shifted upward along a fault on the eastern side of the range.

How does a catastrophic theory relate to these processes? The types of mountains are geological realities supported by abundant evidence. There certainly is room for differing opinions on details, but any geological theory must incor-

porate these basic processes and mountain-building events into its structure. Cross-cutting relationships may indicate at what point in a sequence of geologic events the mountain arose (Fig. 13.12). This is not the same as determining the absolute age of the mountain in years. That is another question. Cross-cutting relationships indicate the relative age of different structures: in this case, which rocks were there before the mountain appeared and which rocks were formed after the mountain arose. These relative ages of rocks in any one area indicate a sequence of events that any theory of geology must explain. Catastrophic theory recognizes this sequence of events but disagrees on how long ago and how fast these events occurred.

Erosion. During and after the uplift of mountains, water flows down the mountains and erodes valleys and canyons and shapes the mountain into a relatively stable structure. Water always goes downhill; even a catastrophic flood won't change these

Figure 13.12
Cross-cutting relationships illustrating how a sequence of geological events can be determined. (1) A granite base was present, then (2) several sedimentary layers were deposited on the level granite base before (3) an uplift raised the granite and sediments to form a mountain. Subsequent sediments formed after the uplift are horizontal. (4) Three of these new sedimentary layers formed and then (5) were cut by a dike of molten rock. (6) Another dike then cut across the sediments and the first dike. Then (7) more sediment was deposited, and (8) all of the sediments shifted along a fault.

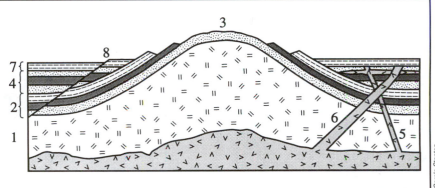

Carole Stanton

laws of nature. Water erosion carves characteristic stream drainage patterns into the landscape (Fig. 13.13) as the water finds its way downslope, eventually to the ocean. How this occurs and how long it takes depends on the nature of the mountain-building process, how fast it happened, and how much water is available to do the job. If the erosion results only from rain water, as a mountain rises very slowly, over thousands or millions of years, the erosion takes a long time. However, if the mountain quickly rises and/or the amount of flowing water increases suddenly and dramatically, the erosion process can occur rapidly.

In modern times, rapid erosion has been observed or inferred in several situations that illustrate what is required to produce it. When Mt. St. Helens erupted in 1980, a large volume of volcanic material was blown out and deposited north of the mountain. Water draining out of Spirit Lake flowed across this volcanic ash, eroding it rapidly.

When erosion occurs on the side of a mountain or through sediment previously uneroded, it continues to cut down through the sediment until it reaches a stable stream profile (Fig. 13.14). High on the slope, the stream valley drops steeply; at lower elevations, it gradually levels off. This stream profile is in equilibrium; sediment in the stream is being eroded and deposited at about the same rate resulting in a very slow net erosion that occurs only very slowly. Events at Mt. St. Helens illustrate what happens when a stream or river has not reached this equilibrium state (Austin 1984). The streams flowing across the new sediment rapidly carved canyons 100 feet deep with typical dendritic drainage patterns. These canyons reached a mature profile very quickly, within a year or much less.

A field near Walla Walla, Washington, has a canyon more than 100 feet deep that was carved through sedimentary rock within a few days when water from an irrigation canal broke through. Also, an eastern Washington area called the Channeled Scablands has a criss-crossed system of large canyons (locally called coolies). These canyons, which are up to 900 feet deep and cut through the

Figure 13.13 Stream drainage patterns. (A) trellis pattern that developed because the ridges of sediment controlled the erosion; (B) dendritic pattern that develops when no geologic structures control the drainage and erosion; and (C) radial pattern developed on a volcano.

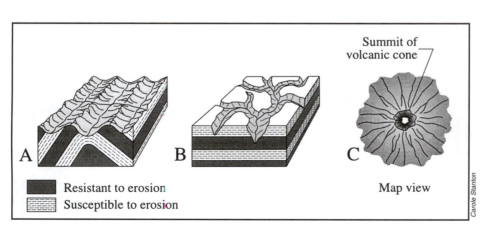

Summit of volcanic cone

A   B   C

Map view

Resistant to erosion
Susceptible to erosion

Carole Stanton

Columbia River Basalt, were apparently carved in a few days during the Pleistocene ice age when giant floods were released from glacial Lake Missoula when an ice dam broke (Bretz 1923, 1927; Baker 1978, 1995). This lake apparently filled up and flooded a number of times, leaving a series of layers of sediment in the flooded areas (Smith 1993).

The processes of erosion that shape the landscape can be observed today and have been an important part of earth history in anyone's theory. A catastrophic theory differs primarily in suggesting that much of the important erosion that has shaped the earth occurred during a major catastrophe and during a still somewhat catastrophic adjustment period afterwards. Such an event would be an ideal situation for rapid erosion and landscape development, slowing down as drainage systems came into equilibrium until they reached the generally stable state and relatively slow pace of erosion on the earth today.

The amount of erosion that has occurred is astonishing. Mountain ranges formed and then largely or completely were eroded away. Some major, existing mountains in North America have experienced heavy

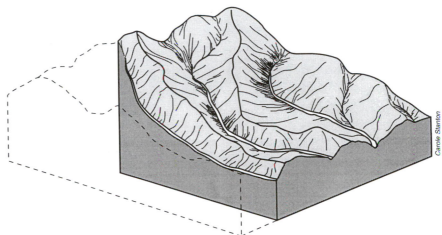

Carole Stanton

erosion. The Rocky Mountains reach maximum heights of about 14,000 feet. But the valleys surrounding the mountains are generally at least a mile high, so the peaks are no more than 9,000 feet above their surroundings. Therefore, the original mountains, before the sedimentary layers were eroded off the mountains and into the valleys, probably were closer to 30,000 feet high (Fig. 13.15) (Love 1960, p. 205). The Appalachian Mountains in eastern United States are no more than 5,000 feet high, usually less, but originally they were as large as the Rocky Mountains and have been eroded down until all that remains are the roots of the original mountains. The catastrophic theory proposes that this significant erosion occurred rapidly during and after the flood when a large amount of water was available to do the eroding.

**Figure 13.14
Cross-section through a mountain with an idealized stable stream profile along the left side of the diagram. Dotted lines outline a part of the mountain cut away to reveal the stream profile.**

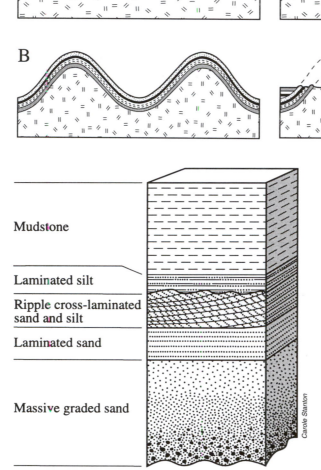

Carole Stanton

Mudstone

Laminated silt

Ripple cross-laminated
sand and silt

Laminated sand

Massive graded sand

Carole Stanton

**Figure 13.15
Cross-sections through the
Rocky Mountains (A) and the
Appalachian Mountains (B),
showing the apparent
original shape, and the
current shape of the
mountains after erosion. The
magnitudes of the original
uplift were approximately
equal, but the Appalachians
are lower because they are
more eroded.**

**Figure 13.16
A complex sequence of
sediments.**

Can This Complex Series of Events Occur Rapidly?

The discussion above proposes that a very complex series of sedimentary deposits were formed, cemented to form rock, uplifted in mountain-building episodes, and eroded to our current landscape—all in a short time. Is this realistic? Fig. 13.16 shows a cross-section through a complex set of sedimentary units. How long would it take to form each of the lower horizontal layers, and then each

of the sloping layers? On top is another series of horizontal layers and a layer of fine mudstone on top of that. Each layer had to be deposited in a manner that allowed it to maintain its identity. How much time is needed after each layer for it to become cemented or compacted before the next layer is deposited?

Some assume that a series of sedimentary events requires a long time. However, the series of deposits shown in Fig. 13.16 is what is called the Bouma sequence—the sequence of sedimentary units that is deposited within a few seconds or minutes as a turbidity current passes over a given spot. As the passing current slows down, it deposits the set of sedimentary structures in the Bouma sequence or some portion of that set (Fritz and Moore 1988, p. 258-265). A complex deposit is not necessarily an indication of a long passage of time.

How long does it take for mountains to form? Modern tectonic processes like movements along faults would take a very long time. Do we have any hard evidence to indicate that it cannot occur rapidly? Because we experience a stable modern world, we tend to assume geologic processes always took a long time. That assumption may not be justifiable.

Today, the overall process of erosion occurs slowly, but it can be extremely rapid in an unstable geologic situation like the eruption of Mount Saint Helens and its aftermath. A global catastrophe, of course, would be the ultimate unstable setting that could yield rapid erosion rates until a new geological balance is reached.

Could sediments become cemented quickly enough to maintain their integrity during all of this rapid upheaval? More research is needed on this question. Some evidence indicates rapid formation of rocks (Wise 1986). Coal has been formed in the laboratory within a year (Larsen 1985), granitic crystals can grow within days (Swanson 1977), and silica-cemented sediment with fossils have been formed in the laboratory within a few months.

Many unanswered questions remain regarding how fast these large-scale geological processes can occur, especially since we have never witnessed such an event. Research in recent decades reveals evidence for increasingly catastrophic geologic processes. I predict this trend will continue. The challenge to a young-earth theory does not seem to be the overall number and complexity of geological events. However, more specific processes do give evidence of requiring time (e.g., growth of stromatolites, deposition of sequences of tidal cycles, growth of coral reefs, recycling of fossils and rocks, etc.). Much more study of such processes and their relation to the geological record is needed.

Glaciation

Another force that has helped to shape the landscape is glaciation (Hamblin and Christiansen 1995, ch. 15; Imbrie and Imbrie 1979; Monroe and Wicander 1992, ch. 18). Geologists can have more confidence in their understanding of glacial processes than is possible in some other areas of geology. No one has ever seen a mountain arise where none was before except for some volcanoes; but in the far north or in high mountain areas, glacial processes and their effects can be observed. One tenth of the earth is still covered with ice, including Greenland, parts of Antarctica, and large areas in northern mountain ranges. The Antarctic ice sheet is 50 percent larger than the United States. Were glaciers much more extensive in the past? Was there really an ice age? To answer these questions, let's review the process of glaciation and the evidence glaciers leave behind. We can then look for this evidence in areas supposedly covered by ice during the ice age.

High up in cold mountain ranges, the snow pack accumulates and compacts into ice. When this ice pack is heavy enough, gravity begins to move it slowly down the mountain. As the ice moves, its weight pushes and drags rocks and sediment along with it, cutting and scouring the underlying rock. This unsorted mass of debris piles up on top of the ice, along the edges of the glacier, and eventually gets deposited along the side of the valley and at the foot of the glacier. The ice continues to move downward and the glacier gets longer until the foot of the glacier reaches an altitude at which the ice is melting as fast as it is moving. It does not get any longer unless the weather turns colder and the ice can move farther downslope. Table 13.3 lists several of the effects that an active glacier has on the land.

We can look for this same kind of evidence in areas where glaciers do not occur today to evaluate the possibility that glaciers were there in the past. It isn't always easy to identify ancient glaciation, since other processes leave some of the same evidence. Deposits of unsorted

sediment (resembling glacial till), striated rocks, and grooved and polished bedrock can be produced by such mechanisms as underwater mud or debris flows or impact of extraterrestrial objects (Crowell 1957; Crowell and Frakes 1971; Dott 1961; Oberbeck et al. 1993; Schermerhorn and Stanton 1963). Consequently, multiple lines of evidence are required to identify ancient glaciation. Landforms—the spatial arrangement of moraines in relation to a U-shaped mountain valley (as seen in Pleistocene and modern glaciation)—are the most definitive, in concert with the other types of evidence.

Modern Distribution of Glacial Evidence

During the Pleistocene ice age, the Sierra Nevada Mountain valleys apparently contained large glaciers like those now found in northern Alaska. In the high valleys of the central Sierra Nevadas are cirque basins along the ridges, just like those produced by glaciers. Down the valleys from those cirques are polished and grooved rock; farther down are accumulations of sediments that exactly fit the characteristics of moraines. These moraines do not occur in small, local valleys, but only in the long valleys that extend far up into the mountains and contain other evidence of glaciation. Moraines are seen most easily along the east side of

Table 13.3
Several of the Principle Types of Evidence Left Behind
by Mountain Glaciers

1. U-shaped valleys. When rivers flow through mountain areas, they carve downward and sediment slumps into the river, producing a V-shaped valley (Fig. 13.17, left). When a glacier moves down a valley, it scours out the sides, producing a U-shaped valley (Fig. 13.17, right).

2. Cirque basins. At the glacier's point of origin, the ice is continually moving down and away from the high mountain ridge. Snow and ice fill in the gap and freeze in the cracks in the rocks. This cracks the rocks even more and, as the glacier moves, the rocks come loose and fall onto the glacier. This process carves out amphitheater shaped basins called cirques, which can be seen at the head of a glacier.

3. Glacial grooves and polish. As the glacier moves down the valley, it carries a large amount of ground-up rock debris and scrapes it against the underlying rock, polishing the rock and cutting grooves oriented along the direction that the glacier is moving.

4. Moraines. The rock debris and soil eroded by a glacier accumulate on the glacier or are pushed along with it. This process does not sort sediment by size of particles or grind off the sharp edges of the rocks as much as flowing water does. Consequently, this unsorted mixture of fine sediment and angular rocks and pebbles called "till" is quite different from water-deposited sediment. Till accumulates along the edges of the glacier in ridges called lateral moraines (Fig. 13.18), at the foot of the glacier in terminal moraines, and where two glaciers meet as a medial moraine. These ridges of unsorted rock debris arranged in specific spatial patterns on and around a glacier are left behind in that pattern in the mountain valley when the glacier melts.

5. Erratic boulders. As a glacier moves, rocks and boulders fall onto the glacier and may be carried far away from their source before the glacier melts, leaving them on the surface. These rocks, called erratic boulders, may be a different rock type from the underlying rock strata.

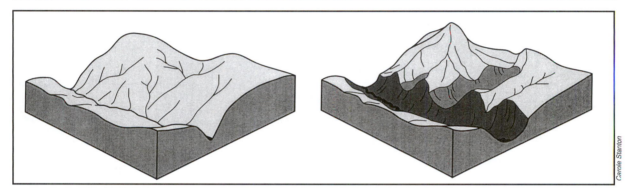

Carole Stanton

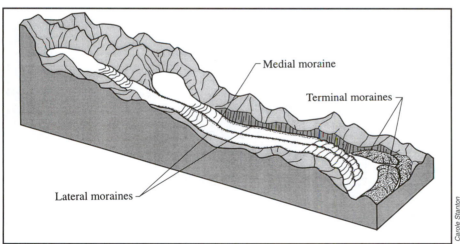

Medial moraine

Terminal moraines

Lateral moraines

Carole Stanton

Figure 13.17
Cross-sections illustrating: (left) a v-shaped river valley, and (right) a U-shaped glacial valley.

Figure 13.18
The arrangement of moraines in a glaciated valley.

the Sierra Nevadas at the mouths of the larger canyons.

Convincing evidence indicates that the Sierra Nevada Mountains were once heavily glaciated. The same evidence also can be found in high mountain ranges in other parts of the world, indicating that ice was once more widespread than it is now.

The ice age, according to theory, not only affected the mountains but also covered extensive northern parts of continents, even where there are no mountains. Does the evidence support this theory of continental glaciation? First, let's recognize that continental glaciation can be observed on the earth today. Greenland and Antarctica support huge continental ice sheets up to a mile thick. Evidence of glaciation can be found in South Dakota and other places. New England has areas of grooved and polished rock, and the grooves just happen to be oriented as one would expect if an ice sheet had moved in from the north. Evidence of glacial action can be found over large areas in northern regions (Fig. 13.19). The types of evidence and their geographic distribution consistently point to the conclusion that essentially all of Canada was covered, and the ice extended down into the United States in Washington, the Dakotas, and extensive areas in northeastern United States. All of Northern Europe, in addition to the mountain ranges, was covered with ice.

The amount of glaciation has fluctuated through history, even after the Pleistocene ice age. Around AD 600, the high passes through the Alps were free of ice. Historical records tell of roads going over these passes from Switzerland to Italy. Today, these same passes are covered with glaciers. From about AD 1450 to 1850, the so-called little ice age occurred (Grove 1988; Montgomery 1990, p. 367; Tkachuck 1983). Historical records from throughout Europe document this period of very cold weather. The Thames River froze over (it doesn't now), along with many other rivers, and agricultural and business records show that warm-

Figure 13.19
The maximum distribution of Pleistocene glaciation.

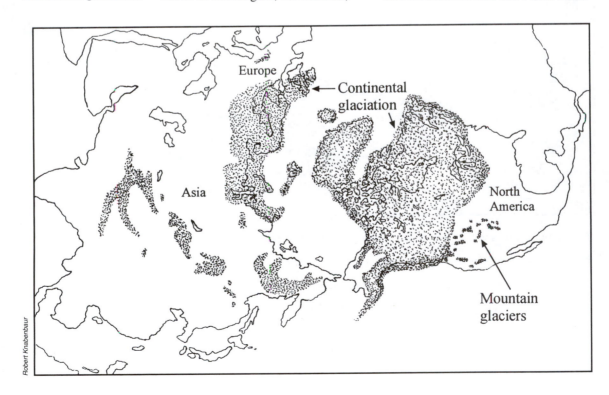

Robert Knabenbaur

weather crops shifted downward in elevation and to the south during that time. Climate, in the long run, is not as stable as we sometimes think.

Two factors are needed to initiate an ice age: (1) cool summers and (2) adequate precipitation. Much of the earth already has cold enough winters, but summers must be cool enough so winter's snow pack does not melt away. Also, winter precipitation must be enough to build up an ice sheet. Large areas of Siberia and Alaska don't show evidence of glaciation. They are cold enough, but apparently they don't receive enough precipitation to generate an ice sheet.

One prominent theory suggests that the cause for these colder conditions is related to factors that reduce the amount of sunlight reaching the earth's surface. During the little ice age, the number of sun spots was greatly reduced. Some believe that this reduces the amount of radiation from the sun.

Large volcanoes can discharge enough volcanic ash into the atmosphere to affect climate. When Mount St. Helens erupted, enormous amounts of ash spewed into the air, and Mount St. Helens was not even a very large volcano. In 1912, Mount Katmai in Alaska erupted, and European weather stations reported lower temperatures for some time afterwards.

The year 1816 is sometimes referred to as the year without a summer (Stommel and Stommel 1979). That year New England had six inches of snow in June and, in fact, reported snow every month of the year. Some think the cool weather was the result of a series of large volcanic eruptions in 1812, 1814, and 1815. These eruptions built up so much ash in the air that it cooled the earth enough to cause the summerless year of 1816. Some have calculated that a drop of a few degrees centigrade in the average annual temperature for the earth is adequate to bring on an ice age. If this is correct, it suggests that if the volcanic eruptions discussed above had been followed by a continuing series of eruptions, another ice age possibly could have begun.

How does catastrophic geology deal with glaciation? The evidence indicates that at one time glaciation was more extensive. A catastrophic theory must account for this. Some individuals attempt to develop theories for the mechanism that would initiate an ice age after the worldwide flood (Oard 1990), implying that conditions at that time were ideal to produce such an event.

Could the extensive volcanic activity during the Tertiary have caused the ice age? Some scientists have considered the possibility. But if the Tertiary covers a period of 60 million years, these eruptions would be too spread out in time to significantly affect world climate. However, if the time span was much shorter, all of this volcanic activity could have created an adequate volume of ash in the air to reduce the sun's radiation and bring on an ice age.

Abundant paleontological evidence indicates that the earth used to be warmer and more uniform in climate than it is now. That evidence is found in Mesozoic and Paleozoic deposits. Even mid-Tertiary deposits hold tropical animal and plant fossils in the arctic (Francis 1991). After that the earth cooled down. A catastrophic theory proposes that the earth was warmer before the flood and cooler after that event. If the earth began to cool off, compounded by extensive volcanic activity, perhaps the setting would be ideal to generate an ice age.

How long would it take to generate the ice age? No one knows for sure, but catastrophic theory predicts that continuing study may indicate that it did not require long ages. Bray (1976), in an article entitled "Volcanic Triggering of Glaciation," states that

> An instantaneous glaciation theory for the formation of the large Pleistocene ice sheets has been proposed by Flohn and by Ives *et al.* It depends on the sudden buildup of a permanent snow cover over sub-Arctic

plateaus. . . . The crucial event in this sudden snow buildup is the survival of snow over a large area for a single summer which then results in a series of feedback reactions leading to the establishment of permanent snowfields and subsequently, icefields. I suggest here that such a survival could have resulted from one or several closely spaced massive volcanic ash eruptions. (p. 414)

Bray is not proposing a worldwide flood as the cause of such an event. His suggestions indicate that at least some scientists feel there is room for discussing how rapidly such an event could begin. There are other lines of evidence that are a problem for catastrophic theory and need much more study, especially the presumed series of Pleistocene climatic cycles with multiple glaciation events (Anon. 1992; Imbrie and Imbrie 1979; Kerr 1992; Winograd et al. 1992).

Stratigraphy - the Geologic Column

The result of the processes we have examined is a sequence of rock formations called the "geologic column" (Fig. 13.20) (Cooper et al. 1990; Hamblin and Christiansen 1995, ch. 9; Stanley 1986, 1993; Wicander and Monroe 1989). Although there is no one place on the earth where rocks representing every part of the geologic column are found in the same sequence, one above the other, a good sampling of the column can be observed at a number of places in different parts of the world. One of these areas is in Arizona and southern Utah (Hamblin and Christiansen 1995, p. 200-201) (Fig. 13.21). The rocks visible at the bottom of the Grand Canyon, in the inner gorge, are Precambrian. At the top of the inner gorge are the first Cambrian rocks. Beginning with the Cambrian, Paleozoic rocks everywhere contain a great diversity of fossils, including all major phyla of animals. Except for some fish scales (Repetski 1978), Cambrian fossil animals are marine invertebrates. The Ordovician and Silurian also contain fish and invertebrate animals, but fish are first abundant in the Devonian which is sometimes called the age of fishes. Trilobites are a widespread, very diverse, and unique part of the fauna of the Paleozoic sediments.

Above the Cambrian formations in the Grand Canyon is a gap, with no Ordovician or Silurian and only a little Devonian. There are formations representing the Mississippian, Pennsylvanian, and Permian. Pennsylvanian and Permian formations contain more invertebrates, amphibians (first found in the Devonian), reptiles (represented by their fossil footprints), and fossil land plants.

All of the Grand Canyon rocks are Precambrian or Paleozoic; but north of the canyon, where the Paleozoic deposits dip toward the north, Triassic deposits are present on top of them. These include the brown Moenkopi Formation and the very colorful Chinle Formation in the Vermillion Cliffs. The Triassic deposits contain dinosaurs and other fossils not present in the Paleozoic rocks. A highway goes north through a gap in the Vermillion Cliffs. Just a little farther north from there, Jurassic rocks appear on top of the Triassic. The Navajo Sandstone is a prominent Jurassic formation, beautifully exposed in Zion National Park, forming part of the cliffs up to two thousand feet. Above that are other Jurassic and Cretaceous layers. Dinosaurs and a number of other extinct reptiles are found only in the Mesozoic era. In some places, the first mammal and bird fossils are also found in the lower to middle part of the Mesozoic. Mesozoic bird and mammal fossils are never common and all represent extinct groups. Of course, the Mesozoic also contains many invertebrate and plant fossils, and the first flowering plant fossils occur in the Cretaceous.

Above the Cretaceous layers in Utah, a portion of the Cenozoic is represented, including the Eocene Wasatch Formation that forms the colorful cliffs and ridges in Bryce Canyon National Park, and a volcanic layer on top of the Wasatch. The most recent sediments are localized

238

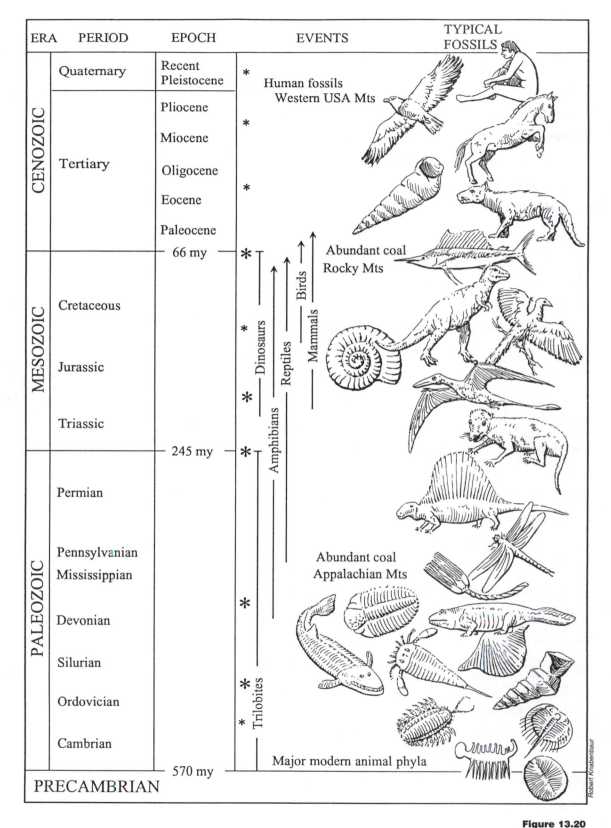

ERA	PERIOD	EPOCH	EVENTS	TYPICAL FOSSILS
CENOZOIC	Quaternary	Recent / Pleistocene	* Human fossils Western USA Mts	
	Tertiary	Pliocene	*	
		Miocene		
		Oligocene	*	
		Eocene		
		Paleocene		
		66 my	* Abundant coal Rocky Mts	
MESOZOIC	Cretaceous			
	Jurassic		*	
	Triassic		*	
		245 my	*	
PALEOZOIC	Permian			
	Pennsylvanian			
	Mississippian		Abundant coal Appalachian Mts	
	Devonian		*	
	Silurian			
	Ordovician		* Trilobites	
	Cambrian		*	
		570 my	Major modern animal phyla	
PRECAMBRIAN				

(Dinosaurs, Reptiles, Amphibians, Mammals, Birds)

Robert Knabenbaur

Figure 13.20
The geologic column and the standard geologic time scale. In this book I am using the radiometric ages from Harland et al. (1989), since it has become an accepted standard. However, more recent work dates the base of the Cambrian at 543 million years and many of the Ediacaran fossils at less than 548 million years (Grotzinger et al. 1995). Some geologists are now using the term Prephanerozoic in place of the more familiar Precambrian.

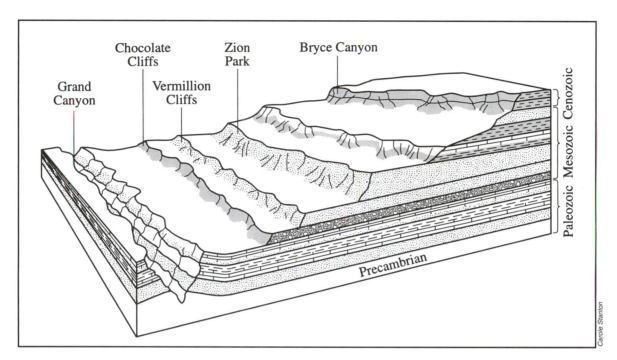

Grand
Canyon

Chocolate
Cliffs

Vermillion
Cliffs

Zion
Park

Bryce Canyon

Precambrian

Paleozoic Mesozoic Cenozoic

Carole Stanton

Pleistocene and Holocene deposits.

Cenozoic deposits, including the Wasatch Formation, contain many fossils of plants, invertebrates, and vertebrates (including birds and mammals), representing types not found lower down. Human fossils are found only in Pleistocene deposits at the top of the geologic column.

Some general trends are seen in the fossil record in the Grand Canyon and elsewhere. The Paleozoic (especially lower Paleozoic) represents predominantly marine environments, the Mesozoic is a mixture of marine and terrestrial, and the Cenozoic represents mostly terrestrial environments. A high percentage of fossils in the Paleozoic are in extinct groups, with the percentage of modern groups increasing toward the upper part of the fossil record (Fig. 9.18). Trends also appear in the

abundance of rock types. For example, limestone is abundant in the Paleozoic and Mesozoic, but its amount drops off higher in the column; very little limestone is forming today.

In northern Arizona and Utah, successive rock layers are exposed in a series of cliffs or hillsides. Fig. 13.21, a cross section through that area, shows the layers dipping down to the north, each layer extending underneath the next exposure above and to the north of it.

Besides exposed rock layers, oil wells can also confirm the geologic column. When an oil well is drilled, bits of rock are brought up from the well. Study of these fragments reveals that the rock layers are underground just as would be predicted from observing the sequence of layers in canyon walls. By using drilling rates,

Figure 13.21
North-south cross section through northern Arizona and southern Utah, showing the sedimentary rocks that form the geologic column in that area.

geologists can predict when the drill will hit a specific layer.

In the Grand Canyon region and in other places, the major parts of the geologic column are exposed in order, layer upon layer. In still other places, only a part of the column is present. Where large portions of the column are represented, the layers with their fossils are found in a consistent sequence, unless faults and overthrusts have caused layers to be moved around.

The sequence of fossils in the rocks apparently is real. Whether we prefer catastrophic geology or conventional geology, the geological column is still a valid description of nature's history book. In fact, the original study and description of the divisions of the geologic column were done largely by creationists. Later, as scientific theories changed after the work of Lyell and Darwin, the original description remained essentially correct. What changed was the interpretation of how the rocks and fossils got that way (Raup 1983). Conventional geology says that the column is the record of 570 million years of geological activity and biological evolution, from the bottom of the Cambrian to the present. The catastrophic geologist says that, at least from the beginning of the Cambrian, the geological record has formed very rapidly. Much

of it (except the upper portion) is a record of activity during a global catastrophe, not of evolutionary time. Some suggest that lower Paleozoic sediments may have formed before the global catastrophe. More research is needed on this point.

Fossils—the Record of Life

How do fossils get preserved? Why do some organisms decay and disappear while others become fossils? In the ocean, many organisms (including mollusc shells, coral, fish, and floating hard-shelled plankton) die and fall to the ocean floor. Other organisms die in lake, stream, or terrestrial environments. If sedimentation occurs and covers them quickly enough, they are likely to be preserved as long as that sediment is not eroded away again. The sedimentation that buries them must be rapid, since animals or plants decay and disintegrate if not quickly preserved. Even if they are in an environment with no oxygen, anaerobic bacteria cause decay unless the specimens are buried rapidly (Allison and Briggs 1991, p. 29-58). Fossils of soft-bodied animals or plants do not form unless they are covered and mineralized within hours or a few days. How soon after fossil organisms were buried can be estimated from the nature of the fossil (Allison and Briggs 1991). A vertebrate animal with its skeleton still articulated must have been buried before decay progressed far enough to separate the body parts—at least within days or weeks, depending on the animal. Most fossils that have soft tissues preserved must have been buried within hours after death. Fossils of intact but scattered bones indicate that the animals decayed and the bones were transported from their original location before burial, but they were not subject to extensive weathering or physical damage. Bones or shells that are badly broken or abraded indicate lengthy exposure and/or transport.

The study of the processes between death and fossilization of organisms is called taphonomy. The basic processes are agreed upon by everyone, no matter what their philosophy. The better preserved a fossil, the more quickly it was taken out of the biotic environment by burial and/or rapid mineralization.

and burial) rather than an evolutionary sequence. This difference is explained by comparing the way the two theories interpret the fossil record. In Figure 13.22, the width of one dark band (biota) indicates the number of groups of living animals on the earth at successive times. The width of the other dark band (fossils) indicates the number of groups of animals that were preserved as fossils at each level in the geological column. According to conventional theory, the band representing biota widens as it goes upward because, as millions of years passed, adaptive radiation occurred in the groups of animals that were living on the earth—evolution produced many new families, genera, and species.

Beginning in the early Cambrian, a number of phyla of living invertebrates were present. As time passed, these animals evolved and adapted to many additional ecological niches.

Figure 13.22
The fossil record as a record of megaevolution. The width of the band on the left is a relative indication of the number of taxa of animals present on the earth at successive times. The diagram at the right represents the number of taxa preserved in the fossil record during the same time periods. There were several mass extinctions of life, and an adaptive radiation after each one, with many new groups of animals evolving. Arrows indicate passage of organisms from biota to the fossil record. The width of the two bands is not to scale. The biota band should be many times wider than the fossil record band.

The Fossil Record, Taphonomy, or Evolution?

An important implication of catastrophic geology is that most of the animal and plant assemblages forming the fossil record represent a taphonomic sequence (sorting by circumstances of death

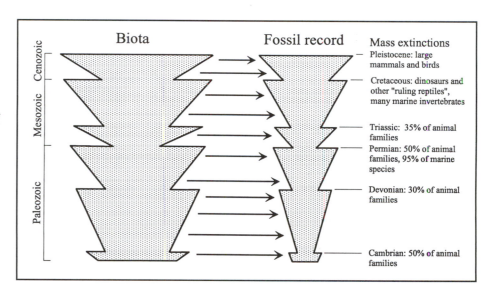

The result was an increase in diversity with many new families and genera. Then, some environmental factor caused many of these to go extinct at the end of the Cambrian. The animals that survived this mass extinction again underwent adaptive radiation until another mass extinction occurred. This process continued through the ages to the present time. At each successive time in earth history, a percentage of the living genera became incorporated into the fossil record as individuals died and were preserved. The width of the fossil band indicates the number of fossils found and is indicative of the relative number of genera alive at successive times in earth history. On a smaller scale, when the animals within a genus or species exhibit progressive change from one strata to the next, as illustrated in Fig. 13.23, it is interpreted as an example of evolution through time.

Fig. 13.24 is a catastrophic geology interpretation of the same data. For the sake of illustration, we will assume that the Paleozoic and Mesozoic were deposited during the global catastrophe and most of the Cenozoic was deposited after the catastrophe. According to this theory, at the beginning of the Cambrian (beginning of the global catastrophe), a very rich biota was living on the earth, including all of the animals represented in the Paleozoic, Mesozoic, and perhaps part of the Cenozoic fossils. Thus, the band labeled biota is very wide at the base. Many of these animals lived in habitats that existed on the earth before the catastrophe but no longer exist because of changed conditions. When the catastrophe began, some types of animals in the biota began to die and to be incorporated into the fossil record. As the Paleozoic deposits accumulated, more and more types of animals, affected by the rising water, added to the fossil deposits. At the end of the Cambrian deposits, some critical stage in the global catastrophe

Figure 13.23
Changes in a fossil animal lineage through time in the fossil record (after Simpson 1953b).

Figure 13.24
The fossil record as primarily a taphonomic record. The band on the left represents the number of genera and species of animals alive on the earth at successive time intervals during and after the flood. The band on the right represents the number of genera and species preserved as fossils at the same successive time periods. Arrows indicate passage of organisms from biota to the fossil record.

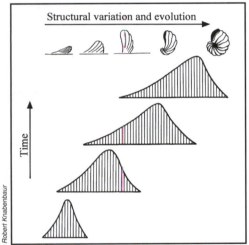

Structural variation and evolution

Time

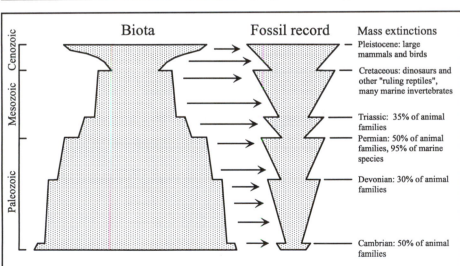

Biota	Fossil record	Mass extinctions
Cenozoic / Mesozoic / Paleozoic		Pleistocene: large mammals and birds
		Cretaceous: dinosaurs and other "ruling reptiles", many marine invertebrates
		Triassic: 35% of animal families
		Permian: 50% of animal families, 95% of marine species
		Devonian: 30% of animal families
		Cambrian: 50% of animal families

was reached, and the last representatives of a number of taxa entered the fossil record. Either all members of these groups had been killed or conditions were no longer favorable to their fossilization. This caused a reduction in the diversity of organisms preserved as fossils. The rising water began to affect previously undisturbed habitats. New types of animals began to be transferred from the biota to the fossil record. The process proceeded as before, until a new crisis was reached. This occurred several times. As a result, the number of groups of animals still alive on the earth gradually decreased throughout the catastrophic process. The sequences of small changes illustrated in Fig. 13.23 resulted from sorting of the organisms by the global catastrophic process, not from speciation.

At the beginning of the Cenozoic, the main part of the catastrophe was over and animals began to spread over the earth again and adapt to the new ecological situations they encountered. Adaptive radiation, in fact, did occur at this time, and the last part of the fossil record documents this sequence of evolutionary events, as discussed in chapters 8 and 12. A reasonable prediction of this theory is that the fossil record is a substantially complete sampling of the types of animals that lived on the earth before the catastrophe began.

The two geologic theories we are comparing use the same data and research methods. They agree on many basics of geological theory and even on a lot of catastrophic geologic activity. One difference stands out in bold relief: the amount of time proposed for the Phanerozoic record—thousands of years compared to 570 million years. How could the data allow such an enormous variation in interpretation?

Many say the data don't allow it; the data point to hundreds of millions of years of geologic time for the fossil record. Nevertheless, my philosophical convictions lead me to predict that as our understanding of the geologic record improves, the balance will shift until the catastrophic theory is best able to explain the data. Even now, the data offer serious challenges to the conventional neocatastrophic theory as well as to catastrophism. If we had all of the data, they would point clearly in one direction. The data available now do not, indicating that many significant discoveries yet await us. Catastrophic theory will succeed only when diligent scientific research

and honesty in dealing with the data are practiced as the theory is utilized for developing testable hypotheses.

The evidence related to geological time is discussed in three categories: (1) scientific trends consistent with or even favorable to catastrophism that are also compatible with neocatastrophism (these lines of evidence are helpful in developing catastrophic theory but are not proof or even necessarily strong evidence for it); (2) evidence against a catastrophic time scale; and (3) evidence against conventional neocatastrophic interpretations of geologic time.

Evidence Favorable to Catastrophic Geology and Compatible with Neocatastrophism

For a century after Lyell, catastrophic interpretations of geologic data were not given serious consideration. The accumulating data finally forced a reconsideration, and the recent trend toward accepting more catastrophic interpretations moves in the direction predicted by catastrophists (Fig. 14.1).

The important question is whether the accumulating evidence will favor a continued strong trend in that same direction or will stop short of pointing to an extensive catastrophe on a global scale. Catastrophism does not rule out any of the possibilities in Fig. 14.1 and suggests that the data for some significant portion of the geologic record are best interpreted by the highest level of catastrophic action.

Geologist J. Harlan Bretz in his study of the Channeled Scablands in Washington state (Baker 1978, 1995) began to break the hold of Lyell's rigid gradualism in geology. This network of channels in eastern Washington are carved hundreds of feet into the Columbia River Basalt. Bretz saw evidence that this was the work of a cataclysmic flood. Resistance to his hypothesis was determined for more than two decades. It finally became clear that Bretz was right—the channels of the Scablands were carved by the sudden draining of about 2,000 cubic kilometers of water from Lake Missoula (Fig. 14.2) when a glacial dam failed. Acceptance of the reality of this event, the great Spokane flood, opened the way for the recognition of

other catastrophic events in geologic history that previously had been overlooked (Albritton 1989; Berggren and van Couvering 1984; Huggett 1990).

In the Atlantic Ocean near Iceland, a new piece of land appeared as a volcano reached above the water and formed the island of Surtsey (Fridriksson 1975). A geologist visiting the island soon after it was formed commented that processes that usually take thousands of years happened on Surtsey in days or weeks. The reason is at least partly apparent. The island formed in the ocean with wave action constantly at work, carving cliffs and beaches and other geologic features. Surtsey shows us how quickly some geologic processes can occur when an abundance of water energy does the work and an abundant input of sediment occurs, as would be the case in a global catastrophe.

Turbidites (Hamblin and Christiansen 1995, p.130-132) are a significant feature of the geological record. Turbidity currents can flow down very low angle slopes or even on the level after they develop momentum. These flows have produced modern submarine fields of turbidites covering thousands of square miles at the mouths of some large rivers. A single turbidite covering nearly 3,600 sq. miles has

Figure 14.1 Sequence of increasing levels of catastrophic processes.

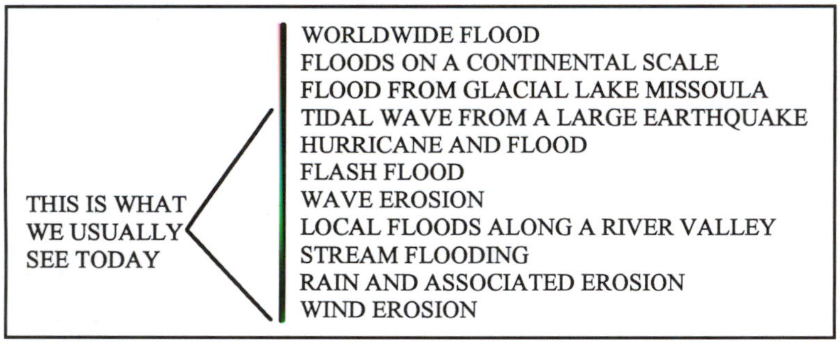

THIS IS WHAT WE USUALLY SEE TODAY

WORLDWIDE FLOOD
FLOODS ON A CONTINENTAL SCALE
FLOOD FROM GLACIAL LAKE MISSOULA
TIDAL WAVE FROM A LARGE EARTHQUAKE
HURRICANE AND FLOOD
FLASH FLOOD
WAVE EROSION
LOCAL FLOODS ALONG A RIVER VALLEY
STREAM FLOODING
RAIN AND ASSOCIATED EROSION
WIND EROSION

been identified. Submarine fans of turbidites and other sediment flows cover 12,000 sq. miles off the mouth of the Mississippi River, 8,000 sq. miles at the Hudson River, and 20,000 sq. miles at the Congo River (Reinick and Singh 1980, p. 468-474). Since the discovery of turbidites, many thousands of sedimentary deposits have been reinterpreted as turbidites. This significant trend has been called the turbidite revolution (Walker 1973). Turbidites are compatible with neocatastrophic theory; and are consistent with the rapid deposition expected by catastrophists.

In 1859, geologist John Wesley Powell and his men were the first known persons to travel by boat through the Grand Canyon. On a subsequent trip in 1871, they took many photographs. In 1968, another geologist, E. M. Shoemaker, made

the same trip and found many of the same camera positions from which Powell took his photos. Comparison of the two sets of photos taken 97 years apart indicate that very little change occurred during that time (Stephens and Shoemaker 1987). Most of the same rocks are in the same places with the same cracks they had in 1871. However, one pair of photos of the same spot in a branch of the Grand Canyon shows a dramatic change. A large volume of rock has been removed from along the river, and other large, new deposits appear. This change occurred recently during a single flash flood. These observations led Shoemaker to entitle a seminar presentation "Nothing Happens in the Grand Canyon Except During a Catastrophe." This is just one example of a general recognition that many geological features form

Figure 14.2
Map of Glacial Lake Missoula and the Channeled Scablands which were carved by the Spokane Flood, initiated by the failure of a glacial dam (after Clark and Stearn 1968).

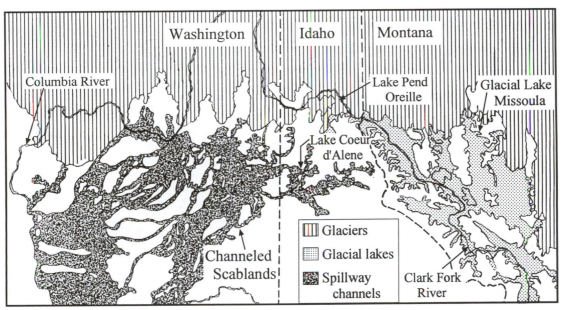

Robert Knabenbaur

rapidly, and then nothing much happens until the next catastrophe. Catastrophic theory goes farther and suggests that, in parts of the geologic record, very little time intervened between these catastrophes.

Megabreccias are sedimentary deposits in which angular rocks (clasts) greater than one meter in diameter occur in a matrix of finer material and smaller rocks, which may or may not be angular. Chadwick (1978) reviewed the literature on a number of very impressive megabreccia deposits—most readily explained by catastrophic theory. Scientists believe most of these deposits occurred under water where buoyancy could reduce the weight of the rocks by a third and thus reduce friction. Some turbidity currents carry large rocks along with them. Kuenen (1950) estimated that clasts up to 100 metric tons can be moved by turbidites. Turbidites containing clasts more than one meter in diameter are found in several countries including western United States, Arabia, and the New Hebrides.

Debris flows are slower, less fluid flows that also do not require a steep slope and can carry clasts of apparently unlimited size. Table 14.1 lists a number of impressive examples of such exotic blocks that have been moved long distances, often tens of kilometers, and up to several hundred kilometers (Chadwick 1978; Conaghan et al. 1976).

During much of the geologic record, large areas of the present continents were low and flat and covered by shallow epeiric seas where abundant marine life was preserved in the accumulating submarine sediments. That is how neocatastrophism interprets the data. Another hypothesis is that the epeiric seas were actually the ancient ocean basins that filled with sediment during the global catastrophe.

Evidence Against a Catastrophic Geology Time Scale

Some mountains are formed by an enormous mass of molten magma intruding into overlying sediment, forming a body of igneous rock called a laccolith (Fig. 13.11). How long does it take for the molten laccolith to cool after it has formed? Some may remember from physics class that some materials gain or lose heat much more slowly than others.

In Hawaii, lava flows several years old are still warm because rock loses heat so slowly. Could those mountain-sized laccoliths already be cool if they formed only a few thousand years ago? This line of evidence seems to indicate a very long time for earth history. Perhaps the earth was here for a long time before life was created, and the laccoliths formed during that period.

That answer doesn't work where cross-cutting relationships indicate that laccoliths formed after some of the Phanerozoic fossil-bearing rocks were formed. This question clearly needs further study. Another question is how the cooling time of laccoliths would be affected if they formed under water.

Specific features of the geologic record seem to require longer time periods than catastrophic geology allows for. Some of these features have been reinterpreted during the rise of neocatastrophism and no longer pose a problem. Others still seem to argue for long periods of time. Coral reefs, stromatolites (algal reefs), or bioherms (similar to reefs) are structures that take at least hundreds of years to grow. If fossil reefs are in their original position of growth at many stratigraphic levels in the fossil record, they present a powerful argument against catastrophic interpretations for that portion of the record (Roth 1979). Many deposits that once were interpreted as reefs have been reinterpreted as debris flows or other non-reef structures. Some large reefs apparently have been transported into position from somewhere else and deposited as megabreccias (which could have grown before the global catastrophe) (Conaghan et al. 1976). Other fossil reefs are still interpreted

Table 14.1		
Large exotic blocks moved by debris flows or slides.		
Location	Geologic age	Size of blocks
Peru	Eocene	10-15 m in diameter, 5000 metric tons
Texas	Paleozoic	30 m in diameter
Oklahoma	Pennsylvanian	100 m in diameter
Venezuela	Tertiary	100 m in diameter, 30 m thick, 1 km long, over 100 m thick
Timor	Miocene	800 m in diameter
Switzerland	Tertiary	500 m long, some overturned
Arabia	Cretaceous	1,600 sq. km, 1,000 m thick
Australia	Devonian	Algal reefs up to 1 km across
Italy	Tertiary	blocks up to 200 sq. km, some upside down
Greece	Tertiary	up to several km long, many upside down

as reefs in position of growth, posing a problem for catastrophism.

Additional features that also seem to require considerable time include stromatolites (Cooper et al. 1990, p. 229-233; Stanley 1993, p.70-71), the several advances and retreats of the Pleistocene glaciers (Imbrie and Imbrie 1979), long series of tidal cycles in Paleozoic sediments (Archer and Kvale 1989; Archer et al. 1995; Brown et al. 1990), and others. Stromatolites are mound-like structures formed by cyanobacteria that begin to grow on rocks or other objects and then form layer after layer as sediment collects on the sticky cyanobacateria. It presumably takes many years to grow a reasonably sized stromatolite.

The sediments containing tidal cycles seem to have been deposited three or four orders of magnitude faster than previously thought (Archer and Kvale 1989; Brown et al. 1990). However, they still appear to contain the record of deposits from ocean tides over several years; thus it seems these deposits could not have occurred during a one-year catastrophe.

Another set of problems can be summarized by asking how a global catastrophe could produce the precision sorting of fossils and sediments that are found in the geological record. More adequate answers are needed for these questions and others like them.

The most serious problem faced by the catastrophic theory is radiometric dating with its 570 million years of time for the Phanerozoic (e.g., see Dalrymple 1991; Harland et al. 1989). Before discussing the implications of these dating methods, let's review the basic principles involved in radiometric dating. All radiometric methods depend on the fact that some isotopes (a particular form of an element) are unstable. Over a period of time, the radioisotope (the unstable parent element) breaks down to form some other element (the daughter product). The rate at which this radioactive decay occurs can be determined experimentally and always follows the same type of decay curve (Fig. 14.3). For example, potassium (^{40}K) decays to argon (^{40}Ar); and in a particular length of time, called the half life, one half of the ^{40}K decays to ^{40}Ar. Intuitively, we might think that in the second half life the rest of it will decay, but not so. In the second half life, half of what is left will decay, and so on, producing the decay curve shown in Fig. 14.3. The half life of unstable elements varies from fractions of a second to millions of years. Those with short half lives are not useful for dating purposes. The half life of carbon 14 (^{14}C) is about 5,730 years; for ^{40}K (potassium), about 1,300 million years. If we can determine the ratio of parent to daughter isotope in a rock sample, we can determine where that ratio fits on the decay curve. That position indicates the age of the rock, if the assumptions of the method are correct and if the rock meets the conditions for valid use of the dating method.

^{14}C dating is different in some important ways from the other

Figure 14.3
The radioactive decay curve illustrating the concept of the half life.

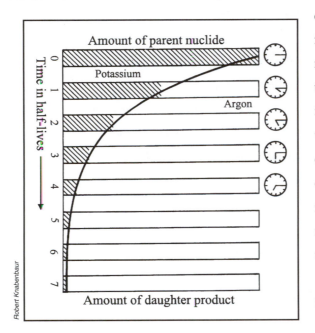

Robert Knabenbaur

methods. Most carbon is ^{12}C, which is stable and is not the source of ^{14}C. ^{14}C originates in the upper atmosphere when cosmic rays strike nitrogen molecules, leading to a change of nitrogen atoms into ^{14}C, some of which combines with oxygen to form carbon dioxide (CO_2). These molecules circulate down into the lower atmosphere (Fig. 14.4). Over time, the ^{14}C, including the atoms that are part of CO_2, decay back to nitrogen. The production and decay of ^{14}C are apparently in equilibrium, so that the ratio of ^{14}C to ^{12}C in the atmosphere is constant. When plants take in CO_2 and use it to synthesize new molecules and plant tissue, they incorporate both the ^{14}C and ^{12}C. Animals eat the plants and, as a result, all live plants and animals contain ^{14}C. A plant or animal no longer takes in fresh ^{14}C after it dies, so the amount of ^{14}C that it contains gradually diminishes as it decays to nitrogen. If we measure the number of radioactive disintegrations per minute in a standard amount of dead tissue and compare it with the decay curve for ^{14}C, we can determine the length of time since the organism died.

The nature of this method places some limitations on how it can be used.

Since it depends on the presence of carbon incorporated from the atmosphere into plants, it is used only for dating plant and animal remains. It can be used only if the organic matter has not been replaced by minerals. Also, because the half life is only 5,730 years, it can be used only for dating fossils less than about 30,000 years old (90,000 with the AMS ^{14}C method). In other words, it only can date fossils in Pleistocene or younger deposits, not fossils older than Pleistocene.

All of the other radiometric dating methods utilize radioactive elements that are found in minerals, not in plant or animal tissue. So they can date certain minerals, but most fossils can only be dated with these methods by dating a layer of lava or other igneous rock near the fossil and

Figure 14.4
The process that produces ^{14}C and incorporates it into plants and animals.

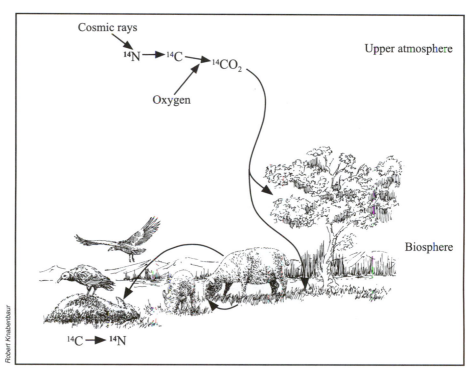

Robert Knabenbaur

using that date to estimate the age of the fossil-bearing sediments. Also, the half lives of these elements are millions of years long, so they are used for dating older materials than can be dated by ^{14}C. The most common of these methods are uranium-lead, potassium-argon, and rubidium-strontium. Miall (1990, p.120-142) contains a helpful summary of the use of these methods in geological dating. Most fossil-bearing rocks cannot be dated with radiometric dating methods. The age of these Phanerozoic deposits is determined primarily by biostratigraphy. This means that the fossils in the rock and in the formations above and below them are compared with the sequence of fossils in other locations to see where it fits in the sequence. Of course, the fossils found in rock can only be used for comparing the sequence of rocks in different locations and don't indicate the age in years of the rocks. Radiometric methods are used wherever possible to date minerals, generally in igneous rocks. These dates provide a time calibration for the biostratigraphic scale. Radiometric dates can be off by several percentage points, even for the more reliable dates; but if the assumptions these methods depend on are correct, they indicate that the

Phanerozoic record occupied well over 500 million years.

Evidence Against a Neocatastrophic Geology Time Scale

Several lines of evidence contradict the time scale and other conditions inherent in uniformitarian or neocatastrophic geology theories. Roth (1986) presented data indicating that rates of sedimentation in the ocean and erosion of the continents are inconsistent with the geological time scale. The amount of sediments being eroded from the continents and deposited in the oceans can be estimated from measurements of the sediment load in major rivers. Estimates range from 8,000 to 58,000 million metric tons/year. From this type of data, estimates of the required length of time to erode our continents to sea level vary from 10 to 34 million years, with 10 million years being a widely accepted figure in the geological literature. The higher rates include adjustments for the assumed increase in recent erosion rates caused by human agricultural practices. Even the slower erosion rates are difficult to reconcile with current geological theory since our continents have not been eroded to sea level as they should have been. Also, there are still mountain ranges like the Appalachians in North America that have been here for about 300 million years, according to radiometric dates, without being eliminated by erosion.

The suggestion that the mountains still exist because of continued uplift from below doesn't seem to be an adequate explanation (Roth 1986). If the uplift of the continents had been sufficient to support such a cycle of continued erosion and deposition, the lower parts of the geological column should have been destroyed, which is clearly not the case. On the other hand, if only the mountains had been continuously uplifting, the sediments deposited along the flanks of the mountains would show that since they would be pushed up along with the mountains. The continuity of the geological record through the Phanerozoic seems to tell us that there has not been a series of cycles of erosion and uplift adequate to begin to account for the discrepancy between current erosion rates and the existence of the continents and mountains. If climates in the past had been much drier than at present, erosion rates would have been a little lower. But it seems more likely that the average conditions have been wetter in the past.

As the rivers erode the continents, the sediment ultimately ends up in the ocean. Conservative estimates of the amount of sediment reaching the ocean would lead to the ocean basins being filled with sediment in

114 to 178 million years (Roth 1986). That has not happened. In large areas of the ocean basins, the sediment thickness averages only a few hundred meters. Major river deltas are not nearly as large as they should be. One suggested solution to this problem is that the sediments are subducted into the deep ocean trenches and carried down into the mantle along plate margins, as proposed in the plate-tectonics model. However, subduction does not occur fast enough to keep up with the sediment flow into the oceans. Also, the sediments from the earth's large rivers are not being deposited in basins containing subduction zones.

Another problem with this type of recycling is that the chemical composition of the sediments does not match the composition of the granitic crust. The rates of erosion of continents and sediment accumulation in the oceans seem to fit better with a much younger Phanerozoic record than is currently accepted by neocatastrophic theory (Roth 1986). As rivers erode, they also carry salts to the ocean. Austin and Humphreys (1990) argue that the amount of salt in the oceans is consistent with an age of the oceans less than about 60 million years, and perhaps much shorter.

Now let's consider a different aspect of erosion in relation to the passing of large amounts of time. A given part of a continental surface is either an upland area that is being eroded or a basin into which sediments are being deposited. Where erosion is occurring, it carves the land into irregular topography as water seeks the path of least resistance in its downhill journey. With this concept in mind, let's take another look at the sedimentation rates discussed in chapter 13 (Fig. 13.3).

Sadler's (1981) data indicate that the fossil record contains only a small fraction of the sediment that would be predicted from modern sedimentation rates. Van Andel's (1981) proposed answer to this problem is that the geological record consists of brief periods of sedimentation separated by long periods of inactivity; or there may be long periods in which sediments are deposited and then much or all of the sediment is eroded before the next sediments arrive. He puzzles over why these events typically leave no record that can be detected. Some evidence of erosion, soil formation, or burrowing by animals should exist, yet the general lack of such evidence is typified by a deposit studied by him in Venezuela.

Two thin coal seams separated by a foot of gray clay were, respectively, of Lower Paleocene and Upper Eocene age. "The outcrops were excellent but even the closest inspec-

tion failed to turn up the precise position of that 15 Myr gap" (p. 398).

There are many known unconformities in the geological record that show evidence of erosion and/or uplift of sediments before the next layers are deposited. But van Andel's (1981) comments are directed to the general lack of evidence for erosional gaps in the record that remains after the evident unconformities have been accounted for. Acceptance of the standard geological time scale is what makes these data puzzling. If we are willing to make that time scale a hypothesis to be tested, the most straight-forward, simplest explanation of the data presented by Sadler and van Andel is that there has not been nearly that much time in the geological record.

Data summarized by Roth (1988) greatly expand the nature of the above problem where gaps in the geological record believed to represent millions of years of time between two consecutive sedimentary formations show little or no evidence that erosion occurred during that time. The Pliocene Ogallala Formation (2-5 million years old) is widespread in central United States. Over an area of 150,000 sq. km it lies directly on top of the Triassic Trujillo Formation (208 million years old). If 200 million years had passed before the Trujillo Formation was covered, there should have been erosion of valleys, gullies, or even canyons besides soil formation and plant growth. However, the contact between the two formations is very flat with only slight evidence of erosion despite the existence of soft units in the Trujillo that should have eroded easily.

If this phenomena were rare, we might pass over it as an oddity that is not pertinent to explaining the record in general. However, this gap is characteristic of what is found frequently in the geological column throughout the world (Roth 1988). Fig. 14.5 compares the erosion that might be expected if long time periods had passed between sedimentary formations with the characteristic appearance of the geologic record, especially in the Paleozoic and Mesozoic, with minimal erosion between formations. Some erosional channels are evident, but the amount of relief is surprisingly small compared to modern topography produced by erosion with the passage of time.

Fig. 14.6 is a cross section through southeastern Utah, illustrating how common these gaps are in a well-studied area. The presumed time gaps are shown in black. In reality, the formations lie on top of one another over large areas without significant erosion between them. They are relatively thin, widespread

layers (vertical exaggeration in the diagram is 16x). Table 14.2 lists a number of additional examples of the same phenomena.

Theories that attempt to explain these uneroded layers below the time gaps have not stood up to careful study. Apparently no modern analogue exists for these very flat areas with little erosion (Roth 1988). Some very arid areas in Australia are quite flat and are believed to represent areas that have been uneroded for millions of years. The most extreme case seems to be Kangaroo Island, which is 140 by 60 km, is extremely flat, and has a surface believed to have been undisturbed for 200 million years. But the very arid condition of these parts of Australia is not at all comparable to the apparent climate of the parts of the fossil record containing the time gaps. Also, the Australian flatlands are not characteristic of the expected results of normal geological processes. These are oddities which are "in some degree an embarrassment to all the commonly accepted models of landscape development" (Twidale 1976, p. 81).

Figure 14.5
Expected (A-D) and actual (E) deposition and erosion patterns at time gaps in the geological record. (A) A series of successive sedimentary deposits. (B) Erosion occurs when the sediments are exposed to water drainage. (C) Sedimentation resumes, filling and preserving the old erosional channels. (D) A second cycle of erosion and deposition. (E) The more usual pattern seen in the geological record, without significant erosion at presumed time gaps. These hypothetical diagrams with variable vertical exaggeration depend on the erosional conditions (from Roth 1988).

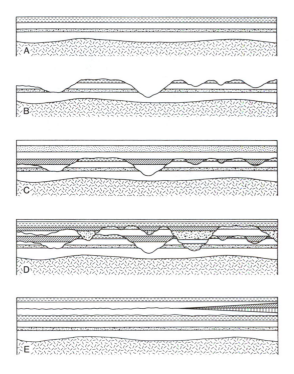

An area like Kangaroo Island is much more easily explained if the time span for its existence was only thousands of years. Catastrophic geology also offers a more natural explanation for the presumed time gaps. This theory proposes that the time spans represented by the gaps would vary from perhaps days to years or hundreds of years at most, depending on whether they occurred during or after the global catastrophe.

I wish to emphasize that the above material does not imply that the geological record does not contain evidence for erosion. On the contrary, evidence shows that significant erosion of sediments occurred as mountain ranges uplifted. Even when there wasn't a large scale uplift of the land, many cases of erosion of channels show up within the rock record. For example, in the Mississippian sediments of the Grand Canyon area are a number of ancient channels averaging over 200 feet deep, with a maximum of 401 feet (Billingsley and McKee 1982) of erosion at several levels in the Grand Canyon sediments (McKee 1982).

Indeed, it would be surprising if a significant geological catastrophe had not eroded significant amounts of sediment at times. The point of the above argument is that, in some places, the amount of erosion is small in spite of the presumed passing of extremely long periods of time. Geological processes on our present earth do not seem to indicate that such a scenario is realistic.

The last line of evidence against neocatastrophic theory

Figure 14.6 Sedimentary layers in south-eastern Utah (clear) and time gaps (black) between the layers. Ages given are in millions of years, according to the geological time scale. Only the names of the major sedimentary formations are given. Vertical exaggeration is about 16x. The horizontal distance is about 200 km, and the total thickness of the layers (clear areas) is about 3.5 km (from Roth 1988).

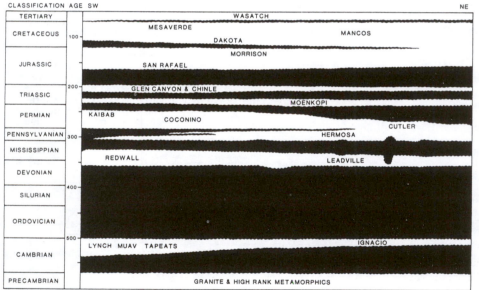

STRATIGRAPHIC HIATUSES IN SOUTHEASTERN UTAH

Table 14.2
A Few of the Observed Time Gaps in the Geological Record
(with little evidence of erosion, listing the location, time span of the gap, and the formations above and below the gap, From Roth 1988)

Location	Time	Formations
Texas	16 my	Late Triassic Tecovas/Permian Quartermaster
Grand Canyon	100 my +	Devonian Temple Butte/Cambrian Muav
Utah	10 my	Triassic Glen Canyon/Triassic Moenkopi
Utah	20 my	Triassic Moenkopi/Permian Kaibab; covers 250,000 sq. km
Australia	5 my	Upper surface of Bulli coal; covers 90,000 sq. km
Switzerland	35 my	Upper Cretaceous
(my = millions of years)		

considered here deals with the large geographic extent of many sedimentary formations compared to the much more localized nature of modern analogues. In the western part of the United States, many dinosaur specimens have been found in the Jurassic Morrison Formation. This formation is interpreted as a fluvial (river and flood plain) and lacustrine (lake) deposit with a fauna rich in dinosaurs. The Morrison Formation can be seen in Dinosaur National Monument in Colorado and Utah. This single formation covers an area from the Canadian border almost to Mexico (Fig. 14.7). The Triassic Shinarump Conglomerate is composed of sand and rounded pebbles in a sand matrix, like a stream deposit, but it covers over 100,000 sq. miles in Utah and adjacent states. In eastern United States, another widespread deposit is the Chattanooga Shale and correlated shale formations which cover a number of states. Another example is coal, which is believed to have formed in swamps as peat accumulated over long periods of time. Some coal layers extend for hundreds of miles. These very large swamps would have to have been very stable for millions of years to accumulate such coal deposits.

Ager (1981), in *The Nature of the Stratigraphical Record,* examines this phenomena in an even broader context. He points out to any who may wish to see this as evidence for Noah's flood that he finds no need for that hypothesis to explain the fossil record. He adds, "Nevertheless, this is not to deny that there are some very curious features about the fossil record" (p. 20). He makes this statement in direct connection with a discussion of the way in which fossils characteristically appear suddenly in the record without ancestors and later disappear to be replaced by different types which also suddenly appear. Clearly he would apply the same caution to other lines of evidence that he presents. He prefers to interpret them in terms of conventional neocatastrophism, though the evidence seems easier to explain in a more catastrophic context.

In his first chapter, Ager describes features of specific parts of the geologic column that are found over very large geographic areas or even worldwide. At the base of the Cambrian is a basal quartzite that is found in most locations, worldwide, typically followed by orthoquartzite, then glauconitic sandstones, then marine shales, and thin limestones. At the base of the Ordovician are prominent quartzites found in many parts of Europe and Africa, and, possibly, are more widespread than that. In the Devonian are continental red sandstones that extend from

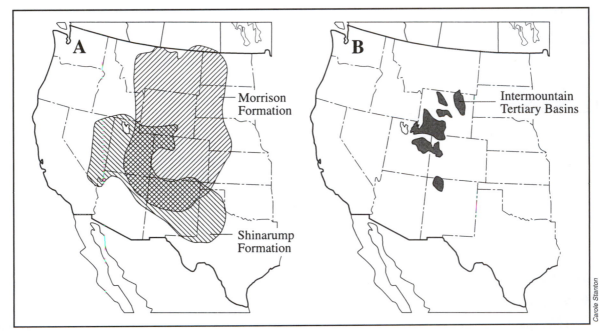

Carole Stanton

Figure 14.7
Distribution of (A) two
widespread Mesozoic formations and (B) a map of the
lower Tertiary sedimentary
basins in the Rocky
Mountain region (after Cook
and Bally 1975; Cooper et al.
1990; Dodson et al. 1980;
Dubiel 1994).

eastern Canada all the way to Iceland, through northern Europe to Russia. The Mississippian Redwall Limestone is a prominent cliff-forming layer in the Grand Canyon. The same type of limestone formation, with similar fossils, is typical of the Mississippian throughout much of North America as far as Alaska and across Europe and into Asia. Pennsylvanian coal deposits are similar in fundamental ways with similar fossil content from eastern North America all the way into Russia. That is a distribution of coal facies that covers 130 degrees of longitude (adjusted for continental drift) or about 2,000 miles. The Triassic in western North America is characterized by a series of red formations. Series of these character-istic Triassic reddish sedimentary layers called redbeds are also found in eastern North America, across

Europe, in Mexico, and possibly in other areas with very similar charac-teristics. Chalk is a very unusual sediment—a very pure coccolith limestone (formed of skeletons of minute organisms)—that is only found at restricted horizons in the geological column. The white cliffs of Dover in England are Upper Cretaceous chalk containing black flints. Virtually the same formation occurs in the Upper Cretaceous from Ireland through many parts of Europe into southern Russia, across southern United States, and in Australia, with the same black flints and character-istic fossils. Ager says, "There has been no other deposit quite like it before or since, except perhaps some Miocene chalks . . ." (p. 2), which are also widespread. Ager only described deposits that he had seen personally. Thus some of these facies may be much more widespread than what he described. In summary, in different parts of the geologic column are characteristic deposits that cover extensive geographic areas and are often identifiably different from sediments in other parts of the column.

Such geographically extensive formations are a common feature of the Paleozoic and Mesozoic. In contrast, North American sedimentary formations in the Cenozoic are more localized, filling basins between the mountains that formed in the Cretaceous or Cenozoic (Fig. 14.7). In the modern world, the types of environments that presumably produced most of these formations cover comparatively small areas. The tremendous geographic extent of many Paleozoic and Mesozoic deposits is so out of character with the depositional environments that occur today that they almost beg for a very different explanation than can be supplied by modern analogues. A hypothesis that seems more consistent with these data is that they were formed by a large-scale catastrophic process, producing unique and widespread types of deposits that were often controlled more by larger regional processes than by local environmental conditions. The process began to wind down during the latter part of the geological column, producing the basin-fill

deposits of the Tertiary, and finally stabilizing to the more localized processes that occur today. A profitable line of research would be a precise quantitative study of the geographic extent of sedimentary formations compared with modern analogues to determine how general the above trends are.

Further Analysis of Dating Methods

Two methods were not discussed above since they are not independent dating methods. Magnetic stratigraphy (Butler 1992; Miall 1990, p. 129-132) is the analysis of evidence for magnetic reversals in fine-grained sedimentary rocks. Magnetic particles in rocks are oriented according to the earth's magnetic field when the rock formed. The earth's north and south magnetic poles have reversed several times in the past, and rocks can be classified as having normal or reversed magnetic polarity (Fig. 14.8). Magnetic reversals have no potential to independently indicate the age of rocks; therefore, the magnetic reversal scale must be calibrated by radiometric dates. If one assumes that the other dating methods are valid, the use of magnetic reversals can help in refining age assignments of rocks.

Humphreys (1986, 1990) has proposed a mechanism for rapid reversals of the earth's magnetic field during the global catastrophe. Some

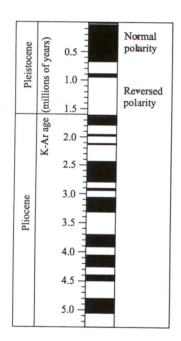

Figure 14.8
Magnetic reversal record in late Cenozoic rocks (after Lemon 1993). During times of normal polarity, the north and south magnetic poles were in the same position as today. During reversed polarity, the positions of the north and south magnetic poles were reversed.

evidence confirms that such reversals can occur within a few days (Coe et al. 1995; Monastersky 1995).

The other method is dating by amino acid racemization. When an organism dies, its amino acids slowly change (racemize) from all L amino acids to a 50/50 mixture of R and L forms. Measurements of the amount of racemization have been used in dating Pleistocene fossils, but the method also is not independent of radiometric dates. The rate "constant" used in calculating ages from amino acid data is not constant. It changes progressively with the age of the fossil by three orders of magnitude (Fig. 14.9) (Brown 1985). If the rate "constant" is kept constant, the method gives dates in the range of a few thousand years (Brown 1985; Brown and Webster 1991).

Carbon 14 Dating

The accuracy of carbon 14 dates is dependent on several assumptions:

1. *The decay rate has always been constant.* (There seems to be no reason to doubt this.)

2. *The amount of CO_2 in the atmosphere has been constant.* Since ^{14}C is produced from nitrogen, not carbon, its production is independent of the amount of carbon in the atmosphere. Consequently, if the amount of CO_2 was higher in the past, it would have diluted the ^{14}C and fossils

would date older than they actually are. It is quite possible that CO_2 was more prevalent in the past, making this a possible source of error.

3. *The amount of cosmic rays entering our atmosphere has been constant.* Possibly the earth originally had a lower rate of cosmic ray bombardment of the upper atmosphere due to a stronger magnetic field and, perhaps, more moisture in the upper atmosphere (although this would have a limited effect), making this another possible source of error in ^{14}C dates (Brown 1979).

4. *Plants take in ^{14}C and ^{12}C unselectively, without preference for ^{12}C.* Some plants do selectively prefer ^{12}C, but it is possible to determine this and correct for it.

Catastrophic geology predicts that a small amount of ^{14}C was in the atmosphere before the global catastrophe. This is based on a theoretical consideration and an empirical observation. The theoretical consideration is the destructive effects of mutations in organisms caused by radiation. Even if that problem has some solution other than a reduction of ^{14}C production, still the observation is that coal and oil yield ^{14}C dates more than 60,000 years, which requires minimal ^{14}C in the atmosphere when the organisms lived that produced the coal and oil, if the catastrophic geology time scale is correct. Brown

(1975, 1979, 1988, 1990, 1994b) has developed a model for relating ^{14}C dates to real time based on this catastrophic theory. According to his model, at the time of the global catastrophe, the mechanism that shielded the earth from excess ^{14}C production was disrupted and ^{14}C levels in the atmosphere began to increase. After a transition period, the level of ^{14}C reached equilibrium at approximately the level observed today (Fig. 14.10). Organisms living during the transition period would date older than they actually are with immediate post-catastrophe ^{14}C ages being in the 40,000 - 70,000-year range. Organisms that died after the curve reached equilibrium would yield ^{14}C ages that are fairly accurate. (One implication of this model is that if someone claims to have wood from the Biblical ark and it has a ^{14}C age of 5,000 years, it is not from the ark. Anything that lived before or immediately after the catastrophe will have a ^{14}C age of greater than 40,000 years, even though it is actually only a fraction of that age.)

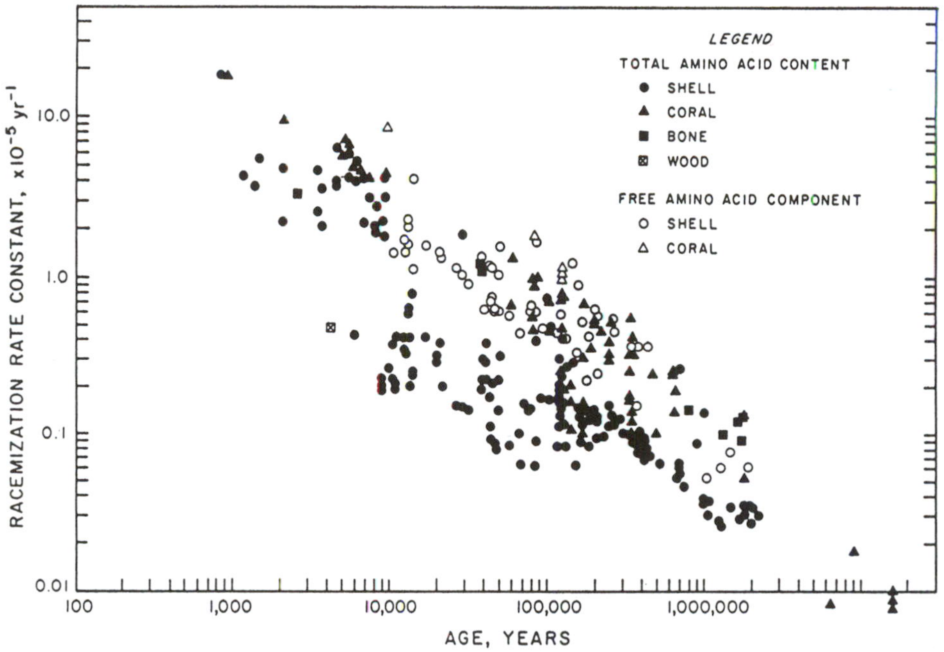

Figure 14.9
Isoleucine racemization rate constant versus associated fossil age as published in the literature (from Brown 1985)

In evaluating these radiometric dating methods, one should think of the entire process including the history of the rock and the laboratory methods and analysis. The ^{14}C cycle begins with the altering of ^{14}N into ^{14}C which becomes mixed with the ^{12}C in the atmosphere. The ratio of ^{14}C to ^{12}C depends on the cosmic ray influx, the amount of ^{12}C, and the tendency of plants to take in different forms of carbon indiscriminately. The result is some proportion of ^{14}C in the tissues of plants and animals which die and become preserved. The scientist collects a sample, determines the number of disintegrations/minute (or in the AMS method, counts the number of ^{14}C atoms), and calculates an age. The scientific procedures for collecting and analyzing samples may be precise and accurate, but the accuracy of the date still depends on the correctness of the assumptions that go into its calculation. Testing those assumptions would require that we know the composition of the atmosphere and the rate of cosmic ray influx during the Pleistocene. Of course, we can't go back and measure those. It is also intriguing that Paleozoic and Mesozoic coal and oil dates with the AMS method (which should be accurate to 90,000 years) give maximum ages between 50,000 and 70,000 years. This indicates that they still have ^{14}C and seem to be younger than 70,000 years (Giem 1997, p. 134-137). This deserves more study.

Other Radiometric Dating Methods

The accuracy of the other radiometric dating methods, such as potassium-argon, depends on three assumptions:

1. *The decay rate has always been constant.*

2. *The rock has remained a closed system*—no chemical exchange with the surrounding medium.

3. *The radiometric clock was set to zero when the rock was deposited in its present location*—all previously existing daughter products escaped at that time (Fig. 14.11) (or were made distinguishable from daughter products formed after deposition).

In evaluating dating methods other than ^{14}C, one should consider the entire process which begins in the earth. The magma at any given point below the earth's crust has some ratio of parent to daughter product, depending on its history. When that magma comes to the surface to form a new deposit, it must lose the daughter products of its radionuclides (resetting the clock to zero) if it is to give us a correct date for the depositional event. After that, no exchange of parent or daughter elements can take place with fluids moving through the rock or its "clocks" will be inaccurate, because the parent/daughter ratio is the result of something other than the amount of time that has passed. The researcher collects a sample, goes through the laboratory procedure to determine the amounts of daughter and parent elements, attempts to determine if the above assumptions have been met, and interprets the date of the rock.

Figure 14.10
Model of the changing level of ^{14}C in the atmosphere after the flood and its effects on the apparent age of organisms (after Brown 1994).

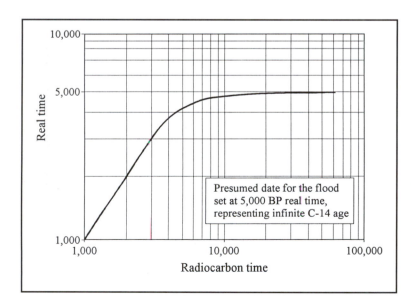

Presumed date for the flood set at 5,000 BP real time, representing infinite C-14 age

Real time — Radiocarbon time

I don't know any reason to doubt the theory of the decay process, the pathways of decay from one isotope to another, or the accuracy of the laboratory procedures for measuring the parent and daughter elements. That does not assure that the resulting geological dates are accurate, however. Several questions seem to need better answers before radio-metric dates are convincing to those of us who view radiometric dating as a hypothesis to be tested rather than as a given truth.

The first question (referring to methods other than ^{14}C) is how sure we can be that any given clock has been set to zero. Evidence in many cases indicates that radiometric dates are too old, by up to several billion years (Brooks et al. 1976; see also Brown 1981—with extensive refer-ence list; Dickinson and Gibson 1972; McDougall et al. 1969; Naeser 1971), giving what is referred to as inherited age. The clock was not set to zero and some percentage of old daughter products were not lost when a new rock formation was deposited.

Is there a truly independent method for determining whether a date is accurate or inherited? That determination must not be based on evaluating whether the date agrees with the already accepted time scale, or circular reasoning comes into play.

How much chemical exchange really occurs as fluids flow through rocks? When such exchange occurs, the affected rock may give an incor-rect radiometric age. Also, if the rock formed by mixing of material from different sources, it gives what appears to be a radiometric "age" that

Figure 14.11 Hypothetical series of events, over a time span of two half-lives, illustrating the process of resetting the potassium-argon radio-metric clock to zero at the time that a lava flow forms. (A) From time 1 to time 2, half of the 40K (potassium) decays to 40Ar (argon). That argon escapes at time 3, and then half of the remaining potassium decays to argon, indicating a time of one half life after the lava flow (from 3 to 4). (B) If the argon that had previously formed in the magma did not escape at the time of the lava flow (time 3), the potassium-argon ratio at 4 would incorrectly indicate an age of two half-lives for the lava flow. The extra "time" is inherited age resulting from extra argon inherited from events before the lava flow.

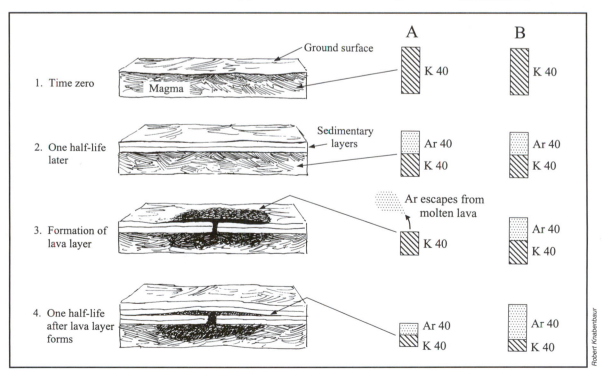

is not a true age, but is the result of the mixing process (Brown 1994a; Shaffer and Faure 1976).

In spite of the above problems, apparently radiometric dating methods give a generally consistent sequence of dates. Even though levels of uncertainty arise about precision (e.g., Miall 1990, section 3.7), at least an approximate correlation occurs between published radiometric dates and the position of a rock in the geological column. Cambrian rocks yield Cambrian dates, not Eocene dates. However, not all dates come out right. Three published time scales for the Jurassic considered that, respectively, 12, 0, and 3 of all the published radiometric dates for the Jurassic were accurate (Miall 1990). It would be important to know on what basis the other dates were rejected. There are ways to determine that some rocks are not suitable for radiometric dating, but how consistently can that be determined?

If a researcher assumes that naturalistic theories are correct and the standard geologic time scale is reliable, then it is valid to use various dating methods as applicable, correcting one against another. If we ask whether the entire concept is correct, we must then have a more independent criteria for judging radiometric dates: methods that allow (1) a reliable decision on the accuracy of a date without any knowledge of what the age of the rock "should" be and (2) a decision about whether a given rock or mineral sample is suitable for use in radiometric dating before it is known what age the sample will yield. This is done whenever possible, but some percentage of samples still yield "incorrect" dates.

I believe that radiometric dating labs are operated by people who are as careful and honest as other scientists, but the points raised here are still valid. A researcher studying the rocks generally knows the stratigraphic position (the expected age) of the samples that he or she collects. If the dating lab personnel know the expected age of a rock sample, they can run the test more efficiently. But our knowledge of human nature tells us that objectivity is enhanced if a researcher doesn't know the expected results before the test is done. Isn't it possible that knowledge of the expected age could influence even the best lab technician or researcher in the decision of the acceptability of a given radiometrically dated sample?

When the two conditions listed above are consistently met, radiometric dating will be a rigorous science, and its conclusions will be more convincing. It is not at all clear that such independent methods are in adequate use at present. The principal exception seems to be cases in which several independent dating methods give the same age for a rock sample (concordant dates). A useful line of research would be to determine which geological eras have produced the most concordant dates.

Catastrophists offer at least two hypotheses for reconciling radiometric dates with a young age for the fossils found within the strata. One suggests that radiometric dates of the Precambrian rocks may be accurate, but ages of younger rocks formed under uniquely catastrophic conditions represent inherited age; consequently, these radiometric ages have no relation to the real ages of the fossiliferous sediments associated with them (Brown 1981). Whether this model explains the sequence of all dates is yet to be tested.

A speculative hypothesis is that, at the time of the flood, an event occurred that destabilized the radioactive elements, speeding up radioactive decay and producing the energy to drive the flood processes (Pearl 1963). That energy could speed up such processes as continental drifting and the rising or sinking of continents. An unavoidable side effect of that process would be that any new rocks formed during that time would date much older than they really are when dated by radiometric methods. Radiometric dating might give relative age, but not absolute age.

Potential problems with this model arise because the event may have produced too much heat which could have destabilized some elements that are not otherwise radioactive. If this happened, it should be possible to find evidence for it.

In summary, radiometric dating, although not an air-tight methodology, is still the strongest evidence for the great age of the fossil-bearing formations. Yet other significant lines of evidence raise doubts about whether that much time passed in the Phanerozoic. The trend toward more catastrophic processes is a movement in the direction predicted by catastrophic theory. The field of geology will be benefited if some earth scientists actively use the catastrophic theory in proposing and testing hypotheses about radiometric dating and geologic history, as long as they use careful scientific methodology and benefit from scientific peer review. The excitement of discovery awaits those who are willing to break new ground in research and look at familiar things from a new point of view. But this viewpoint will still need to account for the radiometric age data.

The Weight of Evidence

We can now add a number of items to our earlier list of evidence in the three categories below. In some cases, it is a matter of opinion which list an item should be placed in, but the following is my list. One cannot realistically make a decision on the strength of a theory based on the length of such lists, since some lines of evidence are far weightier than others. In fact, I have purposely included enough of the best lines of evidence in the two outer lists to make them the same length and to discourage the natural tendency to decide a question according to which list is longer. These lists are merely a way to help organize the information.

Evidence Favoring Intervention and Catastrophism	Neutral Evidence	Evidence Favoring Megaevolution and Neocatastrophism
Lack of fossil intermediates	Microevolution	Biogeography (some)
The problem of originating new body plans	Speciation	Sequence of vertebrate fossils
The problem of originating life	Embryology	Precise sorting of fossils in the fossil record
Sedimentation rates in the modern world and in the rocks	Vestigial organs	Reptile/mammal fossil intermediates
Megabreccias (the larger clasts)	Hierarchical nature of life	Time required for cooling of laccoliths
Small amount of sediments in the oceans	Diverse levels of biological complexity	Glaciation (some of the evidence)
Rate of erosion of the continents	Homology	Fossil reefs (some)
Gaps in the geological record with little or no erosion	"Suboptimal" adaptations	Stromatolites required growth time
Very widespread sedimentary formations	Biogeography (most)	Tidal cycles in sediments
	Archaeopteryx	Radiometric dating
	Record of humans	
	Fish/amphibian "transition"	
	Heterochrony, paedomorphosis, and allometry	
	Regulatory gene evolution	
	Process of formation of rocks and minerals	
	Evidence used for interpreting depositional environments	
	Evidence for water covering more of the continents in the past	
	Mountain building and general patterns of erosion and landscape development	
	Glaciation (most)	
	Fossilization processes	
	Channeled Scablands	
	Abundance of turbidites	
	"Nothing happens in the Grand Canyon except in a catastrophe"	
	Megabreccias (some)	

A Catastrophic Theory of Earth History: General Principles

15

Chapters 15 and 16 present a catastrophic theory of earth history beginning with a discussion of what the original earth may have been like and the concept of a global catastrophe and how some of the geological principles would govern it. Here I present both the philosophical/theological concepts that suggest this unconventional theory and the scientific principles that the theory must account for.

For those who have strong confidence in Scripture, catrastrophic theory involves a specific catastrophe—the Noachian flood. It is especially important to note, in fairness to the authors cited, that many of the authors do not interpret the data in terms of interventionist or catastrophic theory. However, the references are cited for specific data or concepts for which I seek a different interpretation that is still consistent with the data.

Wouldn't it be easier just to accept the long geological time scale and fit creation into that scenario? Probably. But theories outside the accepted norm always seem outrageous at first. And even if they are good theories, they succeed only if some individuals believe in them enough to proceed without any concern for the easy way. The reason for proposing an alternative theory is to maintain internal consistency in the informed intervention paradigm presented here in explaining the stratigraphic distribution of a number of groups of fossils in the fossil record (Fig. 9.18), including the vertebrates (Roth 1980).

At the beginning of the Phanerozoic, the record contains only invertebrates. Then the vertebrates appear, one group at a time, in what is generally interpreted as an evolutionary sequence. If we question the evolutionary explanation, we must provide an alternate one. If a significant part of the fossil record was formed during a worldwide flood, then the sequence of fossils in the record could be the result of sorting processes that buried some groups of organisms before other groups.

Eliminating the flood also eliminates the creation account. Without the flood to provide a mechanism for sorting the animals and plants, the order of the fossils calls for megaevolution to explain the fossil sequence.

In this respect, the two internally consistent approaches are (1) mega-evolution over millions of years of time (along with a philosophy that does not take the Genesis account seriously), and (2) biblical creation with a geologically significant world-wide flood. Both religious and scientific reasons are present for thinking that the second option is worth pursuing seriously. It is consistent with acceptance of Scripture as authoritative in theology, science, and history when it addresses such topics (Hasel 1980b, p. 68).

In evaluating these options, two levels of questions must be addressed:

Question 1—Which is the correct description of the origin of organisms and fossils?

A. Geologic column deposited over millions of years

    No worldwide flood

    Implies megaevolutionary origin of major groups of plants and animals

B. Geologic column deposited rapidly primarily during world-wide flood and postflood transition period, perhaps also preflood

    Major groups of organisms created during creation week

Question 2—If B is correct, how long has it been since creation?

A. 6,000 years

B. 7,000 - 10,000 years

C. 10,000 - 15,000 years

Whatever our choice on question 2, one must not confuse question 2 with question 1 and assume the choice is either 2A or 1A.

Some time in the past, God designed the universe and brought it into being. In the middle of one galaxy among many is a little sun that makes life possible on this earth. On neighboring planets and on Earth's moon, geological processes have been in operation. Meteorites have crashed into their surfaces and made craters of various ages. Some are old with eroded, irregular rims; others have very sharp, smooth rims indicating that they must be of fairly recent origin. Some of the old, eroded craters have young, uneroded craters within them. This evidence indicates a sequence of geological events occurring over some period of time.

The Precambrian deposits on Earth also contain evidence of tremendous geological processes, including cementation, metamorphosis, folding and twisting from the formation of mountains, and subsequent erosion of those mountains. Dynamic geological processes have left their marks on those ancient rocks (Cooper et al. 1990, p. 212-227).

The same basic types of sediment make up the Precambrian and the Paleozoic deposits, but the obvious difference is the relatively few fossils in the Precambrian whereas the

Paleozoic contains an abundance of fossils of structurally complex organisms. Fossils of microorganisms, far down in Precambrian rocks, are presumed to be remains of early life forms. However, recent findings reveal a large biomass of microbes currently living as much as 5 km deep in the earth—even in granite (Gold 1992; Stevens and McKinley 1995). This may make it difficult to be sure about the true age of some fossil microbes.

Did God make our earth and solar system at the beginning of the Biblical creation week? Or did He make it billions of years ago and leave it here in a sort of chaotic state, as Genesis 1 says, "Without form and void" (verse 2)? Some interventionists believe that the sun, moon, and stars didn't exist until day four of our creation week and that the earth did not exist as a body at all until the first day of creation (Exodus 20:8-11).

Others see reason, even in the Bible, for thinking that God created the universe long before creation week. Then at creation week He came down and prepared the earth's surface for life and created life on it (Genesis 1:1, NIV—"Now the earth was formless and empty").

Some would insist that according to the statements in the first two chapters of Genesis, the heavens and the earth that God made at that time are defined there as referring only to this earth. More specifically, "earth" in these cases means the life support system on the earth and the dirt on the ground. "Heavens" are defined as the atmosphere around the earth where the birds fly and the clouds float. Those theological issues aren't settled here, but let's review some of the evidence. The Precambrian rocks show extensive evidence of geological processes that presumably would take a lot of time. The rocks appear to have been cemented firmly and even metamorphosed before the fossil-bearing Phanerozoic deposits were laid down. Meteorite impacts marked the surface. These Precambrian deposits were extensively warped and twisted and folded up into high mountains and then eroded down. The Paleozoic fossiliferous deposits were laid down, originally quite horizontally, on top of these folded and eroded Precambrian sediments (Cooper et al. 1990, p. 212-227).

This is more easily explained if most of the Precambrian represents extensive time for geological processes before the creation week. A suitable life-support system was then constructed on top of the eroded Precambrian surface, with the Precambrian sediments forming the foundation for the reorganized outer crust. At the time of the flood, this new outer crust on top of the

Precambrian was systematically disrupted and deposited to form significant parts of the Paleozoic and Mesozoic rocks.

The explanation that the Precambrian and the rest of the earth did not exist before creation week seems to require very extensive geological processes early on in the flood that we cannot even compre-hend; and these produced the Precambrian deposits before any significant number of organisms were buried and fossilized. Many things are difficult to comprehend, so this diffi-culty does not show it to be false. Nevertheless, it does not appear to be the most likely alternative.

If the Precambrian represents billions of years before creation week, it is easier to explain its structure. It also offers a hypothesis for explaining the radiometric data: Precambrian dates may be accurate unless evidence indicates otherwise, but Phanerozoic radiometric dates are the result of inherited age. As the flood began, the radiometric ages of the early igneous intrusions were not reset—they date at 570 million years or older. Subsequent intrusions during the flood shifted progressively toward younger ages, because of more reset-ting of the clocks or because of systematic changes in the magma chambers. The "radiometric ages" of these flood rocks would indicate relative age, not age in years. It would be unrealistic to expect that this process would affect all rocks in the same way. Many dates would be wrong, but a core of the dates would reflect a reasonable sequence of events (relative-age scale). This hypothesis appears outrageous to many people. But someone needs to devise a way to test it.

The Preflood Earth

What was the surface of the earth like after creation week? We have no direct evidence to answer this question. The few clues available from the inspired writings and geological evidence suggest the following theory to me.

Living things today are very intricately designed with all of their parts beautifully designed to carry out their intended functions. However, the structure of the crust of the earth and its life-support system seem almost haphazard in certain respects. Huge areas of the earth have inadequate rain and can support only a small amount of life. The earth does not look well designed. I hypothesize that the earth in its current changed state is the wreckage of a drowned planet—the remains of what was left after the flood. Perhaps, before the flood, the crust of the earth was as intricately designed as current living things are. The rich fossil record can be interpreted as indicating that before the flood, life on earth was much more abundant than what earth can support now.

Science provides little or no help in determining how the original earth was organized. The best we can do is speculate on the basis of a few Bible texts. We are told that no rain fell before the flood (Genesis 2:5)—perhaps because rain erodes—and the original earth was designed to last forever. An absence of rain requires some important differences in the structure and functioning of the earth's crust. Rain forms when moisture in the atmosphere collects around particles of dust or salt carried up by winds. An absence of rain on an earth with plenty of water would require a very precise climate-control system with fairly even temperature over the earth and very little wind. The fossils indicate that tropical animals and plants were living much closer to the polar regions than they do now, supporting the idea that the earth had a more uniform climate earlier in its history (Francis 1991).

At the flood, things changed very dramatically. In fact, putting together the concept of the flood with the evidence in the rocks indicates that mountains which exist now were formed during the flood, and preflood mountains were destroyed. The existing mountains are not necessarily in the same places as the preflood mountains. It isn't even clear that the continents are in the same places as they were.

Hypotheses of Flood Dynamics

Let's consider the basic principles of what would have to happen to bring on a flood and restore the earth to a habitable condition afterwards. How is the crust of the earth made? Where would the water come from? Where would it go? How would the fossils get to the places where they are now?

Figure 15.1 shows the relationship between the continents, the ocean floors, and the mantle underneath the crust. The earth has land surface that stays above sea level for the same reason that corks float on water. We don't often think of rock as floating, but look again at the diagram of the earth's crust. The continents all have a granitic foundation with a density of about 2.7 compared with the density or specific gravity of 1 for water. Compare that with the basaltic rocks that form the floor of the ocean—a density of about 3—and the mantle below them—a density of about 3.3 (Cooper et al. 1990, p. 8). The continents are formed of a sub-

Figure 15.1
The structural relationships between continents and oceans. Numbers indicate density of the rocks (after Hamblin and Christiansen 1995).

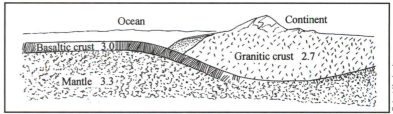

stance different from the floor of the oceans, so they float on the heavier material underneath. This well-balanced system explains why our continents don't sink into the oceanic crust and become covered by water.

If a catastrophic world-wide flood occurred today and carried away the soil and other loose material on the earth, where would it be deposited? On the land or in the oceans? Intuitively, it might seem that most of the sediments, especially the marine sediment, would be deposited in the ocean. But most of the fossil-bearing sedimentary layers (including the bulk of marine deposits) are on the continents. The conventional neocatastrophic theory has an explanation for that evidence. Any catastrophic theory also has to account for the same evidence.

Let's consider several different hypotheses in an attempt to explain these points. Why are these sediments, especially the marine sediments, largely on the continents instead of in the ocean? Where did the water come from during the flood? How could there be enough water to cover the entire earth? Where did the water go after the flood (Ariel Roth, unpublished)?

Why do I suggest several hypotheses? Why not just present the explanation that seems correct? A lot more research is needed before we'll

know the correct explanation. When we get beyond the basic concepts outlined in Genesis, we have only the scientific process to help us fill in the details. Science doesn't properly claim to know "the answer" before it really has "the answer" with the evidence to back it up.

Interventionists, perhaps because of their confidence in the Bible, tend to want the confidence of having the answers to the geological questions as well. But are naturalistic scientists confident of having all the answers? Not if they are thoughtful and well informed. Do they throw out their scientific paradigm if important unsolved problems rise? Usually not. The purpose of science is to work on solving those unsolved problems.

It is not realistic for believers in informed intervention to feel they must have all the answers, that they must be able to prove that they're right and "others" are wrong. Such an approach leads to disappointment when the current idea about the geological details, probably not based on adequate evidence in the first place, runs into new, conflicting evidence. The evolution theory also has run into many problems. Some have called it a theory in crisis (e.g., Denton 1985). Thoughtful evolutionists honestly face these uncertainties and to try to develop a better understanding of how evolution works. A few years ago, Stephen Gould (1980b) wrote an article discussing problems with the neo-Darwinian evolutionary synthesis and presenting alternatives. When addressing the question of what the alternate evolutionary synthesis will be, he stated that on this issue his "crystal ball is a little clouded" by the controversy and the lack of adequate data. Some may be tempted to laugh at evolutionists because they do not have all the answers. To do so is to misunderstand the scientific process. To be scientific is to be honest about our unanswered questions (as Gould was) and to use the questions as a springboard in a search for answers (as he does).

Informed interventionists need this same honesty to face unanswered scientific questions confidently and to recognize that the search for answers is an ongoing process of formulating and testing hypotheses. We don't need more skill at putting down those with whom we disagree. Are creationists who debate with evolutionists mindful that God loves the person they are debating? I hope so.

Let us consider now the concepts and lines of evidence that need to be dealt with to develop a catastrophic theory of geology. As we consider possible explanations of the data, we must be aware that continued research no doubt will change these theories in the coming years. Scripture does not tell us about dinosaurs or Paleozoic sediments; it simply challenges us to look for new ways to explain them.

In 1926, the controversy between the geologist J. Harlan Bretz and the geological community stimulated the president of the Geological Society of America to publish an article entitled "The Value of Outrageous Hypotheses" (Davis 1926; Baker 1978). Any new idea is apt to seem outrageous when first suggested, but "we may be pretty sure that the advances yet to be made in geology will be at first regarded as outrages upon the accumulated convictions of today, which we are too prone to regard as geologically sacred" (Davis 1926, p. 464). I'd like to broaden Davis' concept even more and suggest that catastrophic geology is also a useful "outrageous hypothesis."

These outrageous hypotheses in catastrophic geology, as long as they are also responsible ones, can improve the chances of finding a way to explanations that are consistent with both revelation and geology. The following describes several hypotheses for certain parts of the flood event to stimulate thinking about how these hypotheses could be tested. This follows the approach of multiple-working hypotheses recommended by Chamberlin (1965). If we propose all of the possible hypotheses for a particular phenomenon, we are less likely to settle too quickly for the first one that seems satisfactory. Here, suggested hypotheses deal only with very broad, global aspects of geological processes.

Source of Flood Water, Its Postflood Destination, and the History of Continents

If a world-wide flood occurred on this earth, how could the flood water have covered the highest mountains? There isn't enough water to do that unless the structure of the earth's crust was altered considerably. Some have suggested that a "canopy" of water in the upper atmosphere came down as rain. Whether or not that is a realistic concept, it seems certain that such a canopy would not hold hundreds or thousands of vertical feet of water. Earth's existing water would be able to cover the land only if the continents sank in relation to the ocean floors. It also appears that any preflood mountains were destroyed and existing mountains were formed during or after the flood. The old mountains were covered partly by being eroded away. Another possible result is new mountains rising in some areas while old mountains were still above water.

Removing the water from the land after the flood also depends on changes in the earth's crust. Where did all the water go? It couldn't just evaporate. The atmosphere could hold only a small fraction of the water needed to cause a world-wide flood. Some global process, such as the rising of continents, is needed for the flood water to flow into the postflood ocean basins.

Most sedimentary rocks, including marine deposits, are on the continents. The relatively small amount of sediment in the ocean is all Jurassic or younger. Two general conclusions can be deduced from these observations: (1) Large areas of the continents must have been at low elevation during the flood, forming depressed basins where the sediment was accumulating, or (2) the rock composing existing ocean floors was not formed until late in the flood. Looking back from our stable world with oceans that have stayed in the same place century after century, it is difficult to visualize or understand changes of this magnitude.

Where were the continents before the flood? One hypothesis proposes that the preflood continents were the same as the existing continents, but they sank in relation to the ocean floor during the flood. An alternate hypothesis suggests that continents and oceans traded places during the flood, with shallow preflood oceans filling with sediments and causing them to rise to form new continents.

Is there any way to test these hypotheses? Ultimately, it should be possible. One test that already has been applied (Spencer and Brand 1988; Brand 1989 [unpublished]) seems to falsify the hypothesis that the continents today are in the same place as preflood continents. This test does not ask whether a catastrophic theory or neocatastrophic theory is correct; it is simply part of a process to determine which of the flood hypotheses is more likely to be a realistic option within the overall catastrophic theory.

The test is based on an analysis of the processes necessary to transfer a sequence of faunas and floras from their original location to a sedimentary basin during a global catastrophe and deposit them in a sequence that is consistent at all depositional sites. It focuses in particular on the terrestrial vertebrate faunas. Several assumptions are involved. The first assumption is that at least a major part of the Paleozoic and Mesozoic deposits accumulated in a time frame shorter than the life of almost any individual vertebrate animal. In that scenario, one can assume that any region entirely covered by new marine sediments cannot simultaneously be occupied by terrestrial animals living in their normal habitat. That is to say, any given spot cannot be under the ocean and at the same time support a terrestrial environment for a living assemblage of vertebrate animals.

An examination of paleogeographic maps (Cook and Bally 1975) indicates that, by the end of the Paleozoic, nearly all of North America was covered by marine sediments (Fig. 15.2). Where were the terrestrial vertebrates and plants currently found as Mesozoic fossils in North America living while those marine deposits were being laid down? They couldn't have been living in the central part of North America unless some mechanism could lift them up in the air while the Paleozoic marine sediments were being deposited under them, and then bring them down in sequence to be buried in later sediments. They must have been living somewhere else and transported to their burial sites in North America. One implication of this concept is that many marine

Figure 15.2
The area of North America that was covered by marine sediments (cross-hatched) by the end of the Paleozoic. The Canadian shield consists of exposed Precambrian rocks.

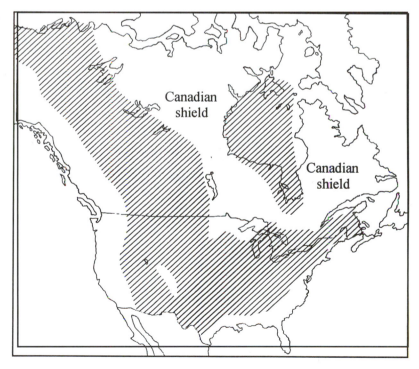

Canadian shield

Canadian shield

organisms were buried more or less in the area where they lived, but the terrestrial organisms were transported, dead or alive, long distances before burial. Another possibility is that both groups were transported some distance, but from different source areas.

The above test seems conclusive, but some critics argue that it may use a database that is not sufficiently precise. They suggest that a more refined analysis may indicate that local higher-elevation areas were available where some animals could have taken refuge for a time. Another criticism is the difficulty of imagining dinosaurs and other animals being transported that far in a flood and still be alive long enough to make footprints in the sediment. The answer to this debate awaits more research.

If the above test is correct, it appears that the preflood continents were not in the same places as the Phanerozoic sediment-bearing parts of existing continents (continental areas outside of the shields in Fig. 15.3). This could imply that the former continents were where the oceans are now and vice versa. How, then, can a continent be a former ocean since granite is normally lighter than basalt? One very speculative idea proposes that the basalt under the former continents was porous, with extensive water channels or aquifers as part of the water distribution system. The net-specific gravity of the basalt plus the water system would have been lower than the specific gravity of granite. Consequently, the honey-combed

Figure 15.3
The location of the shields or areas with no sediments younger than Precambrian.

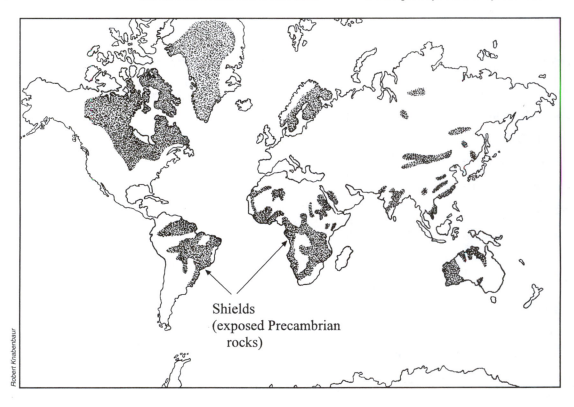

Robert Knabenbaur

Shields
(exposed Precambrian rocks)

continental areas would have risen higher than the granitic base of the ocean floor, keeping the continents above water before the flood.

Another hypothesis, called the expanding-earth hypothesis, may sound really preposterous. But some serious geologists who are not catastrophists believe the earth is larger now than it was in the past (Carey 1976; Mundy 1988). Some catastrophic geologists propose that the expanding-earth model explains the flood.

This hypothesis proposes that, before the flood, the earth was smaller than it is now and the oceans were quite a bit smaller than modern oceans. In this hypothesis, something occurred at the beginning of the flood to cause a phase change in the material composing our earth, thus increasing the mass of that material and changing the size of the earth. This explosive event disrupted the crust of the earth, broke up the granitic crust, and formed new ocean basins into which the flood water drained by the end of the flood.

A third hypothesis (Chadwick, personal communication) begins with a Pangaea-like supercontinent before the flood. It proposes that the shield areas (Fig. 15.3) were the preflood home of at least the upland terrestrial organisms buried late in the flood. A flood model has been proposed by

Austin et al. (1994) which also relates the process to plate tectonics but does not discuss the location of preflood continents.

The Beginning and Conclusion of the Flood

All of these hypotheses have several possibilities for the relationship of the fossils to events at the beginning and end of the flood. What portion of the fossil record contains the remains of animals that lived before the flood and were buried in the primary flood deposits? What portion contains the remains of animals that lived after the flood year ended?

Let's consider some options: (1) No significant net erosion or accumulation of sediments occurred until the sudden onset of the catastrophe at the beginning of the Biblical year of the flood (Fig. 15.4A). (2) Perhaps part of the lower Paleozoic sediment and fossils were deposited in the preflood oceans before the unusual events of the flood began suddenly at the beginning of the flood year (Fig. 15.4B). (3) Stretching that concept, perhaps the earth's stable geological balance began to decay and flood processes began in the lowland areas where no humans were living some time (10 years? 100? 500?) before the sudden acceleration of the flood processes described in the Biblical narrative (Fig. 15.7C).

There must have been a time

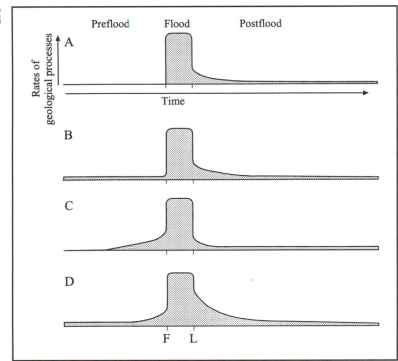

Figure 15.4
Rates of erosion and
sedimentation and other
geological processes before,
during, and after the flood,
according to several options
for processes at the begin-
ning and end of the flood. F
= initial flotation of the ark
and the beginning of the
year of the flood. L = ark
landing and end of the year
of the flood.

(100 years? 1,000 years?) of transition after the ark landed, with catastrophic conditions gradually settling down to the modern state (Fig.15.4A-D shows variations on this concept).

Several possibilities suggest themselves for relationships between the death and fossilization of organisms and the flood events. For instance, when, in relation to the fossil record, did the terrestrial vertebrate animals leave the ark and begin repopulating the earth? Some individuals believe this occurred in the Pleistocene; others place it at the end of the Cretaceous or in the Tertiary. If this repopulation occurred late in the Cenozoic, it implies that such fossil deposits as Tertiary fossil "lakes" and fossil "forests" were not true forests or lakes. They represent transported

material deposited approximately within the year of the flood, and all of the fossil mammals and other terrestrial vertebrates before that event were buried in a sequence controlled by some sorting process in the flood.

If the ark landed at about the end of the Cretaceous or early in the Tertiary, the fossils in the sediments above that level are from organisms that populated the earth after the flood. This implies that many late Tertiary vertebrates are the result of evolution from early Tertiary vertebrates, or that sequences of vertebrates resulted from a sequence of migrations over the earth.

Those options assume that all terrestrial vertebrates were dead approximately by the time the ark landed (Fig. 15.5A). Could some of them still have been alive? Did they survive the main part of the flood on floating debris or on newly formed mountains, and the die out later because of climatic or other changes resulting from the flood (Fig. 15.5B)? We should also consider the possibility that the flood ended at different times in different parts of the earth. Consequently, in such a scenario, the preflood animals didn't all die at the same time.

Orderly Deposition

Even today, while a storm is creating havoc at the water surface, under the water well-ordered deposits of sediment are being produced. This important feature of the sedimentation process is needed to explain the geological record. The flood didn't wash the sediments into the ocean and dump them in a chaotic fashion. The entire geological column is composed of very orderly deposits laid down in a predictable sequence.

This can be illustrated by comparing some modern sedimentary deposits with the fossiliferous rocks in the Phanerozoic record. Today, sand dunes form in the ocean, in deserts, and in other environments. These modern dunes form cross-bedded deposits, and cross-bedded sandstone deposits have the same characteristics as modern deposits. When sand dunes get too steep, the sand slumps (Fig. 15.6A). The same types of slump structures can be seen as fossil slumps in sandstone (Fig. 15.6B). In either underwater sand dunes or desert dunes, the water or air currents may produce ripple marks (Fig. 15.6C). These features are preserved as ripple marks in the rocks (Fig.15.6D) and sometimes cover extensive rock surfaces. Turbidity currents produce characteristic deposits today. In the geologic record, the discrete layers formed by turbidity currents are widespread.

From this orderly deposition, a geologist can study the rock and tell

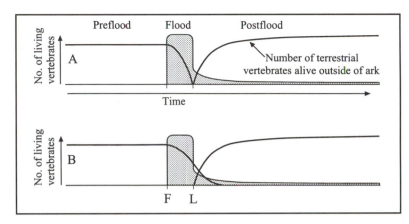

Figure 15.5
Diagram of the models that (A) all terrestrial vertebrates died before the ark landed and (B) that they were not all dead at that time.

in what sedimentary environment it was deposited. The difference between a catastrophic and neocatastrophic theory is largely a matter of time and scale. How rapidly did the geological events occur? What was the magnitude of these events?

Ecological Zonation

During all of this geological activity, animals and plants were being buried. The ecological zonation hypothesis (Clark 1946) (Fig. 15.7) attempted to explain how the fossils were deposited in the order in which they now occur. Our current understanding of this hypothesis leaves many unanswered questions; but until a more satisfactory hypothesis is developed, ecological zonation is a place to begin the process of developing testable hypotheses for the ordering of fossils.

The diagram in Fig. 15.7 is a reconstruction of a possible preflood landscape, based on a synthesis of Biblical information and the fossil record. This hypothesis proposes that

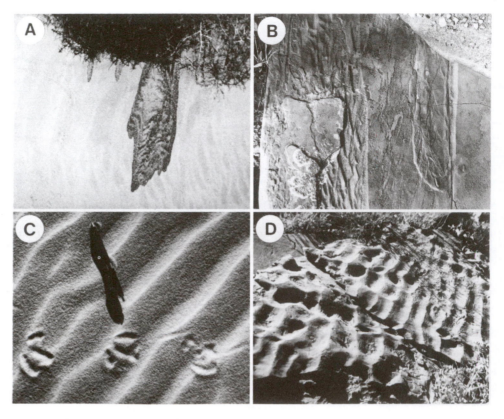

Figure 15.6
(A)Slump on modern desert sand dune; (B) ancient slump in sandstone; (C) modern ripple marks; and (D) ancient ripple marks in sandstone.

there was a system of shallow seas bordered by lowland, swampy environments. Many of the marine creatures from these shallow seas and almost all of the plants and animals from the lowland habitats are now extinct.

A little farther from the sea, but still in the warm, humid lowlands, other habitats were occupied by dinosaurs, pterosaurs, and other extinct reptiles. Plesiosaurs and other now extinct aquatic reptiles lived in some of the middle elevation bodies of water. The higher elevations were home to most of the mammals and birds, the flowering plants, and other organisms more familiar to us.

One should keep this picture in mind while considering this hypoth-esis. When the ocean waves started to disrupt the land and to produce sediments, the marine creatures that lived on the bottom of the sea were most likely to be buried first. Of course, in the fossil record, the marine organisms do appear first. Sometime later, some of the bottom-dwelling fish were overcome by the turbid water and were buried. Amphibians and reptiles living on the shore were caught and buried a bit later. As the water continued to rise, it destroyed different habitats one after another.

When the water rose to the eleva-tion of the Mesozoic animals' habitat, it overcame some of these animals. Their carcasses were buried in the newest sedimentary deposits. As the

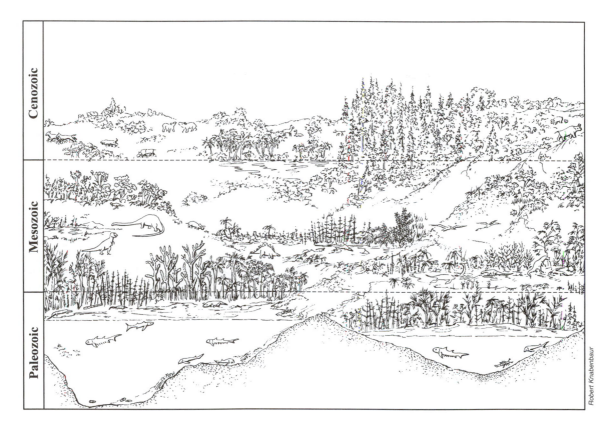

Robert Knabenbaur

Figure 15.7
The ecological zonation
hypothesis showing the
relationship between a
hypothetical preflood
landscape and the sequence
in which the fossils were
preserved in the geological
column (after Clark 1946).

water rose higher, it caught and buried other types of animals, finally reaching the elevations where most of the mammals lived.

If we take our current, modern-day ecology and superimpose it on the flood, however, an ecological zonation model won't work. The data from the fossil record tell us the ecology was different before the flood in some important ways.

One major difference is that a broad category of preflood habitats did not become reestablished after the flood. The plants and animals from these habitats (represented primarily by the Paleozoic and a portion of the Mesozoic fossils) are virtually extinct.

I propose that these extinct habitats, including a system of shallow seas, were in a warm, lowland environment. The great variety of animals and plants which lived in this environment did not survive the flood and could not live on the changed earth after the flood.

Perhaps these shallow seas were part of the climate-control mechanism in the then warmer earth. Unique faunas and floras were adapted for that environment. The mammals (including human beings) and birds, the angiosperms (flowering plants), the modern groups of reptiles and amphibians, and the teleost fish lived in the cooler upland areas. Perhaps that is why we don't find them in the lower parts of the fossil record. This hypothesis suggests that the post-flood world was populated primarily by upland organisms that were better prepared to survive on the cooler earth. This may also explain why the farther back we look in the fossil record, the larger the percentage of extinct organisms.

The concept that the preflood ecology (vertical sequence of life zones) would be one factor affecting the fossil sequence is a hypothesis based on the fossil record. However, it seems clear that the burial of a vertical succession of life zones would not be an adequate mechanism for producing the fossil sequence. Some other factors would have to sharpen the sorting effect of the process.

If we rank organisms according to their likelihood of being buried early in the fossil record, we would expect oceanic fish to be buried first since they live at the lowest elevation. Of course, fish can be found at all elevations, even up in mountain streams, but this ranking system is based on where the first representatives of a given group are likely to be buried (Table 15.1).

A second factor is how animals would react to the flood. Some animals' behavior is very rigid and stereotyped. They would likely stay where they were used to staying and would have little chance to escape. More intelligent and adaptable animals would recognize something

was wrong and make an effort to escape. Fish are the least intelligent and adaptable in their behavior. The amphibians come next, and then the reptiles, the birds, and, lastly, the mammals.

The third factor to consider is mobility of land vertebrates. Once they became aware of the need to escape, how capable would they be of running, swimming, flying, or riding on floating debris? Amphibians would be the least mobile. Reptiles would perform somewhat better but wouldn't be equal to the mammals' mobility, due largely to low metabolic rates. Birds, with their wings, would have the best expected mobility.

These three factors tend to support each other (Table 15.1). If they were working against each other, the order of the vertebrates in the fossil record would be more difficult to explain. Since they all do work together, it is somewhat realistic to suggest that the combination of these three factors could contribute significantly toward producing the general sequence we see in the fossil record.

Other fossil groups are more of a challenge to the ecological zonation theory. For example, why is there no flowering plant pollen below the Cretaceous? What is the explanation for the sequence of different types of foraminifera (one-celled marine organisms) in marine deposits? Why aren't at least a few mice or sparrows in Paleozoic or Mesozoic deposits? In other words, why did animals and plants from "higher zones" not mix with those in "lower zones" during the massive river and valley flooding that must have been going on? The mammals also pose some important questions. If the Cenozoic was postflood, where are the preflood mammal fossils including the preflood humans? Were they not preserved in the fossil record? If the lower Cenozoic was flood deposit, did the upper Cenozoic mammals all evolve from lower Cenozoic mammals after the flood?

Other factors significantly must have influenced the time at which many groups met their demise. As the catastrophic destruction progressed, we would expect changes in the chemistry of seas and lakes—from mixing of fresh and salt water—and contamination by leaching of other chemicals into the water. Each species of aquatic organism would have its own physiological tolerance for these changes. The result could be a sequence of mass mortalities of different groups as the water quality changed. Changes in turbidity of the water, pollution of the air by volcanic ash, or changes in air temperature could have similar effects.

If much of the Cenozoic was deposited postflood, then ecological zonation is not relevant to the order of fossils in that part of the column. Also, if the lower Paleozoic was formed preflood, then ecological zonation wouldn't be involved, at least not in the form suggested by Clark. Ecological zonation is a useful concept to begin with in catastrophic theorizing, but reality is likely to be much more complex than was originally envisioned.

Table 15.1
Factors Affecting Burial of Vertebrates in a Flood

Numbers indicate rank order in which they would be expected to be buried, as predicted by the ecological zonation hypothesis. A low number indicates that the first burials of members of that class would be expected to occur early, in relation to first burials of other vertebrate groups, if the indicated factor was the determining one. Ecology = successive elevations in a hypothesized preflood ecology; behavior = intelligence and behavioral adaptability.

	Ecology	Behavior	Mobility	Mean
Birds	4	4	4	4.0
Mammals	4	5	3	4.0
Reptiles	3	3	2	2.3
Amphibians	2	2	1	1.7
Fish	1	1	--	0.7

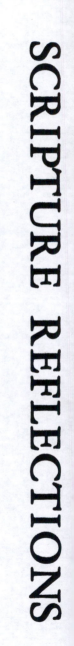

SCRIPTURE REFLECTIONS

with Mary Sharon

Sunday - October 15th

6:00 p.m. - Lounge

(Refreshments will
be provided.)

A Catastrophic Theory of Earth History: Interpreting the Historical Record

16

Early Flood

This chapter presents an approach to interpreting the evidence in terms of what may have happened during a global geological catastrophe. The process begins at the start of the flood (bottom of the Paleozoic or in the upper Precambrian [e.g., Austin and Wise 1994]) and continues through the flood and subsequent events to the modern world. It is unrealistic to be more specific about the beginning of the flood until much more research is done to develop the theory further. This discussion illustrates how a catastrophic theory can deal with the data and yield more specific, testable hypotheses. Chapter 14 addressed the question, "Do the data point more clearly to catastrophism or neocatastrophism?" This chapter doesn't attempt to prove catastrophism; it simply gives alternate, catastrophic explanations of data for which neocatastrophism also may have good explanations.

As the flood began, earth's geological balance was disrupted and, apparently, new ocean currents began to transport and redeposit ocean sediments as the lower Paleozoic deposits. The animals which could not escape would be buried and preserved as fossils. Many others did escape and were buried later. In the meantime, invertebrate animals were alive and moving around. This is demonstrated by the presence of abundant fossil burrows and trails (Fig. 16.1) throughout the geologic column, including many trilobite trails, feeding marks, and resting marks where the animals dug into the sediment to rest while hidden in the mud (Clarkson 1993, p. 362-366; Seilacher 1967— these authors describe the animal trails but not their relation to a flood).

Animals that live within sediment continually burrow through more and more sediment, destroying the original layering (Bromley 1990). This activity is called bioturbation. In the modern world, the activity of burrowing animals in

Figure 16.1
Representative trace fossils of invertebrate animals, including (A) burrows in the sediment and (B) crawling traces or trails of trilobites (after Bromley 1990; Frey 1975).

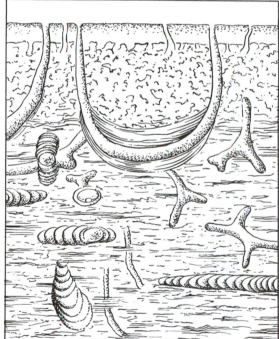

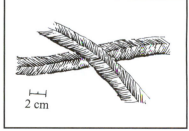

2 cm

Robert Knabenbaur

underwater sediment results in the total bioturbation of that sediment so none of the original layering or other sedimentary structures remain (Fig. 16.2, D & E). If sediments preserved as rock have not been 100 percent bioturbated, that feature requires explanation (Bromley 1990, p. 200-204). Much of the sedimentary rock record has not been completely bioturbated. Some of the sediments have trace fossils only in the top portion of individual sedimentary units (Fig. 16.2, B). Incomplete bioturbation or no bioturbation results if the sediments cannot support animal life (e.g., if they lack oxygen) or if they were deposited so rapidly that the animals had no time to do their work (Fig. 16.2, A and B). Much of the sediment deposited during a global catastrophe would be deposited too quickly for complete bioturbation. Rock layers with some bioturbation represent the passing of at least a few hours for the animals to walk around and leave their footprints or burrow in the sediment before the next layer was deposited. A careful study of the distribution of bioturbated sediment through the geological record is important for understanding the relationship between specific sediments and a global catastrophe. Another important question is where so many animals came from during a flood to produce all of the existing bioturbation.

The first abundant fossil fish found in the Silurian and Devonian deposits were mostly armored fish; many were bottom-dwelling (benthonic) (Carroll 1988, p. 27, 46). Their probable behavior pattern of hiding from danger on the sea floor would not be helpful for surviving a sudden influx of sediment. As a result, they were the first vertebrates buried.

The movement of water on a global scale deposited sediment over extensive areas, producing the widespread sedimentary formations with similar formations of the same geological age spread over many parts of the world (as described in ch.14). This catastrophic theory offers an explanation for the long gaps of many millions of years in the geologic record. The rock formations were deposited in a rapid sequence of events; no significant period of time elapsed between the deposition of the layers above and below the supposed gap.

Study of the rock record on a large geographic scale has identified an interesting pattern (Fig. 16.3) of six cycles of sedimentation across the North American continent, separated

Figure 16.2 Relationship between bioturbation (animal traces) and sediments. In (A) the sediments were deposited rapidly with no time for bioturbation—or else erosion removed the tops of sedimentary units, removing the traces. In (B) some time allowed for bioturbation after some of the units were deposited; (C) indicates more time after some units were deposited. Almost all of (D) and all of (E) have the original sedimentary structures removed by bioturbation, as would be expected if the deposits were produced slowly under conditions favorable to animal life (after Bromley 1990).

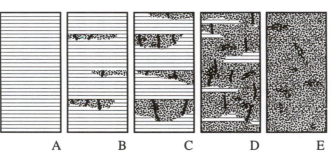

A   B   C   D   E

Carole Stanton

mid-continent by unconformities or times not represented by any rocks (Dott and Prothero 1994). The same pattern continues worldwide with some variation in details (Dott and Prothero 1994). This phenomenon merits more study and has the potential to yield important insights into large-scale processes during the global catastrophe. In a catastrophic theory, the unconformities would represent lowered water level or a change of sediment source areas. This resulted in no sediment in the unconformities, but long periods did not elapse.

In the mid-Paleozoic (early in the catastrophe), the process of mountain building began in some places, producing new mountain ranges like the Appalachian Mountains. The present-day Appalachians are the eroded remains of tremendous uplifts. Why are they so low and eroded into rounded hills while the western mountains are so much higher and more jagged (Fig. 16.4)? The Appalachian Mountains were formed in the Paleozoic. The Rocky Mountains were uplifted much later at the end of the Mesozoic, and the Sierra Nevadas were formed in the late Cenozoic.

The Appalachians formed early in the flood with plenty of time for

water to erode them. The western mountains formed later and apparently near the end of the flood, so they didn't have much opportunity to

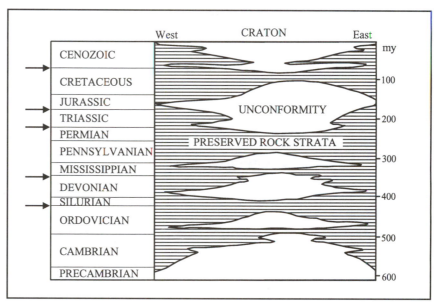

Figure 16.3
Relationship between preserved rock record and major unconformities across North America, with arrows indicating the stratigraphic position of major mass extinctions (adapted from Dott and Prothero 1994).

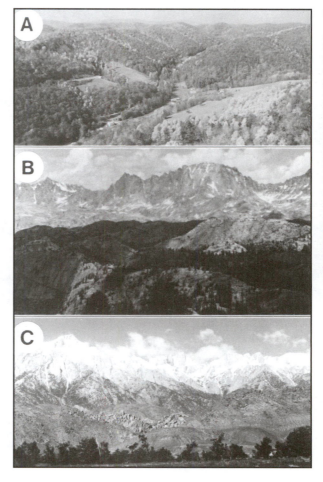

Figure 16.4
(A) The Appalachian Mountains are usually 2,000 to 4,000 feet high with a maximum height of 6,684 feet (photo by Stephen J. Shaluta, Jr.; used by permission of the West Virginia Division of Tourism). (B) The Rocky Mountains reach heights of 14,000 feet. (C) The highest peak in the Sierra Nevada Mountains is Mt. Whitney, 14,494 feet (central peak in photo).

erode. The geographic distribution of coal follows this same east-to-west pattern (Fig. 16.5). This sequence of events during the flood is fascinating, but these theories are not developed sufficiently enough to know just what they mean.

The Carboniferous (Mississippian and Pennsylvanian) coal fields of eastern North America appear to represent the remains of the lowland swampy area along the shores of pre-flood oceans. The swamps were populated with Paleozoic plants, amphibians, reptiles, and other animals (Fig. 16.6). Many of the Carboniferous plants have features that seem to indicate they were floating plants unable to grow in soil. Their roots have air spaces in them, making them more suitable for growing in water. This suggests an alternate possibility. These plants actually may have been part of extensive floating islands (Austin 1979). According to this hypothesis, animals living on these floating masses of plants on the water were easily disrupted and deposited to form coal seams interspersed with other sediments transported in from surrounding areas. In either case, the Carboniferous contains the remains of lowland life zones that evidently came to an end early in the flood, since their fossils do not persist throughout the fossil record.

Some coal deposits contain upright fossil

Figure 16.5
The distribution of coal in the United States (from Montgomery 1990), and the locations and geological age of major mountain ranges.

Figure 16.6
A reconstruction of a Carboniferous swamp environment based on the fossils found in sediments.

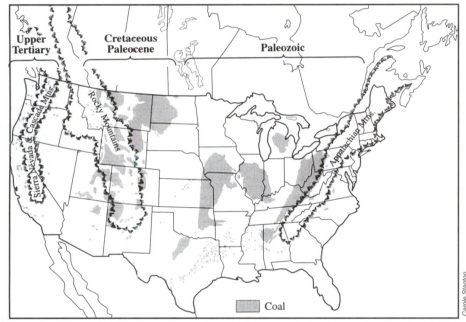

Carole Stanton

Mark Ford

trees. Catastrophic theory predicts that these trees were washed into these spots and buried. Some of the upright Paleozoic fossil trees are hollow and contain the fossilized carcasses of amphibians that fell into the stumps and were buried there.

Fossil vertebrate footprints also are common in middle and upper Paleozoic deposits (Brand and Florence 1982), indicating that the animals were quite active on the new sediments before they were killed or buried. Numerous amphibians or reptiles left their footprints on Permian cross-bedded sandstones like the Coconino Sandstone in Arizona (Fig. 16.7), the Lyons Sandstone in Colorado, the De Chelly Sandstone in Utah, and similar sandstones in Europe, Africa, and other places (McKeever 1991). These tracks are much the same around the world, most of them going up the slopes of the dunes. Where did they go when they got to the top?

One suggestion proposes that this occurred during the flood and the water current washed the animals out of their natural habitat into an area where pure sand was being deposited. As the animals tried to go back where they came from, they were often going up the lee sides of the dunes against the current.

Mesozoic (Middle to Late Flood) Deposits

As the flood continued, its waters encountered other life zones with characteristic animals. Mesozoic deposits contain the remains from preflood lowlands dominated by dinosaurs and other large reptiles. Perhaps they aren't found in the

**Figure 16.7
Fossil vertebrate tracks in the cross-bedded Coconino Sandstone of northern Arizona.**

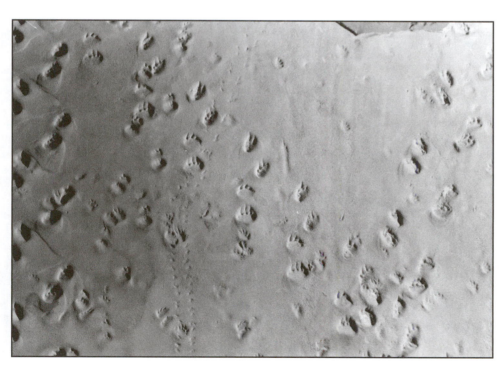

Paleozoic because they lived inland from the swamps. They also may have been more mobile and could escape further. At many different levels in the Mesozoic deposits, additional types of dinosaurs and other animals appear in the rocks for the first time as they were affected by the flood water at differing times (see Fig. 9.18). These include swimming reptiles such as plesiosaurs and ichthyosaurs, and flying reptiles, or pterosaurs.

The first mammals and birds were buried in the Mesozoic. Mesozoic bird fossils are rare and in extinct orders. The Mesozoic mammals (Fig. 16.8) are all small (mouse to rat size), all in extinct groups, and none are common as fossils (Carroll 1988, ch. 18; Lillegraven et al. 1979). The plants in the Mesozoic are a little more familiar to us than the Paleozoic plants, but many are in extinct groups and the flowering plants do not appear until the Cretaceous.

According to this catastrophic theory, the groups of animals that began appearing toward the end of the Mesozoic seem to represent either ones that could escape the flood waters longer than the others or organisms that lived at higher elevations with the late Mesozoic plants in the cooler, upland environments.

The geological column shows a sequence, from mainly marine deposits at the bottom to terrestrial in the upper part. The Paleozoic marine organisms living in the ocean began to be buried early in the flood. As the flood progressed, more terrestrial animals and plants were transported in and buried. After the decline of the flood water, most of the Cenozoic deposits were terrestrial.

The distribution of limestone fits naturally into a flood theory since limestone is most abundant in the Paleozoic and Mesozoic. The amount of limestone decreases up the geological column. This suggests that conditions favorable to large deposits of limestone were prominent before and

Figure 16.8 Two types of Mesozoic mammals: (left) a shrew-sized mammal, *Megazostrodon*, and (right) *Ptilodus*, a multituberculate with tooth cusp patterns quite different from other mammals (after Savage and Long 1986).

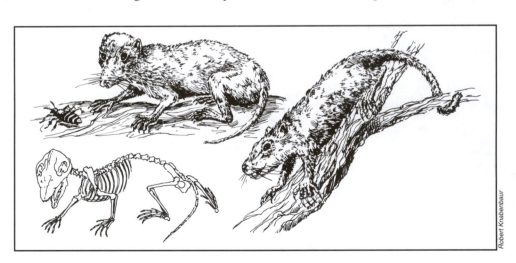

Robert Knabenbaur

during the flood, but are much less common in the modern world.

Fossil tracks and burrows made by invertebrate animals continue to be common throughout the geological column. Many are similar to modern animal tracks and burrows (Bromley 1990; Donovan 1994). This evidence implies that during the flood, many invertebrate animals were moving around. They weren't all suddenly killed and buried. Many continued to live for a time and were able to burrow up through the sand. If there was a quiet period of time, even a few hours, the live animals would make burrows. If sediment accumulated over the burrow, some would try to burrow up through it, leaving escape burrows. Others would swim up in the water and come down on top of the next layer.

Perhaps temporary shore lines formed during the flood with the water line staying at one point for some time. We would expect animals during these times to seek habitats most like the ones they were used to. Those that burrow in the mud in deep water would do so, and others would seek their preferred habitat. If this happened during the

flood, their new homes wouldn't last long. Soon they would have to move on or get buried, but some burrows left behind would become trace fossils.

Many amphibians and reptiles were also active, leaving footprints during the middle part of the flood. Brand and Florence (1982) summarized the available data on stratigraphic distribution of vertebrate tracks. More recent literature reports an abundance of new fossil track sites. These new discoveries still seem to fit the stratigraphic pattern reported by Brand and Florence.

Amphibian footprints are almost entirely limited to the upper Paleozoic, the Triassic, and the lower Jurassic (Fig. 16.9). These early flood footprints are the right size and shape to have been made by the now extinct Paleozoic amphibians. By the end of

**Figure 16.9
Stratigraphic distribution of fossil reptile and amphibian tracks and body fossils (from Brand and Florence 1982).**

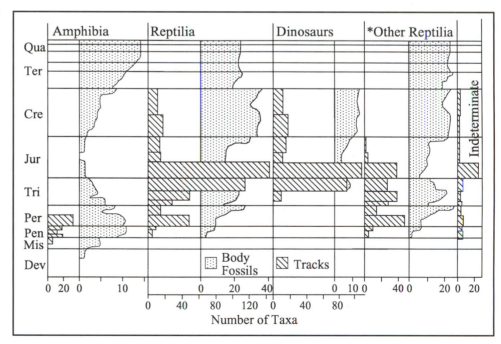

the early Jurassic, almost no more amphibian footprints are found, and very few have been fossilized since then. The greatest diversity of reptile footprints occurs in the Triassic and early Jurassic, but body fossils (bones) are most abundant higher up in the Cretaceous and Tertiary. Apparently, early in the flood they were actively walking or running over the new deposits. Dinosaur tracks are quite diverse in the Triassic and early Jurassic. However, the greatest diversity of their body fossils is in the Cretaceous. Dinosaur tracks are very abundant and yield insight into the life of these animals (Gillette and Lockley 1989; Lockley 1991; Lockley and Hunt 1995; Thulborn 1990).

Fossil tracks of small dinosaurs and other reptiles almost came to an end by the mid-Jurassic, but abundant large dinosaur tracks appear in the late Mesozoic (Brand and Florence 1982). Why have almost no amphibian or reptile tracks (compared with Paleozoic and Mesozoic) been preserved in all of the Cenozoic? Perhaps so many more fossil reptile and amphibian footprints occur earlier in the fossil record because of the unique catastrophic sedimentary conditions that existed during the flood. Those unique conditions did not occur after the Mesozoic, so fewer reptile and amphibian tracks are in more recent (postflood) deposits.

The overall picture shows abundant vertebrate-animal activity recorded in early flood deposits; but by the end of the Jurassic, most of the vertebrates still making tracks were the large dinosaurs. Other tetrapods were mostly dead or were not in areas where new sediments were being deposited. Instead, their carcasses were buried. By the end of the Cretaceous (late flood?), even the large dinosaurs and their tracks came to an end.

Here, a major question needs more study. How did the terrestrial animals get to their burial sites? How come they were alive and well enough to make many footprints? As pointed out earlier (Fig 15.2), some evidence seems to indicate they were transported long distances. The abundant evidence of animal activity poses a problem for that interpretation.

Other evidences of animal behavior can be found in flood or postflood fossils. Some fossil fish have other fish in their stomachs or in the process of being swallowed. These fish were killed and buried so suddenly that both fish skeletons are perfectly preserved. The activities of predators and scavengers during and after the flood probably had a significant impact on the fossil record.

Some vertebrate fossil deposits appear to be entirely composed of bone fragments from predator dung or owl pellets (Dodson and Wexlar 1979; Mellet 1974).

Another evidence of normal behavior is the presence of fossilized reptile nests full of eggs, sometimes containing fossil embryos. Abundant dinosaur nests and eggs have been found on several continents, sometimes on several successive sedimentary layers (Carpenter et al. 1994; Gillette and Lockley 1989, p. 87-118; Hirsch 1994; Horner 1982; Horner and Weishampel 1989).

One hypothesis for interpreting these in a catastrophic framework suggests that perhaps female dinosaurs retained their eggs within their bodies until the eggs were almost ready to hatch, as some modern reptiles do (Goin et al. 1978). When the season for egg-laying arrived, they would search for a place to build a nest. The land surface during the flood was not all under-water all the time (as evidenced by the numerous animal tracks on mudflat environments), so the dinosaurs built nests on an exposed surface and laid their eggs. The next inflow of sediments catastrophically buried the nests (nests of eggs would be well-preserved only by rapid burial). When the land was again exposed, some of the still-surviving dinosaurs would build more nests and lay eggs. This could happen repeat-edly, resulting in several levels of nests in the same geographic area. This story certainly should not be taken as a final answer, but it is a hypothesis to be tested.

Marine deposits are more abundant in the Cretaceous than in earlier parts of the Mesozoic (Fig. 13.10). In fact, the flood waters may have reached their highest point at about that time, destroying preflood upland areas. Some have suggested that upland seas were destroyed at this time. The animals and sediments in those seas were deposited as a new group of marine deposits in the Cretaceous. These proposed upland seas apparently differed in some respects from the lowland seas, since important differences are noted between the Cretaceous and the Paleozoic marine animals (Fig. 9.18).

Late Flood Earth Movements and Mountain Building

Abundant evidence indicates that the continents were not always where they are now. Catastrophic theory must deal with the theory of plate tectonics (Cooper et al. 1990, ch 1; Hamblin and Christiansen 1995, ch. 3, p. 18-22; Monroe and Wicander 1992, ch. 13; Stanley 1993, ch. 6, 7). At one time, apparently, the conti-nents were all close together. They gradually spread apart until they reached their present positions on earth. The nice fit between the continents (at the edges of the continental shelves) on both sides of the Atlantic supports this theory (Fig. 16.10). Also, the mid-oceanic ridge runs down the middle of the Atlantic Ocean, paralleling the contour of the continents on either side. Similar ridges in other oceans (Fig. 16.11) follow the contour of other continental plates that are believed to have been moving away from those ridges. How did this happen? The theory is that a slow movement of hot magma underneath the earth's crust in the mantle began to move the continents apart, producing a crack in the earth's crust. Magma slowly flowed up through the crack and formed a new

ocean floor and the mid-oceanic ridge as the continents continued to move apart (Fig. 16.12).

As the continental plates move over the earth, there are places where two plates collide with each other. The theory says that one of the plates will ride up on top of the other, and the edge (always the oceanic plate) that is being overridden will be pushed down into the mantle. Just as the theory predicts, the deep oceanic trenches occur at places where oceanic plates are being shoved down into the earth by collision with a continental plate. The epicenters of recorded earthquakes are clustered along the areas where plates are colliding (Fig. 16.3). Another type of evidence supporting the theory of continental movement is the match of fossils and types of rock on adjacent continental plates (Fig. 16.10).

Plate tectonics also offers an explanation for the origin of mountain ranges. At the point where two plates collide, one would expect the earth to be buckled and folded by the force of the impact. We do find that major mountain ranges are parallel to the edges of plates that are in collision with other plates—the Andes Mountains in South America, the Alps in Europe, the Rockies in North America, and the

Figure 16.10
The fit between the continents before the formation of the Atlantic Ocean (after Monroe and Wicander 1992). Also shows the distribution of fossil mesosaurs on both sides of the Atlantic Ocean (after Hallam 1972).

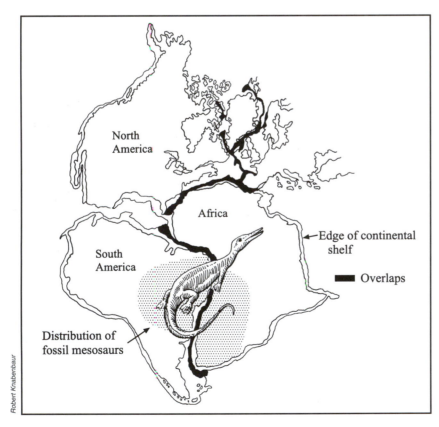

North America

Africa

South America

← Edge of continental shelf

■ Overlaps

Distribution of fossil mesosaurs →

Robert Knabenbaur

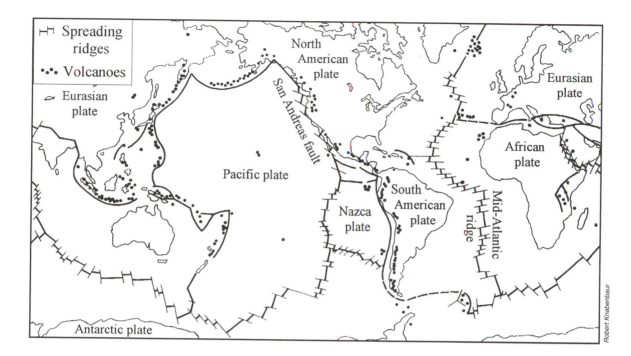

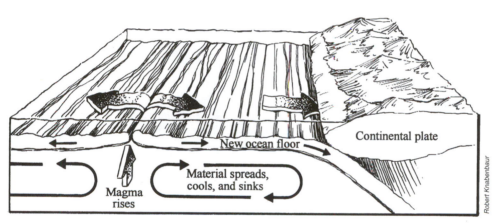

Robert Knabenbaur

Himalayas in Asia. The evidence for plate tectonics includes much more than is summarized here.

The significant amount of continental movement that must be included in our catastrophic theory requires more rapid movement than neocatastrophic concepts of geology accept. If this process took 1,000 years, a continental movement of 2,000 miles would require an average speed of 1.2 feet/hour. The process seems to have begun near the end of the flood and continued for a while afterwards. The greatest difficulty with this hypothesis is posed by the physical effects of moving continent-sized plates that fast. This unanswered question may be related to the question of how the laccoliths could cool down so quickly. A model for rapid plate tectonics during the flood has been proposed by Baumgardner (1986, 1990, 1992, 1994a, 1994b, 1994c) and Austin et al. (1994).

In North America, the Rocky Mountains formed during the late

Figure 16.11
The continental plates and spreading ridges showing where ocean floor is forming (after Monroe and Wicander 1992).

Figure 16.12
A cross-section through a portion of the earth's crust showing the presumed movement of magma that moves the continents and produces new ocean floor (after Montgomery 1990).

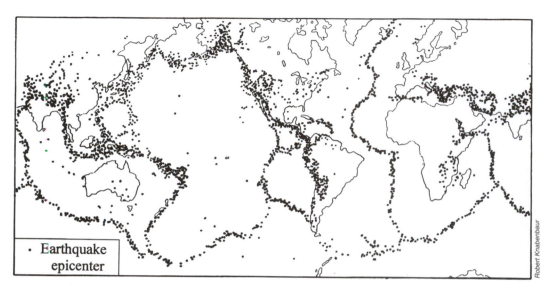

Robert Knabenbaur

· Earthquake
epicenter

Robert Knabenbaur

**Figure 16.13
Locations of modern earthquakes which are primarily
along the contacts between
continental plates (after
Montgomery 1990).**

**Figure 16.14
Cross-section illus-
trating the formation of
an overthrust. The
sedimentary layers are
pushed from the left,
buckle to form an
overthrusted mountain,
and erode to the
modern form of the
mountain (see Fig.
16.15) (after Eardley
1965).**

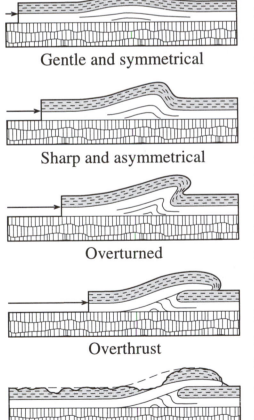

Gentle and symmetrical

Sharp and asymmetrical

Overturned

Overthrust

Overthrust showing erosion

Mesozoic and early Cenozoic.
Another major episode of coal formation was associated with the Rocky
Mountain uplift (Fig. 16.5). In some
places, a formation or series of formations evidently was broken at a fault
zone and then the strata on one side
were pushed up and over the top of
the same strata on the other side of
the fault (Fig. 16.14, 16.15) to form
an overthrust (Hatcher 1995, ch. 11;
Monroe and Wicander 1992, p. 393-
394). One result of an overthrust is
that older rocks are sitting on top of
younger rocks. A number of these
exist around the world, and a large
part of the Canadian Rockies is a
gigantic overthrust belt (Fig. 16.15).
In a global catastrophe in which
continents are actually moving around
the earth, it's no big surprise that
some rock strata have slid right over
other rock for many miles.

Late Flood and Postflood

Exactly where in the fossil record the
initial year of the flood ends is
especially difficult to determine. It is
probably somewhere between the
Cretaceous and the Pliocene—a big

range of uncertainty. Much more work is needed before we have an adequate understanding of how to relate the end of the flood to the Cenozoic fossil record. How much of the Cenozoic represents flood deposits? How much of it is a transition period after the flood before things settled down? In this book, I have placed most of the Cenozoic in the postflood period. That is only a working hypothesis. Other options must be kept in mind.

It's unlikely that the flood ended suddenly or that the survivors found the earth dry, calm, and back to normal. The geological data seem to indicate that catastrophic activity gradually tapered off until the earth's crust reached a state of equilibrium with only slow changes occurring during the last few thousand years. All we can deduce from the Bible is that, after the year of the flood, enough dry land surrounded the Mountains of Ararat to support the people and animals. (Note that the Bible says mountains of Ararat, not Mount Ararat. The mountain currently called Mount Ararat apparently did not get that name until about the 12th century AD [Spencer and Lienard 1988, unpublished]. Mount Ararat is probably not where the ark landed).

Carole Stanton

When the flood was ending and during the transition period after the flood, a lot of water was moving around on the earth. The newly formed landscape was not yet in equilibrium and tremendous erosion could occur rapidly. Probably much of the present spectacular scenery—like the Grand Canyon, the San Juan River meanders, and many other canyons and cliffs—were carved during the time after the flood. Steve Austin (1994) has proposed a hypothesis for the carving of the Grand Canyon by catastrophic draining of a large inland lake. Experiments by Koss et al. (1994) indicate that when a continental area is underwater and the water level drops to expose the land, one result is the carving of canyons or valleys similar to the Grand Canyon. They didn't invoke a catastrophic theory in their discussion, but a global catastrophe would explain where all that water came from.

Figure 16.15
Photo of overthrust strata in the Canadian Rockies. Sediments above the thrust fault have moved toward the right, over the top of older strata below the fault. Subsequent erosion has removed part of the sediment, leaving these remnants.

The Rocky Mountains began to develop in the Jurassic, but the process continued as the Cretaceous and early Cenozoic deposits were forming. During the uplifting of the mountain ranges, erosion removed the sediments that formed the tops of the mountains. Today it's evident that the sedimentary rock formations that once crossed these areas have been tilted up against the slopes of the uplifted mountains (Fig. 16.16) and eroded off the mountain tops to expose the granite that forms the high peaks in these ranges.

By the end of the flood, the original climate-control system had been modified and the earth began to cool off during the Cenozoic. This change occurred gradually, and during the Eocene, tropical plants and animals still were being fossilized in the Arctic (Francis 1991).

Extinctions

At several points in the fossil record, often called crises in the history of life, an especially large number of groups of animals went extinct (Fig. 16.3; 13.24) (Carlisle 1995; Donovan 1989; Chaloner and Hallam 1989). At the end of the Permian, at least half of the types of animals that occurred as fossils in the Paleozoic rocks went extinct. Clams occur in the Paleozoic and other clams in the Mesozoic, but they are not the same kinds of clams. The Paleozoic species became extinct just as some whole groups did—for example, the trilobites.

One prominent extinction came at the end of the Cretaceous (Carlisle

Figure 16.16
Sedimentary layers tilted up along the flank of a folded mountain.

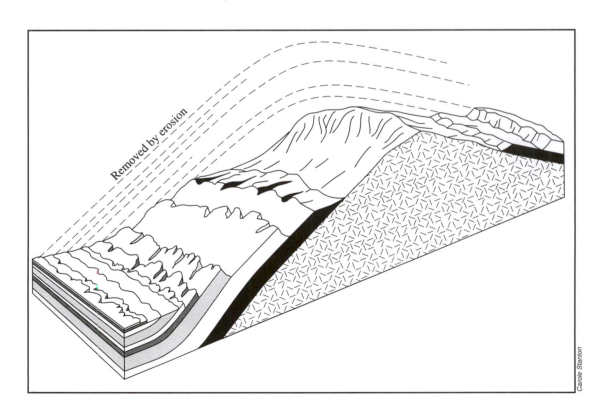

Carole Stanton

1995; Stanley 1993, p. 388-393). All of the large reptiles, including the dinosaurs, went extinct. The pterosaurs and the swimming reptiles such as plesiosaurs, ichthyosaurs, and others also went extinct, along with many types of marine invertebrates.

Neocatastrophic theory proposes that at these times of crisis, something changed, such as climate, and the animals couldn't cope with it; many types were wiped out. A prominent theory proposes that some of these crises were caused by catastrophic asteroid impacts on our earth (Chaloner and Hallam 1989, p. 421-435; Glen 1990; Gould 1989b; Stanley 1993, p. 389-393; Ward 1995) and/or massive volcanic activity (Kerr 1995a). Animals that were left colonized the earth and evolved into new forms to fill the now empty niches.

Catastrophic geology proposes, on the other hand, that these crises occurred when the flood reached some critical point and the remaining members of certain groups of organisms were all killed and buried. A life zone may have been destroyed. For example, the lowland swamps that were inhabited by some Paleozoic creatures were destroyed. Thus the deposition of sediments and organisms from these lowland areas came to an end. Deposits forming afterwards no longer contained fossils

from that life zone. In some cases, a group of organisms went almost extinct, and those individuals that survived the extinction avoided getting buried and fossilized. They are not found as fossils in later rocks, but they are still alive today. An example is the Coelacanth fish that was thought to have been extinct for 60 million years, but has been found living in the ocean near India.

The distributions of mass extinctions in the fossil record have an intriguing relationship to the continent-wide pattern of rocks and major unconformities. The most significant mass extinctions were during or at the end of major or minor episodes of sedimentation across the continents (Fig. 16.3). This is another feature that deserves more study.

The extinction at the end of the Cretaceous is especially interesting. Why did the dinosaurs go extinct? Paleontological theory is currently grappling with this post-Cretaceous extinction. The catastrophic theory perhaps does a little better. While we also do not know exactly what happened, it isn't too hard to imagine some critical stage in the flood when the dinosaurs and some other animals were no longer able to survive. Perhaps an asteroid impact was at least part of the process that caused the extinction to occur at that time. The animals died out or were too decimated to reestablish themselves after the flood. At least they did not live long enough to leave a fossil record.

The widespread deposits that were common in the Paleozoic and Mesozoic (as described in chapter 14) do not occur in the Cenozoic in North America. The Rockies had pushed up, forming valleys between the ranges. Much of the Tertiary sediment (Fig. 16.17) in North America is in the west, partly filling these valleys (Fig. 14.7B) and spilling over onto the plains to the east and west. They contain abundant mammal fossils which were rare in Mesozoic deposits. Bird fossils are also more common and diverse in the Tertiary.

Vertebrate fossils are often found as accumulations of transported bones. Even those who are not catastrophists recognize evidence that most if not all of our mammal

deposits represent animals that were washed into their current location by water. Some fossil-bearing deposits show obvious evidence of rapid deposition, at least in local floods, while others are usually interpreted as accumulating over a period of time in a river or lake system. Catastrophic theory proposes that the overall process occupied a much shorter time span. However, each deposit must be examined to determine how it was deposited and where it fits in the flood/postflood sequence of events.

The sediments help to provide clues about the environment in which they were deposited. Taphonomy, the study of the processes between death of an organism and its fossilization (Allison and Briggs 1991; Behrensmeyer and Hill 1980; Briggs 1995; Donovan 1991; Lyman 1994), also yields insightful information. An animal that was buried quickly after it died produces an articulated fossil skeleton; but if it decomposes for months, the bones disarticulate. The disarticulated bones may be scattered, damaged, and/or transported and mixed with other bones. Shells of invertebrate animals become abraded or otherwise damaged when transported by water. Others, still in very good shape

Figure 16.17
The Eocene Bridger Formation in Wyoming which contains numerous fossil vertebrates and invertebrates.

when they were deposited and fossilized, indicate that they did not experience much transport. This information yields insights into the history of fossil deposits. A catastrophist honestly searching for truth must pursue these studies of sedimentology and taphonomy with as much care and objectivity as any other scientist. A catastrophist also enters such studies alert to the possibility that there may not be any modern analogues on as large a scale as the flood processes that produced some sedimentary deposits and doesn't have an *a priori* preference for processes that occupy long periods of time. We have never observed a modern erosional event on the scale of the Channeled Scablands. J. Harlan Bretz (who doesn't believe in a biblical flood) was successful in interpreting the evidence in the Scablands (Baker 1978) because he was evidently more open-minded than other geologists of his day to the possibility of a more catastrophic process than is seen in modern analogues.

Flood Survival and Postflood Biogeography

At some point during the deposition of the Cenozoic formations, animals began spreading over the earth and establishing themselves on the new landscape. How did they get where

they are now? Did they all leave the ark and find their way to new homes? This topic is a significant challenge that catastrophic theorists must address. First, we should recognize that the story of the ark involves only a small portion of the animals and none of the plants. The spread of plants apparently depended on seeds that were carried far and wide by flood water and then landed, sprouted, and survived in areas where the environment was right for them. Could it be that some seedlings or other plants also survived long enough in the water or on floating debris to settle in the mud and grow?

Marine animals had to make their own way. They were in the water, their own element, and survival and geographic spread depended on their ability to tolerate such conditions in the water as turbidity, chemical changes, temperature changes, and destruction of breeding grounds which, for many animals, is one of the most critical and specific requirements for completing their life cycle.

Fresh-water organisms faced a different type of challenge since it appears that some suddenly found themselves in salt water. The effect of this mixing of waters leaves many questions unanswered. One hypothesis to consider is that, as large fresh-water bodies spill out onto the rising ocean, the less dense fresh water may not mix quickly with the salt water and it stays on top long enough to provide a temporary refuge for fresh-water organisms. Perhaps, too, many animals have a greater potential for adaptation to changing water conditions than we have recognized.

The terrestrial invertebrates probably had more options for survival. An enormous amount of floating plant debris, perhaps even floating islands, would mean that animals could live on for a long time during the flood until they landed on a newly emerged land surface. This would be especially true for upland organisms whose environments were the last to be uprooted during the flood. The groups of organisms affected last during the flood spent the shortest time in the water before finding new homes. These would be the groups most likely to survive into the new postflood world. The sequence of events in the geological record suggests that new mountains were appearing before the old land surface was all destroyed. The flood was a complex event. Thus, even though the preflood mountains were covered (and no doubt destroyed), we can't necessarily assume that all the land was covered at the same time. This would favor the survival of many organisms that could find shelter on the available land.

The biggest questions involve the terrestrial vertebrates. These seem to be the animals described as making their way to the postflood earth on the ark. Did modern biogeographic distributions of the terrestrial vertebrates result from the spread of all of these groups from the ark in Asia Minor to their present location? It wouldn't be too hard to explain the horses, elephants, rabbits, and a variety of others, but what about the kangaroos and numerous other marsupials of Australia, the tree-dwelling sloths of South America (they cannot walk effectively on the ground), or the pocket gophers that live only in North America? Did the complex of closely related rodent families found only in South America all stick together as they avoided other continents and made their way together to, and only to, South America? This situation is complicated further by the fact that their fossil relatives also are found only in South America.

A large number of mammal families have a fossil record and modern distribution limited to only one continent. Did they travel from the ark and return only to their original home without even leaving any fossils along the way? This could happen by chance for a few families, especially if their home was a continent readily accessible to Asia Minor. However, 59 families of mammals fit this pattern (Table 16.1), and the continents with the highest percentage of endemic families are Australia and South America, two continents that are farthest removed from Asia Minor and the most difficult to reach from there.

The geographic distribution of reptile groups does not show the pattern so characteristic of mammals. Based on a preliminary analysis of the data, the distribution of reptiles appears to be consistent with the hypothesis that their modern distribution could have resulted from a spread from one point on the globe. Modern groups of amphibians do not have an adequate fossil record to address this question.

The fossil record of endemic bird families does not match the modern geographic distribution of those same families. Families that are now endemic to one continent tend to have a fossil record in other continents as well. Modern bird distribution seems to be explained more by birds' superior long-distance migration than by biogeographic history (Feduccia 1994 [oral presentation and written material]). The biogeographic problem is most acute for mammals.

After carefully analyzing this issue, I conclude that the current distribution of at least the terrestrial mammals from their spread, and under their own power, from Asia Minor is refuted by the above cited

data (Brand 1982; Gibson and Brand 1983 [unpublished papers]). Perhaps the God who initiated the flood and brought the mammals to the ark also involved Himself in concluding the process by distributing the mammals so that the repopulation of the earth would proceed in a balanced fashion. Whether or not other possibilities are compatible with Scripture needs further study. The choice between such interpretations is strictly philo-sophical, but science can be used to analyze patterns of animal movement after the initial point. Science can only deal with concrete data on geographic distribution patterns and hypotheses about patterns of movement of the animals as revealed by data, not with ultimate questions about causation.

Whatever the mechanism, animal distributions tend to show a consistent pattern throughout the fossil record. Distribution patterns in the preflood

Table 16.1
Number of Endemic Mammal Families in Six Paleogeographic Regions (Compared with total number of mammal families)

Paleogeographic Region	Total Families	Endemic Families	
		No.	% of total
Neotropic (S. & C. America)	39	24	62
Australian	16	14	88
Nearctic (N. America)	23	2	9
Ethiopian (Africa)	37	13	35
Oriental (SE. Asia)	31	4	13
Palearctic (Europe & Asia)	32	2	6
Total	101	59	58

Note: In this study "endemic" is defined as a family with its modern and pre-Pleistocene fossil distribution limited to that same paleogeographic region. Some families that have no living forms, but have a fossil record reaching into the Pleistocene, are included. Only terrestrial forms are considered.

world are not accessible to us. We don't know how much the fossil record was affected by animals being carried long distances during the flood before they were buried. The catastrophist can pursue biogeographic study with the assumption that the early fossil record of various groups indicates a pattern of burial activity during the flood. The more recent fossil record and modern distribution patterns reveal migrations and speciation events since that time, many of which can be related to such geological processes as glaciation, formation, and colonization of islands; changes in sea level; etc. These processes can be studied by methods useful to biogeographers working under different paradigms.

Post-flood Evolution

After the flood, conditions were ideal for rapid speciation. The earth was largely empty with many niches to be filled. The animals were spreading over the empty earth, becoming isolated in ecological pockets in valleys, in mountain ranges, and on new islands. Catastrophic geology proposes that new species were forming rapidly as animals and plants adapted to changed conditions on the earth, and modern biogeographic patterns—modern distribution of species and higher groupings—were established at this time. For example,

a group of salamanders apparently spread down through the Sierra Nevada and Coast Range mountains of California and adapted to the conditions they encountered there (Fig. 8.6). Some populations of salamanders moved into caves and became adapted to that environment—even becoming blind because their eyes were useless in a dark cave.

The volcanic islands of Galapagos and Hawaii apparently formed after the flood. Several groups of animals have gotten to these and other islands, perhaps on floating debris on the oceans. Speciation then occurred on the islands.

The chipmunks spread over Asia, where one species still lives today, and to North America (or the reverse). Perhaps they came across what is now known as the Bering Straits. Evidently, land connected Asia and North America at one time. The chipmunks scattered over North America and developed into separate species in different mountain ranges and other ecological pockets. The voles, like the chipmunks, speciated simultaneously in many places. A large number of species and even genera resulted through the operation of microevolution and speciation processes in these and other animal groups.

Kurt Wise (1989) has developed an interventionist version of punctuated equilibrium that makes fruitful predictions about the patterns in the fossil record. Characteristically, fossil species abruptly appear in the fossil record (no transitions from ancestral species) and exhibit stasis (no substantial morphological change through time). In a catastrophic theory in which at least much of the Paleozoic and Mesozoic were deposited rapidly in a flood, exceptions to abrupt appearance and stasis in fossil species should appear, if at all, in the Cenozoic sediments since they were deposited more slowly. That prediction seems to be confirmed, since the fossils that come closest to violating abrupt appearance and stasis are unicellular organisms in the Cenozoic. These organisms have short generation times (less than a year) which also facilitate rapid change in a relatively short time.

After the flood, coral reefs apparently began to grow. Some of these reefs, such as Enewetok Atoll in the Pacific Ocean, have a depth of 1,405 m from the basaltic rock of the ocean floor to the top of the reef. Can a reef grow that much in a few thousand years? Coral doesn't grow if it is more than 50 m below the ocean surface. So the Enewetok reef must have begun growing when the ocean was quite shallow and continued growing as the ocean bottom gradually subsided. These would be ideal circumstances for rapid growth of coral, perhaps even adequate to grow the Enewetok reef in 3,400 years (Roth 1979).

Cenozoic Basin Deposits

A lot of volcanic activity went on during and after the flood process. The volcanoes produced ash deposits, lava flows, or deposits of volcanic breccia. The Yellowstone deposits are mostly breccia and ash from volcanic eruptions rather than lava flows. In other places, extensive deposits originated as molten lava flowed from long fissures and formed extensive basalt plateaus (Rampino and Stothers 1988) (Table 16.2). A notable example is the Columbia River Basalt, a series of thick layers covering eastern Washington and Oregon (Fig. 16.18). This enormous deposit of lava dwarfs anything we see happening today, but it is small compared to lava deposits in other areas. The only area where this type of deposit is still forming is in Iceland.

During the Eocene, the trees of the Yellowstone fossil forests were

Table 16.2 Basalt plateaus Data from Monroe and Wicander (1992)		
Basalt Plateau	Area (km2)	Average thickness (m)
Snake River Plain, Idaho	50,000	
Columbia River basalts, NW United States	164,000	1,000
Deccan Traps, India	500,000	1,000
Parana Plateau, Brazil	1,200,000	650
Karroo basalts, South Africa	2,000,000	700
Siberian Platform, USSR	2,500,000	360
Northern Australia	400,000	1,000
Great Lakes Region, USA & Canada	100,000	Up to 5,000

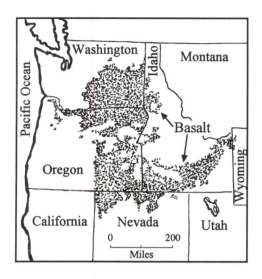

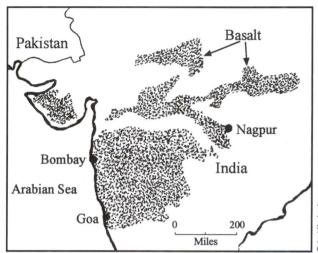

**Figure 16.18
The distribution of (left) the
Columbia River Basalt in
northwestern United States,
and (right) a large basalt
field in the Deccan Plateau
in India (after Longwell et
al. 1969).**

being buried (Coffin 1979a, 1979b, 1992; Fritz 1980; Ritland and Ritland 1974; also see list in ch. 5). Perhaps they were deposited while this area was still under water, or at least while there was enough rain and standing water to produce mud slides down the sides of the volcanoes, burying the trees as has happened at Mt. St. Helens.

About the same time (in the Eocene), deposits of fine-grained volcanic sediments and coarser sediments eroded from adjacent mountains were filling the valleys to the south and southeast in Wyoming,

Utah, and even Colorado. These volcanic sediments formed the flood-plain sediments in the Wasatch and Bridger Formations. A few volcanic layers also settled in the lake that occupied part of the same basin and formed the Green River Formation with its millions of fossil fish, shore-line reefs formed by stromatolites, and other fossils.

The upper Tertiary holds more direct evidence of bird and mammal activity that must have been postflood, including corkscrew-shaped burrows of extinct giant beavers. Many types of mammal footprints also are found in Tertiary deposits (especially upper Tertiary). Almost all of them were made by carnivores, ungulates (hoofed mammals), or elephants. Fossil-bird footprints are not as common as mammal prints, but the majority of those that have been found are also in upper Tertiary deposits (Fig. 16.19). Many of these footprints

**Figure 16.19
The stratigraphical distribution of fossil bird and
mammal tracks (from Brand
and Florence 1982).**

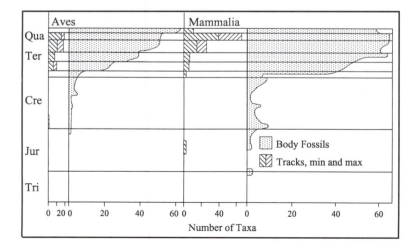

probably can be interpreted as post-flood fossils. One might ask why there aren't at least a few tracks in flood deposits lower in the geologic column. Perhaps there are. Some bird and mammal tracks are found in Mesozoic deposits, and at least two papers in the paleontological literature report fossils that look just like bird tracks. However, since they are found in Paleozoic formations, they are labeled merely as unidentified tracks (Gilmore 1927; Sternberg 1933) (Fig. 16.20).

A great diversity of bird and mammal fossils occurs in the Cenozoic (although bird fossils are usually not abundant). The upland areas of the preflood world logically would be the last habitats to be destroyed by the flood waters. It appears that this is where most of the birds and mammals lived. Several other groups of modern organisms have stratigraphic distributions very similar to those of birds and mammals (Fig. 9.18). Perhaps a number of these groups were largely inhabitants of the preflood upland regions. Apparently, many groups of preflood animals and plants did not survive long in the cooler postflood world.

The Ice Age

The Pleistocene clearly represents events that occurred after the flood. Something happened to change the climate, bringing on the Pleistocene glaciation. After that episode, earth's climate finally warmed up again and the ice melted back to expose more land. It appears that there may have been a few cycles of retreat and advance of the glacial front. When all the ice was on the land, enough water was frozen up in the glaciers to lower ocean levels as much as 300 feet.

During and after glaciation, large lakes developed in western North America. In eastern Washington state, the Channeled Scablands resulted from the rapid draining of one of these lakes, Lake Missoula (Fig.

Figure 16.20
Two bird-like tracks from Paleozoic sediments (after [A] Sternberg 1993 and [B] Gilmore 1927).

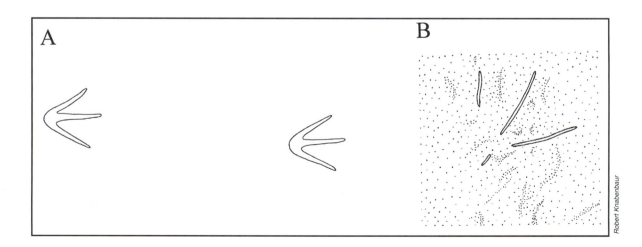

Robert Knabenbaur

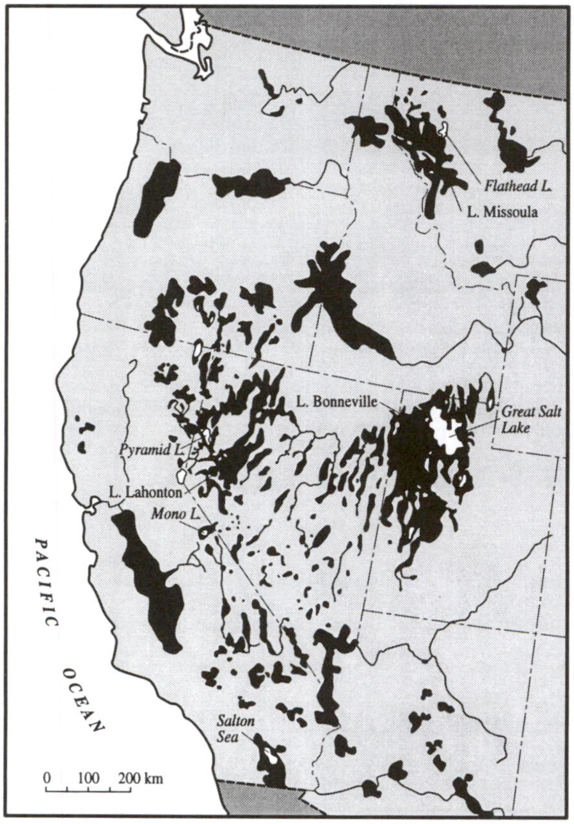

Larson 1978, p. 370) (Fig. 16.21).

The shorelines of these Pleistocene lakes can be seen in the desert basins in Nevada, and especially in Utah along the Wasatch Mountains (Fig. 16.22) from Salt Lake City south to Provo and beyond. Interventionists sometimes cite these old shorelines as evidence of the receding waters of the flood. But the flood waters certainly must have been gone before glaciation, and these shorelines are from the receding of the glacial waters.

At the same time, the earth's crust was readjusting after glaciation. The tremendous weight of the ice pushed the earth's crust down. As the ice melted, the land rebounded, rising slowly to a new stable position. In some places, a significant elevation change took place, even in the last 2,000 years, as can be seen in Italy (Fig. 16.23). The ruins of a Roman

Carole Stanton

Figure 16.21
Pleistocene lakes that filled basins in western United States at the end of the ice age (after Foster 1969).

14.2). The Great Salt Lake once covered a large part of western Utah, almost down to Arizona, and is called Lake Bonneville. Many desert valleys in California, Nevada, and Utah were also filled with water (Birkeland and

Figure 16.22
Old shorelines (arrow) of ancient Lake Bonneville, north of Salt Lake City, Utah.

Carole Stanton

market, within a few blocks of the ocean, are now partly under water. These buildings were above sea level in the second century AD. Then they sank slowly until during the Middle Ages when marine, boring animals made their burrows in the stone columns 18 feet above the floor level of the structure. Before 1500 A.D., the area began to rise again. Now it is under only a few feet of water (Birkeland and Larson 1978, p. 510-511). These ancient buildings in Italy provide evidence of continuing adjustments of the earth's crust long after glaciation.

Glaciation had a profound influence on the climate in the northern hemisphere. When northern Europe and North America were covered

with ice, the rest of Europe and eastern North America were covered mostly by tundra and coniferous forest. As the glaciers melted, the plant communities moved north until today tundra is found only in the far north and on mountain peaks. The coniferous forest is in the mountains and in northern Canada. Most of Europe and eastern North America are covered by deciduous forest (Dott and Prothero 1994, p. 529, 530) (Fig. 16.24).

The changes in climate were accompanied by changes in the distributions of animals. In North America, the muskox and a very little animal, the arctic shrew, are found now only in the northern part of Alaska and Canada. Pleistocene fossils of muskox

Figure 16.23
Roman ruins near Naples, Italy, showing evidence of submergence and more recent rise above sea level (after Longwell et al. 1969).

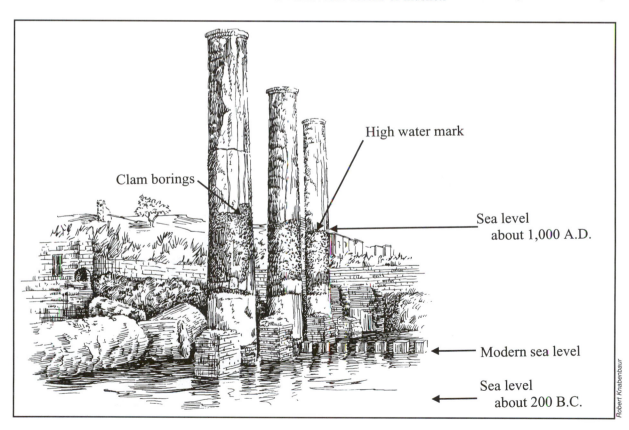

Clam borings

High water mark

Sea level about 1,000 A.D.

Modern sea level

Sea level about 200 B.C.

Robert Knabenbaur

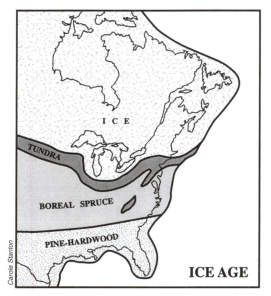

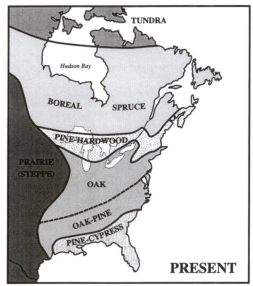

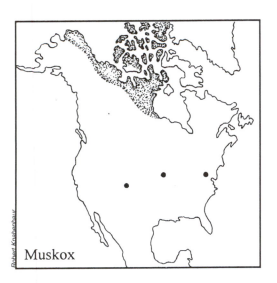

Muskox

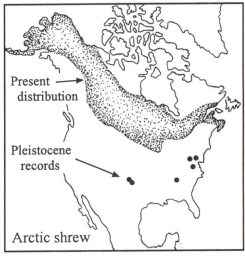

Present distribution

Pleistocene records

Arctic shrew

Figure 16.24 Distribution of vegetation types in eastern North America during the ice age and present distribution (after Dott and Prothero 1994).

Figure 16.25 Modern and Pleistocene distribution of the arctic shrew and the muskox (after Hibbard et al. 1965).

and arctic shrews, from glacial times, can be found much farther south in central United States (Fig. 16.25) (Hibbard et al. 1965). It appears that since the glaciers disappeared, the climate has changed accordingly. The life zones have all moved northward. Neocatastrophism and catastrophism agree on this basic sequence of events, but catastrophism proposes that they occurred over a much shorter time span.

Post-Flood Humans and Other Fossils

In North America during the Pleistocene, a fauna of large game animals comparable to the type of fauna that now exists in Africa populated the land. At that time, the area near Wilshire Blvd. in Los Angeles looked quite different from today. Mammoths, mastodons, wild horses, lions similar to African lions, wolves, saber tooth cats, huge ground sloths, dire wolves, camels, and other exotic, wild mammals were roaming the area (Stock 1956). A variety of birds lived there also, including vultures and a type of condor larger than our modern condor. An impressive accumulation of skeletons of these animals was preserved in the tar pools now called the La Brea tar pits.

All of these animals lived in North America post-flood. We don't know why these large animals went extinct. Mastodons or other fossil animals have been found with arrowheads stuck in them, and other evidence implicates humanity in their death (Stanley 1993, p. 469-470).

All known human fossils have been found in the Pleistocene. One human fossil site called Mummy Cave is east of Yellowstone National Park, near Cody, Wyoming. Apparently, ancient Indians camped at this spot during their travels, and charcoal from their campfires and artifacts such as arrowheads were left behind. Sediment covered these areas and other Indian parties camped at the same site on top of the new sediment. In this way, a sequence of fossil-bearing layers was produced over a period of perhaps several thousand years. On one level, a mummified person was found, giving the cave its name. Some believe that the deposits at Mummy Cave accumulated over a period of nine to ten thousand years. We can propose it didn't take that long, and that after the flood the

climate was wetter and sediments were accumulating more rapidly than they do today. The layers still represent the passage of time associated with changes in the human cultures that left their artifacts behind. For instance, the arrowheads definitely change as we explore up through the layers.

Many unanswered questions about ancient humans still remain. Why do no human fossils appear in deposits considered to be flood deposits? Were there actually so few humans then? Did the antedeluvians all escape long enough to decay on the surface after the flood? Perhaps future discoveries will help to answer these questions.

Modern Processes and the Study of the Flood Deposits

When the flood was over, the earth went through a long period of readjustment. The earth's crust came much closer to being in equilibrium. The geological processes of erosion and sedimentation slowed to more gradual or sporadic rates. Mountain-building processes and other major readjustments of the earth's crust are no longer occurring at rates noticeable to us.

Today, rivers slowly cross the landscape, carving out wide meanders and then cutting them off during storms, leaving oxbow lakes. Windstorms blow dust and sand and produce new sedimentary deposits, including desert sand dunes. Ocean waves round off pebbles and grind them smaller, finally producing sand, and the waves and currents shift the sand and make new sedimentary deposits. The coastline erodes, and we can measure how fast it erodes. Earthquakes occur, and their strength and location can be measured. Volcanic lava flows and other types of volcanic eruptions are observed. They do not seem to occur on a scale that they have in some cases in the geological record, but the basic processes are the same. We can all watch on TV as prime residential areas in California slump into the ocean and flash floods in the desert slowly add more sediment to the alluvial fans along the hills.

These processes (modern analogues) help us to understand the past, but they also have all been studied during the recent, relatively stable, part of earth history (according to catastrophic theory). As a result, they introduce a strong bias towards the interpretation that ancient rocks were deposited slowly, over very long periods of time. It is possible also that some natural bias exists against deeper water sedimentary processes, since it is more difficult to study the details of modern deep-water deposits than shallower water or terrestrial deposits. The study of modern analogues yields many valuable

insights, but catastrophic geology argues mainly with the rates of geological processes determined from such analogues.

In recent decades, the data have led science to recognize that the deposition of the rocks involved much more catastrophism than was previously thought. Catastrophic geology, which does not make the *a priori* assumption of millions of years of time, predicts that continued research will indicate still far more catastrophic geologic processes than have been currently envisioned. I even suggest that researchers who are open to that possibility ultimately will be more successful in understanding earth history.

The basic concepts of this catastrophic theory suggest a series of events that could have happened. Many things still lack answers, just as other scientists are also without answers. I can't wait to see how the accumulating data will change and improve our catastrophic theories in the coming years, making them more effective in explaining the geological events of the past. Research can be directed toward two different issues: (1) the improvement of the catastrophic theory and (2) attempted tests between catastrophic and neocatastrophic theory. Many areas of research can contribute to the development of catastrophic theory when it is entered with a willingness to use that theory to suggest hypotheses and test them. Some central topics of research that come to mind include (1) a study of any indicators of sea level at various stages in the geological column; (2) a study of the sequence of paleoenvironments, one geological basin at a time, for comparison with flood theories; (3) a development of a 3-dimensional model of the movement of sediments and organisms during the flood process; (4) a quantitative study of the extent and nature of unique and widespread deposits, on a global scale; (5) the study of paleocurrents over large areas; (6) an analysis of indicators of animal activity in relation to sedimentation; and (7) a study of taphonomy to evaluate such things as which fossil deposits were formed rapidly. More detailed research also may be needed on the structure and origin of some fossils currently called reefs, stromatolites, etc. Austin et al. (1994) suggest additional research questions to solve.

Research which tests whether catastrophic or neocatastrophic theory provides better explanations for the data should be directed especially to the items in the two outer lists at the end of chapter 14. Other research suggestions were made at the end of chapter 12. And consider these suggestions: a study of fossil reefs to evaluate the strength of the evidence that they are true reefs and are buried in their original growing position, or whether some of these reefs could have been transported as large blocks—as suggested by Conaghan et al. (1976). It probably would be valuable to analyze the geographic and stratigraphic distribution of fossil reefs in relation to theoretical reconstructions of preflood oceans to determine which of these fossil structures could have grown before the flood. Further analysis of the origin and distribution of stromatolites and other apparent indicators of the passage of time (independent of radiometric dating) is also needed, along with more general quantitative analysis of the time gaps in the rock record and of evidence for large scale erosion and its distribution in the geologic record.

Individually we face the important decision of what to do with the alternative paradigms of earth history. On the one hand is the scenario developed by naturalistic science, of life arising and evolving by itself over several billion years. Many thousands of scientists use this concept as the basis for interpreting all their evidence. It has worked very well and appears to be a stable, reliable explanation for earth history and the history of life.

On the other hand, some believe that although major portions of that standard scientific paradigm are on the right track, other significant aspects are not. Those of us who are of that persuasion are convinced that, if we open our minds to new ideas and testable hypotheses suggested by the biblical story of origins, this approach ultimately will lead to an even more successful explanation for the history of life and of the earth. This implies that some segments of scientific theory that now appear to be solid are going to break down in the future in the face of continuing accumulation of evidence.

The latter, interventionist

paradigm promotes vigorous research in all areas of science. Progress is made by opening our minds to new possibilities generally excluded from consideration by the rules of naturalistic science rather than by ridiculing or downgrading the ability of science and scientists. This work must be done with the highest standards of scientific quality. Elton Trueblood (1958) set an important objective before us when he stated that

> the religious scientist has more reason to be careful of his evidence than has the nonreligious scientist, because he is handling what is intrinsically sacred. Shoddiness, for him, is something to spurn because it is a form of blasphemy.

Based on the foregoing, I suggest the following summary of current scientific theory (the lists below are representative and are not intended to be complete):

1. *Fields of science that are not affected by the assumptions of interventionism or naturalism* and can progress with equal effectiveness under either paradigm—fields that do not focus on the study of history—are:

Anatomy
Physical chemistry
Physiology
Organic chemistry
Biochemistry
Physics
Molecular biology
Animal behavior (most)
Medical science
Ecology

2. *Areas of scientific theory that attempt to explain history and are accepted by interventionists* as worthy of our confidence—with the normal changes expected as science advances—are:

Genetics of microevolution and speciation, and macroevolution at lower taxonomic levels (at least genera)

Analysis of phylogenetic pathways of biological change at the level of subspecies to approximately genera (not involving the evolution of new structures or physiological systems)

Genetic analysis of behavioral changes outlined in sociobiology theory (not including any interpretations that depend on naturalistic assumptions)

Geological and paleontological processes that can be studied in the modern world, and recognition of these processes in the geological record (as long as we understand that modern analogues may not represent the entire range of processes occurring in the past)

The geological and paleontolog-ical sequence of events that can be determined by evidence in the rocks

3. *Areas of scientific theory that attempt to explain history and are predicted by interventionists* to be unreliable—ultimately to be refuted by new evidence—are:

The time scale for events in at least the Phanerozoic portion of the geological record

The origin of life by natural processes, without informed intervention

Megaevolution—the evolution of new life forms, new body plans, and significant new structures by natural processes.

These lists demonstrate that interventionism is in harmony with most of science. The areas of disagreement are the time scale for the history of life on earth and the concept that life can originate without intelligent input and can evolve into new life forms by mutation and natural selection or any similar process. The reality of microevolution and speciation is based on a strong body of evidence. In contrast, the biological evidence for megaevolution is slim, and will remain very weak until it can be convincingly demonstrated that new, coordinated, adapted complexes of genes can arise by a process that begins with random mutations and then proceeds only by the natural-selection processes available in nature. Until that can be empirically demonstrated, the possibility of the infinite complexity of life arising by itself, remains an intellectually unsatisfying idea to many.

Without the sequence of appearance of life forms in the rocks, the concept of megaevolution would have little firm evidence to support it; but the strong evidence of that sequence of fossils demands an explanation. Is the Phanerozoic geological record the result of catastrophic activity in a short time frame or of 570 million years of evolution? Recognition of more catastrophic geological processes is an important trend in science. It is consistent with young-earth interventionist expectations; however, many challenges remain.

Whether a person thinks the interventionist theory of a catastrophic geologic record is worth pursuing depends largely on whether he or she has more trust in God's communication to us, or more confidence in human scientific theories of earth history. The explanation of the fossil record is significant to the Christian because of its implications for the nature and future of humankind. If life is the result of evolution (either naturalistic evolution or theistic evolution), then humans have been evolving and improving, man did not fall from a perfect state, and a Savior was not needed to redeem us. But if life, including humans, was created perfect, and humans fell from that perfect state, then the Bible account of a Savior who died to save us means everything.

Try to imagine yourself back in the time of Noah. The people living then probably were very intelligent; maybe they studied science in great depth, since many of them had over 900 years in which to study. Picture Noah working on his ark with the usual crowd of hecklers gathered around. Not only were the curious bystanders laughing at him, but the scientists were presenting him with the data showing that his predicted flood was impossible. Noah listens thoughtfully and says, "Yes, I have examined that data myself, and have tried to understand how the flood could happen. I don't have an explanation to give you, but I believe that God is smarter than we are." Noah then proceeds to drive the next peg into his ark.

Today, I believe that God is still smarter than we are—smart enough to communicate truth to us in spite of the humanity of the Bible writers. We like to have answers for everything, but we don't have answers for all the questions about earth history. We will be much better off to recognize that the limitations in the available evidence and in the amount of time we have for research on these issues makes it unrealistic to expect scientific answers for all of our questions in the near future.

To me, the exciting thing is that, when we allow the Scriptures to aid us in developing hypotheses about earth history, we can successfully use these hypotheses to guide us in productive scientific research. Popper (1959) stated, "Only . . . in our subjective faith can we be 'absolutely certain'" (p. 280). To expect science to provide that type of certainty is not the answer to our biggest questions. Scientific findings also do not indicate that we should abandon trust in God. We can have confidence in our relationship with Him and in His communication to us. I see reasons to believe that, if we do trust Him, that belief will help us to be good scientists.

Glossary

Abiogenesis   The naturalistic origin of life by combining inorganic molecules into increasingly complex organic molecules, until a living organism results.

Adaptive radiation   The evolution from a single ancestral species of a variety of forms that occupy somewhat different habitats.

Allele   Any of several different gene forms that could exist at a given position on a chromosome (e.g., different alleles for different eye colors).

Allometry   One or more body parts grow at a different rate than the overall growth rate of the organism (e.g., animals in a small species have horns 5 percent as long as their bodies, and those in large species have horns 15 percent as long).

Altruistic behavior   Behavior that benefits another individual at some cost to the individual performing the behavior.

Amino acids   The building blocks of proteins. Twenty different amino acids are in the proteins of living organisms. These amino acids combine in chains of a specific sequence to make a protein.

Analogous   A characteristic present in two or more groups of organisms but not present in their presumed ancestor, implying that the character evolved independently in each group.

Benthon   Organisms that live on the bottom of a body of water.

Biogeography   The study of the distribution of organisms over the surface of the earth, and the processes that produced that distribution.

Biota   The combined total of living organisms in a given area.

Bioturbation   The mixing and stirring of the sediment by organisms as they burrow through it or walk on it.

Body plan   The overall structural organization of a group of organisms. The arthropod body plan includes a jointed external skeleton, jointed appendages, and internal organs inside of its several body segments.

Catastrophism   The theory that a significant portion of the geologic structure of the earth was formed in a global catastrophe of short duration—years rather than millions of years.

Cladistics   An approach to the study of systematics (classifying and naming of organisms) based on evolutionary theory. Evolutionary principles are used to identify ancestor-descendant relationships, which in turn are the basis of the classification. Also called phylogenetic systematics.

Class   A biological systematic unit that includes one or more orders of organisms (e.g., the class Mammalia includes the mammals, which are placed in about 20 orders).

Coccolith   Microscopic calcium carbonate skeletal elements of minute floating marine organisms. Accumulations of coccoliths form chalk and deep-sea oozes.

Control   (see experimental control)

Convergence   The process by which a characteristic evolves independently in different groups of organisms (i.e., their structure converges toward being more similar than their ancestors were).

Craton   The portion of a continent that has been stable through much of geologic time. The North American craton includes most of the continent, except the far west and the east coast.

Creationism   The belief that life was created by an intelligent God.

DNA   The organic molecule (deoxyribonucleic acid) consisting of a long chain of building blocks called nucleotides, that form the genetic information in the chromosomes of almost all living cells. There are four types of nucleotides, and each set of three nucleotides (a codon) along the DNA form a code that specifies a particular amino acid in a specific protein.

Deduction   A logical process that uses a generalization as a basis for interpreting the data in a particular case.

Endocrine   A system of ductless glands that produce hormones, which control growth and development and regulate body functions such as metabolism.

Enzyme   An organic molecule (a protein) that serves as a catalyst to speed up the rate of a specific biochemical reaction inside a living cell.

Eukaryote   A living organism made of cells that have a nucleus containing its DNA. Most living things are eukaryotes (see prokaryote).

Evolution   The process of change in organisms through time; descent with modification.

Experimental control   A standard in an experiment against which the experimental group can be compared. For example, the effects of an experimental diet fed to one group of rats (the experimental group) can be evaluated by comparison with the effects of a known and tested diet fed to another group of rats (the control group).

Facies   A distinctive rock type, formed in a particular environment or by a specific geologic process (e.g., marine facies formed in the ocean, freshwater facies, deep water facies, shore facies, etc). A continuous rock formation may grade laterally from one facies to another, depending on the environment in which it was deposited.

Family A biological systematic unit consisting of one or more genera of organisms (e.g., the Family Canidae includes the dogs and their relatives). Several families form an Order.

Fitness The ability of an organism to pass its genes on to the next generation through successful reproductive efforts.

Fluvial deposit A deposit of sediment laid down by flowing water in rivers or streams.

Founder effect When a small group of individuals becomes isolated from others of its species and founds a new species, the characteristics of the new species will reflect the characteristics of the founder group. If the founders are larger than average, the new species will be larger than the ancestral species.

Gene flow The movement of genes through a population, by movement of individual animals or plant seeds or pollen in each generation.

Genetic drift Random genetic changes in a species or, more specifically, random changes in gene frequencies in a population.

Genetic variability The variability of traits within a population (e.g., variation in size of individuals within the same species).

Genome The total complement of genetic material of a given organism.

Genus (*pl.* genera) A biological systematic unit consisting of one or more species of living organisms (e.g., the genus *Canis* includes the dogs and wolves). Several genera form a family.

Geologic column The sequence of rock formations, one above the other, from the oldest rocks (at the bottom) to the youngest, that form part of the outer crust of the earth.

Glaciation The formation and movements of ice in mountain glaciers or continental ice sheets.

Gradualism The concept that biological and/or geological change occurs only slowly and gradually.

Heterochrony Changes in the timing of embryological developmental processes, resulting in the acceleration or slowing of the development of a particular developmental or structural feature. Three types of heterochrony are neoteny, paedomorphosis, and progenesis.

Homology (homologous) A similarity between two organisms due to (1) similarity in embryological development or (the following are interpretive definitions) (2) inheritance of the feature from a common ancestor, or (3) similarity due to a common plan used by the Designer of life.

Homoplasy A similar characteristic that is shared by two groups of organisms but does not meet the criteria of a homology; an analogy; a feature believed to have evolved independently in each group (convergence).

Igneous rock Rock that forms by cooling of molten or partially molten material (e.g., granite or volcanic lava).

Inclusive fitness The ability of an organism to pass its genes directly to the next generation through its own offspring and indirectly through the offspring of relatives who share many of the same genes that it has.

Induction A reasoning process that begins with individual observations and uses these to develop generalizations.

Informed intervention (interventionism) The paradigm or philosophy that accepts the possibility of Divine intervention in history, especially in the origin of life forms.

Kin selection Natural selection through animal behaviors that will improve the reproductive success primarily of close relatives (e.g., alarm calls given by squirrels living close to many relatives, thus improving the chances that these relatives will escape danger).

Lacustrine deposit A deposit of sediment laid down in the quiet water of a lake.

Macroevolution Evolutionary change above the species level. Includes all that comes under the definition of megaevolution plus changes sufficient to be called a new genus.

Megaevolution Evolutionary change into new families, classes, or phyla of organisms.

Metabolism The sum of the chemical reactions within a cell or organism which release heat and energy. The rate of metabolism varies according to temperature and/or internal control by the organism.

Metamorphic rock Rock formed by alteration of other rocks by temperature or pressure, usually resulting from burial under a thick overburden of additional rock.

Microevolution Small scale evolutionary changes that produce variation within a species of organism.

Natural selection The individuals in a population that are best able to survive and reproduce in their environment pass on more of their genes to succeeding generations than other individuals.

Naturalism The scientific paradigm or philosophy that only considers hypotheses or theories that do not require any divine intervention in the functioning of the universe at any time in history.

Neocatastrophism The modern geological paradigm that recognizes the evidence for catastrophic processes, but places these events in a time frame of hundreds of millions of years in evolutionary time.

Neoteny The retention of formerly juvenile features into the adult life of an organism. In some species of salamander, the gills (normally a juvenile feature) remain functional in adults.

Niche The role of an organism in its environment. For an animal, this includes where it lives; what it eats; when, where, and how it gets its food; and its relationships to other types of organisms.

Nucleic acids   The building blocks that link together in long chains to form DNA and RNA.

Ontogeny   The embryological development of an organism; the sequence of developmental events during that process.

Order   A biological systematic unit consisting of one or more families of organisms (e.g., the Order Rodentia, which is one order in the Class Mammalia, includes all the rodents).

Overthrust   Large-scale lateral movement of rock along a fault, pushing the rock over other, younger, rocks for distances generally measured in kilometers.

Paedomorphosis   The retention of ancestral juvenile characters into later stages of embryological development.

Pangea   A hypothesized supercontinent early in Phanerozoic history, that was composed of all of the present continents joined into one.

Paradigm   A broad, explanatory scientific theory; a framework for interpreting evidence, such as the heliocentric theory or the theory of naturalistic evolution.

Phanerozoic   That part of the geologic column containing abundant life—from the Cambrian to the present.

Phylogeny   The evolutionary history of a group of organisms.

Phylum (plural - phyla)   A biological systematic unit consisting of one or more classes of organisms (e.g., the Phylum Chordata consists of the animals with backbones).

Plate tectonics   A global theory of the structure and changes of the earth's crust, in which the outer crust is divided into a number of plates that move in relation to one another (continental drift). The movements of these plates are involved in the generation of earthquakes, volcanoes, and mountain ranges.

Primeval soup   Ocean water in which organic molecules were accumulating and where abiogenesis is presumed to have occured.

Progenesis   Alteration of embryological timing so that sexual maturation is reached by an organism that is morphologically juvenile.

Prokaryote   A cell without a distinct nucleus. Bacteria and some other simple organisms are Prokaryotes (see eukaryote).

Propositional truth   In theology, specific, true, and objective information or concepts, such as the Ten Commandments or the history of life's origins, that can be communicated by God to His prophet.

RNA   A form of nucleic acid (ribonucleic acid) that is involved in protein synthesis and in carrying genetic information from the DNA to sites of protein synthesis.

Reef   A mound-like structure built by calcareous organisms, especially corals, and consisting largely of their remains.

Ribosome   Small organelles present in cells that are the sites of protein synthesis.

Scientific revolutions   The process by which a new paradigm or theory replaces another one after a crisis reveals problems in the old theory and a successful competitor wins the allegiance of the scientific community.

Sedimentary rock   Rock formed by erosion of other rock; this eroded sediment is transported into a basin and deposited as layers.

Shield   An area of exposed basement rocks (generally Precambrian) not covered by sediments (e.g., the Canadian Shield in eastern Canada).

Sociobiology   The application of evolution theory to the explanation of animal behavior, with the assumption that all behavior is the result of evolution.

Speciation   The evolution process that produces a new species.

Species   Organisms of a population that normally in nature do not reproduce with other populations of similar organisms.

Stromatolite   A structure—usually mound-shaped—composed of a series of layers of sediment trapped one layer upon another by organisms, mostly blue-green algae that grow on their surface.

Taphonomy   Study of the processes that produce a fossil, including death of the organism, that determine whether it will be buried and in what condition, changes that cause fossilization, and alterations to the organism that occur after it is fossilized.

Turbidite   A distinctive deposit of sediment produced by a turbidity current, a rapid flow of water and sediment usually down a very gentle slope under water.

Uniformitarianism   The concept that geological processes occur by the action of natural laws that are always the same, and by processes that can be observed today. Charles Lyell also included the now rejected concept that these processes are always slow and gradual (gradualism).

References

Ager, D. V. 1981. *The Nature of the Stratigraphical Record.* 2nd ed. New York: John Wiley and Sons.

Alberch, P. 1985. Problems with the interpretation of developmental sequences. *Systematic Zoology* 34:46-58.

Albritton, C. C. Jr. 1989. *Catastrophic Episodes in Earth History.* New York: Chapman and Hall.

Allison, P. A., and D. E. Briggs. 1991. *Taphonomy: Releasing the Data Locked in the Fossil Record.* New York: Plenum Press.

Amabile-Cuevas, C. F., and Marina E. Chicurel. 1993. Horizontal gene transfer. *American Scientist* 81:332-341.

Anderson, D. 1982. Sex machines. *Science Digest* 90(4):74-77, 96.

Anonymous. 1992. Devil's Hole plays devil's advocate. *Geotimes* 37(12):7.

Archer, A. W., and E. P. Kvale. 1989. Seasonal and yearly cycles within tidally laminated sediments: An example from the Pennsylvanian of Indiana, U.S.A. *Illinois Basin Studies* 1:45-6.

Archer, A. W., G. J. Kuecher, and E. P. Kvale. 1995. The role of tidal-velocity asymmetries in the deposition of silty tidal rhythmites (Carboniferous, eastern interior coal basin, U.S.A.). *Journal of Sedimentary Research* A65:408-416.

Arthur, W. 1984. *Mechanisms of Morphological Evolution.* New York: John Wiley and Sons.

Ashton, E. H., R. M. Flinn, and R. K. Griffiths. 1979. The results of geographic isolation on the teeth and skull of the green monkey (*Cercopithecus aethiops sabaeus*) in St. Kitts - a multivariate retrospect. *Journal of Zoology (*London) 188:533-555.

Asimov, I. 1964. *A Short History of Biology.* Garden City, NY: The Natural History Press.

Austin, S. A. 1979. *Depositional Environment of the Kentucky No. 12 Coal Bed (Middle Pennsylvanian) of Western Kentucky, with Special Reference to the Origin of Coal Lithotypes.* Ph.D. Dissertation, Pennsylvania State University.

——. 1984. Rapid erosion at Mount St. Helens. *Origins* 11:90-98.

——. 1994. *Grand Canyon: Monument to Catastrophe.* Santee, CA: Institute for Creation Research.

——, and D. R. Humphreys. 1990. The sea's missing salt: A dilemma for evolutionists. *Proceedings of the Second International Conference on Creationism*, 2:17-33.

——, D. R. Humphreys, L. Vardiman, J. R. Baumgardner, A. A. Snelling, and K. P. Wise. 1994. A catastrophic plate tectonics: A global flood model of earth history. *Proceedings of the Third International Conference on Creationism. Technical Symposium Sessions.* 609-621.

——, and K. P. Wise. 1994. The pre-flood/flood boundary: As defined in Grand Canyon, Arizona and eastern Mojave Desert, California. *Proceedings of the Third International Conference on Creationism. Technical Symposium Sessions.* 37-47.

Avers, C. J. 1989. *Process and Pattern in Evolution.* New York: Oxford University Press.

Baker, A. J. 1987. Rapid genetic differentiation and founder effect in colonizing populations of common mynas (*Acridotheres tristis*). *Evolution* 41:525-538.

Baker, V. R. 1978. The Spokane flood controversy and the Martian outflow channels. *Science* 202:1249-1256.

——. 1995. Joseph Thomas Pardee and the Spokane flood controversy. *GSA Today* 5:169-173.

Bakker, R. T. 1985. Evolution by revolution. *Science* 85:72-80.

Barash, D. 1974. The evolution of marmot societies: A general theory. *Science* 185:415-420.

——. 1979. *The Whisperings Within.* New York: Penguin Books.

Barrick, R. E., and W. J. Showers. 1995. Oxygen isotope variability in juvenile dinosaurs (*Hypacrosaurus*): Evidence for thermoregulation. *Paleobiology* 21:552-560.

Barth, K. 1936-1969. *Church Dogmatics.* 13 volumes. Bromiley, G. W., and T. F. Torrance (eds.). Edinburgh: T. and T. Clark.

Baumgardner, J. R. 1986. Numerical simulation of the large-scale tectonic changes accompanying the flood. *Proceedings of the First International Conference on Creationism*, 2:7-31.

——. 1990. 3-D finite element simulation of the global tectonic changes accompanying Noah's flood. *Proceedings of the Second International Conference on Creationism*, 2:35-45.

——. 1992. 3-D numerical investigation of the mantle dynamics associated with the breakup of Pangea. Abstract of a paper presented at the annual meeting of the American Geophysical Union. *Eos supplement, AGU Transactions* 73:576. (A commentary on this presentation was published in *Geotimes* 38 (3):9, 1993; Computer replicates Pangea's breakup.)

——. 1994a. Thermal runaway in the mantle. Abstract of a paper presented at the annual meetings of the American Geophysical Union. *Eos supplement, AGU Transactions* 75:687.

——. 1994b. Computer modeling of the large-scale tectonics associated with the Genesis flood. *Proceedings of the Third International Conference on Creationism. Technical Symposium Sessions.* 49-62.

——. 1994c. Runaway subduction as the driving mechanism for the Genesis flood. *Proceedings of the Third International Conference on Creationism. Technical Symposium Sessions.* 63-75.

Behe, M. J. 1996. *Darwin's Black Box: The Biochemical Challenge to Evolution.* New York: The Free Press, A Division of Simon and Schuster.

Behrensmeyer, A. K., and A. P. Hill, eds. 1980. *Fossils in the Making: Vertebrate Taphonomy and Paleoecology.* Chicago: University of Chicago Press.

Bellis, M. A., and Baker R. R. 1990. Do females promote sperm competition? Data for humans. *Animal Behaviour* 40:997-999.

Bentley, D. R., and Hoy R. R. 1972. Genetic control of the neuronal network generating cricket *(Teleogryllus gryllus)* song patterns. *Animal Behaviour* 20:478-492.

Benton, M. J., ed. 1993. *The Fossil Record 2.* New York: Chapman and Hall.

Berggren, W. A., and J. A. van Couvering, eds. 1984. *Catastrophes and Earth History: The New Uniformitarianism.* Princeton, NJ: Princeton University Press.

Berta, A. 1994. What is a whale? *Science* 263:180-181.

Berthold, P., and U. Querner. 1981. Genetic basis of migratory behavior in European Warblers. *Science* 212:77-79.

Bertram, B. C. R. 1975. Social factors influencing reproduction in wild lions. *Journal of Zoology, London* 177:473-482.

Billingsley, G. H., and E. D. McKee. 1982. Pre-Supai buried valleys. In E. D. McKee, ed. The Supai Group of Grand Canyon (p. 137-153). *U. S. Geological Survey Professional Paper* 1173.

Birkeland, P. W., and E. E. Larson. 1978. *Putnam's Geology*. 3rd ed. New York: Oxford University Press.

Bradley, W. L., and C. B. Thaxton. 1994. Information and the origin of life. In J. P. Moreland, ed., *The Creation Hypothesis* (p. 173-210). Downers Grove, IL: InterVarsity Press.

Brand, L. R. 1970. *Vocalizations and Behavior of the Chipmunks (Genus Eutamias) in California.* Doctoral Dissertation, Cornell University.

——. 1974. Tree nests of California chipmunks (*Eutamias*). *The American Midland Naturalist* 91:489-491.

——. 1976. The vocal repertoire of chipmunks (Genus *Eutamias*) in California. *Animal Behaviour* 24:319-335.

——. 1979. Field and laboratory studies on the Coconino Sandstone (Permian) vertebrate footprints and their paleoecological implications. *Palaeogeography, Palaeoclimatology, Palaeoecology* 28:25-38.

——. 1982. The Genesis flood and the biogeography of the vertebrate animals: Or how did the kangaroos get to Australia? Unpublished paper.

——. 1985. Can science and religion work together? *Origins* 12:71-88.

——. 1989. Transport of fossils during the flood. Unpublished paper.

——. 1992. Reply: Fossil vertebrate footprints in the Coconino Sandstone (Permian) of northern Arizona: Evidence for underwater origin. *Geology* 20:668-670.

——, 1996. Variations in salamander trackways resulting from substrate differences. *Journal of Paleontology* 70:1004-1010.

——, and R. C. Carter. 1992. Sociobiology: The evolution theory's answer to altruistic behavior. *Origins* 19:54-71.

——, and J. Florence. 1982. Stratigraphic distribution of vertebrate fossil footprints compared with body fossils. *Origins* 9:67-74.

——, and L. J. Gibson. 1993. An interventionist theory of natural selection and biological change within limits. *Origins* 20:60-82.

——, and R. E. Ryckman. 1968. Laboratory life histories of *Peromyscus eremicus* and *Peromyscus interparietalis*. *Journal of Mammalogy* 49:495-501.

——, and R. E. Ryckman. 1969. Biosystematics of *Peromuscus eremicus, P. guardia, and P. interparietalis*. *Journal of Mammalogy* 50:501-513.

——, and T. Tang. 1991. Fossil vertebrate footprints in the Coconino Sandstone (Permian) of northern Arizona: Evidence for underwater origin. *Geology* 19:1201-1204.

Brandes, C. 1991. Genetic differences in learning behavior in honeybees (*Apis mellifera capensis*). *Behavior Genetics* 21:271-294.

Branscomb, L. M. 1985. Integrity in science. *American Scientist* 73:421-423.

Bray, J. R. 1976. Volcanic triggering of glaciation. *Nature* 260:414-415.

Breithaupt, B. H. 1990. Eocene mammals from the Fossil Butte Member of the Green River Formation, Fossil Basin, Wyoming: Chronological and environmental implications. Abstract of a paper presented at the Geological Society of America, Rocky Mountain Section, 43rd annual meeting, Jackson, Wyoming. *Abstracts and Programs* 22(6):4.

Brescia, F., S. Mahlman, F. Pellegriai, and S. Stambler. 1974. *Chemistry: A Modern Introduction*. Philadelphia: W. B. Saunders.

Bretz, J. H. 1923. The Channeled Scablands of the Columbia Plateau. *Journal of Geology* 31:617-649.

——. 1927. Channeled Scabland and the Spokane flood. *Journal of Washington Academy of Science* 17:200-211.

Briggs, D. E. G. 1995. Experimental taphonomy. *Palaios* 10:539-550.

Bromley, R. G. 1990. *Trace Fossils: Biology and Taphonomy*. Boston: Unwin Hyman.

Brooks, C., D. E. James, and S. R. Hart. 1976. Ancient lithosphere: Its role in young continental volcanism. *Science* 193:1086-1094.

Brown, M. A., A. W. Archer, and E. P. Kvale. 1990. Neap-spring tidal cyclicity in laminated carbonate channel-fill deposits and its implications: Salem Limestone (Miss.), south-central Indiana, U.S.A. *Journal of Sedimentary Petrology* 60:152-159.

Brown, R. H. 1975. C-14 age profiles for ancient sediments and peat bogs. *Origins* 2:6-18.

——. 1979. The interpretation of C-14 dates. *Origins* 6:30-44.

——. 1981. Geo and cosmic chronology. *Origins* 8:20-45.

——. 1985. Amino acid dating. *Origins* 12:8-25.

——. 1988. Implications of C-14 age vs. depth profile characteristics. *Origins* 15:19-29.

——. 1990. Correlation of C-14 age with the biblical time scale. *Origins* 17:56-65.

——. 1994a. Mixing lines - considerations regarding their use in creationist interpretation of radioisotope age data. *Proceedings of the Third International Conference on Creationism. Technical Symposium Sessions.* 123-130.

——. 1994b. Compatibility of biblical chronology with C-14 age. *Origins* 21:66-79.

——, and C. L. Webster. 1991. Interpretation of radiocarbon and amino acid data. *Origins* 18:66-78.

Buchheim, H. P. 1994a. Paleoenvironments, lithofacies and varves of the Fossil Butte Member of the Eocene Green River Formation, southwestern Wyoming. *Contributions to Geology, University of Wyoming* 30:3-14.

——. 1994b. Eocene Fossil Lake, Green River Formation, Wyoming: A history of fluctuating salinity. In B. L. Garces and J. G. Aquilar, eds. Sedimentology and geochemistry of modern and ancient saline lakes (p. 239-247). *SEPM (Society of Sedimentary Geology) Special Publication* No. 50.

Bultmann, R. 1960. Is exigesis without presuppositions possible? In M. Ogden, ed., *Existence and Faith*. New York: World Publishing.

Butler, R. F. 1992. *Paleomagnetism*. Boston: Blackwell Scientific Publications.

Cain, A. J. 1989. The perfection of animals. *Biological Journal of the Linnaean Society* 36:3-29.

Cairns, J., J. Overbaugh, and S. Miller. 1988. The origin of mutants. *Nature* 335:142-145.

Carey, S. W. 1976. *The Expanding Earth*. New York: Elsevier Scientific Publishing.

Carlisle, D. B. 1995. *Dinosaurs, Diamonds, and Things from Outer Space: The Great Extinction*. Stanford, CA: Stanford University Press.

Carpenter, K., K. F. Hirsch, and J. R. Horner, eds. 1994. *Dinosaur Eggs and Babies*. New York: Cambridge University Press.

Carroll, R. L. 1988. *Vertebrate Paleontology and Evolution*. New York: W. H. Freeman.

Carson, H. L. 1975. The genetics of speciation at the diploid level. *American Naturalist* 109:83-92.

——, and R. G. Wisotzkey. 1989. Increase in genetic variance following a population bottleneck. *American Naturalist* 134:668-673.

Chadwick, A. V. 1978. Megabreccias: Evidence for catastrophism. *Origins* 5:39-46.

——. 1981. Precambrian pollen in the Grand Canyon - a reexamination. *Origins* 8:7-12.

——, and T. Yamamoto. 1984. A paleoecological analysis of the petrified trees in the Specimen Creek area of Yellowstone National Park, Montana, USA. *Palaeogeography, Palaeoclimatology, Palaeoecology* 45:39-48.

Chaloner, W. G., and A. Hallam, eds. 1989. *Evolution and Extinction*. London: The Royal Society.

Chamberlin, T. C. 1965. The method of multiple working hypotheses. *Science* 148:754-759. (See also *Journal of Geology* 103:349-354, 1995; a reprint of the above article with an introduction by D. C. Raup)

Clark, H. W. 1946. *The New Diluvialism*. Angwin, CA: Science Publications.

——. 1966. *Crusader for Creation*. Boise, ID: Pacific Press.

Clark, M. E. 1979. *Contemporary Biology*. 2nd ed. Philadelphia: W. B. Saunders.

Clarkson, E. N. K. 1993. *Invertebrate Palaeontology and Evolution*. 3rd ed. New York: Chapman and Hall.

Coe, R. S., M. Prevot, and P. Camps. 1995. New evidence for extraordinarily rapid change of the geomagnetic field during a reversal. *Nature* 374:687-691.

Coffin, H. G. 1976. Orientation of trees in the Yellowstone petrified forests. *Journal of Paleontology* 50:539-543.

——. 1979a. The organic levels of the Yellowstone petrified forests. *Origins* 6:71-82.

——. 1979b. The Yellowstone petrified forests. *Spectrum* 9(4):42-53.

——. 1983a. Erect floating stumps in Spirit Lake, Washington. *Geology* 11:298-299.

——. 1983b. Erect floating stumps in Spirit Lake, Washington; reply. *Geology* 11:734.

——. 1983c. *Origin by Design*. Washington, DC: Review and Herald Publishing Association.

——. 1987. Sonar and scuba survey of a submerged allochthonous "forest" in Spirit Lake, Washington. *Palaios* 2:178-180.

——. 1992. The puzzle of the petrified trees. *Dialogue* 4(1):11-13, 30, 31.

Conaghan, P. J., E. W. Mountjoy, D. R. Edgecombe, J. A. Talent, and D. E. Owen. 1976. Nubrigyn algal reefs (Devonian), eastern Australia: Allochthonous blocks and megabreccias. *Geological Society of America Bulletin* 87:515-530.

Cook, T. D., and A. W. Bally (eds.). 1975. *Stratigraphic Atlas of North and Central America*. Prepared by the exploration department of Shell Oil Co. Princeton, NJ: Princeton University Press.

Cooper, J. D., R. H. Miller, and J. Patterson. 1990. *A Trip Through Time: Principles of Historical Geology*. 2nd ed. Columbus, OH: Merrill Publishing.

Corbet, G. B., and J. E. Hill. 1991. *A World List of Mammalian Species*. New York: Oxford University Press.

Crick, F. 1981. *Life Itself*. New York: Simon and Schuster.

Crick, F. H. C., and L. E. Orgel. 1973. Directed panspermia. *Icarus* 19:341-346.

Cromer, A. 1993. *Uncommon Sense: The Heretical Nature of Science*. New York: Oxford University Press.

Crowell, J. C. 1957. Origin of pebbly mudstones. *Geological Society of America Bulletin* 68:993-1010.

——, and L. A. Frakes. 1971. Late Paleozoic glaciation: part IV, Australia. *Geological Society of America Bulletin* 82:2515-2540.

Dalrymple, G. B. 1991. *The Age of the Earth*. Stanford, CA: Stanford University Press.

Darwin, C. R. 1859. *On the Origin of Species*. London: John Murray.

Davis, W. M. 1926. The value of outrageous hypotheses. *Science* 63:463-468.

Dawkins, R. 1986. *The Blind Watchmaker*. New York: W.W. Norton.

Dayhoff, M. D. 1972. *Atlas of Protein Sequence and Structure*. Vol. 5. Silver Spring, MD: National Biomedical Research Foundation.

De Duve, C. 1995. The beginnings of life on earth. *American Scientist* 83:428-437.

De Sousa, M. 1989. Warning: Scientists are becoming too much like chefs. *The Scientist* 3(1, January 9):9, 11.

Denton, M. 1985. *Evolution: A Theory in Crisis*. Bethesda, MD: Adler & Adler.

Dessauer, H. C., G. F. Gee, and J. S. Rogers. 1992. Allozyme evidence for crane systematics and polymorphisms within populations of sandhill, sarus, Siberian and whooping cranes. *Molecular Phylogenetics and Evolution* 1:279-288.

Diamond, J. M. 1981. Flightlessness and fear of flying in island species. *Nature* 293:507-508.

Dickinson, D. R., and I. L. Gibson. 1972. Feldspar fractionation and anomalous Sr^{87}/Sr^{86} ratios in a suite of peralkaline silicic rocks. *Geological Society of America Bulletin* 83:231-240.

Dilger, W. C. 1960. The comparative ethology of the African parrot genus *Agapornis*. *Zeitschrift fur Tierpsychologie* 17(6):649-685.

——. 1962. The behavior of lovebirds. *Scientific American* 206:88-98.

Dobzhansky, T. 1973. Nothing in biology makes sense except in the light of evolution. *The American Biology Teacher* 35:125-129.

Dodson, E. O., and P. Dodson. 1985. *Evolution: Process and Product*. Boston: PWS Publishers.

Dodson, P., and D. Wexlar. 1979. Taphonomic investigations of owl pellets. *Paleobiology* 5:275-284.

Dodson, P., A. K. Behrensmeyer, R. T. Bakker, and J. S. McIntosh. 1980. Taphonomy and paleoecology of the dinosaur beds of the Jurassic Morrison Formation. *Paleobiology* 6:208-232.

Donovan, S. K., ed. 1989. *Mass Extinctions*. New York: Columbia University Press.

——, ed. 1991. *The Processes of Fossilization*. New York: Columbia University Press.

——, ed. 1994. *The Paleobiology of Trace Fossils*. Baltimore: The Johns Hopkins University Press.

Dott, R. H., Jr. 1961. Squantum "Tillite", Massachusetts - evidence of glaciation or subaqueous mass movements? *Geological Society of America Bulletin* 72:1289-1306.

——, and D. R. Prothero. 1994. *Evolution of the Earth*. 5th ed. New York: McGraw-Hill.

Drickamer, L. C., and S. H. Vessey. 1992. *Animal Behavior*. 3rd ed. Dubuque, IA: Wm. C. Brown Publishers.

Dubiel, R. F. 1994. Triassic deposystems, paleogeography, and paleoclimate of the western interior. In M. V. Caputo, J. A. Peterson, K. J. Franczyk, eds. *Mesozoic Systems of the Rocky Mountain Region, USA* (p. 133-168). Denver, CO: Rocky Mountain Section, SEPM (Society for Sedimentary Geology).

Dunbar, C. O. 1961. *Historical Geology*. 2nd ed. New York: John Wiley and Sons.

Dunford, C. 1970. Behavioral aspects of spatial organization in the chipmunk, *Tamias striatus*. *Behaviour* 36:215-231.

Eardley, A. J. 1965. *General College Geology*. New York: Harper and Row.

Eaton, J. E. 1929. The by-passing and discontinuous deposition of sedimentary materials. *American Association of Petroleum Geologists Bulletin* 13:713-761.

Eaton, T. H., Jr. 1970. *Evolution*. New York: W. W. Norton.

Eibl-Eibesfeldt, I. 1975. *Ethology: The Biology of Behavior*. 2nd ed. New York: Holt, Rinehart and Winston.

Eiseley, L. C. 1955. Was Darwin wrong about the human brain? *Harper's Magazine* 211(No. 1266, November):66-70.

——. 1979. *Darwin and the Mysterious Mr. X.* New York: Harcourt Brace Jovanovich.

Eldredge, N. 1982. *The Monkey Business: A Scientist Looks at Creationism.* New York: Pocket Books (Washington Square Press).

——. 1986. Review of Evolution: A Theory in Crisis, by Michael Denton. *Quarterly Review of Biology* 61:541-542.

——, and S. J. Gould. 1972. Punctuated equilibria: An alternative to phyletic gradualism. In T. J. M. Schopf, ed. *Models in Biology* (p. 82-115). San Francisco: Freeman-Cooper.

Encyclopedia Britannica. 1952. *Great Books of the Western World.* Vol. 16, *English Translation.* Chicago: Encyclopedia Britannica.

Endler, J. A. 1986. *Natural Selection in the Wild.* Princeton, NJ: Princeton University Press.

Ewer, R. F. 1968. *Ethology of Mammals.* London: Elek Science.

——. 1973. *The Carnivores.* Ithaca, NY: Cornell University Press.

Feduccia, A. 1994. Tertiary bird history: Notes and comments. In D. R. Prothero and R. M. Schoch, *Major Features of Vertebrate Evolution* (p. 178-189). Short Courses in Paleontology, Number 7. A Publication of the Paleontological Society. Oral presentation of this material was at the annual meeting of the Geological Society of America, October, 1994.

——, and H. B. Tordoff. 1979. Feathers of *Archeopteryx*: Assymetric vanes indicate aerodynamic function. *Science* 203:1021-1022.

Feyerabend, P. 1978. *Against Method.* New York: Verso.

——. 1987. *Farewell to Reason.* New York: Verso.

Fischman, J. 1995. Were dinos cold-blooded after all? The nose knows. *Science* 270:735-736.

Fisher, A. 1991. A new synthesis comes of age. *Mosaic* 22(1):1-17.

Fontdevila, A. 1992. Genetic instability and rapid speciation: Are they coupled? *Genetica* 86:247-258.

Ford, E. B. 1964. *Ecological Genetics.* New York: John Wiley and Sons.

Foster, R. J. 1969. *General Geology.* Columbus, OH: Charles E. Merrill Publishing.

Francis, J. E. 1991. Arctic Eden. *Natural History* 100(1):56-63.

Frey, R. W. 1975. *The Study of Trace Fossils.* New York: Springer-Verlag.

Fridriksson, S. 1975. *Surtsey.* New York: John Wiley and Sons.

Fritz, W. J. 1980. Reinterpretation of the depositional environment of the Yellowstone "fossil forests." *Geology* 8:309-313.

——, and J. N. Moore. 1988. *Basics of Physical Stratigraphy and Sedimentology.* New York: John Wiley and Sons.

Frodeman, R. 1995. Geological reasoning: Geology as an interpretive and historical science. *Geological Society of America Bulletin* 107:960-968.

Futuyma, D. J. 1983. *Science on Trial.* New York: Pantheon Books.

——.1986. *Evolutionary Biology.* 2nd ed. Sunderland, MA: Sinaur Associates..

Gale, G. 1979. *Theory of Science.* New York: McGraw-Hill.

Gibbons, A. 1996. On the many origins of species. *Science* 273:1496-1499.

Gibson, L. J. 1987. Do DNA distances reveal avian phylogeny? *Origins* 14:47-76.

——. 1994. Pseudogenes and origins. *Origins* 21:91-108.

——, and L. Brand. 1983. Post-flood dispersal of mammals: Testing two models. Unpublished paper.

Giem, P. A. L. 1997. *Scientific Theology.* Riverside, CA: La Sierra University Press.

Gillette, D. D., and M. G. Lockley. 1989. *Dinosaur Tracks and Traces.* New York: Cambridge University Press.

Gilmore, C. W. 1927. Fossil footprints from the Grand Canyon. Second contribution. *Smithsonian Miscellaneous Collections* 80(3):1-78.

Gingerich, P. D., S. M. Raza, M. Arif, M. Anwar, and X. Zhou. 1994. New whale from the Eocene of Pakistan and the origin of cetacean swimming. *Nature* 368:844-847.

Glen, W. 1990. What killed the dinosaurs? *American Scientist* 78:354-370.

Goin, C. J., O. B. Goin, and G. R. Zug. 1978. *Introduction to Herpetelogy.* 3rd ed. San Francisco: W. H. Freeman.

Gold, T. 1992 . The deep, hot biosphere. *Proceedings of the National Academy of Sciences, USA* 89:6045-6049.

Goodstein, D., and J. Goodstein. 1980. The scientific method. *Engineering and Science* (Calif. Inst. Technology) 44(1):23-28.

Gorr, T., and T. Kleinschmidt. 1993. Evolutionary relationships of the Coelacanth. *American Scientist* 81(1):72-82.

Gould, S. J. 1965. Is uniformitarianism necessary? *American Journal of Science* 263:223-228.

——. 1977. *Ontogeny and Phylogeny.* Cambridge, MA: Belknap Press of Harvard University Press.

——. 1980a. *The Panda's Thumb: More Reflections in Natural History.* New York: W.W. Norton.

——. 1980b. Is a new and general theory of evolution emerging? *Paleobiology* 6:119-130.

——. 1984. Lyell's vision and rhetoric. In W. A. Berggren and J. A. Van Couvering, eds. *Catastrophes and Earth History: The New Uniformitarianism.* Princeton, NJ: Princeton University Press.

——. 1987-88. The verdict on creationism. *The Skeptical Inquirer* 12(2):184-187.

——. 1989a. *Wonderful Life.* New York: W. W. Norton.

——. 1989b. An asteroid to die for. *Discover* 10(10):60-65.

——. 1994. Common pathways of illumination. *Natural History* 103 (12):10-20.

——. 1995. Of it, not above it. *Nature* 377:681-682.

Grande, L. 1984. Paleontology of the Green River Formation, with a review of the fish fauna. 2nd ed. *Geological Survey of Wyoming, Bulletin* 63:1-333.

——, and H. P. Buchheim. 1994. Paleontological and sedimentological variation in early Eocene Fossil Lake. *Contributions to Geology, University of Wyoming* 30:33-56.

Grant, V. 1991. *The Evolutionary Process.* 2nd ed. New York: Columbia University Press.

Greene, J. C. 1959. *The Death of Adam.* Ames, IA: The Iowa State University Press.

Grotzinger, J. P., S. A. Bowring, B. Z. Saylor, and A. J. Kaufman. 1995. Biostratigraphic and geochronologic constraints on early animal evolution. *Science* 270:598-604.

Grove, J. M. 1988. *The Little Ice Age.* London: Routledge.

Hall, E. R. 1981. *The Mammals of North America.* 2nd ed. New York: John Wiley and Sons.

Hallam, A. 1972. Continental drift and the fossil record. *Scientific American* 227(5):56-66.

Hamblin, W. K., and E. H. Christiansen. 1995. *Earth's Dynamic Systems.* 7th ed. Englewood Cliffs, NJ: Prentice Hall.

Hamilton, W. J., and H. W. Mossman. 1972. *Human Embryology.* Baltimore: Williams and Wilkins.

Hampe, A. 1960. La competition entre les elements ossent du zengopode de Poulet. *Journal of Embryology and Experimental Morphology* 8:241-245.

Harland, W. B., ed. 1967. *The Fossil Record*. London: Geological Society of London.

Harland, W. B., R. L. Armstrong, A. V. Cox, L. E. Craig, A. G. Smith, and D. G. Smith. 1989. *A Geologic Time Scale*. New York: Cambridge University Press.

Hasel, G. F. 1974. The polemic nature of the Genesis cosmology. *Evangelical Quarterly* 46:81-102.

———. 1980a. Genesis 5 and 11: Chronogeneologies in the biblical history of beginnings. *Origins* 7:23-37.

———. 1980b. The meaning of the chronogeneologies of Genesis 5 and 11. *Origins* 7:53-70.

———. 1980c. *Understanding the Living Word of God*. Mountain View, CA: Pacific Press.

———. 1985. *Biblical Interpretation Today*. Washington, DC: Biblical Research Institute, General Conference of Seventh-day Adventists.

———. 1994. The "days" of creation in Genesis 1: Literal "days" or figurative "periods/epochs" of time? *Origins* 21:5-38.

Hatcher, R. D., Jr. 1995. *Structural Geology*. 2nd ed. Englewood Cliffs, NJ: Prentice Hall.

Hibbard, C. W., D. E. Ray, D. E. Savage, D. W. Taylor, and J. E. Guilday . 1965. Quaternary mammals of North America. In H. E. Wright, Jr. and D. G. Frey, eds. *The Quaternary of the United States*. Princeton, NJ: Princeton University Press.

Hill, J. E., and J. D. Smith. 1984. *Bats: A Natural History*. Austin, TX: University of Texas Press.

Hillis, D. M., and C. Moritz. 1990. *Molecular Systematics*. Sunderland, MA: Sinauer Associates.

Hinegardner, R. 1976. Evolution of genome size. In F. J. Ayala, ed., *Molecular Evolution* (p. 179-199). Sunderland, MA: Sinauer.

Hirsch, J., and T. R. McGuire. 1982. *Benchmark Papers in Behavior*. Stroudsburg, PA: Hutchinson Ross Publishing.

Hirsch, K. F. 1994. The fossil record of vertebrate eggs. In S. K. Donovan, ed. *The Palaeobiology of Trace Fossils* (p. 269-294). Baltimore: The Johns Hopkins University Press.

Holmes, W. G., and P. W. Sherman. 1983. Kin recognition in animals. *American Scientist* 71:46-55.

Hopson, J. A. 1994. Synapsid evolution and the radiation of non-Eutherian mammals. In D. R. Prothero and R. M. Schoch, eds., *Major Features of Vertebrate Evolution* (p. 190-219). Short Courses in Paleontology, Number 7. A Publication of the Paleontological Society.

Horner, J. R. 1982. Evidence of colonial nesting and 'site fidelity' among ornithischian dinosaurs. *Nature* 297:675-676.

———, and D. B. Weishampel. 1989. Dinosaur eggs: The inside story. *Natural History*, December, 98:61-67.

Hou, L., Z. Zhou, L. D. Martin, and A. Feduccia. 1995. A beaked bird from the Jurassic of China. *Nature* 377:616-618.

Hrdy, S. B. 1974. Male-male competition and infanticide among the langurs (*Presbytis entellus*) of Abu, Rajasthan. *Folia Primatologica* 22:19-58.

———. 1977a. *The Langurs of Abu: Female and Male Strategies of Reproduction*. Cambridge, MA: Harvard University Press.

———. 1977b. Infanticide as a primate reproductive strategy. *American Scientist* 65:40-49.

Huggett, R. 1990. *Catastrophism: Systems of Earth History*. New York: Edward Arnold.

Humphreys, D. R. 1986. Reversals of the earth's magnetic field during the Genesis flood. *Proceedings of the First International Conference on Creationism*, 2:113-125.

———. 1990. Physical mechanism for reversals of the earth's magnetic field during the flood. *Proceedings of the Second International Conference on Creationism*, 2:129-143.

Hutton, J. 1795. *Theory of the Earth With Proofs and Illustrations*. 2 vols. William Creech, Edinburgh. (Reprinted 1959. H. R. Engelmann (J. Cramer) and Wheldon and Wesley, Weinheim)

Hyde, G. M., ed. 1974. *A Symposium on Biblical Hermeneutics*. Washington, DC: Biblical Research Committee, General Conference of Seventh-day Adventists.

Imbrie, J., and K. P. Imbrie. 1979. *Ice Ages: Solving the Mystery*. Cambridge, MA: Harvard University Press.

John, B., and G. L. G. Miklos. 1988. *The Eukaryote Genome in Development and Evolution*. Boston: Allen and Unwin.

Johnson, D. H. 1943. Systematic review of the chipmunks (genus *Eutamias*) of California. *University of California Publications in Zoology* 48:63-148.

Johnson, M. W. 1953. The copepod *Cyclops dimorphus* Kiefer from the Salton Sea. *American Midland Naturalist* 49:188-192.

Johnson, P. E. 1991. *Darwin on Trial*. Downers Grove, IL: InterVarsity Press.

Johnston, R. F., and R. K. Selander. 1964. House sparrows: Rapid evolution of races in North America. *Science* 144:548-550.

Keeton, W. T., and J. L. Gould. 1986. *Biological Science*. 4th ed. New York: W. W. Norton.

Kerr, J. A. 1992. A revisionist timetable for the ice ages. *Science* 258:220-221.

———. 1995a. A volcanic crisis for ancient life? *Science* 270:27-28.

———. 1995b. Did Darwin get it all right? *Science* 267:1421-1422.

Kitcher, P. 1982. *Abusing Science: The Case Against Creationism*. Cambridge, MA: The MIT Press.

Kneller, G. F. 1978. *Science as a Human Endeavor*. New York: Columbia University Press.

Kollar, E. J., and C. Fisher. 1980. Tooth induction in chick epithelium: Expression of quiescent genes for enamel synthesis. *Science* 207:993-995.

Koss, J. E., F. G. Ethridge, and S. A. Schumm. 1994. An experimental study of the effects of base-level change on fluvial, coastal plain and shelf systems. *Journal of Sedimentary Research* B64:90-98.

Krebs, J. R., and N. B. Davies. 1987. *An Introduction to Behavioural Ecology*. 2nd ed. Sunderland, MA: Sinauer Associates.

Krynine, P. D. 1956. Uniformitarianism is a dangerous doctrine. *Journal of Paleontology* 30:1003-1004.

Kuenen, P. H. 1950. Turbidity currents of high density. *Reports of the 18th International Geological Congress, London 1948* Part 8:44-52.

———, and C. I. Migliorini. 1950. Turbidity currents as a cause of graded bedding. *Journal of Geology* 58:91-127.

Kuhn, T. S. 1957. *The Copernican Revolution*. Cambridge, MA: Harvard University Press.

———. 1970. *The Structure of Scientific Revolutions*. 2nd ed. Chicago: University of Chicago Press.

———. 1977. *The Essential Tension*. Chicago: University of Chicago Press.

Kyriacour, C. P. 1990. The molecular ethology of the *period* gene in *Drosophila*. *Behavior Genetics* 21:191-211.

Landau, M. 1990. Protein sequences and Denton's error. *Creation/Evolution* 9(2):1-7.

Landgren, P. 1993. On the origin of 'species': "Ideological roots of the species concept. In S. Sherer, ed., *Typen des Lebens* (p. 47-64). Berlin: Pascal-Verlag (Studium Integrale).

Langridge, J. 1987. Old and new theories of evolution. In K.S.W. Campbell and M. F. Day, eds. *Rates of Evolution* (p. 248-262). London: Allen and Unwin.

Larsen, J. 1985. From lignin to coal in a year. *Nature* 314:316.

Laudan, L. 1981. *Science and Hypothesis: Historical Essays on Scientific Methodology.* Boston: D. Reidel Publishing.

Lemon, R. R. 1993. *Vanished Worlds: An Introduction to Historical Geology.* Dubuque, IA: Wm. C. Brown Publishers.

Lenski, R. E., and J. E. Mittler. 1993. The directed mutation controversy and neo-Darwinism. *Science* 259:188-194.

Lester, L. P., and R. G. Bohlin. 1989. *The Natural Limits to Biological Change.* 2nd ed. Dallas, TX: Probe Books; Word Publishing.

Lillegravin, J. A., Z. Kielen-Jaworowska, and W. A. Clemens, eds. 1979. *Mesozoic Mammals.* Berkeley: University of California Press.

Lockley, M. 1991. *Tracking Dinosaurs.* New York: Cambridge University Press.

——, and A. P. Hunt. 1995. *Dinosaur Tracks and Other Fossil Footprints of the Western United States.* New York: Columbia University Press.

Lodish, H., D. Baltimore, A. Berk, S. L. Zipursky, P. Matsudaira, and J. Darnell. 1995. *Molecular Cell Biology.* 3rd ed. New York: W. Freeman.

Longwell, C. R., R. F. Flint, and J. E. Sanders. 1969. *Physical Geology.* New York: John Wiley and Sons.

Love, J. D. 1960. Cenozoic sedimentation and crustal movement in Wyoming. *American Journal of Science* 258-A;204-214.

Lovtrup, S. 1987. *Darwinism: The Refutation of a Myth.* New York: Croom Helm.

Lowe, D. 1994. Abiological origin of described stromatolites older than 3.2 Ga. *Geology* 22:387-390.

Lubenow, M. L. 1992. *Bones of Contention: Creationist Assessment of Human Fossils.* Grand Rapids, MI: Baker Book House.

Lyell, C. 1892 *Principles of Geology, or the Modern Changes of the Earth and Its Inhabitants Considered as Illustrative of Geology.* 11th ed. 2 vols. New York: D. Appleton.

Lyman, R. L. 1994. *Vertebrate Taphonomy.* New York: Cambridge University Press.

Macbeth, N. 1971. *Darwin Retried.* Boston: Gambit.

MacFadden, B. J. 1992. *Fossil Horses.* New York: Cambridge University Press.

Marler, P. R., and W. J. Hamilton. 1967. *Mechanisms of Animal Behavior.* New York: John Wiley and Sons.

Marsh, F. L. 1941. *Fundamental Biology.* Lincoln, Nebraska: Author.

——, 1976. *Variation and Fixity in Nature.* Mountain View, CA: Pacific Press.

Maynard Smith, J. 1989. *Evolutionary Genetics.* New York: Oxford University Press.

——. 1992. Byte-sized evolution. *Nature* 355:772-773.

——, and G. R. Price. 1973. The logic of animal conflict. *Nature* 246:15-18.

Mayr, E. 1970. *Populations, Species, and Evolution.* Cambridge, MA: Belknap Press.

——, 1996. The modern evolutionary theory. *Journal of Mammalogy* 77:1-7.

McDougall, I., H. A. Polach, and J. J. Stipp. 1969. Excess radiogenic argon in young subaerial basalts from the Auckland volcanic field, New Zealand. *Geochimica et Cosmochimica Acta* 33:1485-1520.

McKee, E. D. 1982. Erosion surfaces. In E. D. McKee, ed., The Supai Group of Grand Canyon. *U. S. Geological Survey Professional Paper* (p. 155-176): 1173.

McKeever, P. J. 1991. Trackway preservation in eolian sandstones from the Permian of Scotland. *Geology* 19:726-729.

McKinney, M. L., and K. J. McNamara. 1991. *Heterochrony: The Evolution of Ontogeny.* New York: Plenum Press.

McMillen, S. I. 1984. *None of These Diseases.* Rev. ed. Grand Rapids, MI: Fleming H. Revell.

Medawar, P. 1984. *The Limits of Science.* New York: Oxford University Press.

Mellett, J. S. 1974. Scatological origin of microvertebrate accumulations. *Science* 185:349-350.

Mettler, L. E., T. G. Gregg, and H. E. Schaffer. 1988. *Population Genetics and Evolution.* Englewood Cliffs, NJ: Prentice Hall.

Miall, A. D. 1990. *Principles of Sedimentary Basin Analysis.* 2nd ed. New York: Springer-Verlag.

Miller, S. L. 1953. A production of amino acids under possible primitive earth conditions. *Science* 117:528-529.

——, and H. C. Urey. 1959. Organic compound synthesis on the primitive earth. *Science* 130:245-251.

Miyamoto, M. M., and M. Goodman. 1986. Biomolecular systematics of eutherian mammals: Phylogenetic patterns and classification. *Systematic Zoology* 35:230-240.

Moffatt, A. S. 1989. A challenge to evolutionary biology. *American Scientist* 77:224-226.

Monastersky, R. 1995. Earth's magnetic field follies revealed. *Science News* 147:244.

Monroe, J. S., and R. Wicander. 1992. *Physical Geology.* New York: West Publishing.

————. 1995. *Physical Geology.* 2nd ed. New York: West Publishing.

Monroe, K. R. 1996. *The Heart of Altruism: Perceptions of a Common Humanity.* Princeton: Princeton University Press.

Montgomery, C. W. 1990. *Physical Geology.* 2nd ed. Dubuque, IA: Wm. C. Brown Publishers.

Moody, P. A. 1962. *Introduction to Evolution.* New York: Harper and Brothers.

Moore, R. 1964. *Evolution.* New York: Time-Life Books.

Moore, R. C. 1958. *Introduction to Historical Geology.* 2nd ed. New York: McGraw-Hill Book.

Moreland, J. P. 1989. *Christianity and the Nature of Science.* Grand Rapids, MI: Baker Books.

——, ed. 1994. *The Creation Hypothesis.* Downers Grove, IL: InterVarsity Press.

Morell, V. 1996. Starting species with third parties and sex wars. *Science* 273: 1499-1502.

——, V. 1997. Predator-free guppies take an evolutionary leap forward. *Science* 275:1880.

Mundy, B. 1988. Expanding earth? *Origins* 15:53-69.

Naeser, C. W. 1971. Geochronology of the Navajo-Hopi diatremes, four corners area. *Journal of Geophysical Research* 76:4978-4985.

Nalley, R., E. Wilson, M. Batten, R. Wilder, N. Solomon, L. Koromvokis, H. Newton, and R. Trivers. 1982. Sociobiology: A new view of human nature. *Science Digest* 90(7):61-69.

National Academy of Sciences. 1989. *On Being a Scientist.* Washington, DC: National Academy Press. 22.

——. 1995. *On Being a Scientist.* 2nd ed. Washington, DC: National Academy Press. (Copies of this publication, produced by the National Academy of Science, can be purchased from National Academy Press, 2101 Constitution Ave., N.W., Washington, DC 20418.)

Natland, M. L., and P. H. Kuenen. 1951. Sedimentary history of the Ventura Basin, California, and the action of turbidity currents. *Society of Economic Paleontologists and Mineralogists Special Publication* 2:76-107.

Neufeld, B. 1975. Dinosaur tracks and giant men. *Origins* 2:64-76.

Nichol, F. D., ed. 1953. *Seventh-day Adventist Bible Commentary*. Vol. 1. Washington, DC: Review and Herald Publishing Association.

Nicolis, G., and I. Prigogine. 1977. *Self-organization in Nonequilibrium Systems*. New York: John Wiley and Sons.

Novacek, M. J. 1994. Whales leave the beach. *Nature* 368:807.

Nowak, R. 1994. Mining treasures from "junk DNA." *Science* 263:608-610.

Numbers, R. 1992. *The Creationists*. New York: A. A. Knopf.

Oard, M. J. 1990. A post-flood ice-age model can account for Quaternary features. *Origins* 17:8-26.

Oberbeck, V. R., J. R. Marshall, and H. Aggarwal. 1993. Impacts, tillites, and the breakup of Gondwanaland. *Journal of Geology* 101:1-19.

Oldroyd, D. 1986. *The Arch of Knowledge: An Introductory Study of the History of the Philosophy and Methodology of Science*. New York: Methuen.

Oliwenstein, L. 1990. Fossil Fraud. *Discover* 11(1):43-44.

Olson, S. L., and A. Feduccia. 1979. Flight capability and the pectoral girdle of *Archeopteryx*. *Nature* 278:247-248.

Opadia-Kadima, G. Z. 1987. How the slot machine led biologists astray. *Journal of Theoretical Biology* 124:127-135.

O'Rahilly, R., and F. Muller. 1992. *Human Embryology and Teratology*. New York: John Wiley and Sons.

Oster, G., and P. Alberch. 1982. Evolution and bifurcation of developmental programs. *Evolution* 36:444-459.

Ostrom, J. H. 1994. On the origin of birds and of avian flight. In D. R. Prothero and R. M. Schoch, eds. 1994. *Major Features of Vertebrate Evolution* (p. 160-177). Short Courses in Paleontology, Number 7. A Publication of the Paleontological Society.

Packer, C. 1977. Reciprocal altruism in olive baboons. *Nature* 265:441-443.

Parsons, P. A. 1987. Evolutionary rates under evolutionary stress. *Evolutionary Biology* 21:311-347.

——. 1988. Evolutionary rates: effects of stress upon recombination. *Biological Journal of the Linnaean Society* 35:49-68.

Patterson, C. 1981. *Evolutionism and creationism*. Unpublished lecture presented at the American Museum of Natural History, New York.

Pauling, L. 1964. *College Chemistry: An Introductory Textbook*. 3rd ed. San Francisco: W. H. Freeman.

Pearl, H. F. 1963. *A re-evaluation of time-variations in two geochemical parameters of importance in the accuracy of radiocarbon ages greater than four millennia*. Master's Thesis, Pacific Union College.

Plomin, R., J. C. DeFries, and G. E. McClearn. 1990. *Behavioral Genetics: A Primer*. 2nd ed. New York: W. H. Freeman.

Popper, K. R. 1959. *The Logic of Scientific Discovery*. New York: Harper & Row.

——. 1963. Science: Problems, aims, responsibilities. *Federation Proceedings* 22: 961-972.

Press, F., and R. Siever. 1986. *Earth*. 4th ed. New York: W. H. Freeman.

Price, G. M. 1906. *Illogical Geology*. Los Angeles: The Modern Heretic.

——. 1923. *The New Geology*. Boise, ID: Pacific Press.

Prothero, D. R. 1990. *Interpreting the Stratigraphic Record*. New York: W. H. Freeman.

——, and R. M. Schoch, eds. 1994. *Major Features of Vertebrate Evolution*. Short Courses in Paleontology, Number 7. A Publication of the Paleontological Society.

——, and F. Schwab. 1996. *Sedimentary Geology*. New York: W. H. Freeman.

Provost, E. 1991. Nonnestmate kin recognition in the ant (*Leptothorax lichtensteini*): Evidence that genetic factors regulate colony recognition. *Behavior Genetics* 21:151-167.

Rampino, M. R., and R. B. Stothers. 1988. Flood basalt volcanism during the past 250 million years. *Science* 241:663-668.

Raup, D. M. 1983. The geological and paleontological arguments of creationism. In L. R. Godfrey, ed. *Scientists Confront Creationism* (p. 147-162). New York: W. W. Norton.

——. 1986. New ideas are 'guilty until proved innocent'. *The Scientist* 1(1):18-19.

Reanna, D. C. 1985. The origin, nature and significance of genetic variation in prokaryotes and eukaryotes. In K.S.W. Campbell and M. F. Day, eds. *Rates of Evolution* (p. 235-247). Boston: Allen and Unwin.

Reichenbach, H. 1968. *The Rise of Scientific Philosophy*. Berkeley, CA: University of California Press.

Reinick, H. E., and I. B. Singh. 1980. *Depositional Sedimentary Environments*. 2nd ed. New York: Springer Verlag.

Repetski, J. E. 1978. A fish from the Upper Cambrian of North America. *Science* 200:529-531.

Retallack, G. J. 1994. Were the Ediacaran fossils lichens? *Paleobiology* 20:523-544.

Revkin, A. C. 1989. March of the fire ants. *Discover* 10(3):71-76.

Reynaud, C., A. Dahan, V. Anquez, and J. Weill. 1989. Somatic hyperconversion diversifies the single V_H gene of the chicken with a high incidence in the D region. *Cell* 59:171-183.

Reznick, D. N., F. H. Shaw, F. H. Rodd, and R. G. Shaw. 1997. Evaluation of the rate of evolution in natural populations of guppies (*Poecilia reticulata*). *Science* 275:1934-1937.

Rice, R. 1991. *Reason and the Contours of Faith*. Riverside, CA: La Sierra University Press.

Ricker, J. P,. and J. Hirsch. 1988. Genetic changes occurring over 500 generations in lines of *Drosophila melanogaster* selected divergently for geotaxis. *Behavior Genetics* 18:13-25.

Ridley, M. 1993. *Evolution*. Boston: Blackwell Scientific Publications.

Ritland, R. M., and S. L. Ritland. 1974. The fossil forests of the Yellowstone region. *Spectrum* 6(1/2):19-66.

Romer, A. S. 1962. *The Vertebrate Body (Shorter Version)*. Philadelphia: W. B. Saunders.

Roth, A. A. 1965. The value of scientific information. Unpublished paper.

——. 1979. Coral reef growth. *Origins* 6:88-95.

——. 1980. Implications of various interpretations of the fossil record. *Origins* 7:71-86.

——. 1986. Some questions about geochronology. *Origins* 13:64-85.

——. 1988. Those gaps in the sedimentary layers. *Origins* 15:75-92.

——. 1990. Flood stories - can they be ignored? *Origins* 17:51-55.

Rothrock, P. E., and M. E. Rothrock. 1987. Christianity and E. O. Wilson's mythology of scientific materialism. *Perspectives on Science and Christian Faith* 39(2):87-93.

Roubertoux, P. L., and M. Carlier. 1988. Differences between CBA/H and NZB mice on intermale aggresion. II. Maternal effects. *Behavior Genetics* 18:175-184.

Sadler, W. M. 1981. Sediment accumulation rates and the completeness of stratigraphic sections. *Journal of Geology* 89:569-584.

Savage, R. J. G., and M. R. Long. 1986. *Mammal Evolution*. London: British Museum (Natural History).

Schaeffer, F. A. 1972. *Genesis in Space and Time*. Downers Grove, IL: InterVarsity Press.

Scherer, S., ed. 1993. *Typen des Lebens*. Berlin: Pascal-Verlag (Studium Integrale).

Schermerhorn, L. J. G., and W. I. Stanton. 1963. Tilloids in the West Congo geosyncline. *Quarterly Journal of the Geological Society of London* 119:201-241.

Schleiermacher, F. 1821-1822. *The Christian Faith*. Edinburgh: T. and T. Clark. (A 1928 translation by H. R. Mackintosh and J. S. Stewart, of *Glaubenslehre*.)

Schwabe, C. 1985. On the basis of the studies of the origins of life. *Origins of Life* 15:213-216.

——. 1986. On the validity of molecular evolution. *Trends in Biochemical Sciences* 11(7):280-283.

Seilacher, A. 1967. Fossil behavior. *Scientific American* 217(2):72-80.

——. 1984. Late Precambrian metozoa: preservational or real extinctions? In H. D. Holland and A. F. Trendall, eds. *Patterns of Change in Earth Evolution* (p. 159-168). Berlin: Springer-Verlag.

Shaffer, N. R., and G. Faure. 1976. Regional variation of $^{87}Sr/^{86}Sr$ ratios and mineral compositions of sediment from the Ross Sea, Antarctica. *Geological Society of America Bulletin* 87:1491-1500.

Shea, W. H. 1978. The unity of the creation account. *Origins* 5:9-38.

——. 1984. A comparison of narrative elements in ancient Mesopotamian creation-flood stories with Genesis 1-9. *Origins* 11:9-29.

——. 1989. Literary structural parallels between Genesis 1 and 2. *Origins* 16:49-68.

——. 1991. The antediluvians. *Origins* 18:10-26.

Sherman, P. W. 1977. Nepotism and the evolution of alarm calls. *Science* 197:1246-1253.

Sigma Xi. 1991. *Honor in Science*. Research Triangle Park, NC: Sigma Xi, The Scientific Research Society. 41 p. (Copies of this booklet can be purchased from Publications Office, Sigma Xi, The Scientific Research Society, P. O. Box 13975, Research Triangle Park, NC 27709.)

Simpson, G. G. 1953a. *The Major Features of Evolution*. New York: Columbia University Press.

——. 1953b. *Life of the Past*. New Haven: Yale University Press.

Smith, G. A. 1993. Missoula flood dynamics and magnitudes inferred from sedimentology of slack-water deposits on the Columbia Plateau, Washington. *Geological Society of America Bulletin* 108:77-100.

Spencer, L., and L. R. Brand. 1988. Testing flood models. Unpublished paper.

Spencer, L., and J. Lienard. 1988. Noah's Ark: A critical literature review. Unpublished paper.

Spieth, P. T. 1987. Review of evolution: A Theory in Crisis, by Michael Denton. *Zygon* 22:252-257.

Stanley, S. M. 1986. *Earth and Life Through Time*. New York: W. H. Freeman.

——. 1993. *Exploring Earth and Life Through Time*. New York: W. H. Freeman. (A condensed version of Stanley 1986)

Stearn, C. W., R. L. Carroll, and T. H. Clark. 1979. *Geological Evolution of North America*. 3rd ed. New York: John Wiley and Sons.

Stebbins, G. L. 1971. *Processes of Organic Evolution*. 2nd ed. Englewood Cliffs, NJ: Prentice-Hall.

Stephens, H. G., and E. M. Shoemaker. 1987. *In the Footsteps of John Wesley Powell*. Boulder, CO: Johnson Books.

Sternberg, C. M. 1933. Carboniferous tracks from Nova Scotia. *Geological Society of America Bulletin* 44:951-964.

Stevens, T. O., and J. P. McKinley. 1995. Lithoautotrophic microbial ecosystems in deep basalt aquifers. *Science* 270:450-454 (also see news note on p. 377).

Stock, C. 1956. *Rancho La Brea*. 6th ed. Los Angeles County Museum, Science Series, No. 20, Paleontology No. 11.

Stommel, H., and E. Stommel. 1979. The year without a summer. *Scientific American* 240(6):176-186.

Strahler, A. N. 1987. *Science and Earth History - the Evolution/Creation Controversy*. Buffalo, New York: Prometheus Books.

Swanson, S. E. 1977. Relation of nucleation and crystal-growth rate to the development of granitic textures. *American Mineralogist* 62:966-978.

Terzian, C., and C. Biemont. 1988. The founder effect theory: Quantitative variation and mdg-1 mobile element polymorphism in experimental populations of *Drosophila melanogaster*. *Genetica* 76:53-63.

Thaxton, C. B., W. L. Bradley, and R. L. Olsen. 1984. *The Mystery of Life's Origin: Reassessing Current Theories*. New York: Philosophical Library.

Thewissen, J. G. M., S. T. Hussain, and M. Arif. 1994. Fossil evidence for the origin of aquatic locomotion in archaeocete whales. *Science* 263:210-212.

Thulborn, T. 1990. *Dinosaur Tracks*. New York: Chapman and Hall.

Tkachuck, R. D. 1983. The little ice age. *Origins* 10:51-65.

Trefil, J. 1991. Whale feet. *Discover* 12(5):44-48.

Trivers, R. L. 1971. The evolution of reciprocal altruism. *Quarterly Review of Biology* 46:35-57.

Trueblood, E. 1958. *The Yoke of Christ*. New York: Harper and Brothers.

Twidale, C. R. 1976. On the survival of paleoforms. *American Journal of Science* 276:77-95.

Valentine, J. W. 1966. The present is the key to the present. *Journal of Geological Education* 14(2):59-60.

——. 1992. The macroevolution of phyla. In J. H. Lipps and P. W. Signor, eds., *Topics in Geobiology* (F. G. Stehli and D. S. Jones, series eds.). *Origin and Early Evolution of the Metazoa* (10:525-553). New York: Plenum.

——, and C. A. Campbell. 1975. Genetic regulation and the fossil record. *American Scientist* 63:673-680.

——, and D. H. Erwin. 1987. Interpreting great developmental experiments: the fossil record. In R. A. Raff and E. C. Raff, eds., *Development as an Evolutionary Process* (p. 71-107). New York: Liss.

van Andel, T. H. 1981. Consider the incompleteness of the geological record. *Nature* 294:397-398.

Villee, C. A. 1977. *Biology*. 7th ed. Philadelphia: W. B. Saunders.

Walker, R. G. 1973. Mopping up the turbidite mess. In R. N. Ginsburg, ed., *Evolving Concepts in Sedimentology* (p. 1-37). Baltimore, MD: Johns Hopkins University Press.

Wallace, R. A. 1973. *The Ecology and Evolution of Animal Behavior*. Pacific Palisades, CA: Goodyear Publishers.

Ward, P. D. 1995. After the fall: Lessons and directions from the K/T debate. *Palaios* 10:530- 538.

330

Watts, W. W. 1976. Christ and science. *Journal of the American Scientific Affiliation* 28:9-11.

Weaver, W. 1961. The imperfections of science. *American Scientist* 49:99-113.

Webster, C. 1986/87. Glaciers: A progeny of earth's climate. *Geoscience Reports* (No. 8):1-3.

Weiner, J. 1995. Evolution made visible. *Science* 267:30-33.

Wheeler, G. W. 1974. The most unique creation story of the ancient world. *These Times* 83 (10):2-34.

——. 1975. *The Two-Tailed Dinosaur: Why Science and Religion Conflict over the Origin of Life*. Nashville, TN: Southern Publishing Association.

Whitcomb, J. C., Jr., and H. M. Morris. 1961. *The Genesis Flood*. Philadelphia: The Presbyterian and Reformed Publishing.

Wicander, R. and J. S. Monroe. 1989. *Historical Geology*. New York: West Publishing.

Wiedershiem, R. 1895. *The Structure of Man: An Index to His Past History*. London: McMillan.

Wiley, E. O., D. Siegel-Causey, D. R. Brooks, and V. A. Funk. 1991. *The Compleat Cladist: A Primer of Phylogenetic Procedures*. The University of Kansas Museum of Natural History, Special Publication No. 19.

Wilson, D. E., and D. M. Reeder, eds. 1993. *Mammal Species of the World*. 2nd ed. Washington: Smithsonian Institution Press.

Wilson, E. O. 1975. *Sociobiology: The New Synthesis*. Cambridge, MA: Belknap Press of Harvard University Press.

——. 1978. *On Human Nature*. Cambridge, MA: Harvard University Press.

——. 1980a. *Sociobiology - The Abridged Addition*. Cambridge, MA: Belknap Press of Harvard University Press.

——. 1980b. The relation of science to theology. *Zygon* 15:425-434.

Winograd, I. J., T. B. Coplen, J. M. Landwehr, A. C. Riggs, K. R. Ludwig, B. J. Szabo, P. T. Kolesar, K. M. Revesz. 1992. Continuous 500,000-year climate record from vein calcite in Devils Hole, Nevada. *Science* 258:255-260.

Wise, K. 1986. How fast do rocks form? *Proceedings of the First International Conference on Creationism,* 2:197-203.

——. 1989. Punc eq creation style. *Origins* 16:11-24.

——. 1994. The origin of life's major groups. In J. P. Moreland, ed., *The Creation Hypothesis* (p. 211-234). Downers Grove, IL: InterVarsity Press.

Woodward, T. E. 1988. Review of Evolution: A Theory in Crisis, by Michael Denton. *Perspectives on Science and Christian Faith* 40:240-241.

Zimmerman, E. C. 1960. Possible evidence of rapid evolution in Hawaiian moths. *Evolution* 14:137-138.

Index